UPRISING

STEPHEN GAPPS is a public historian working to bring Frontier War histories into broader recognition as Australia's First Wars. In 2011, he was awarded the NSW Premier's History Award for regional and community history. Stephen's *The Sydney Wars: Conflict in the early colony 1788–1817* was the inaugural winner of the Les Carlyon Award for the writing of military history (2020). He is also the author of *Gudyarra: The first Wiradyuri war of resistance – The Bathurst War, 1822–1824* (2021), and is an editor of *The Australian Wars*, the book of the award-winning documentary series, forthcoming.

'Stephen Gapps' work is a significant contribution to truth-telling in Australian history.' **ANITA HEISS**

'A great and much needed account. And yet another loud cry to break the great Australian silence.' **JOHN MAYNARD**

'For all Australians to truly understand their history, the Australian Wars need to be a prominent part of our national story. At a time when we need to think deeply about how the past impacts our future, *Uprising* is essential reading.' **RACHEL PERKINS**

'This is a must-read! *Uprising* is a landmark book at the forefront of the new and exciting scholarship about the Australian Wars. In a brilliant synthesis, Gapps draws together his deep research with extensive consultation with Elders and local knowledge holders and, just as importantly, his detailed understanding of the country in contention.' **HENRY REYNOLDS**

UPRISING

WAR IN THE COLONY OF NEW SOUTH WALES, 1838–1844

STEPHEN GAPPS

NEWSOUTH

UNSW Press acknowledges the Bedegal people, the Traditional Owners of the unceded territory on which the Randwick and Kensington campuses of UNSW are situated, and recognises the continuing connection to Country and culture. We pay our respects to Bedegal Elders past and present.

A NewSouth book
Published by
NewSouth Publishing
University of New South Wales Press Ltd
University of New South Wales
Sydney NSW 2052
AUSTRALIA
https://unsw.press/

Our authorised representative in the EU for product safety is
Mare Nostrum Group B.V., Mauritskade 21D, 1091 GC Amsterdam,
The Netherlands (gpsr@mare-nostrum.co.uk).

© Stephen Gapps 2025
First published 2025

10 9 8 7 6 5 4 3 2 1

This book is copyright. Apart from any fair dealing for the purpose of private study, research, criticism or review, as permitted under the *Copyright Act*, no part of this book may be reproduced by any process without written permission. Inquiries should be addressed to the publisher.

 A catalogue record for this book is available from the National Library of Australia

ISBN: 9781742238029 (paperback)
        9781742239125 (ebook)
        9781761178351 (ePDF)

Cover artwork Original artwork by Blak Douglas, 2024
Cover design Luke Causby, Blue Cork
Internal design Josephine Pajor-Markus

All reasonable efforts were taken to obtain permission to use copyright material reproduced in this book, but in some cases copyright could not be traced. The author welcomes information in this regard.

Contents

Introduction	'Rebellion is war: that is the cardinal principle'	1
PART ONE	**Uprising**	
CHAPTER ONE	'An exterminating warfare'	19
CHAPTER TWO	The Battle for Big River	42
CHAPTER THREE	The Battle of Broken River	59
CHAPTER FOUR	Re-taking the Murrumbidgee River	82
CHAPTER FIVE	The Battle of Meewah	102
CHAPTER SIX	'These Tribes vowed vengeance'	116
PART TWO	**The Counteroffensive**	
CHAPTER SEVEN	'This deed of blood'	135
CHAPTER EIGHT	Murdering Island and Poison Waterholes Creek	157
CHAPTER NINE	'A commission to wage war against the aboriginal natives'	168
CHAPTER TEN	'Come on you white buggers!'	187
CHAPTER ELEVEN	'It now became evident that they must be conquered'	206
EPILOGUE	'The blacks interfere with the profits of grazing'	217
Acknowledgments		233
Bibliography		235
Notes		251
Index		312

Cultural warning and readers' note

Due to the vast range of these stories, from Benalla to Brisbane, it was not possible to talk to everyone I wanted to or to cover some events in the detail I wished. I hope that this book sparks more local and detailed work of future historians of the Australian Wars.

Covering such a vast area also means some Aboriginal names may be incorrect, contested or have several spellings or usages. I have endeavoured to use generally accepted standards where possible and apologise in advance for any errors.

The first section of this book mainly covers Aboriginal victories in war. The second section deals with the colonial counteroffensive against the uprisings along the colonists' 'frontier'. Readers are warned that this section in particular contains graphic details of massacre events and language from the past that may be considered inappropriate today.

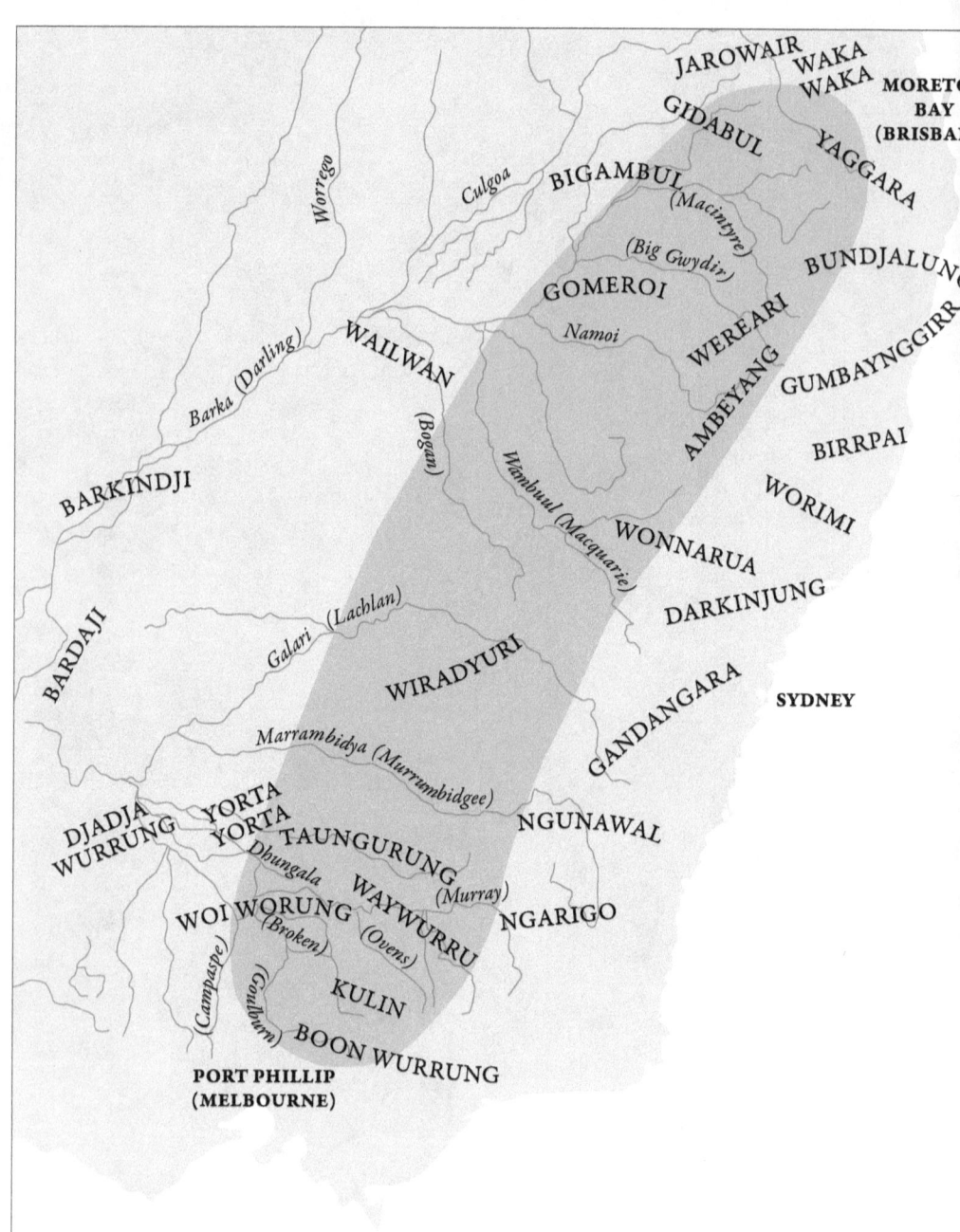

The Uprising, 1838 to 1844

The approximate main areas of conflict between colonists and Aboriginal people between 1838 and 1844. Not all First Nations and groups in southeast Australia are highlighted, only the main groups mentioned in the book.
The maps are representational and intended to provide an overview of locations and Country.

INTRODUCTION
'Rebellion is war: that is the cardinal principle'

The Battle of Broken River

In April 1838, a group of stockmen with all their supplies loaded high on bullock drays, along with several thousand sheep and cattle, were heading south from near present-day Goulburn, through Waywurru Country into Taungurung Country near Benalla in what was to later become the colony of Victoria. Eighteen men, mostly convicts or ex-convicts under the charge of overseer Frederick Crossley, formed a long, winding column that was known at the time as an 'overlanding party'. They travelled at the pace of the sheep and cattle, not going too far each day, stopping at places with good water and plentiful kangaroo grass to rest their precious stock.

The men and their cattle and sheep were part of what one writer recalled in 1906 as 'the time of the great invasion'. According to the journalist and historian Donald Alaster McDonald, they were 'all making like the Israelites for their land of promise' and 'broke into the virgin lands of Port Phillip at all points'. As they rode, 'the seeding grasses rustled against their stirrup irons'. This party were like many others, a kind of advance guard. The financers and men in charge – who were being called 'squatters' as they occupied what they believed was empty land – would follow later to supervise the building of a cattle or sheep station or 'run'.[1]

These 'overlanders' were following the river systems of Wiradyuri Country beyond Narrungdera (current day Narrandera) and across the Murrumbidgee and Murray rivers south into the homelands of the Kulin peoples. They were but one group of many overlanders at this time, spreading out like tendrils across the vast lands of what in 1836

Major Thomas Mitchell had enticingly called 'Australia Felix' (fortunate or happy Australia) in a huge arc around present-day central, north and western Victoria. By 1837, overlanding parties were slowly but surely driving their sheep and cattle through the Upper Campaspe, Gisborne and Mount Macedon, and by early 1838, the Upper Goulburn River areas.

A well-financed operation could claim a huge swathe of Aboriginal land. They merely had to set up huts and mark out stock runs. Later perhaps, occupancy might become ownership. In the meantime, owning the land beyond the 'limits of location' or 'settled districts' did not matter. These were grazing lands being used to make money. If these enterprises were uninterrupted in getting their bales of fleece back to Sydney or Port Phillip (Melbourne), squatters could make their fortunes out of wool that in 1836 had never seen such high prices. It was a relatively low investment for a potentially high return.[2]

The group of overlanders heading south with Overseer Crossley were under the charge of two young brothers with a surname that would echo down the ages across northeastern Victoria and well beyond, George and William Faithfull. William remained at their base at Goulburn and George rode ahead to catch up with his overlanding party. George halted at the Ovens River, where he thought he could establish a run on the Oxley Plains, and sent his overseer Crossley ahead with a column of cattle, sheep and stockmen to seek a river and pasture that his brother could come and occupy.

Crossley halted at a place that the people who lived there called Marangan – what the Europeans first called 'Swampy River' and 'Winding Swamp' and later, 'Broken River'. After crossing the river at present-day Benalla, the overlanders came under a fierce attack by a large force of warriors. Despite having six firearms among the eighteen men, Crossley and his stockmen were almost annihilated. Eight were killed and the rest ran for their lives.[3]

Introduction

'Benalla's secret'

Many years later, in 1906, the dogged local historian Samuel Uren asked around the township of Benalla trying to 'solve the mystery of the Faithfull brothers massacre'. According to Uren, no-one in Benalla in the early 1900s seemed to 'know anything about it' and quite incredibly, they were all sure it did not happen 'within 25 miles of Benalla'. Others told him to leave it alone as 'this mystery is a Benalla secret'.

In 1945, he wrote a second account of the battle and its aftermath, which he called 'Benalla's secret'. In this version, he added detail of the two survivors who made their way to Colonel Henry White's station. White had gathered men, and as Uren wrote:

> They returned to the scene [the] next day and found the natives having the greatest feast of their lives, on the site now known as the Benalla Gardens. The relief party slaughtered many of the natives and burned them on the spot to hide all trace of their unlawful act. Many other natives escaped to safety.[4]

It is no wonder Benalla locals wanted to keep the 'Benalla secret' a secret. Somewhere in the beautifully kept Benalla Botanic Gardens on the banks of Marangan and the edge of the main road through the town may well lie the charred bones of people found 'feasting' on the Faithfulls' dray loads of provisions.

When Uren began to investigate the 'Benalla secret' he found local stories that suggested the bodies of the stockmen had been buried at an old red gum near Arundel Street, known as the 'Faithfull Tree'. Uren had stirred the town into action. After some digging at the tree, 'a skull, leg and arm bones, shoulder-blades, and portions of vertebrae, these being apparently the remains of one of the murdered men' were found. Then 'the skeletons of two men were quickly exhumed, a third later'. When a Dr Nicholson examined the remains, he 'found a mark where the man had been struck with a spear in the shoulder-blade from behind. On the back of the skull was evidence of a tremendous blow, which had cracked the skull right round'.[5]

Just the year before, in 1906, the *Benalla Standard* newspaper had published a story that was headed the 'Fight of the Broken River'. There could now be no denying the event occurred in Benalla. However, a spear 'in the shoulder-blade from behind' and a blow 'on the back of the skull' suggested the men were killed in cold blood. A subsequent newspaper report titled 'The Faithfull Massacre' soon became etched in local memory.[6]

The stockmen were not, as the widely accepted definition of a massacre notes, 'defenceless'. As military historian Chris Clark notes, 'there is no reason to view this incident as anything other than a battle which the Aborigines won'. In fact, as we shall see, it was one of the great Aboriginal military victories in the entire Australian Wars. But in 1838, the death of eight white men in one fell swoop sent shivers down the spines of isolated frontiersmen. It also sent shockwaves through the entire colony of New South Wales. The battle at Broken River appeared to indicate to both the squatters and the colonial authorities and military that a 'general rising' by Aboriginal people had begun.[7]

A 'general rising' was the greatest fear of the stockmen on the frontier. As the journalist and early historian George Burnett Barton recalled in 1896:

> When the news of the fight at the Winding Swamp between Faithfull's party and the blacks was brought into Melbourne by Crossley it caused a general feeling of alarm, for everyone was more or less interested in the fate of the Overlanders. Several parties were known to be on the road, and it was naturally supposed that if one of them was attacked and slaughtered the rest would soon share the same fate ... The details of the affair led people to suppose that several tribes had returned to make the attack, and if that was the case, there would probably be a general rising among them, and every station hut would become a scene of plunder and bloodshed.[8]

Barton called it a fight. Yet the 'Faithfull Massacre' story continues to be told. It became part of squatting legend. In 1920, in his history of

Introduction

squatting in the Murray River region, Arthur Andrews noted that 'many murders and other outrages' were conducted by Aboriginal people and 'in this part especially, the memory of the "Faithfull Massacre" is not likely to be forgotten'. How right Andrews was. Even the recent online map 'Colonial Frontier Massacres, Australia, 1788 to 1930' follows the well-worn story and (in 2024) represents it as one of the few blue dots on the map – a massacre of Europeans.[9]

The conflict from 1838 to 1840 in northeast Victoria has rarely been seen by historians (let alone those still calling the Battle at Broken River the 'Faithfull Massacre') as a co-ordinated resistance. Local historian Harry Parris, however, stands out. He told his audience at a meeting of the Historical Society of Victoria in July 1950 that the Battle at Broken River 'can be considered as an organised attempt by a combination of more than one tribe to dispute the right of white people to enter their country'. Harry had it right back in 1950. Sadly, we have failed to do much about telling this story of resistance ever since.[10]

The regional Victorian town of Benalla is better known today as part of 'Kelly Country'. It is just down the road from Glenrowan, where the bushranger Ned Kelly and his gang conducted their famous last stand. There are no monuments or plaques to Aboriginal resistance in Benalla. There are several plaques to white men who were killed by warriors. As Benalla Aboriginal History Group member Hamish McPherson notes, 'rarely discussed is the dramatic period of hostilities between Aboriginal people and settlers that had occurred some forty years earlier'. Historian and nearby Euroa resident, Kate Auty, has drawn attention to a Benalla street named after Major James Winnett Nunn, who has, as we will see, been associated with a massacre far to the north near Moree. Aunty Cheryl Cooper of Benalla is tired of her town remembering the deaths of eight white stockmen rather than the people who fought them. She has been campaigning for several years to have the name Faithfull Street changed.[11]

'The blacks are in open rebellion'

George Barton was correct. Victory at the Battle of Broken River was not an isolated incident. In fact, it signalled the beginning of arguably the greatest military counteroffensive on Australian soil in Australian history, with tens of thousands of warriors fighting against the occupation of their homelands. In 1847, the self-styled colonial 'observer' Alexander Harris remarked that during the early 1840s there had been 'an entire line of active hostility' along the 'whole boundary' of the colony of New South Wales. Harris called it a 'rising' and 'so perfect and so simultaneous was this "rising", as it may be properly enough called', that it was obviously conducted in a 'mutual understanding ... by the whole line of natives tribes from north to south'. Harris was suggesting 'the rising' occurred over a vast area from Port Phillip (Melbourne) to the Darling Downs near Moreton Bay (Brisbane). He believed it must have been co-ordinated by all these nations across vast distances as it was 'so perfect and simultaneous'.[12]

Many other contemporaries said much the same thing. In 1854, the journalist and early historian of New South Wales Roderick Flanagan wrote in the grandly named newspaper *Empire* that this uprising 'belongs to the history of the country'. Despite his fine words, it was actually *written out* of the history of this country. By the 1850s, speeches about progress and future prosperity of the burgeoning colony utterly drowned out such 'history of the country'.

Flanagan believed the uprising occurred between 1842 and 1845 (though, as we shall see, it began earlier and peaked in 1840 to 1842, though extended in southeast Queensland far longer). His graphic description is worth quoting in full:

> The simultaneous aggressive movement of the Aborigines throughout the entire colony, and along its boundaries, commenced in 1842, and continued through the two or three succeeding years, belongs to the history of the country. For more than two years the warfare which the blacks waged upon the stations situated along the boundaries of the colony, from one extreme to the other, was

universal, implacable, and incessant. So simultaneous, indeed, and so general was the movement, that, did we not know, from the habits and condition of the blacks, that such a thing would be impossible, a belief would be encouraged that the onslaught of the Aborigines on the lives and property of the settlers was the result of a perfect organisation, effected with all the aids of negotiation, secret intrigue, and general assemblies. From Wide Bay to Port Phillip, the organization seemed to extend, and scarcely a day elapsed without tidings reaching the city of some remote station being driven in, some flock driven away or speared, some shepherd or hutkeeper being wounded or killed. To add to the horror excited in the minds of the people in the several stations, by the alarming situation in which they found themselves placed, tribes of blacks who had hitherto lived on the most peaceful or friendly terms with the whites, became all at once transformed into their most bloodthirsty enemies, while other tribes hitherto unknown or unheard of within the limits of the colony, came in from the wilderness to join in the war which their brethren were waging.[13]

As Flanagan pointed out, in the early 1840s, anyone taking note of the weekly reports of conflict in the various colonial newspapers could have seen this. For example, in September 1843, a *Sydney Herald* correspondent who had just returned from the Murray River reported that 'the blacks in that neighbourhood' were 'committing the most daring outrages ever recorded'. The newspaper bemoaned that 'of late we have had to record so many daring outrages committed by the blacks upon the lives and properties of the settlers'. Just a few days later, far to the north in southern Queensland, the same paper reported that at Moreton Bay, 'the blacks are in open rebellion, and are determined, from their well-devised proceedings, to drive the settlers from that district'.[14]

Flanagan and Harris were not alone in understanding the early 1840s as a co-ordinated uprising, a period of Aboriginal rebellion against the colony. Flanagan, who most unusually for the time made a point of writing about Aboriginal people as *part* of Australian history, pointed to the reports from the 'Protectors of Aborigines' that they, 'and the friends of the aborigines in general, maintained that the outbreak of the blacks' was an 'explosion of long-pent feelings of revenge and hatred towards the whites, resulting from a long course of violence and injustice'.[15]

In 1857, the self-styled adventurer Frederic de Brébant Cooper described how around 1841, a 'coalition of several tribes' operated against colonists from north-western New South Wales to south-west Queensland. The term 'rising' or 'uprising' was often used to describe resistance warfare at other times as well. In 1852, the term 'a general rising' was used in Queensland to describe a projected offensive around the Wide Bay area on the coast north of present-day Brisbane and along Kgari-Fraser Island. As the *Moreton Bay Courier* announced in April that year, 'it is anticipated that there will be a general rising amongst the aborigines in this part of the colony this winter; stations on the River having been attacked at three different points almost simultaneously'. In 1854, the Commissioner for Crown Lands for the Wide Bay district, Arthur Edward Halloran, reported that 'the whole of the Wide Bay tribes have been combining in large numbers and have sent messages to me ... to say that as soon as the bunya bunya was ripe they intended to take all the sheep in the district and kill all the white men'.[16]

Even into the late 19th and early 20th centuries the idea of a 'rising' or 'uprising' was not quite erased in white memory of the Australian Wars. In the 1890s, a Queensland squatter, Nehemiah Bartley, reminisced about how 'many a terrible melee took place' in what he called 'the war of '43 to '55'. Bartley believed this was a general 'uprising' that extended from southern Queensland as far south as Victoria, and that each 'tribe' had communicated their intent to their neighbour. So too, James Gormly, writing in 1921 about 'Exploration and Settlement in Australia', noted that 'in 1838 the blacks became most hostile to the new settlers in many parts of N.S.W. (which then included Port Phillip District and Moreton Bay, now Victoria and Queensland) when a number of white men were killed by the natives'. Gormly was clear they were so aggressive that 'the government authorities in Melbourne became alarmed about the safety of the settlement there'. Gormly also noted rather ominously that 'reinforcements' were slow to arrive, but that 'in the meantime, the settlers and others proved themselves equal to protecting themselves'.[17]

Introduction

In 1938, in one of those typical local history stories of the days when 'the blacks were troublesome', yet another journalist and historian, Clem Lack, wrote in the *Courier-Mail* about 'A pitched battle of the early days'. According to Lack, across the Darling Downs in southern Queensland in 1843, 'the blacks were rising' and 'intended to spear all the commandants, fence off the roads, stop the drays travelling over the range, and starve the "jackeroos" [strangers]'.[18]

So, if it was commonly agreed by squatters in the 1840s, journalists in the 1850s, and later writers and other observers that in the early 1840s there was an 'open rebellion' – in effect a great and combined defensive war along hundreds and hundreds of kilometres of Aboriginal land – why do we know so little of this today? Some historians have seen the period 1838–1842 as 'the climax of the Frontier War', solely due to the intensity and extent of the squatters' land grabs at this time.

Yet the idea that Aboriginal warriors could not co-ordinate or combine into large forces has held sway for many years. Some historians have lamented that 'Aboriginal fighting skills' were not 'matched by organisational capacity', nor did they have 'inter-tribal military links', making it easier for colonists to pick them off one by one. They supposedly did not have an economy that created surpluses 'to feed a warrior class'. Apparently, they also lacked 'military leaders and support systems'.

In fact, they had all this and more. As we shall see, united resistance warfare across vast distances was conducted by allied military leaders with surpluses (often of herds of cattle and sheep and sometimes stockpiled grain). Traditional alliances were mobilised against colonists, and new ones were formed.[19]

One of the few historians to consider the Australian frontier wars as involving 'uprisings', Roger Milliss, noted in 1992 that the Gomeroi (also written Kamilaroi, Gamilaroi, Gamilaraay) conducted 'a determined guerrilla resistance for more than a quarter of a century that flared into periodic uprisings'. But historians have generally been suspicious of descriptions of frontier warfare as 'uprisings' or 'rebellions' – as if a slippery language was being used to cover up the fact that this was indeed a period of war between sovereign states, but one that could not be admitted as such. While squatters and others repeatedly claimed they were fighting a war, the authorities did not dare say so. If war was formally declared against Aboriginal people it would have undermined British claims to possession of the entire country. Aboriginal people were British subjects, so any attacks and threats to 'kill all the white men' was internal rebellion and that was that. No one took much notice of whether Aboriginal people believed they had declared war on the whites.[20]

Yet Harris, Flanagan and other contemporaries could easily comprehend this 'uprising' as a 'war'. It was commonly understood in military legal terms that an uprising, or internal rebellion, was in fact, war. As William Finalson wrote in his treatise on martial law in 1868, 'rebellion is war: that is the cardinal principle'. In combatting rebellion, as in combatting war, 'equal measures', according to Finalson, were required. Mid-19th-century colonial authorities and those men pushing cattle and sheep beyond the boundaries of the colony deep into Aboriginal lands had little time for the semantics of war. They all knew that when they were confronted by warfare, they met it with equal measures of warfare.

In many cases the measures were clearly disproportionate. The massacre of Aboriginal people by armed parties of squatters and stockmen became a standard practice. At times it should be seen as a standard military tactic – especially when the authorities formally tasked squatters far beyond the reach of military or police with their own defence. But the fact that colonists resorted to massacres also highlights their desperation. It highlights the widespread extent of Aboriginal resistance to the colonial juggernaut of sheep, horses and armed men that was rolling across their Country.[21]

'Signal-fires ... had sprung up on many hills'

There is no doubt that Aboriginal warriors could unite forces across vast distances. It is now well understood by archaeologists, anthropologists and historians that there was a vast network of trade routes throughout Australia, trading in goods, but also ceremonies and stories. The strange omission from all these decades of important work is that the single biggest threat to these peoples' existence – the great pastoral invasion – was, in the 1830s, undoubtedly a critical part of these communications. So too was a major response to the invasion – resistance.[22]

Many of these stories today have remained with Aboriginal people. Elders and knowledge holders consulted for this book all agreed that communication of news travelled far and travelled fast. Gomeroi man Uncle Paul Spearim notes that the Gomeroi travelled south into Wonnarua (the Hunter Valley region) and Gandangara lands (Blue Mountains and Southern Highlands) and north to the Bunya Gathering in south-east Queensland – a vast area of over 1000 kilometres.[23]

It has been well documented in the past how 'confederations' or 'associations' were made between groups for large hunts, food gathering and sharing, ceremonies and dispute resolution. Some confederacies such as the Ngarrindjeri association of eighteen 'tribes' were ongoing, while others came together for specific purposes. Others came together in times of urgency and distress. In Tasmania, by 1828 after several years of conflict, many bands or large clan groups were so reduced by disease and fighting that those who were left amalgamated. The leader Kickerterpoller described to the grazier and newspaper editor Gilbert Robertson how before 1828, twenty clans of the Oyster Bay nation had united and that warfare was being conducted 'by all the tribes in a body' under the leadership of Tongerlongeter. In 1830, the colonists so desperately hunting Palawa warriors were told by one of their Palawa guides that Palawa people had 'suspended their own internal broils, and formed a regular systematic plan of offensive aggressions against the white colonists'. It could not have been made much clearer to the so-called 'roving parties' trying to stop the Palawa attacks. They were told by Palawa 'that the different tribes had leagued together sinking their own disputes and [were] determined to exterminate the whites if possible'.[24]

Some colonial observers noted how warriors united on a tactical level as well. In South Australia in 1862, one 'overlander' described how a body of 300 warriors had 'collected within eight miles' and attacked his expedition:

> (They) attacked our little camp twice in one afternoon in two
> different mobs of about 100 strong each, and, from the signal-fires
> that had sprung up on many hills ... we had most unpleasant proof,
> not only of their capabilities of conceiving, but of executing
> 'a concentrating movement' with most disagreeable rapidity.[25]

Communication by the colour, shape and direction of smoke was both rapid and complex. Rather than 'smoke signals', Uncle Paul Spearim prefers to call them fire messages, as the material burned and type of fire determined the smoke. Sometimes, in between the fire messages, 'runners' would pass messages on. In early 1838, Charles Bonney had joined Joseph Hawdon's overlanding party attempting to reach the new settlement in South Australia. He described how from the junction of the Murrumbidgee and the Murray, 'the natives used to assemble to see us pass, and send forward messengers to tell the next tribe of our approach'.[26]

There are many examples of rapid and widespread communication and the formation of alliances. The Kulin confederacy in southern central Victoria were reported by squatters to have extensive and rapid communication networks that reached hundreds of kilometres inland. As historian Fred Cahir notes, envoys were sent on journeys far into other nations with information of 'important economic, political and ceremonial meetings'. On occasion, a thousand people were seen gathered in present-day Melbourne. Performances of song and dance that did not need language to convey story gradually travelled long distances across many different language groups. They often told of news that emanated from hundreds, sometimes thousands of kilometres away.[27]

Initiation ceremonies of boys into manhood saw large gatherings of hundreds of people often coming from vast distances. As Uncle Bill Allen Junior notes, like the Gomeroi, Wiradyuri had ties stretching from Dhungutti Country on the north coast of New South Wales down to the Snowy Mountains and across the Murrumbidgee River in the south. Ceremonial and other meetings served to reinforce social ties, but also to exchange information. They were still observed by early anthropologists in the 1890s who recorded people travelling to ceremonies with other groups who spoke completely different languages. Message sticks were sent hundreds of kilometres around to prepare for ceremonies. Long before the first Europeans began to travel across their lands, the peoples right across the huge expanse of what we now call the Murray-Darling basin had a vast and complex communication network. Could a message, news or information travel from present-day Benalla to Brisbane?[28]

Bringing people together over hundreds if not thousands of kilometres was nothing unusual. Historian Ray Kerkhove points out that 'the Bunya festival [northwest of modern-day Brisbane] alone involved delegates and networks of messaging spanning 1000 to 1400 kms'. Songlines that used the night sky could stretch even further. Some have been reported spanning from the Central Desert near present-day Alice Springs right across to the north coast of present-day New South Wales. Considering all this potential communication and travel, Alexander Harris's 'entire line of active hostility' communicated along the 'whole boundary' of the colony of New South Wales from modern-day Queensland to Victoria doesn't seem far-fetched at all.[29]

Dharawal Elder Aunty Glenda Chalker notes the continuity of communication networks among Aboriginal people down to this day. A few days after the Appin Massacre south of Sydney on 17 April 1816, a large group of Dharawal people had gathered at 'the rocks at the back of Mr. Kennedy's Farm' nearby. As Aunty Glenda notes, 'Rest assured, by 22nd April, it would have been widely known about the massacre among the people, from far and wide. The Koori grapevine existed then and still does today'.[30]

'A parcel of regular humbugs'

The squatters knew something was different in the late 1830s. They could no longer rely on Aboriginal labour to help them cut bark or cross rivers as they had in the early 1830s. According to many squatters, the newly appointed Protectors of Aborigines were to blame. In April 1839, David Henry Wilsone wrote in a letter to his brother back home in Glasgow:

> The Natives ... are becoming very impertinent and frequently most troublesome, from the injudicious lenity almost on all occasions shown to them by the Government, making them suppose that they may injure the whites with impunity.[31]

By May 1840, Wilsone's 'Upper Wirrobbee' run in the Port Phillip district came under attack. He blamed the Governor as well as the Protectors:

> The Blacks have been very annoying to us, having attacked our stations 2 times within the last 6 weeks & succeeded in carrying away guns, pistols, clothing, bedding, & provisions. Our people gave them chase, but they succeeded in getting away. This is allowing to the disgraceful manner we have been treated by the Governor of N.S. Wales & Protectors of the Blacks, a parcel of regular humbugs.[32]

Others blamed the trial and execution of seven white men for the June 1838 Myall Creek Massacre. The fact that white men could actually be hanged for killing black people apparently gave Aboriginal people, as Flanagan scathingly wrote, 'a belief that they were to be saved from violence under all and every circumstance, and that a feeling had sprung up among them, that from some mysterious cause, they were thenceforward especial objects of care with the King of Great Britain'. Flanagan caustically continued: 'The settlers and their friends openly attributed the blame' for 'the violent warfare carried on, on the frontiers of the colony, with spear and musket' to the Myall Creek trials and the 'Protectorate of the Aborigines'. Numerous letters to newspapers chorused that the colonial government was being far too soft on Aboriginal people and this was why they were suddenly attacking the squatters with impunity, right across the entire frontier.[33]

Introduction

Rivers and resistance

Among 'the colonists whose interests were involved in the matter' as Flanagan called the letter-writing squatters and their financiers, few if any suggested this was a fight back against the occupation of Aboriginal lands. By 1840, squatters had occupied a continuous, if patchy, belt from Port Phillip (Melbourne) in the south to the Darling Downs (west of Brisbane) in the north. From 1838 to 1842, the hundreds of reports of conflict in newspapers, journals, letters and records quite precisely match this huge sweep of Country. Importantly, they match broad swathes of land centred on the rivers and waterways of the vast Murray-Darling basin.

This connection of Country, rivers and resistance has rarely been noted by historians. However, it has been seen as critical by First Nations people. According to Wiradyuri Elder Uncle James Ingram, the Murrumbidgee River was 'not a boundary', but a 'responsibility'. It belonged to all Wiradyuri clans. The river was more than a physical entity and had important spiritual significance. According to Uncle James, the Lizard clan or 'Narinjera' had 'the same totem' as many other clans along the river. All these clan groups 'would have united as a body' in bringing hundreds of warriors together in 'defence of the river' that was at the heart of their Country.

The raids and attacks and killing of cattle and sheep followed a path – a path along the Murrumbidgee River 'from Narrandera to Gundagai'. As Uncle James notes, the Riverine Red Gum could only be found along this waterway. These giant old trees and their river habitats were incredibly important to southern Wiradyuri people. They provided so much: canoes, shields and water carriers, to name a few. They created places for animals. They provided shade and shelter. According to Uncle James, in the great fightback of the southern Wiradyuri around 1840, the river and its richness was what Wiradyuri wanted back.[34]

...

This is a story of the fightback to regain control of the rivers, the lifeblood of Country. It follows the push back by warriors along the Murrumbidgee. It follows battles on the Ovens, Goulburn and Broken Rivers. It continues west and north along the Wambool, Bogan, Namoi and up to the Big River, now known as the Gwydir. It continues along smaller waterways such as Waterloo Creek, and moves along waterholes and reedy river bends where battles were fought and terrible forms of revenge sought.

At times, Aboriginal resistance warfare was a slow and persistent affair, chipping away at the heart of the colonisers' ventures – their sheep and cattle. So too, lone shepherds and stockmen were picked off here and there, which terrified the other station hands. At other times it broke out into what can only be called total war. The term Frontier Wars was coined by historians to reflect the nature of warfare that occurred over vast areas and long time periods. It utterly fails to reflect these periods of all out, total war, a war for, as Uncle Bill Allen Junior calls it, the defence of homelands.

At certain periods where large allegiances of warrior forces occurred or there were co-ordinated simultaneous conflicts such as in the late 1830s and early 1840s, rather than a 'frontier', there was what might be better considered as a front – a military front line between two forces at war – where a co-ordinated and widespread counterattack occurred. What follows is the story of the most significant, protracted, widespread and bloody of these major fightbacks in the Australian Wars – The Uprising of 1838 to 1844.[35]

PART ONE
Uprising

CHAPTER ONE
'An exterminating warfare'

'Levy war against the enemy in a vigorous manner'

In late 1834, a gang of bushrangers raided the 'Jamison station', the furthest along the Namoi River. The Namoi begins to the west of present-day Uralla in inland northern New South Wales. It meanders south, then west through Manilla and Gunnedah, then swings north to Boggabri and Narrabri. It once fed mighty sweeping grass lands and now mostly feeds the giant cotton fields heading west to Wee Waa, then southwest above the Pillaga Scrub before flowing through Walgett, where it joins the Barwon River. In a grand sweeping arc, it passes mostly through Gomeroi Country.

At the time, the 'Jamison station' was undoubtedly the squatting run furthest from any township in the colony of New South Wales. It was probably the most remote outpost in the entire British empire. The station's owner, Sir John Jamison, was of course not there in 1834. Apart from his 'Regentville' country estate near Penrith in western Sydney, he owned or leased the largest amount of land in the colony at the time. Jamison sent his employees to the Namoi. He had much business to do attending horse races at the Sydney Turf Club, running the Sydney College school and being president of the Agricultural and Horticultural Society of New South Wales.

According to Jamison's overseer on the Namoi station, George Biddles, in December 1834 five bushrangers bailed up the stockmen who worked at the station at their huts. At far-flung outstations deep in Aboriginal land, all stockmen were well-armed. Jamison's workers decided to fight and, after a gun battle with Biddles's men, two of the bushrangers, 'McDonald and Lynch', were killed. Three others fled. They headed away from all the other stations upriver and followed the Namoi deep into Gomeroi Country, where few if any white people had

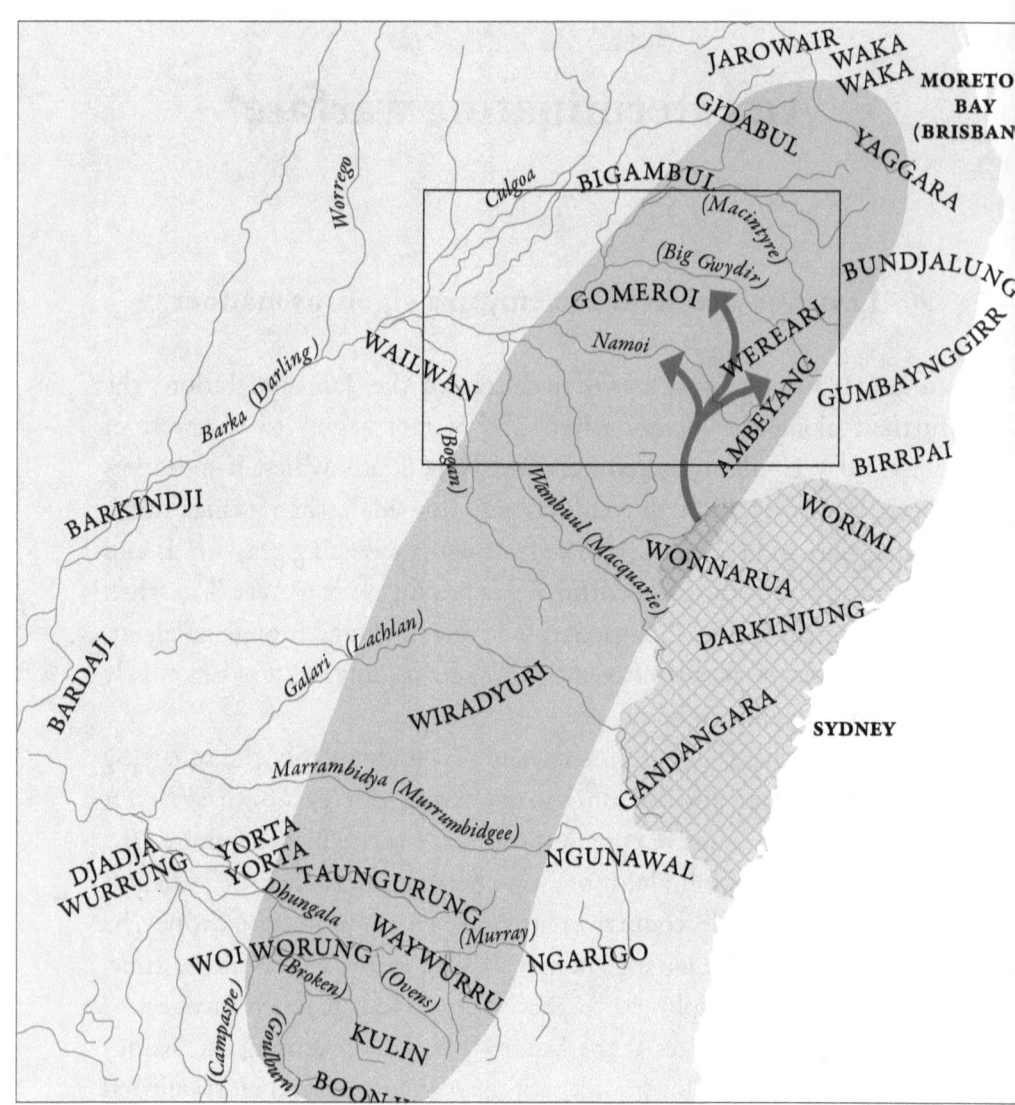

Northwest New South Wales, late 1830s
The 'Settled Districts' are indicated by hatching.
The movement of squatters, stockmen and stock marked with arrows.

been before. They may have chosen this direction to escape a pursuit by the Mounted Police that would be sure to follow. But somewhere beyond present-day Wee Waa they were 'harried and attacked', as another of Jamison's stockkeepers, William Thomas, later reported, by 'native blacks' in 'great number'.

According to Thomas, he was told these warriors were of 'gigantic stature (seven feet in height)' and 'great ferocity'. Thomas learned from 'Natty, the Namoie chief' what had happened to the bushrangers. Natty had been 'informed by native blacks' further down river 'that one of the gang of white robbers had been shot by their own party, and two tumbled down [killed] by the natives'.[1]

McDonald and Lynch's ill-fated gang may also have headed deep into Aboriginal lands in the hope of finding some allies. In the 1830s, settlers were raising concerns about bushrangers and warriors combining forces. In June 1835, the editor of the *Sydney Gazette* was worried some escaped convicts and a party of military deserters had teamed up with warriors and were raiding and roaming with impunity in the Upper Hunter Valley:

> That beautiful district the Hunter seems destined to be the frequent theatre of turbulence and atrocity, not only from the convicts, but the aboriginal natives, who seem to have imbibed an hostility to the British which it will require much activity and toil wholly to subdue.

In mid-1835, four men, 'Cockie, Scrammy Headed Jackey, Baker and Jemmy', were outlawed and a £60 reward was placed on their heads for attacking and plundering a station on the Williams River. In another of the so-called 'dreadful outrages' by the 'native blacks' at the Williams River, 'five of Mr. Mackenzie's servants' were killed and according to the *Sydney Gazette*, 'the blacks are said to be led by four bushrangers'.

The editor of the *Gazette* went on to describe this 'turbulence and atrocity' as 'rebellion'. And this rebellion against the Crown was especially dangerous if reports were true of a 'union of a band of free men armed at all points, with the natives and convicts'. Usually, in most districts of the colony, asserted the editor, it had been the British stockmen and convicts who instigated violence against Aboriginal people. But this was different. He could only think of one other instance (apparently ignoring Tasmania), at Bathurst in 1824, where there had been such 'a continued and determined animosity like that prevalent for some years past, among the aborigines along the extended chain of out-stations which border upon, and lie beyond, the officially recognised line of colonization'.[2]

*

The great uprising of 1838 to 1844 did not begin overnight. It was not a 'storming of the barricades' moment but a long build-up through the early 1830s. Even as early as 1827, when the first tentative push into Gomeroi Country began, Benjamin Singleton's men at 'Tarrimanbaj' (at that point one of only three stations formed across the entire Liverpool Plains) had come under attack by what they reckoned were 200 warriors. Eleven stockmen held them off and 'a considerable number' of warriors were killed. Around 1828 Joseph Onus's run 'Borambil' in the Upper Mooki Valley also came under attack from 'hundreds' of warriors. It was later claimed that the well-armed stockmen killed 200 of them.[3]

By the early 1830s, the sons of those families who had taken Wiradyuri lands across the Bathurst Plains – Cox, Lawson, Blaxland – as well as the sons of the Hunter Valley, Hawkesbury and Macdonald River settlers, were now moving north into the Liverpool Plains. By 1835, reports of conflict and violence across the plains increased. In that year, the editor of the *Sydney Herald* noted that to the north of the Hunter River region there were reports of an 'exterminating warfare, on the part of the combined blacks and bushrangers'. In June, this war apparently continued 'with unabating virulence'.[4]

A party of mounted police was sent to the Williams River, to the north of the lower Hunter Valley, but the 'enemy' had moved to the Paterson River. However, one of the bushrangers who set out on a 'reconnoitring expedition' for the 'blacks and bushrangers' was captured by 'Mr. A. Park, and committed to gaol by Mr Townshend, J. P.' To his captor's surprise, this man, 'covered with rags, and in a most filthy and squalid condition' soon 'discoursed most eloquently on his rights as a free subject'. This was no escaped convict bushranger. He boldly 'talked of his right to choose his own company, and threatened Mr. Park with a prosecution in the Supreme Court'.

After being taken into custody he apparently 'changed his tone, said he had been kept a prisoner by the blacks, and gave information where they were encamped'. With this, 'the police, assisted by a strong body of armed settlers and their servants' headed to the encampment and after what the editor of the *Sydney Herald* described as 'a slight resistance', the police captured two men and identified one of them as having been 'concerned in the late outrages'. But the main party was still at large and they brazenly attacked the sheep station of Magistrate Townshend – the very man who committed their eloquent and free white comrade to gaol. They also killed two of Townshend's shepherds.

The colonists in the region blamed the Mounted Police, who they believed were 'afraid to fire on the blacks' because their 'sergeant' (actually Lieutenant Nathaniel Lowe) had been on trial previously 'for killing some blacks'. No mind, the Hunter Valley and Williams River colonists 'set about firstly, purchasing arms and ammunition at Maitland' so they could be 'resolute in self defence'.

They also wanted 'to get an assurance for the shooting of all blacks'. According to a settler from the Williams River writing to the *Australian* newspaper, 'the latter is, in all our opinions, the readiest way of quieting the country'. The now well-armed Williams River settler believed 'the only effectual manner of coming at them, would be to protect our property, and let the Settlers, Stock-keepers, and Government Men, turn out and take the bush, and find out their camp, and when there at night to broadside them'.

No one in the 1830s could argue New South Wales didn't have a free press – one willing and able to publish a call for wholesale murder. Other less outright genocidal squatters called for a military force to be sent to the area. The enthusiastic Mr Park travelled to Sydney to petition the Governor for military aid. With the newspapers calling for Aboriginal blood, Governor Bourke soon assented and 'ordered Major Croker and fifty men of the 17th Regiment, to proceed to the scene of disturbance'. The editor of the *Sydney Herald* was full of praise for the governor and pleased that 'Major Croker is armed with full instructions and authority to levy war against the enemy in a vigorous manner'.

The 'war against the enemy' had shifted a gear. The joining of black and white 'insurgents' was a huge threat to the remote regions of the colony. Perhaps it should have been expected that, as had happened before, escaped convicts would team up with warriors. In the 1790s, John Wilson (who lived with Aboriginal people for an extended period) and William Knight had joined Pemulwuy's warriors around Sydney. There were other examples. But when the editor of the *Sydney Herald* heard that 'free men as well as Convicts are found to join the blacks', this was truly shocking news.[5]

There was no law against it. Any British person could wander into the bush and not return to 'civilisation'. And many did, often unintentionally by shipwreck or becoming lost. Some such as William Buckley spent long years living with Aboriginal people, accepted into their society and families. But a shipwreck or being lost was understandable. There now seemed to be people choosing to live outside European society and work with Aboriginal people. Surely, pleaded the *Sydney Herald* in June 1835, the government must do something about this?

By August, they had. The Legislative Council passed an act that classed all free colonists living beyond the pale of the colony as illegal 'vagrants'. The act was designed to capture all sorts of people from runaways to sly-grog sellers and bushrangers, but it now also covered free men who chose to live with Aboriginal people. They could now be captured and imprisoned. Any rights to 'choose their own company' beyond the settled districts were gone. The terms of the Act were published widely: 'any person, not being a black native, lodging or wandering in company with the black natives of this colony, who shall not give a good account to the satisfaction of any justice that he hath a fixed place of abode' could be declared a vagrant. One possible source of recruits in attacks on the colonists had, it seems, been closed off.[6]

In August, the 'blacks of Williams' River ... resumed their depredations, stopping and plundering carts and robbing huts'. One report noted 'a party of them armed with muskets went to a Settler's station, drove the men from their sheep, and robbed the huts of three muskets and every thing portable'. The *Sydney Herald* blustered: 'now that the blacks are possessed of so many fire-arms, they are of course much more formidable than ever'.[7]

The 'blacks of Williams' River' were not just more formidable, but were on the offensive. There were several reports of gun battles between warriors and stockmen. The settler who wanted to 'find out their camp, and when there at night to broadside them' was quite alarmed by their skill and tactics. He noted 'they show a good deal of tact' and 'in their second attack on Myles's station; they formed two parties, one of which appeared in front of the huts and fired, the men turned out to meet them, then the others who were behind marched and took possession of their station, so that they were between the two parties of blacks and of course had no alternative but to win the race [flee]'.[8]

There was a scourge of bushranging across inland New South Wales during the 1830s. At Bathurst, after convict stockworkers had been given arms to 'defend themselves' against a fierce onslaught by the Wiradyuri in 1824, the number of firearms in circulation among a large convict population led to a spate of violence and robberies. It culminated in the so-called 'Bathurst Rebellion' of 1830, the largest armed rising by convicts since the Castle Hill Uprising in 1804. In desperation, Governor Bourke wrote to London for permission to hand out rewards to convicts who protected their masters' property. By 1835, convicts were effectively being recruited to fight back against escaped convicts. And they were also to be rewarded for defending their masters' property and stock against attack from warriors.[9]

Clarke of the Kindur

The convict George Clarke, son of a London comb-maker and thus nicknamed 'The Barber', bolted from his assigned master Benjamin Singleton on the Liverpool Plains around 1828. His memoirs are notoriously embellished, but he was accepted into the Gomeroi north of the plains, near present-day Boggabri. He apparently learned the language and had two wives. Barber, 'tatooed' with initiation scars, took it upon himself to lead warriors on cattle raids and build stockyards to house their supplies of beef. Several convicts joined him. At first they were in Gomeroi lands far from white settlement. But by 1830, the squatters and stockmen were closing in.

In 1831, Clarke and Gomeroi warriors were raiding cattle and robbing homesteads as far south as Maitland in the Hunter Valley. When he was finally captured and sent to Bathurst gaol, the strikingly named Ensign Lauderdale Maule of the Mounted Police took down an account of his adventures. Clarke regaled Maule with stories of a great river he called the 'Kindur', flowing through luxuriant pastures. When he got wind of it, the soldier-turned-surveyor Major Thomas Livingstone Mitchell was most interested. Mitchell soon set off on what he thought might be the discovery of a great inland sea.[10]

Mitchell's expedition came across the remnants of Clarke's house surrounded by a village of numerous Gomeroi gunyahs. The yards were strewn with bullock bones that, as Mitchell wrote, plainly showed 'the object of the stock-yard and that of the Barber's alliance with the Aborigines of these parts'. The nearby water source is still known as Barbers Lagoon today.

Mitchell was more concerned with finding Clarke's 'big river'. He travelled on, desperately hoping that the huge system of smaller rivers all ultimately flowing south to the Darling and Murray rivers (annoyingly for Mitchell, recently charted by Charles Sturt) led to some great inland sea, rather than the ocean. He was wrong. Clarke's 'Kindur' river that, according to him, emptied into the ocean or a vast inland sea may well have been a great expanse of flood waters. Mitchell pushed his bullocks and horses on, increasingly concerned by fires across the grasslands all around – to him this was a sign 'the invisible blacks, the Barber's allies, were not well disposed to us'.[11]

Escaped convicts and warriors made many alliances at this time. They occurred deep in the bush and there are few surviving records or stories of how and why this happened. The fear of them joining forces, however, is widely recorded. The alliance with 'The Barber' certainly gave the

Gomeroi insights into how and where to strike in their raids and attacks, as well as practical experience in managing such a wonderful mobile food supply as sheep and cattle. They were using metal axes even before the first venturers deep into Gomeroi Country arrived near present-day Narrabri. And Gomeroi who had never seen Europeans apart from Clarke before shouted in English at Thomas Mitchell's party's approach: 'white fellow, white fellow'.[12]

'They know well enough ... their land is going to be taken away'

By 1830, the Wiradyuri, Gomeroi and other peoples across inland New South Wales were being invaded by an unseen enemy – disease. George 'The Barber' Clarke had witnessed it first-hand. In 1832, Mitchell's party were at Borambil Creek (near present-day Willow Tree) and saw a 'tribe', 'extremely ill, being affected with a virulent kind of small-pox'. In July 1835, Mitchell was at Lake Poopelloe near present-day Wilcannia when he came across 'three large tombs of the natives', nearly 2 metres high. Mitchell wrote he 'could scarcely doubt, that these tombs covered the remains of that portion of the tribe, swept off by the fell disease, which left such marks on those who survived'. He was talking about smallpox.[13]

From around 1830 the disease had travelled far ahead of the colonists who had brought it with them. Smallpox appeared in the Hunter Valley, where it killed around half of those Wonnarua who had survived the loss of their homelands to sheep farmers in the 1820s. It moved unseen, from clan to clan, along the riverways right across to South Australia. When naturalist and painter George French Angus travelled out from Adelaide in 1845 he noted that smallpox had depopulated the banks of the Murray River 'for more than a thousand miles'. Some Wiradyuri understood it to be the powerful magic of distant enemy tribes. Others soon saw the connection between smallpox and the Europeans.[14]

With such devastation, when the squatters began their great land rush in earnest in the mid-1830s, what chance was there for any kind of fightback? It seems the disease forced some groups to move or unite with others. Mitchell's party, who in 1832 saw a 'tribe' with smallpox, noted they had moved from their homelands and were 'strangers in the land to which they had resorted'. In his recent study of the Murray-Darling basin, Quentin Beresford notes that after smallpox, Aboriginal people had become 'so powerless' it placed them 'at a distinct disadvantage in resisting the European invaders'. It was certainly a disadvantage. But as they began to steal more and more firearms, ally with bushrangers and feast on sheep and cattle, Aboriginal people were certainly not 'powerless'.[15]

The so-called 'Wild tribes beyond the Bogan' were definitely fighting back. In early 1835, an exploring party led by 'Mr. C. Coxen, who arrived in this Colony with orders from the Zoological Garden, London', had pushed 100 miles past the last station on the Namoi River. Here they were unimpressed by the 'dead level' country where 'not a hill was visible'. They also found their reception, even though they had 'some tame blacks' with them, to be 'very hostile'. After warriors threw spears at them and harried them constantly, attempting to cut out one or two of the party at a time, Coxen's hired men refused to go on. As the *Sydney Monitor* put it, they 'refused positively to proceed any further – threatening to abandon him if attacked by the ferocious natives'.[16]

In July 1835, the *Gazette* reported on 'particulars' that had reached Bathurst 'of the murder of one of Major Mitchell's exploring party, at Bogan Creek, ninety miles from Boru [Boree]'. The *Gazette* called them 'the "Mial" or wild tribes beyond Bogan'. As Mitchell wrote, 'the conduct of several of these tribes was very extraordinary. To conciliate them was quite hopeless, but not from any apprehensions on their part. On the contrary, the more we endeavoured to supply their real wants and show good will towards them, the more they seemed to covet what was utterly useless to them, and the more they plotted our destruction'.

When Mitchell's party camped by the Baaka-Darling river just below where today's town of Bourke is, he built a timber construction grandly named after the governor, 'Fort Bourke'. As Mitchell wrote:

> the position was naturally good, overhanging the river, and commanding a good run for the cattle; but I strengthened it as a

place of defence against the natives, by cutting down the few trees on it, and erecting a block-house large enough to contain all our stores and equipment.[17]

Major Mitchell was the archetypal explorer of inland Australia – a military man. He made military-style missions into unknown and potential enemy lands; as he himself wrote in 1832: 'it is as well ... to be guarded, and we are as much so as if traversing the country of a civilised enemy'. When he felt his party under threat he fired rockets in the air or ordered volleys of musket fire 'by way of giving them an idea of what could be done by us if requisite'.[18]

Almost all the well-known explorers were ex-military, or they lapped up Sturt's treatise on how to conduct an expedition. Sturt urged inland travellers and convoys of sheep and cattle to operate as military units. In 1835 he published 'Obstacles that attend travelling into the interior of Australia' in various newspapers. Sturt noted such handy points as that:

> ... at every station [campsite] so arrange your drays and provisions that they may serve as a defence in case of your being attacked [and] ... it is absolutely necessary to establish nightly guards, not only for the security of the camp, but of the cattle ... it is essential to have a force strong enough to maintain an obstinate resistance against any number of savages, where no mercy is expected.

The ex-military officer, schooled in warfare in Napoleonic Europe and North America, was clear and 'decidedly of the opinion that no party could long remain in the distant interior without some fatal collision with the natives, which would be attended with the most deplorable consequences'.[19]

Building a fortification such as Fort Bourke might have made it worse for Mitchell's party in the long run. In August 1836, a writer to the *Commercial Journal* noted that the 'hostility of the natives only arose when the indications of occupation of their territory appeared by the establishment of a depot, and the return of the party'. He suggested that travellers who kept their march, and 'the heads of their flocks, turned to the westward' would 'disarm hostility, and meet with every facility to progress'. He urged squatters to look like they were just passing through Aboriginal lands.

A very different observation was made by the squatter-turned-politician Thomas McCombie, who 'claimed a long acquaintance with Aboriginal people'. In evidence to an 1845 inquiry into the condition of Aboriginal people, McCombie suggested that when Aboriginal people (in present-day northern Victoria) 'saw Sir Thomas [Mitchell] with horses, and mules, and men all armed ... they know well enough when their land is going to be taken away from them'.[20]

At one point on his vast journeys through Aboriginal lands, Mitchell's party 'had a re-contre [encounter] with the natives ... and in repelling their attacks, two blacks were killed'. When it looked like warriors were about to attack, Mitchell operated the only way he knew – in military fashion. With a vastly outnumbered party, a classic form of defence is attack. As squatters were to also work out, with terrible consequences, a pre-emptive strike with firearms was a sure way of stopping warriors in their tracks. One writer to the *Australian* suggested it was in fact necessary in order to 'awe and force the insurgent natives to more peaceable conduct'.[21]

Mitchell later faced scrutiny and criticism over these killings and his 'driving' another group across a river. He was ultimately exonerated in an exhaustive inquest that came down on the side of 'self defence'. Still, the widespread condemnation of Mitchell's attacks in the press was a warning to those who might shoot first and ask questions later. The squatters and others who conducted such attacks were now less likely to crow about them in the newspapers.[22]

'Ten stand of arms and ammunition, and one sword'

Several years earlier, in 1829, Hamilton Hume and Charles Sturt had been welcomed along the Baaka-Darling River. But by 1835, things had changed. Mitchell's party was not welcome in Barkindji, Bardaji,

Murrawari, Nyemba and Nyirrpa Country. Squatters were not welcome along the Bogan River right through Wiradyuri and Gomeroi Country. In July that year, the *Gazette* reported that right along the Bogan River warriors 'have commenced a series of aggressions which have created alarm amongst the stations bordering on that remote spot plundering the huts with impunity and outrage, and in some cases spearing the hut keepers'.

The squatters along the lower Macquarie and Bogan Rivers were then banned from taking up further runs in the area. The colonial authorities said they could not offer any police or other protection for them at such remote locations. The fearsome 'Bogan Blacks' had won a significant victory. No further squatters entered the area until the Bathurst pastoralist William Lee illegally did so in 1841. And when he did, three of his men were soon dead.[23]

Indeed, conflict was so widespread at this time that 'friendly' locals had become a feature of advertisements for land sales. 'One Hundred One Acre Allotments' were advertised in August 1836 'at Kempsey, near Commandant's Hill, on the banks of the River McLeay'. Among the selling points such as river access and cedar forests was the inducement that 'the Natives in that quarter are exceedingly friendly'.[24]

They certainly weren't in many other places. In February 1836 the *Gazette* urged the government to take action against 'several tribes of the interior'. The editor believed that 'a timely shew of determination by the authorities would no doubt go far towards stifling all bellicose symptoms in their infancy'. When two white men were killed at Port Phillip, a letter writer to the *Sydney Herald* suggested the 'annihilation of the whole body of Port Phillip natives' would not do justice for the death of two white men.[25]

Throughout 1836, conflict across the colony of New South Wales from north to south was being reported in all the newspapers. The *Sydney Monitor* noted:

> The Blacks, it is said, are again becoming troublesome at the upper districts of Hunter's River; and it would appear ... that in the country to the southward, they are also committing outrages.

From the circumstance of their having so many arms with them, it is probable that some bushrangers may have joined, and are now leading them.

The *Monitor* printed a letter from 'Nenah Farm' on the Bila Galari or Lachlan River, dated 18 January 1836. One hundred warriors had come from the Murrumbidgee 'in search of the Warwick Blacks'. After shooting at some Wiradyuri who were working at the neighbouring station and then ransacking the squatter's house, they left. According to the letter writer at Nenah, 'they had ten stand of arms and ammunition, and one sword, spears in abundance, and other instruments of war'.[26]

Across inland New South Wales at this time, a force of ten firearms was a powerful one. Rarely did Mounted Police patrol in larger units, and settlers had to organise between often distant stations to bring that many firearms to bear. The idea that warriors did not take up firearms should be dismissed. At Port Phillip (to become Melbourne) in June 1836, the first item on the agenda of 'a first general meeting of the inhabitants' was 'that all attempts [to] teach the Aborigines the use of fire-arms should be henceforth religiously abstained from'. But it was too late. As we shall see, there were many instances of warriors using guns in battle in the 1830s and beyond.[27]

'The Messrs., Hall have been obliged to abandon the station'

During 1836, warriors were forcing squatters to leave new runs and look elsewhere in 'less dangerous' locations. Brothers Thomas, Ebenezer and Mathew Hall had reaped the windfall of their parents George and Mary's land grants along the upper Hawkesbury River. Like many of the Hawkesbury settlers, the Halls sent their young 'native born' sons north to the Hunter Valley, and then the Liverpool Plains. By the mid-1830s, the Big River even further to the north beckoned and the Halls established a run at Bingara, not far from Myall Creek. Squatting ventures were often family affairs, calling upon those who could be trusted. Hall's family connections included his nephew John Henry Fleming, whose name was to become connected with Myall Creek forever.

The Big River picks up flow from its headwaters near Uralla and snakes through the rolling hills around Bingara. The large flats between the hills were perfect cattle and sheep country and the Hall brothers decided it was a good place to set up a station. Within a few days they had built a bark hut. But then the Hall brothers suffered 'a dreadful outrage committed by the blacks'. One evening, 'a party of blacks, about twelve in number paid a visit to the station where they remained for a few hours', obviously scouting the hut for numbers of men and firearms. As the *Colonist* newspaper described it:

> on the following day, the Messrs. Hall, who were alone in the hut, their men having gone out to split timber in the bush, observed a party of blacks probably about fifty in number, armed with spears, waddies, and tomahawks approaching, and suspecting from their appearance and menacing gestures that their intentions were not the most amicable, it was thought advisable to make preparations for their reception, should they show any symptoms of a hostile disposition. While Mr. Hall was procuring a supply of powder and shot from the box in which they were kept, the blacks attacked the hut and launched several spears at himself and at his brother one of which grazed his eyebrow, but fortunately did him no material injury. A shot was fired in return, which wounded one of the blacks, and seeing preparations for more they scampered off.

The Hall brothers feared the worst for their two assigned servant stockworkers. When they found them, 'the corpse of one of the men lay on the ground dreadfully mangled, scarcely a feature in his face being distinguishable'. The other was severely wounded but survived. The *Colonist* declared that 'the Messrs., Hall have been obliged to abandon the station, and to look out for another in some less dangerous locality'. The brothers headed further north to the Mehi River near present-day Moree.

Thomas Hall set about establishing a new station he called 'Wee Bolla Bolla' on the Mehi River. His nephews Joseph and John Fleming followed suit and set up 'Mungie Bundie' nearby. They seem to have remained on guard, perhaps vengeful about being forced from their Big River run. As we shall see, John Fleming was soon to join the campaign of Major Nunn's Mounted Police near Moree, and then led his own campaign, perhaps more aptly described as a rampage, at Myall Creek.[28]

In the grandly named New England region, conflict was escalating. To the east of Bingara, the higher altitude tableland with a more European climate was prized by squatters. But they were not able to take Ambēyang lands without a fight. The *Sydney Times* reported in October 1836 that 'the Blacks are very troublesome at New England, (Invermein) destroying cattle, and not sparing, but spearing their owners'. Several stockworkers had been killed. The newspaper called for 'some active measures' to be 'adopted by the settlers under the sanction of the government, for the protection of their own lives and property from their sable neighbours'. According to the newspaper, the armed settlers simply needed a police magistrate in charge and the settlers could then be trusted to look after their own defence.[29]

A common thread in the increasing conflict was revenge against white retaliation. According to the reminiscences of Susan Young, daughter of one of the first squatters in the area, at the Macdonald River station near present-day Walcha, squatters put arsenic in milk and gave it to Ambēyang people. Another 'story passed down' about 'Terrible Vale' station, just south of present-day Uralla, was that 'a large number of Aborigines were killed near the creek'. The station was apparently named after the head stockman, who was known as 'Terrible Billy'. He was reported 'a ruthless bully of the local Aborigines' and many 'were supposedly shot by Terrible Billy who was greatly feared in the Terrible Vale area and further south'. Today, the scenic drive called Thunderbolt's Way after the bushranger Captain Thunderbolt and the New England Highway that passes by Thunderbolt's Rock are well signposted for tourists. The Macdonald River and Terrible Vale Creek killings are not.[30]

What was clear in the late 1830s across the New England tableland and west toward present-day Moree was that massacring Aboriginal people was becoming a common white response to raids and attacks on stockmen and stock.[31]

'They evinced decided hostility towards the incoming settlers'

By 1837, conflict was reported across a vast swathe of land from the Central Coast to Port Stephens and Port Macquarie, and inland to the Upper Hunter Valley, the Liverpool Plains, and the New England region. Below the tablelands, raids and attacks had been increasing since 1835 when at Kiripit (now Rawdon Vale, west of present-day Gloucester), five convict workers were killed, 'attacked singly and in open daylight'. The 'body of one was never recovered'. Apparently, 'the perpetrators were the Barrington River natives'. Only one white man escaped 'after a [running] fight of over 25 miles [roughly 40 kilometres]; the last spear was thrown almost in sight of Underbank House' to the northwest of present-day Dungog.

On the coast, there was also a 'decided hostility towards the incoming settlers'. The Birrpai (Biripi) and Worimi – the 'branch of the tribe inhabiting the Cape Hawke district and those located along the Barrington River valley' were reported to have combined in attacks. According to a much later account, 'the Cape Hawke natives came into open conflict at Waterloo, on the Upper Wallamba – resulting in a bloodless victory for the natives'. The Wallamba River flows from the ranges east of Gloucester toward the coast at present-day Forster-Tuncurry. Today, a road along the upper reaches of the river is still called Waterloo Road, undoubtedly named after the 'bloodless victory'. There are no other details, yet the fact this recalls an Aboriginal victory is rare among the many other places called 'Waterloo' across New South Wales. Most are named after white victories in battle, or massacres.[32]

The deaths of the five stockmen killed at Kiripit went down in local history as the Rawdon Vale Massacre. It seems they had no firearms, as it was reported much later that one man 'fought his last great fight armed only with a paling'. In northern New South Wales in 1837 retaliation and massacre were being conducted tit for tat and there were now no holds barred.

In fact, the Rawdon Vale Massacre was a retaliation for an earlier massacre that Australian Agricultural Company stockworkers had conducted. The company had established a 'heifer station' at 'Baker's Creek, 12 miles northeast of Gloucester, now known as Upper Ghangat'. Some cattle were speared and the rest taken, 'driven through the wild brushes at the head of the Myall, almost to the foreshores of Port Stephens'. The company's workers were not armed – it actually had its own kind of military force, something akin to the British East India Company's, though not on so grand a scale. The company employed a small body of 'time expired soldiers' as a kind of private police force. When settlers around the Port Stephens area organised 'punitive bands' to hunt down warriors, the company's 'militia' joined them. But they could not patrol all the outstations. Unarmed and alone in their huts, the convict workers at Baker's Creek 'mixed arsenic in dampers and placed them where the natives had easy access to them. The result was deadly to the natives. The black warriors lay down and died all around'.[33]

By 1837 attacks had become bolder. News of stockworkers being killed spread rapidly across the colonies. The editor of the *Launceston Advertiser* wrote in March:

> In letters from Port Macquarie, (New South Wales,) dated 12th of February, we regret to learn that three free servants, employed by Mr. Alex. McLeod as sawyers and splitters, have been murdered by the native blacks. Four men inhabited the hut which the natives attacked, and out of the four only one escaped to bear the dreadful tidings to their employer.

The *Sydney Herald* summed it up in December that year:

> Letters have been received from the Northern parts of the Colony, which state, that the Blacks are murdering the shepherds and stockmen with impunity. These letters also inform us, that the same tribe of Blacks are destroying the cattle by hundreds.[34]

In October it was reported two stockmen were killed on the Liverpool Plains and that 'a variety of outrages' had been 'committed lately by the aborigines among the stock-stations at the outskirts of Liverpool Plains'. It was concerning that groups of warriors were combining:

> Several tribes of the blacks, it appears, have for some time been congregated together in that vicinity and have speared a considerable number of cattle, the property of various persons.

Convict workers for 'Mr. Bowman of Richmond' had 'fallen victims to their ferocity'. The inevitable calls came for 'the Government' to 'lose no time in dispatching some of the military to aid the residents in that vicinity in reducing the savages to order'.[35]

Far to the south, on the great expanse of the 'Maneroo Plains' or Monaro Tableland in present-day southeast New South Wales, more conflict was occurring. In November 1836, Ngarigo warriors had some success in destroying the plans of squatters on their lands. The *Australian* newspaper reported that 'the blacks are troublesome, on account of their continually spearing cattle, as many head have been found in the gullies with only a small-portion of the carcase consumed [sic]'. Apparently, 'several gentlemen' were contemplating leaving the Monaro Plains to 'proceed overland to Port Phillip'.[36]

'The cunning of the Elders'

In 1837, a 'new chum' in the colony and self-proclaimed 'adventurer', James Balfour, chose some Aboriginal land on the Bogan River to 'take up a run'. He, like many, had been lured to inland New South Wales by reports of the opportunities for young men with a little means to make a huge profit in sheep. Balfour set up a company, 'Balfour and Co.' and soon occupied two stations on the river. One was named 'Mudall' after the people who lived there. Commissioner for Crown Lands Francis Allman later said that of all the 'tribes' in the area, they were the 'fiercest of all'. Five stockmen had already been killed on the two runs that were supposed to make the 'Balfour and Co.' fortune.[37]

Balfour's 'Bogan station' didn't last long. After an incident where the 'Bogan Blacks' attacked him and he was only saved by the intervention of a 'Macquarie black', Balfour decided to leave his station and passed it on, as he said, 'to a gentleman who entertained a better opinion of the blacks'.

Balfour thought himself lucky. He and his neighbours were plagued by 'cattle and sheep stealing' that was, he wrote, 'so common ... that thousands of sheep and hundreds of cattle' had been taken 'in daylight from their white protectors, and sometimes the shepherds killed'. Balfour was incensed that 'in a district where the [white] population did not exceed 1,000 there were, in less than twelve months, twenty white men butchered'.[38]

Balfour echoed growing claims by squatters that squarely placed the blame for these attacks on 'misguided philanthropists'. Balfour later wrote in his 1845 handbook for prospective immigrants *A Sketch of New South Wales* that 'proper protection for the herds, flocks, and men, in the distant localities' was a drawback to squatting and needed to be addressed by the colonial government.

Despite spending six years in the colony, Balfour's account of 'the Australian Natives' is superficial. But the embittered Balfour noted several key elements of the attacks on his Bogan River stations that pointed to an organised resistance. He was exasperated by a level of planning in the cattle and sheep raids and attacks on stockmen. He believed these 'atrocious crimes', as he called them, were 'devised by the cunning of the elders of the Australian tribes' and 'executed by the strength and activity of the young men [sic]'.[39]

'A range of Sheep-walks' and land 'ready for the plough'

In just three years between 1835 and 1838, colonists took more Aboriginal land than in the previous fifty years. It was a frenzied land grab – the fastest occupation of First Peoples' land in the entire colonial world. In October 1835 Governor Bourke reported to the new Secretary for the Colonies, Lord Glenelg, that 'the Wool of New South Wales forms at present, and is likely long to continue [to be] its chief wealth'. After some hesitation, largely brought on by the reformist zeal growing in Britain that had urged the British to withdraw from Xhosa lands after the sixth Cape Frontier War in modern-day South Africa, Glenelg agreed. He authorised the expansion into Aboriginal lands.[40]

Until 1835, the colonial office had encouraged a policy of restraint over the growing colony. Lord Glenelg was a known social reformer and supporter of evangelical philanthropists; for him, restraining squatters was both financially prudent and humane. The 'limits of location' were to be enforced. Colonists who went beyond the limits of settlement effectively dragged the British empire with them, as had been seen in India, South Africa and North America. This was just too expensive to administer. And it was causing a headache from the liberals and humanitarians who were beginning to highlight the downsides of colonialism. Surely, they asked, there was plenty of land for the Colony of New South Wales within the great expanse of the so-called 'settled districts' of the Nineteen Counties – all 22.8 million acres of it?[41]

Yet numerous glowing reports of the lands the squatters were heading into kept crossing Lord Glenelg's desk in London. He was now quite convinced that 'the whole surface of the Country exhibits a range of Sheep-walks'. According to Glenelg, New South Wales was 'marked out by Nature for a Pastoral country' and when these 'Sheep-walks' were 'occupied in large Masses' they were 'of almost unrivalled value for the production of the finest description of Wool'. Glenelg could not ignore the wealth of the empire, and Aboriginal people paid the price. As the highest colonial authority, he gave the green light to occupy more and more Aboriginal lands.

The lure of wool was great. And wool was the perfect export for the far-flung colony. It could be brought long distances on bullock drays and stored and shipped for months on sea voyages. In 1836 it accounted for two-thirds of exports from the colony and at a peak price of 2 shillings per pound. It meant the colony might soon pay for itself, and even generate a tidy profit.

To make 'sheep walks' viable, Aboriginal land, or what the British had decided was now Crown Land, was to be sold. The British decided that this money – £116 000 for 374 000 acres of land in 1836 – would fund an immigration scheme assisting 'married artisans and labourers'. Now, the more land claimed and sold meant more and more people arriving in the colony, and more and more people drifting to the sheep stations where labour was in demand.[42]

But there was a problem. Squatters were moving around the outback like wandering nomads, seeking greener pastures along the next river or over the next range. If one run failed, they simply moved on to another. Glenelg worried that this giant 'Sheep-walk' placed the 'Shepherd and Herdsmen and all their associates in labour' far away from the 'Seat of Government'. No laws, argued Glenelg, could 'repress the spirit of adventure and speculation' such as had occurred at Port Phillip in 1835 by two of the greatest speculators of the age – John Batman at Port Phillip and Benjamin Boyd at Twofold Bay. It appeared to Glenelg that these men, even though they might have done it illegally, had 'converted an unproductive Waste into two great and flourishing Provinces'. With such a result for the colony, Glenelg pressed Governor Bourke that 'local Government' should 'place itself at the head of the undertakings in which the unauthorised Settlers have engaged'. It needed to provide 'guidance and direction of enterprises'. The colony needed to catch up with the speculators and their stockworkers on the frontier.[43]

The governor and his advisors in the Executive Council (the largest landowners and sheep farmers in the colony among them) came up with a plan. It was becoming more expensive for the government to reign in this land grab than to allow it. Governor Bourke proposed establishing 'Townships and Ports' that would surely diminish 'the evils of dispersion'. They would become centres of 'Civilisation and Government'. The land sales to government would fund their administration and 'guidance'.

In late 1836 the colonial government opened the floodgates. In July the oddly named 'Act to restrain the unauthorised occupation of Crown Land' was passed. Regulations for the Act released in October announced a £10 per annum licence could be granted for running sheep and cattle outside the Nineteen Counties. And in November, Major Thomas Mitchell's report on his travels through the Murray River region was published in the *Government Gazette*, for 'general information'. It was soon printed in every colonial newspaper over the following two weeks. Mitchell proudly reported that his party had traversed 'a region more extensive than Great Britain, equally rich in point of soil, and which now lies ready for the plough in many parts, as if specially prepared by the Creator for the industrious hands of Englishmen'. For Mitchell it was God, not Aboriginal people, who had 'specially prepared' these lands. There would be no stopping the squatting rush now.[44]

The wealth and growth of New South Wales relied upon the 'wide expanse of native Herbage', as Governor Bourke called it, that was fuelling a huge economic boom in wool. In 1836 the colony's entire expenditure on the people whose lands they were taking was in the form of blankets at a cost of £904. Income to the colonial coffers that same year from land sales produced more than £130 000. The former penal colony was now itself shackled to the private enterprise of turning Aboriginal land into 'a range of Sheep-walks'.[45]

CHAPTER TWO
The Battle for Big River

'The blacks call the Mounted Police "soldiers"'

Squatters constantly complained about the mounted police. They were regarded as quite useless in preventing raids on sheep stations and too scared of going on trial for killing 'blacks'. Yet the mounted police were seen in the settled districts as having something dashing and gallant about them. No cavalry regiments had ever been stationed in the Colony of New South Wales. Infantry who joined the mounted police had the opportunity to be part of an institution that was adored at home in England – the cavalry of empire. Men had the opportunity to wear a distinct uniform and a low-slung light cavalry sabre to official and social engagements in Sydney. It certainly attracted men from the infantry stationed in two-year rotations across the British colonies – there were no problems recruiting. Being part of a 'colonial cavalry' had more appeal than being a plodding redcoat foot soldier at the far end of the British world.

But it was hard work riding the Australian bush. Trying to ride down escaped convicts, bushrangers and Aboriginal warriors over hundreds of kilometres through the outback was certainly not the most enjoyable part of the job. Yet riding back into town, dusty, dirty, and reeking of a hard-fought and dangerous campaign must have felt like a well-earned bonus.

One of the main duties of the mounted police was to be in effect the bodyguard of the lands commissioners as they traversed great realms under their jurisdictions, sorting out competing claims, taking censuses and investigating raids, attacks and killings. As the squatter Edward Curr noted in 1841, commissioners had 'duties of a composite judicial and military character'. Curr was taken aback by the military appearance of the mounted police:

The Battle for Big River

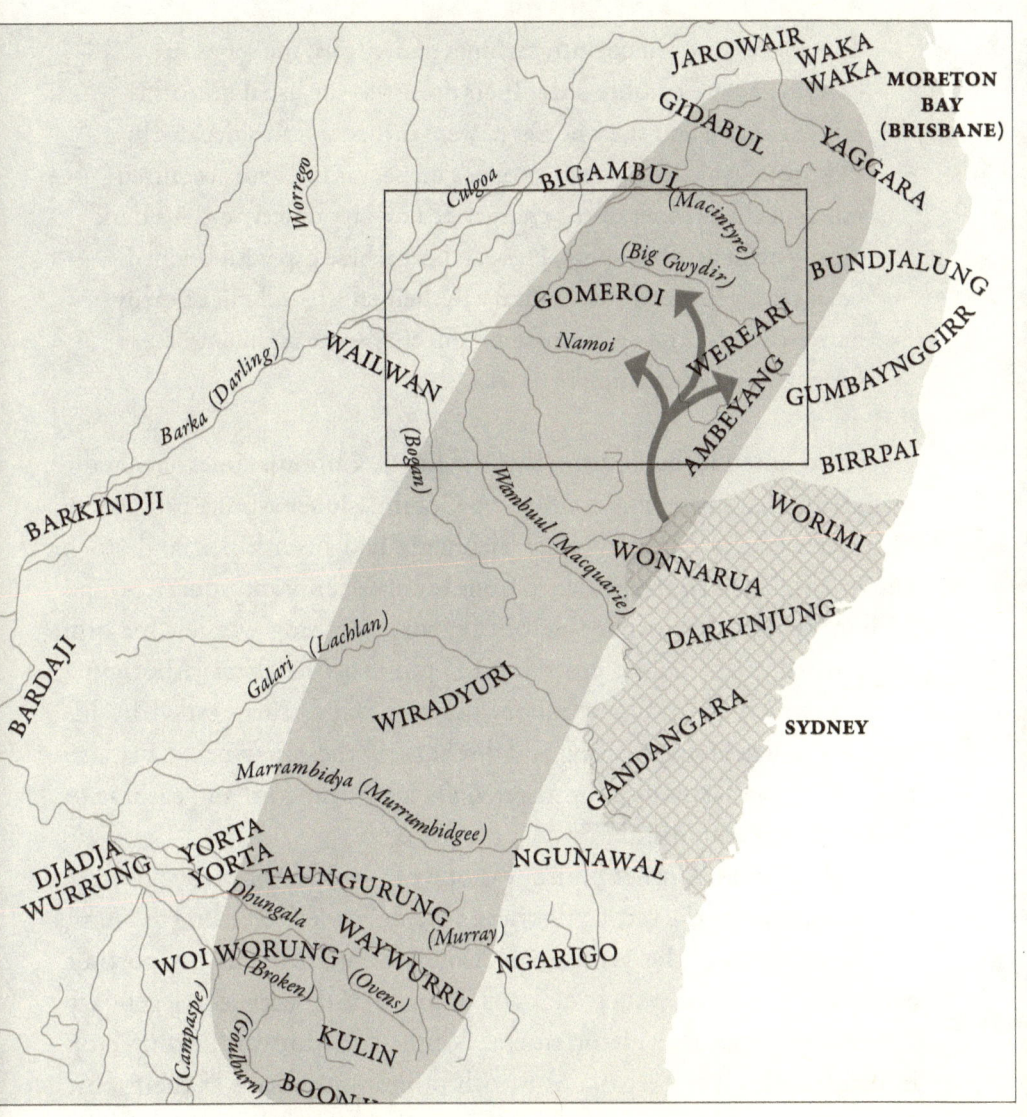

Northwest New South Wales, late 1830s

> The police were armed with carbines and pistols, the sergeant carrying a cavalry sabre only. Their dress was the usual uniform of their corps; and their horses ... were turned out in a decidedly military way ... The Commissioner's horse was likewise accoutred much in the manner of the charger of a cavalry officer, and his dark green costume, fixed spurs, Hessian boots, blue cap with braided band etc., were decidedly military in their effect, and might easily have passed for the uniform of an officer of some regiment of irregular mounted rifles.[1]

Curr also noted rather scathingly how Lands Commissioners generally operated when there was conflict. A Commissioner would proceed to 'the scene of the outrage' (after shepherds had been killed and stock destroyed), listen to the evidence from the shepherds and squatters, and without hearing the other side of the story, 'nothing was left for him as guardian of the public peace but to appear before them [Aboriginal people], which he did at a gallop, sabre in hand, surrounded by his troopers industriously loading and discharging their carbines'. Curr also noted 'they occasionally administered justice with sword and carbine to the wrong tribe in mistake'.[2]

Major James Winnet Nunn was one of these law enforcers beyond the boundaries of the settled districts. Joseph Fowles's painting of Nunn clearly shows how the 'Australian Mounted Infantry', as his portrait called the mounted police, claimed a connection with the legendary British cavalry of the Victorian era. Nunn struts forward, riding crop in hand, with all the regalia of British military uniforms at their most extravagant (the sharpshooting and trench warfare of the Crimean War in the 1850s was to be a lesson for officers in their increasingly impractical and easily targeted finery). Born into a military family that had little distinction beyond his father becoming a lieutenant rather late in life, Nunn was in many ways typical of military careerists during the great period of opportunity in the expanding British empire. Fowles painted Nunn in a classical pose – pointing to the lands behind him he'd had a part in conquering. It is no coincidence they are grazing lands nestled in a range of hills. This connected his role as an officer of the mounted police with settling Aboriginal land as part of empire.³

In the 1830s the mounted police were selected from the regiments stationed in the colony – 'the best behaved men and the smartest ... the very best men we have' noted Lieutenant Colonel Henry Breton. Technically, their actions were not part of their regimental duties, and thus have not been seen as part of the military history of the colony, nor of Australia. However, Aboriginal people made no distinction between police and military. As Lieutenant of Mounted Police George Geddes McKenzie Cobban noted at the Namoi and Big Rivers, 'soldiers' were what 'the blacks call the Mounted Police'.⁴

'There are a thousand Blacks there'

As we have seen, by 1837, squatters had pushed out from the Liverpool Plains along the Peel and Namoi rivers. Within a year, Jamison's run, which had been attacked by bushrangers in 1836, was no longer the furthest along the Namoi. Cyrus Doyle had stopped his sheep at Narrabri, the Loder brothers at Wee Waa and then Merah, and George Hall's sons took Gomeroi land near Sydney merchant Charles Smith's 'superintendent's claim' over 'Greenhatch Creek'. Many of these forays were led by employees of the growing numbers of men with money in Sydney. The financiers of these operations generally awaited news before heading deep into the bush to inspect the investments they had speculated upon. They were also a little concerned that their supply of free labour might be soon coming to an end as calls to end convict transportation grew. The land rush was ratcheting up. The area around the Liverpool Plains was getting more and more crowded. The next step for overlanding parties was toward bushranger 'The Barber' Clarke's 'Big River'.⁵

Gomeroi raiders had consistently harassed the men who were taking up runs along the Big River. A stockman by the name of 'Major' Fitton who worked on the Hall station on the Big River later described just how:

> ... up to that time [December 1837] the blacks in that part of the Country had been very troublesome. Five stockmen and shepherds had been murdered by them ... and a great many Cattle had been killed and speared, and sheep also. These outrages caused a very hostile feeling against them, in fact no one considered it safe to go about, spears and boomerangs were constantly thrown at us.[6]

As Gomeroi man Boe Spearim notes, warriors would often 'respond to some breach of Gomeroi law or protocol'. Much of the hostility no doubt originated in the stockmen using their firearms to capture Aboriginal women. After Commissioner Bingham reported how a stockman had almost certainly been killed because of this, Lieutenant George Geddes McKenzie Cobban was despatched to the area around present-day Coonabarabran. The energetic Cobban pushed on from Marsden's station to James Walker's 'Barradean' run and then on toward the Barwon River, 'several days journey beyond any Stations'. He failed to find any trace of the four men he was after, 'Tallboy, Milballal, Good Morning and Chatty, all of the Burigaly Tribe', according to James Nobbs at the Marsden station on Baradine Creek. What he did find was evidence of yet another white man, possibly a bushranger, living with Aboriginal people far beyond the furthest outstation.[7]

There were reports of other attacks right along the Namoi River. The newly appointed Commissioner of Crown Lands for the Gwydir district, Alexander Paterson, had been ordered to 'perambulate the District ... going from Station to Station' from his base at Jerry's Plains in the upper Hunter Valley. He was to obtain a census of the white population over a huge and largely undefined area that he was now responsible for from the Liverpool Plains north and west to the Peel and Namoi rivers. When Paterson toured the area between October and December, he wrote urgently back to the Colonial Secretary, but not about the census.[8]

Paterson found himself touring a landscape of fear and desolation. Earlier, his neighbouring Commissioner, Bingham, had been shocked to find stockmen 'taking and Keeping by force the Black Native women' by using the firearms they were given to protect themselves. Bingham had written to the Colonial Secretary Edward Deas Thomson about this 'prevailing habit' in the outstations and, by September, Thomson had duly published a proclamation promising to punish those who had taken this 'abominable and unchristian' action. Yet a proclamation in the *Government Gazette* had little impact in the far-flung 'remote Districts'.[9]

Constant attacks by Gomeroi warriors had halted the squatters in their tracks. In November, Paterson made it to Loder's station, then the furthest along the Namoi, just past present-day Wee Waa. He wrote to the colonial secretary that 'the Blacks are so numerous and daring that the men have all quitted the station from fear, and left the Cattle to their fate'. Every station along the way had suffered from 'depredations'.

After reaching the very far end of the known British world in this area in 1837 (apart from reported 'wild white men' further west) Paterson turned back to the northeast, heading for Bowman's station on Terry Hie Hie Creek before hitting the Big River. Paterson would have passed near a large ceremonial bora ground, a 'Great Ancestral Bora', still today of great significance to Gomeroi people, just near present-day Terry Hie Hie village. It was near to where Bowman had rather unceremoniously stopped his sheep and cattle and established a run.[10]

Paterson noted that the Gomeroi had killed even more cattle here than at the Namoi, and it was 'getting worse every day'. He found the remains of six bullocks at one campsite and twenty-eight sheep at another. Hundreds of warriors were eating very well. This was Major Mitchell's worst nightmare – that if Aboriginal people obtained a ready supply of cattle they would be very hard to defeat in battle. As Mitchell wrote, 'they might increase in number and ... become formidable and implacable enemies'.[11]

At Cobb's station near present-day Warialda, Paterson was shown some spears and boomerangs gathered from where two of Cobb's men had been killed. One of the spears was apparently removed from a dead man's forehead. The station hands were keen to show the Commissioner just how bad things were. But then in a most unexpected turn of events, while looking at the weapons, one of the stockmen calmly raised a gun and shot another stockman through the breast while saying 'this is the sort of spear'. He was later tried for murder and sent to a lunatic asylum. It seems a kind of madness had descended upon the stations in Big River Country.[12]

'A dreadful massacre'

Perhaps the shooter was not so insane. Perhaps he was making a point about how guns were the real killers on Big River Country. And perhaps he had spiralled into madness from being part of a massacre party and witnessing the slaughter of Gomeroi women and children. What Paterson either didn't find out or did not reveal, were reports of a massacre that had led to the attacks. Always with an ear out for reports of the mistreatment of Aboriginal people, the missionary Lancelot Threlkeld at Lake Macquarie near Newcastle later noted that 'two shepherds of Mr Cobb's station, Anambah ... were unfortunately murdered by the Blacks'. Threlkeld had heard that this was 'in consequence of the atrocities being committed against the Blacks by the stockmen in another part of the country, which drove them towards Mr Cobb's station, where they met the two shepherds and wreaked their vengeance, in retaliation, on the unhappy sufferers'. Threlkeld said he was 'informed by one who was there at the time of the catastrophe'. This person told him that the stockmen 'armed themselves, overtook or came upon the tribe, found some with clothes of the murdered shepherds on their backs, whom they hewed to pieces with their hatchets, and killed others'.[13]

Another story filtered through to Paterson's replacement, Commissioner Edward Mayne. In February 1839, Mayne was told about a 'dreadful massacre', reputedly 'done in revenge for another outrage of a similar kind upon the blacks'. He had been taken to the site, not far from Cobb's station, on a 'high mountain'. Mayne understood it to be 'known by the name of Gravesend, from the number of appearances of graves'.

Like a jagged sentinel, Mount Gravesend overlooks the present-day small and sleepy township of Gravesend. There is no signpost or marker indicating why it was given its name. Perhaps this is understandable. There was no official or other report of these events, beyond what Mayne and Threlkeld had 'heard' over a year later. Despite Mayne announcing around '200' graves there in evidence to a Legislative Council Committee dealing with policing in June 1839, nothing was done to investigate. By then, it could easily be placed in the 'too hard basket' as the event had occurred two years before.[14]

Somewhere in Big River Country Paterson had obtained a guide, only noted by him as 'a boy' who told Paterson 'he had no wish to join his tribe again as they would kill him'. The young outcast took the Lands Commissioner to where people, only described as 'the tribe', had camped. They counted the remnants of 250 fires. The young man told Paterson there would have been four people at every campfire. It appeared that around a thousand Gomeroi were on the move.

As Gomeroi man Uncle Paul Spearim notes of what he calls the 'Gomeroi 500', they might not have all been warriors. Thanks to the squatters it was now even more possible for such a large number of people to actually gather and then travel together – they had mobile food supplies of sheep and cattle. And the sheep and cattle just kept on coming – like some kind of magic pudding to be eaten again and again.[15]

At Bell's station on the Big River, Paterson was told one of the shepherds had been set upon by a number of warriors 'brandishing tomahawks and spears about his head'. He said he believed he would have been killed 'had he not told them that the Soldiers ... were on their way up'. They robbed him, let him go and then told him 'they did not care for the Soldiers, that they were not afraid of them'. The Big River warriors were defiant.[16]

Even worse tidings were to come. Paterson's young guide told him that 'there are three white men with them painted like the Blacks'. He took Paterson to show him proof. They went to 'a hut in the mountains evidently constructed by white men':

> The wall plates were morticed and pegged down, the bark put up with green hide, the door hung with hide hinges, and berths for sleeping in put up.

Paterson was most concerned. He believed the main cause of Aboriginal attacks in Big River Country was 'white men being with them urging them on to these outrages'. Perhaps they were opportunistic escaped convicts, or bushrangers. Perhaps these outcasts thought that in the insanity that now prevailed across the Big River stations they stood a better chance of survival if they were allied with the Gomeroi.[17]

'We shall be driven from our stations'

When Paterson's letters finally reached Sydney, the Colonial Secretary and the acting Governor (after Governor Bourke's departure in early December) stepped in. Secretary Thomson and Lieutenant-Colonel Snodgrass ordered the head of the mounted police, Major Nunn, to report to Government House. Snodgrass and Thomson were now armed with a series of letters from Lands Commissioners Henry Bingham and Alexander Paterson. They had also received letters from the pastoralists of the Hunter Valley who had established runs at the Big River. James Glennie had written to Robert Scott that if something was not done soon on the Gwydir (Big) River 'we shall be driven from our stations'. Robert Scott duly wrote to Colonial Secretary Thomson about the 'disturbed state of the Country' and pleaded with the Governor to do something about it.[18]

By November 1837, the colonial authorities were in an uproar. Only days before, in late October, they had celebrated the ascension of Queen Victoria to the throne, pledging their allegiance with cannon fire and a grand military parade headed by Major Nunn and, in lieu of any British cavalry, a detachment of his mounted police. Now, newspapers were crying out that in the 'Northern parts', 'hordes of runaway convicts' were on the loose and 'the Blacks are murdering the shepherds and stockmen with impunity'. The Executive Council had been informed that numbers of stockmen were dead and many 'acts of violence, rapine and murder' had occurred at Big River during 1837. The Council believed these were so extreme 'as to authorise and require the employment of an Armed Force to repress them'.[19]

The 'Armed Force' was of course to be the highly mobile mounted police. On 19 December Lieutenant-Colonel Snodgrass told Major Nunn to waste no time in proceeding to the Namoi, Gwydir and Big rivers (the same river). The Lieutenant-Colonel had fought in the Peninsular Campaign during the Napoleonic Wars – the campaign where guerrilla warfare was given its name. Snodgrass was not renowned as a colonial administrator. But he was highly respected as a soldier. According to Nunn, he told him:

there are a thousand Blacks there, and, if they are not stopped, we may have them presently within the boundaries.

It seems the acting Governor believed the warriors might cut a swathe through the outstations beyond the limits of location, and then enter the nineteen counties. This was unthinkable – a force of 1000 warriors actually moving against the so-called settled districts. And such an embarrassment to a colony about to celebrate fifty years of existence and beginning to believe in its important (wool-based) status as part of the British empire. But if these warriors had a ready food supply in sheep and cattle wherever they went, why couldn't they be very soon 'within the boundaries'?

Paterson's report and Snodgrass's assessment of it gave Nunn's orders a palpable sense of urgency. His written orders were to 'examine into and repress' the 'aggressions' of these warriors. There was no mention of any 'aggressions' on the part of the white population. In Nunn's orders there were echoes of many previous British military campaigns to 'strike terror' into Aboriginal populations. After all, the established colony inside the nineteen counties of New South Wales was, it seems, about to be invaded.[20]

When Snodgrass told Nunn 'there are a thousand Blacks there' this was based on four people per campfire. While this might have been a large warband of warriors, it might well have included women, older men and children. War bands often travelled as family groups. Women had an important role in traditional combat. One combat witnessed by a squatter in the late 1830s described how women joined a pursuit 'and did good service with their bungwall sticks, which they handled like quarter-staves, and made the heads of many of the retreating Jockeroos [stockmen] rattle'. As Wiradyuri woman Aunty Leanna Carr notes, the role of women in warfare was important in many ways, from supplying food to retrieving weapons during combat. Importantly, they were also 'critical in decision making'. And around the Big River, they might well have had enough of the 'prevailing habit' of, as Commissioner Bingham described it, stockmen 'taking and Keeping by force the Black Native women'.[21]

The Gomeroi were a large and powerful nation estimated to have been around 12 000 strong when the first squatters edged cautiously along their riverways in the late 1820s. By 1838, Gomeroi warriors had several years to refine their tactics of raids and attacks on outstations and stock. And they seemed happy to enlist auxiliary white outcasts.[22]

Their language was spoken across what has been called a confederacy of tribes or nations that stretched from the back of the Hunter Valley up to Moree and from Tamworth out towards Walgett. Like the Wiradyuri, the name Gomeroi (or Gamilaroi) is based on a suffix attached to the word kamil- (gamil), meaning 'no'. And like the Wiradyuri before them around Bathurst in 1824, the Gomeroi were now certainly saying 'no' to any more white people and their sheep and cattle.[23]

The Europeans first called Gomeroi lands 'Big River country', but the river was inextricably linked to other rivers and waterways. The Big River, mistakenly thought to be separate from the Gwydir, flows into the Barwon which meets the Namoi near present-day Walgett. From the back of the New England tableland and the Liverpool and Nandewar ranges, these rivers were the lifeblood of a massive area of open forests and plains. Camped out on the river today, there is no way of understanding it in any other manner – the roads follow it, the trees snake along beside it, the animals flock to it. Rivers were, and are, the lifeblood of inland New South Wales.[24]

In 1831, Thomas Mitchell was impressed with the 'park-like vistas' around the Barwon River. All sorts of edible herbs and grasses flourished in the vast fields, described by Lands Commissioner Paterson as 'luxuriant pasture' and 'Country of the richest description'. Gomeroi people ground goolah grass into flour and baked this into cakes like a damper. They made a bread from kangaroo grass seeds. Cattle and sheep fed voraciously on these grasses, herbs and yams that had been farmed in abundance right across Gomeroi Country for millennia. While the first Europeans in Gomeroi Country might not have seen the great floods that periodically swept through, at the right time, it certainly must have seemed, as Paterson enticingly called it, 'Country of the richest description'.[25]

Along the Big River, Thomas Mitchell had also been impressed by Gomeroi 'Villages of bowers' as he called them, with strongly made conical houses 'tastefully distributed among drooping acacias and casuarina'. The villages gave Mitchell an idea of not only the shelter they provided but projected an idea of 'comfort and happiness'. He was also impressed with the men described as giants by some, 'tall and well formed' by surveyor Allan Cunningham, and who Mitchell thought were 'the finest looking men of their race' he had seen.[26]

As Uncle Paul Spearim notes, the Gomeroi were well-travelled and well-informed of events hundreds of kilometres outside their Country. There was a network of fire signal stations at high points such as Mount Kaputar and Burning Mountain. For Uncle Paul it was wii (fire) and duu (smoke) that was the heart and soul of Gomeroi Country and 'kept us safe'. Warriors were renowned for raiding into the Wonnarua and other lands around the Hunter Valley. The Gomeroi also traded their acacia-wood spears for stone axe-heads across the Hunter region. Some travelled to the Bunya Gatherings in present-day southern Queensland and others had strong links with the Wiradyuri. By 1838, the Gomeroi were no doubt very well-informed about the squatters pushing out from the Liverpool plains and along their creeks and waterways. They would have been informed about the victories along the Bogan River, with squatters abandoning their runs. They might well have been informed of the southern Wiradyuri fightback that, as we shall see, had begun along the Murrumbidgee River. And they would have known of the constant flow of squatters and their sheep that, despite these victories, kept on coming in through all these neighbouring lands.[27]

'A great state of alarm'

We can only guess at Major Nunn's enthusiasm as he left Government House on 19 December 1837; fuelled by the urgency of a threat to the colony, fraught with a long journey at the height of summer in the distant bush, perhaps tinged with excitement by the possibility of a military campaign. Nunn was still a 'new chum' in the colony but he might well have heard of the impressive warriors of the Big River. He wrote very little on the whole affair – uncharacteristically of the British military, his later report lacked important detail. Within ten days of the meeting with his commander at Government House, Nunn set off from the police outpost at Jerry's Plains in the Hunter Valley with a detachment of around twenty troopers and an Aboriginal guide known only as 'Jacky'.

They headed north, aiming to cross the Peel and Namoi Rivers in a big sweep before they reached the Big River. At Invermein, their ranks were swollen by a detachment of Sergeant Lee and five men. If Nunn asked any of the many stockmen he was to meet over the next weeks about the 'Blacks of the Big River', as a military man would almost certainly do, he may well have been given descriptions of their stature and military capabilities.[28]

There was no need to ask the men at Charles Smith's station, where Joseph Greenhatch the overseer welcomed the troopers. Nunn was regaled with tales of warriors' attacks by all the stockmen there. Greenhatch obliged the major by sending his stockmen out with police reconnaissance detachments. They soon returned with news of a large Gomeroi camp on the nearby Namoi River. The stockmen guided Nunn's men through the night. When they got near, Nunn ordered them to move quietly toward the sleeping camp. In the breaking light they mounted and charged in. Some people tried to escape into the river but the camp was surrounded. Several shots were fired but apparently only as warnings. It was one of very few dawn raids in Australian history that did not end in a massacre.

It was a confusing situation for all concerned. The Gomeroi were told through 'Jacky' that they had to give up anyone who had killed stockmen or stolen or killed cattle or sheep. There were apparently two groups – one from the Namoi River and another from the Horton River. It seems the Namoi people pointed to the others and Nunn took fifteen of them into custody.

Back at Greenhatch's run, the two prisoners among them who had been named as murderers of Hall's men escaped during the night. One man, known to stockworkers as 'Doherty', was shot and killed by a trooper guarding them. Nunn said later it was 'satisfactory' to know 'that the man who was shot was the actual murderer of Mr. Hall's servant'. It was rough justice for someone who, in the confusion that reigned around Greenhatch's, might well have been innocent.[29]

Lieutenant Cobban thought the man's death was unfortunate but also saw a bright side – he hoped it would deter others 'from committing further outrages'. Nunn wanted to press on to the Big River or the 'Guyder' as he called it, as this was where 'the ravages were stated to be greater'. The rest of the prisoners were released except for one, who was kept as a guide. According to Cobban, he 'promised' to lead the troopers 'to the other tribe of the Guyder [Gwydir] blacks'. Apparently this man 'knew the blacks on the Big River who had been committing the murders in that neighbourhood and their Country', as Cobban unwittingly called it.

Nunn pushed on to Bell's station on the Horton River. Here, the station was in 'a great state of alarm' and a stockman told the troopers that the warriors nearby who had accosted him said they were not afraid of 'the soldiers'. Cobban was sent out to investigate. On the edge of the Nandewar Ranges, Cobban's detachment came across some warriors 'perched upon ledges and rocks quite inaccessible'. As the troopers looked up at them from the gully below, the warriors 'jeered and 'shouted defiance'. Cobban said 'all our efforts to take these people failed'. Whether that included a few pot-shots at them in their rocky defences, he did not say. He returned to Nunn empty-handed.

Nunn was keen to get to the Big River. The party moved on to Cobb's station on the Gwydir (at this time the upstream name for the Big River). Here they found a scene of 'confusion' and 'disorder'. Sheep were actually starving because shepherds would not leave their huts. It seems Nunn worked to calm the shepherds' fears at every stop along the way and sent out detachments to scour the bush. The sight of a force of cavalry certainly seems to have meant Gomeroi warriors vanished. It also comforted terrified stockmen who soon went back to work on Cobb's station.

Historians have seen the horse as a key factor in European victories in the open terrain of plains and grasslands. They have also suggested that the most successful areas of Aboriginal resistance occurred in 'regions of dense bush or mountains'. This was certainly true in some places such as the Sydney region during the 1810s and in Tasmania in the 1820s and 1830s. It seems obvious. Yet a closer look at the river Country of the vast Murray-Darling basin shows that not just mountains and dense bush are good terrain for guerrilla warfare. The thick scrub alongside a winding river, impenetrable reeds and boggy marshes, the steep sides of a river bank that no horse will plunge down – these were all useful to warriors defending their Country from mounted forces.[30]

Nunn was told that at Hall's run on Bingara Creek, stockworkers were being assailed by 'spears and boomerings' and 'no one considered it safe to go about'. But after resting his horses and gathering supplies, the major also heard from Cobb's superintendent, James Lamb, that the warriors who attacked Hall's and killed two shepherds were 'at some distance in the interior'. Lamb said he had tracked them but gave up the chase. Nunn later said he 'considered it my duty to pursue the tribe who had been committing these outrages' and headed down the banks of the Big River.[31]

Nunn had gathered some 'guides', men with local knowledge. 'Mr. Lamb, Mr. Hall [who had come across from Bingara] and Mr. Scott's men' had joined the troopers. Around 16 January he set off with these reinforcements, making an extremely powerful party of at least thirty armed, mounted men, possibly more. They reached the end of the line, Marshall's station, then the 'lowest station on the Big river'.

Here they came across four people who unwittingly, or perhaps under pressure, indicated where the people Nunn's men were hunting were camped. The pursuit continued to a deserted camp, but fresh tracks of 'a very numerous tribe' led them on. The troopers saw smoke up ahead and they prepared for battle, but were disappointed to find only a burning log.

As 26 January dawned, in far-off Sydney, it was time to celebrate the jubilee – fifty years since the colonists had arrived at Sydney Cove. Being a Friday, 26 January was declared a public holiday and thousands of Sydneysiders flocked to the harbour to see cannons fired and a regatta of sailing boats. Festivities continued well into the evening with fireworks and patriotic toasts to the new queen, as well as plaudits to the 'prosperous Colony', one of the 'brightest jewels' in the crown of a 'Queen on whose dominions the sun never sets'.[32]

Once the sun had risen on the banks of what Nunn and Cobban called 'Bogy' creek, fresh tracks led them to a 'large body of water'. Soon after, Cobban saw 'a great number of blacks' camped across the water from them. Such a large lagoon in the middle of a vast, often dry landscape was obviously an important place for Gomeroi people. Even today it teems with wildlife. It was almost certainly what in 1832 Thomas Mitchell had called 'Snodgrass Lagoon' in honour of the man who was now Nunn's commanding officer and acting governor. The lagoon sits at the end of what was to be named Waterloo Creek, around 50 kilometres south-west of the current-day town of Moree.[33]

Cobban took some men and circled back to a crossing point in order to flank the 'great number of blacks'. Nunn remained on the other bank to capture any who might try to escape through the water. People in the camp scattered. Nunn described the bush as 'so open the men could ride through' but it was certainly not clear terrain. Cobban thought the trees and scrub meant that when fighting began, 'each man was acting for himself'.

Cobban soon came upon a man armed with two spears. He spurred his horse on and tried to run him down, but the wily warrior ducked under his horse. Cobban wheeled around and heard a trooper shout 'take care, sir, he is spearing you!' just as the trooper fired his pistol at the man. Then Cobban heard a call: 'Damn them, they have speared Hannan!' and heard others call: 'They have also speared the Officer!'

Corporal Patrick Hannan recalled that he tried to 'apprehend the first black man I saw' and did not shoot him 'as our orders from Major Nunn were to take prisoners, but not to fire unless in self-defence'. Whether Hannan was later trying to defend the troopers' actions or not, he was certainly surprised that the 'first black man' he saw 'turned suddenly and thrust a spear into the calf of my leg'. The defiance Gomeroi warriors had earlier shouted to Nunn's men from the rocky crags of the Nandewar Ranges had turned to action.

On the banks of what was to become known as Waterloo Creek, the hunters were themselves now under attack. Nunn's decision to split his force could have been a huge mistake. Half his men were under attack, cut off from their support and out of sight in scrubby terrain. Normally, the massed firepower of muskets was the key to British success in such conflict. Now it was every man for himself. Around the same time that crowds of Sydneysiders were streaming home from the 26 January celebrations on the harbour, the Battle for Big River lay in the balance.

CHAPTER THREE
The Battle of Broken River

'Sheep and cattle mania'

In the autumn of 1838, as we have seen, the Faithfull brothers had sent their overseer, James Crossley, south with seventeen stockmen and all their supplies on bullock carts, along with several thousand sheep and cattle. They were heading into Taungurung Country near present-day Benalla in north-east Victoria, seeking land to set up a station. Crossley's party were following 'Major Mitchell's Line' – essentially the wheel marks of Thomas Mitchell's carts that had trundled through there in 1836. It was still a rough track, much of it first marked by the bushman Hamilton Hume, the former sea captain William Hovell and a party of convicts in 1824. It was soon grandiosely called the 'Port Phillip Road'. The Sydney to Melbourne freeway, once known as the Hume Highway, still largely follows the same route.[1]

Squatter Charles Hotson Ebden had reached the Murray River (near present-day Albury) by mid-1836. In 1837 he employed Charles Bonney to drive 10 000 sheep to the growing township at Port Phillip. Just a year after his journey through 'Australia Felix', the wheel ruts of 'Major Mitchell's Line' had become a road that was described as 'good all the way' and there was, for the moment at least, 'plenty of native grass for the horses'. Many regarded such 'a certain and speedy communication' between Port Phillip and Sydney as sure to lead to the new southern outpost's prosperity.[2]

In February 1838, Acting Governor Snodgrass reported to Lord Glenelg that a detachment of seven mounted police and a party of land surveyors to assist in marking out the growing township that would become Melbourne had travelled 'efficiently' along the Port Phillip Road. Indeed, there was now a contracted mail service and Snodgrass reported

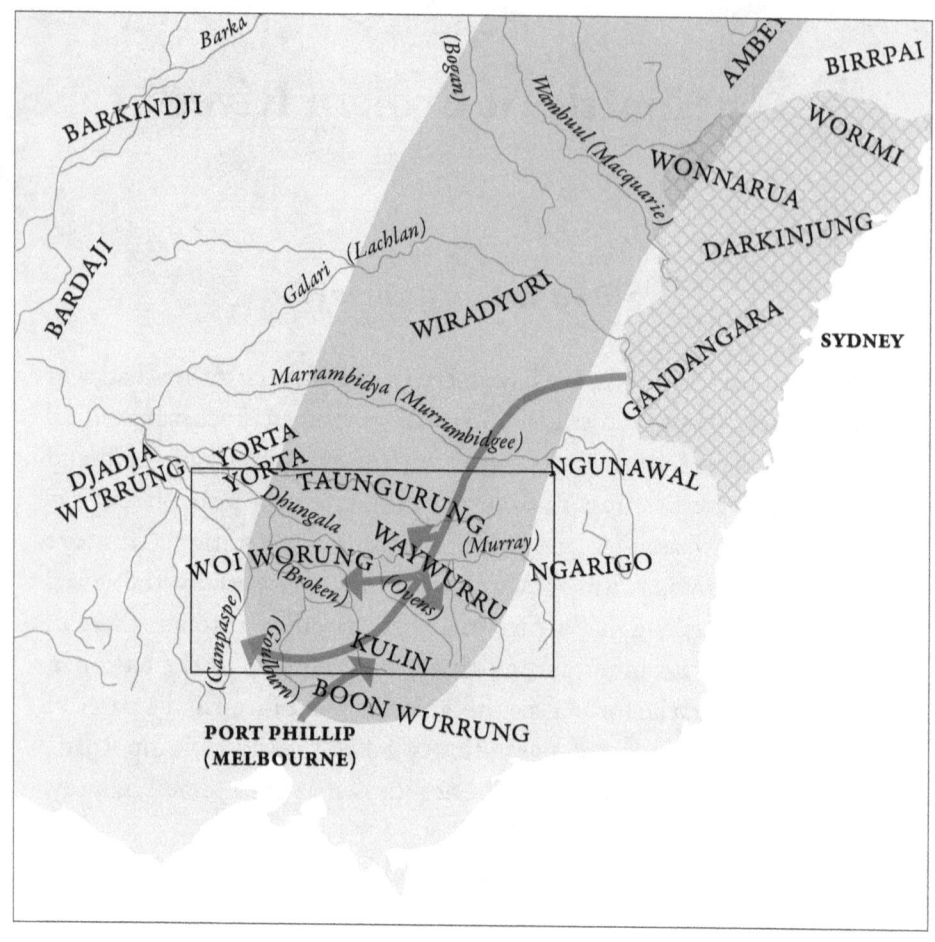

Northeast Victoria, late 1830s
'Settled Districts' are indicated by hatching.
The movement of squatters, stockmen and stock marked with arrows.

that 'the road [is] now travelled daily without difficulty or danger by those who are removing their sheep and cattle to this new country'.[3]

At first, between Mitchell's journey in 1836 and mid-1837, the overlanders generally kept heading south, keen to supply Port Phillip with beef. Yet in April 1837, the well-funded and well-named Alexander Fullerton Mollison set off from his station, Uriara, on the Murrumbidgee River with two overseers, forty-nine servants, 5000 sheep, 634 cattle, twenty-eight bullocks and twenty-two horses. After travelling some

400 miles (644 kilometres) he decided to stop on the Coliban River, between Mount Macedon and Mount Alexander, and set up a station, Tarringower. Others soon followed. Colonel JC White, William Bowman and Dr George Mackay all began to get their men to cut timber and strip bark for huts on their chosen grazing lands around the Oxley Plains. No longer were overlanders overlanding. By early 1838 it must have been quite clear to the Woiwurrung and Taungurung that these people and their cattle and sheep were there to stay.[4]

George and William Pitt Faithfull were backed by their father, William Faithful senior, who had arrived in the colony a humble private in the New South Wales Corps. He left the Corps, took his due land grant and prospered from farming at the Hawkesbury River. Success bred success and by 1834 he had received more land and helped his sons establish a merino sheep station, Springfield, at what was soon to become the township of Goulburn. By 1836, the smart money was heading further south, following Major Mitchell's dream.[5]

In fact, the move south was described almost as a kind of 'madness'. The Scottish firebrand Presbyterian clergyman John Dunmore Lang described the late 1830s as a period of 'sheep and cattle mania'. Lang – ever concerned with the low moral standards of New South Wales – believed a 'madness' had 'seized on all ranks and classes' in the colony who were purchasing sheep and cattle and heading beyond the 'limits of location.' Ex-convicts could make their fortunes taking their masters' stock deep into Aboriginal land. Many then used their hard-earned wages to set up their own stations. Well before the gold rushes of the 1850s, there were a series of 'land rushes' across New South Wales.[6]

In April 1838, George Faithfull farewelled overseer James Crossley and his seventeen men, 3472 sheep and 395 cattle. Faithfull himself was to follow after with another party of eight men and even more sheep. He and his brother William had directed Crossley to choose some Aboriginal land on the Oxley Plains.

While their workers might have been relatively cheap assigned or ex-convicts, the Faithfull brothers had certainly put some money into the venture. Crossley's drays were stocked with tons of flour and barrels of tobacco and salted meat. Perhaps confident in the imposing presence of such a large convoy of men, horses, bullock drays and cattle and sheep, not all of Crossley's men were armed with firearms – there were five muskets and a pistol between the eighteen men. While George Faithfull was to bring up more weapons, it proved to be a learning curve for future overlanders. Every single stockman needed a gun.[7]

The Faithfull brothers and Crossley might not have read Charles Sturt's 1835 'Obstacles that attend travelling into the interior of Australia', where he warned it was 'essential to have a force strong enough to maintain an obstinate resistance against any number of savages, where no mercy is expected'. Crossley and his employers may have been confident the increasingly well-travelled Port Phillip Road was not now as dangerous as it might have once been.[8]

At the Ovens River, near present-day Wangaratta, Crossley's long column of sheep, cattle, horses and drays stopped at the river crossing. In the first few years of squatters driving into Aboriginal lands south of Goulburn and north of Port Phillip between 1836 and 1838, the land owners actually offered the Europeans a good deal of assistance, including finding the best pastures, and ferrying people and goods across rivers with bark canoes.

But there might well have been some other kind of engagement with the people at the Ovens River. Later, in mid-1840, Lands Commissioner Bingham noted that 'the natives of the Ovens River from their recent communication to me ... have a strong dislike to a man named William Thomas ... This man did live with Mr. Faithful and was with some of the party in the rear at the time of the affray at the Broken river'. So too Bingham wrote, 'The natives have likewise a great enmity to ... a Man named William Brown [who] was with Mr. Faithful's party in the rear when that affair took place'. Bingham also said a man, 'Simon', 'one of their Chiefs on the Hume [Murray] River', told him that 'on the first settlement of the whites on the Ovens River that the whites killed and shot many of them'.[9]

Aboriginal women told Bingham some further detail about the dreaded William Thomas, who had worked with the Faithfulls at Wangaratta – though he was not part of the party that was at the head of the column at Broken River in 1838. Bingham described how 'the Gins [women] have been heard singing their war-song at Barweigee Creek [Barwidgee Creek near present-day Myrtleford] near the Ovens Plain'. Bingham transcribed the song as:

> William Thomas was a saucy fellow set his Dogs at poor Black fellow and one of them fastened on him and the black native speared the Dog, and rejoiced.

Bingham was also told that the 'melancholy scene on Mr. Faithful's men in the vicinity of the Broken River' had arisen 'from the highly improper Conduct of a person named "O'Brien": the overseer, who had one of the Black Gins and promised her a Lamb – and then would not give it, and her black fellow was beat[en]'. Another of the Faithfull stockworkers, 'a man named Samuel', informed Bingham he had 'no doubt of the fact' this occurred. It seems then, that O'Brien had offered a lamb to a woman for sex, refused to give it to her and then beat her husband. Both men did not travel on with the other stockworkers to Broken River and remained at Wangaratta.[10]

Megan Carter is a descendant of Ovens River Waywurru man 'Brangy'. Megan describes the men who were assigned to or worked with the Faithfulls as 'just brutal men' and some such as Benjamin Reid as 'absolute barbarians who took delight in hurting Aboriginal people'. These ignorant stockworkers, who often delighted in finding people regarded as one rung below them in British society, were led by squatters who were often veterans, or the sons of veterans, of the Napoleonic Wars. Their fathers were heroic figures under whose shadows they lived, and they wanted to cut out their own piece of fame and wealth. As Megan notes, putting these two types of men together in occupying Aboriginal land was 'a recipe for disaster'.[11]

'Millions of murrnong'

In just three years, from 1835 to 1838, more than 300 000 sheep had been brought into or bred in the Port Phillip District around present-day Melbourne. Such competition for Aboriginal land meant that by 1837, pastoralists were also heading north toward the Murray River. In 1840, in Djadja Wurrung land that was to be called the Loddon district, the Assistant Protector of Aborigines Edward Parker remarked that 'the very spots most valuable to the Aborigines for their productiveness – the creeks, water courses, and rivers – are the first to be occupied'.[12]

The 'Protectors of Aborigines' could see the problem, but they could do little about it. As Chief Protector George Augustus Robinson noted in January 1840 when he was touring the Loddon district, 'Mr Munro said [when he first arrived in the district] there were millions of murrnong or yam, all over the [Campaspe] plain and that the kangaroos were so abundant that they came up to the door of their tent ... emu were also abundant and near their tents. That was only 18 months ago; now there are none to be seen. The sheep drive them away. Yet this is a proof that the natives have been deprived of a large portion of their support and subsistence'.[13]

In 1838, the people who had lived along the middle stretches of the Broken River for millennia were part of what might be thought of as a loose confederacy. Assistant Protector William Baylie was at Murchison in 1843. His descriptions of people of the Goulburn River area provide some insight into both those who lived in the Broken River area in 1838, and those who were their allies. Baylie wrote that 'the *Youngillums*' [Yowen-ilam] lived 'about the Broken, Devil's and Ovens River, mixing with the Murray blacks on the eastern side'. Several groups across the Kings, Broken, Devil's and Ovens rivers were undoubtedly in an alliance – in Melbourne in 1843 Protector William Thomas noted them as camping together and separate from the other 'Goulburns'.[14]

The reasons for an attack on Crossley's party of overlanders were numerous. Across the region, the Taungurung (Daung Wurrung) and Ngurai Illum Wurrung of the Goulburn and Ovens River valleys and the Waywurru (Waveroo) were under increasing pressure from overlanders and their stock pushing south and west from the Murray River. What at first might have seemed containable had become intolerable.[15]

William Faithfull later revealed another possible reason, writing, 'this is not the first outrage committed here by the Blacks – two of

Mr Tooths' men were killed a short time since, and the skeletons of two white men were found within the last three months – supposed to have been Bushrangers'. While the party was at the Ovens River in early April, two cattle had been speared and some of Faithfull's men 'fired at them [warriors] and they disappeared into the scrub'. Perhaps they hit their mark and vengeance was smouldering. Just days before, to the south-west at Pyalong near present-day Seymour, warriors had raided the Bowman and Mollison stations. The magistrate at Port Phillip, Captain William Lonsdale, said later in July 1838 he was 'inclined to think these blacks are some of those who were concerned in the attack upon Mr Faithfull's party'.[16]

After a few days at the Ovens River, with conflict swirling around his overlanding party, Crossley decided to move on. On 6 April the overlanders headed through an area of open forests toward a place the people who lived there called Marangan. Before an artificial lake was constructed for the town of Benalla in 1973, the river broke into a series of watercourses which in summer would dry out into separate waterholes. It was known by the Europeans as the 'Swampy River' or 'Winding Swamp' before the name 'Broken River' was settled upon.[17]

One of the few local historians to investigate what occurred at Broken River in 1838, Samuel Uren, described how from 'the rising ground near the Butter Factory in Mitchell Street' Benalla, 'a panorama of billabongs, lagoons, [and] meanders would meet the eye'. A Benalla resident and school teacher in the early 1900s, Uren noted how 'the surplus water in flood time formed a swamp wherein the watercourse proper lost itself, water remaining in the lagoon for some time'. These deep holes, masses of reeds and fast-flowing swells so confused one of Thomas Mitchell's party in 1836 that he drowned while trying to find the Surveyor General a crossing point.[18]

Marangan has been identified as the heartland of the Yeerun-illam group of the Taungurung (Taung Wurrung), and there are accounts of Marangan as a meeting place. In his 1906 'History of Benalla', Samuel Uren obtained information about events of 1838 from Jim Brown, 'a son of one of the number of the party', John Brown. Uren wrote that 'at certain periods as many as 400 blacks would meet together in the vicinity of Benalla to hold a corroboree'. Uren was certain that Benalla was 'the meeting place of various tribes and the scene of many a [traditional] battle'.[19]

Megan Carter notes that the present-day Winton Wetlands just northeast of Marangan were also an important resource and gathering place – though in 1838, these wetlands were dry. But Marangan was never dry. It was the centre of a rich place full of fish, crayfish, mussels, turtles, ducks, kangaroos, wallabies, possum and vast fields of murrnong or native yams across the areas where the river broke its banks during floods.

Even in 1906, as the *Benalla Standard* newspaper reported, locals could still see 'many fantastic shapes cut into the bark of the trees ... the shape of the cut showing plainly that a canoe has been taken out of it' and on other 'giant eucalypts which grow along the banks of the river that passes through the heart of the town ... the black man's shield is clearly out lined. Then, again, higher up the tree are the holes, made by the natives, from which the opossums were dragged'. Marangan certainly was an important place for the groups who gathered there or nearby on ceremonial or hunting occasions. On the grassy riverbanks beyond the reeds and sedges that lined the river's edge in swathes and under the shade of the huge flooded-gum trees, numerous campfires would have been the centre of dances, stories, exchanges, disputes and alliances.[20]

In 1837, some of the first overlanders in the area, Henry and John Howey – according to early newspaper accounts, 'pioneer pastoralists along the "Major's Line"' – came across a gathering of 'no less than 800 Aboriginal fighting blacks of the famed Broken River tribe camped on the banks of the river' at Benalla. Another local history from 1906 called them 'a powerful and treacherous tribe of natives, known as the Merangan tribe'. The Howeys believed the warriors were holding a 'bora' or ceremony, so these were in fact people from various groups gathered, rather than just the 'Broken River' or 'Merangan tribe'.

In the Howeys' overlanding party was a William Piper, later named 'pioneer Piper' in a Benalla newspaper. When the overlanders camped on the river in the midst of hundreds of 'the famed Broken River tribe', Piper apparently 'fired a bullet into a gum tree ... to show what could be done with fire arms, much to the amazement of the sable warriors'. Piper went on to become the police magistrate at Benalla and in the 1890s the tree was 'still standing near the bridge' across the Broken River. Piper's action of displaying the fire and effect of a musket was regarded by some locals in the 1860s as a sort of foundational event and a Union Jack was attached to a pole next to the tree where he fired 'the historical bullet'.[21]

'Monsters in human form'

By the time Crossley and his overlanders arrived at Broken River in April 1838 there had been a steady flow of overlanders into the wider region, with many in 1836 enticed by bringing highly profitable cattle to the Port Phillip settlement. There had also been a series of attacks and settler reprisals in the area. In late 1837, the squatter Fitzherbert Miller Mundy had established the first station on Taungurung Country around Pyalong, just west of modern-day Seymour.[22]

It seems in 1837 his brothers, Lieutenant Alfred Miller Mundy and Charles Fitzroy Miller Mundy, along with Lieutenant George Brunswick Smyth, took the opportunity of being posted with their regiment to Port Phillip to overland stock there. When they arrived, the Mundy brothers and Smyth were to become famous by playing the first cricket match and are regarded as founders of the Melbourne Cricket Club (MCC).

In December 1839 the ever-diligent Assistant Protector Dredge took down a conversation he had with a Taungurung man he called 'Bulgetheroon' about what had happened when many of his people were 'killed by Mr Mundy and other whites'. Bulgetheroon told Dredge 'the men had gone to look out opossum when they fell in with Mr Mundy'. According to Bulgetheroon, Mundy told them to 'go with him and they would give him plenty of flour'. The grateful Taungurung then 'took it to their fires and made "big one – big one" cake [damper]'.

Then, while they were 'in the act of eating it Mr. M.__ [Mundy] and other white men rode down upon them and shot several of them dead'. The exact number, Dredge could not make out, but he was certain from Bulgetheroon's testimony it included 'men, women and children'.

It seems Mundy, keen to set up a station with no interruptions and, isolated, deep in Aboriginal land, decided the military maxim of a 'pre-emptive strike' was the order of the day.

Bulgetheroon said he hid himself 'under a cliff by the side of the creek – where he heard the [musket] balls whistle over him'. Dredge angrily wrote down Bulgetheroon's account in his diary: 'This is another instance of the savage barbarity of "White Gentlemen" toward the unprotected and persecuted blacks'. Dredge continued:

> The wholesale Murder, like many others of a similar character took place in the bosom of the solitary forest. No human eye witnessed it save that of the murderers – and those who escaped their fiendish fury.

James Dredge was an intelligent and compassionate Wesleyan Methodist preacher, well suited to the albeit strange and almost pointless task of Assistant Protector of Aborigines. On instructions from Lord Glenelg, the Secretary of State for the Colonies, in 1838 a Protectorate of Aborigines had been established and a number of men like Dredge chosen to live among Aboriginal people, learn their languages, watch over their rights and 'protect them from acts of cruelty, oppression and injustice'. Importantly, Protectors were to 'faithfully represent their [Aboriginal peoples'] wants, wishes or grievances'. Dredge certainly attempted to.[23]

But his was a lonely voice in the colonial world of 1830s New South Wales. He noted the outrageous inconsistency that Aboriginal people were 'held amenable to our laws, and are punished for the violation of them' but they are 'considered incompetent to tell their own tale of woe [in court] even under the circumstances of so horrifying a character' as Bulgetheroon had outlined to him.

Dredge wondered no more at the 'sneering manner' in which Mundy (who he now openly called a 'brute') had previously spoken to him about 'the Aborigines'. When Dredge asked Mundy if he thought 'the blacks troublesome', Mundy told him 'he thought they would not trouble him again in a hurry – that he had given them a punishing they would not readily forget'.

Bulgetheroon and his people certainly did not forget. Dredge, who had set up his Protectorate 'station' at Michelton (Mitchellstown) on a bend in the Goulburn River south of present-day Ngambie, noted that 'they continue to breathe vengeful threats at the remembrance of his [Mundy's] name'. Dredge himself called Mundy and his co-killers 'monsters in human form'.

Lieutenant George Brunswick Smyth went on to gain a promotion as captain in the mounted police and Lieutenant Alfred Miller Mundy became a politician. Today, their relationship to one of the Mundy brothers at Pyalong is not mentioned in the text accompanying the portraits that adorn the walls of the 'Foundation Gallery' at the MCG. Historian Jacqui Durrant finds nothing unusual in this: 'I do not think there are many early settlers who weren't engaged in violence. The whole founding of Victoria is steeped in blood'.[24]

'We shall all be killed if we do not send these blacks away'

Warriors raided Pyalong Station, the scene of Mundy's killing spree, several times during early 1838. So too, just a few days before Crossley's party headed off from the Ovens River, they raided Bowman and Mollison's stations on the Coliban and Upper Campaspe rivers in Djadja Wurrung Country. Writing in July, Captain William Lonsdale, the Port Phillip Police Magistrate, was 'inclined to think these blacks [of the Pyalong and other raids] are some of those who were concerned in the attack upon Mr Faithfull's party'. While Pyalong was a fair journey to Broken River, around 130 kilometres, this was not unknown Country for the Djadja Wurrung, and most certainly Taungurung people would have heard of the 'vengeful threats at the remembrance of his [Mundy's] name'. Richard Flanagan's 1854 observation that 'The Rising', as he called it, was an 'explosion of long-pent feelings of revenge and hatred towards the whites, resulting from a long course of violence and injustice' certainly rings true in the first incursions of trigger-happy squatters into northeastern Victoria in the late 1830s.[25]

When Crossley's column arrived on the banks of the Broken River at Marangan on 6 April and set up camp, they were soon met by ten Aboriginal men. According to local historian Uren, who interviewed the son of one of the party, the overlanders were struck by how 'the aborigines were quite different' from those they had met previously on their journey south. Those 'fishing and hunting between the River Ovens and the Broken River were fierce, courageous, numerous, and were guided solely by their own tribal laws'. They certainly had some experience of Europeans. Some of the Aboriginal men who turned up to Crossley's camp at Marangan were wearing European clothes and spoke some English. Among them was a man named 'Charlie' who said he was from Port Phillip and was described as a leader of the group.[26]

Crossley and others later noted that the stockmen all treated Charlie's group 'kindly' and gave them food. On Sunday 8 April, just near where a weir has since been built at Benalla and where the railway bridge now stretches high above, the overlanders got their stock across the 'Winding River' and made camp on the other side, deciding to rest the animals for a couple of days.[27]

Counting sheep is not a straightforward task, but it seems the convict and ex-convict drovers now had some good experience at it – they managed to find that eight sheep from the 3472 were missing. Sheep don't wander from their flocks, so Charlie and his men were instantly suspected of taking them. Perhaps Charlie and the other warriors thought the overlanders would not miss a mere eight out of 3742 sheep. Surely that was plenty for all to share. Still, Crossley had no proof, and bullock driver William Walker later recalled that the overlanders, just like 'pioneer Piper' had done almost on the same spot months before, then proceeded to give Charlie and his men a demonstration of their firearms.

As Walker stated, 'we showed them the use of our arms'. It seems, though, that they already well understood firearms and this display had little effect as the next day, ten more Aboriginal men joined Charlie's group. Now the stockmen were even more on their guard. Among the thick reeds that line the banks of Marangan and the river, the stockmen found a cache of spears – reported by Crossley as '80 or 100' (but by others as around twenty), and 'shifted them to another place'. Then, an Aboriginal man was spotted brazenly taking a sheep from the flocks.

Ticket-of-leave man Thomas Bentley believed an attack was imminent. He claimed some experience in these matters and suggested the fact there were no women in the group meant they had warlike plans. He prophetically warned the rest of the party that 'we shall all be killed if we do not send these blacks away'.[28]

But the overlanders had firearms. Overseer Crossley was confident that 'one shot fired over the heads of a thousand blacks would cause them all to flee in terror'. Still, that night, Crossley didn't seem as confident; he ordered the Aboriginal men to lie on the ground within sight while William Walker stood 'mounting sentry' with a firearm over them throughout the night.[29]

The next day, the stockmen confronted Charlie, as William Read (or Reid) recounted, 'we desired him to take his tribe away'. However, they refused to move. Read 'and two other men ... then drew back with our muskets'. Perhaps Read meant they cocked their muskets ready to fire, or they moved away to an obvious firing position. Whichever, Charlie and his men 'then walked toward the spot where the spears had been concealed, and not finding them sent up a shout and ran away'. According to Walker, Charlie lingered at the camp for a short time and seemed to him to be saying that 'there were 1000 others nearby'. Their confidence around the overlanders' camp suggests Walker was correct in understanding what Charlie was saying – there were indeed large numbers of warriors nearby.[30]

'They seldom attack, but when they are sure of overpowering'

On the morning of Wednesday 11 April, just after the clearing of the light fog that often shrouds Marangan and burns off quickly in the sun, around 9 am the overlanders prepared to move out. Crossley might have felt their display of firepower and stealing the men's spears had worked and they would not dare attack. He did not later remark on seeing any 'smoke signals' as was later mentioned in John Brown's version of his father's story of events, but then most Europeans had no idea that Aboriginal people used fire and smoke to communicate. The stockworkers would probably not have read Thomas Mitchell's account of his journey in the region in 1836, where he noted that 'by the smoke which arose from various parts, we perceived that the aborigines were watching'.[31]

Crossley sent the shepherds ahead with their slightly depleted flock, while the rest of the party remained to pack the drays and yoke the bullocks. He had just split his party into two groups. If there was a perfect time to attack, this was it.

Around 10am the shepherds were about half a mile (roughly 805 metres) ahead of the bullock drays and cattle when William Read heard one of the shepherds shouting 'Murder! A man has been speared!' Crossley and five or six of the men grabbed three muskets and ran towards them, leaving John Clay with the fourth musket to guard the drays. Crossley also had a pistol.[32]

As they ran toward the shepherds, Crossley saw John Bass lying wounded on the ground. Crossley believed there were 'from 150 to 200 natives in all directions round in a threatening attitude'. As William Read recounted, 'About 20 blacks met us before we reached the shepherd and [they] began to shout and throw spears at us'.

Thomas Bentley then aimed and fired 'and a native fell'. Read then 'took a gun from the overseer and fired also as the blacks approached'. William Bateman (or Balmain) fired too, but missed. They both reloaded and fired again, but as Bateman recalled, 'the blacks closed us in' and 'about twelve of us' decided to run. Bentley had managed to kill a warrior; he stopped to reload and fired again, but Bateman said, 'I have not seen him since'. William Faithfull later said that when the warriors attacked, 'the first they speared was the only good marksman'.[33]

As the affair was reported in the *Sydney Gazette* in May:

> Bentley, fired his gun in the air, thinking that such a display would intimidate them: but it had no effect. The blacks still came forward, cautiously sheltering themselves behind the trees in their path, until, when within near approach of the adverse party, one came

forward and was in the act of deliberately poising his spear, when Bentley shot him dead, and was himself, immediately after, pierced with three spears. This unfortunate man was last seen desperately fighting with the butt end of his musket.

Among readers of the *Gazette*, a newspaper steeped in British stories of colonial bravado against all odds, Bentley was considered a heroic figure – pierced with spears and fighting on. Whether that was actually the case or not is uncertain – no survivor mentioned it.

The *Gazette* report continued:

The combat now became general; spears flew in all directions, and several shots were fired without effect, owing to the caution exercised by the blacks of interposing the trees between themselves and the defensive party, but still gradually closing upon the latter. It was now seen that further resistance would be of no avail, and that in flight lay the only chance of safety – as the blacks continued to increase in numbers as they advanced.[34]

Crossley later said he saw 'about forty' of the warriors go straight past them toward the drays and then 'commenced ransacking them'. With warriors in between the two groups of overlanders, the shepherds were forced to flee away from the other stockmen and headed south. William Walker recounted that 'they threw spears at us, and not being armed we ran away with the overseer and several others'. Crossley said they ran through the bush for a few miles, pursued all the way, until some of the men could run no further. According to Crossley, Read gave in first and 'was immediately speared by two of the natives'. Crossley heard Edward Laycock, John Fannan and William Mackay say 'we cannot run further – let us die together!'

Not all the men had run. John Clay hid in the reeds near Marangan watching what he believed were a hundred men looting the drays before he could escape on what must have been a frightening, lonely journey back to the Faithfulls' camp at Wangaratta, about 50 kilometres away. Two other men, Thomas Thatcher and his assistant, had been rounding up the cattle and were on horseback. They galloped off to the north and then rode back toward Wangaratta.

William Read told a somewhat different story to overseer Crossley. Read said Crossley turned and fled with four or five other men while Read took the overseer's gun and fired. He called on Crossley to stop but he and the others kept running. Read saw Fannan lying on the ground with a spear in his back, and then Read was speared three times in the body and thighs, beaten around the head, and left for dead. He dragged himself under one of the drays and fell unconscious, waking the next morning to find Fannan still alive, barely. Read staggered back along the road north for a few miles until he was met by George Faithfull and the stockman Thatcher.

Walker said he saw 'John Freeman speared, then Bass, then John Hargrave, and after, Joseph Smith'. The remaining men then split up, Crossley, Bateman and Welsh headed toward the Goulburn River and Walker and John Brown toward Colonel White's station on the Ovens River. Crossley believed Walker and Brown could not have escaped as most of the warriors pursued them. But soon after, they broke off the attack and the two men made it to the relative safety of Colonel White's station of tents and bark huts.[35]

Andrew Gibson (George Faithfull's brother-in-law, who had a station at Goulburn) was later told that 'many of the natives spoke English, and whilst in pursuit called out after the men several well-known English oaths'. The *Sydney Monitor* newspaper was more explicit, reporting that they 'called out, in their pursuit, that the fugitives were white b——s. [bastards]'.[36]

Crossley and his men had been utterly routed. Their stock was dispersed across the countryside and their drays and supplies plundered. Seven men lay dead. It was a complete victory for the warriors. Their attack showed a high level of timing, co-ordination and tactics, with different groups targeting the advance party, cutting off the two parties from each other, and attacking the drays and pursuing fleeing stockmen. They also had a huge superiority of numbers.[37]

The *Sydney Gazette* received a report that was certain it was a pre-planned, co-ordinated attack:

The survivors of Mr. Faithful's party strenuously persist in denying that any act on their part provoked the commission of the outrage; indeed, from their statement, it would appear to have been a deliberately formed scheme, which had been in contemplation for some time previously.

The editor of the *Gazette* suggested that previous overlanders were to blame and 'some party that preceded his, must have excited the blacks to the commission of so horrible an outrage.' Generally, the colonists were convinced warriors only attacked for revenge. The Europeans could not, or would not, believe that such attacks could be made in defence of Aboriginal homelands.[38]

'We retreated to the Ovens River'

Historian Jacqui Durrant has 'no doubt that the Faithfull incident was coordinated between Waywurru and Taungurong, and that knowledge of those events would have shortly reached most spheres of Kulin influence'. Waywurru and Taungurung warriors were known to have had strong ties. While the western Waywurru had ties with Wiradyuri to their north, the Taungurung did not. Apart from the Waywurru, other Kulin groups had few ties with Wiradyuri, so at this point there was hardly a possibility of an allied Wiradyuri force being involved. But as Durant notes, the Taungurung were certainly well aware of what was coming down Major Mitchell's line of road. Even if they had an enmity with Wiradyuri, their allies the Waywurru did not. Waywurru were a go-between for Taungurung and Wiradyuri, but Wiradyuri and Taungurung did not travel onto each other's Country. Despite this, knowledge, stories and tales of heroic deeds and battles with whites could travel through various Countries via the complex, criss-crossing networks of enmity and friendship.[39]

Further detail of how the attack transpired and just how co-ordinated it was came from William Faithfull. He was heading south from his family's Springfield station in Goulburn to assess the losses in stock and goods when at the Murrumbidgee River he met two of the stockmen who had been 'engaged in the affray'. Faithfull said they told him (as he wrote in a letter to Andrew Gibson in Goulburn) the attack was by at least 300 well-armed warriors 'with not an old man among them'. Half of them had launched an assault on the shepherds while the rest were 'ranged and drawn up' about 100 metres away, 'kept as it were in reserve'. The vanguard of the attack had sheltered in trees before 'rapidly closing in on the camp'. When the stockmen fled, 'in making a rush through the line of Blacks these opened a passage for the men and as they passed, they were speared right and left by at least 150 natives'. In what might well have been an adaptation of traditional combat to anti-colonial warfare, the warriors had opened their lines, creating a gauntlet for the white men to run through, and be speared at will.[40]

By the 1830s the military capabilities of war bands or fighting groups were well known. Charles Sturt noted how distinguishable leaders or 'chiefs' commanded groups, and according to Sturt, 'turned from time to time to direct their followers'. The warriors at Broken River certainly used tactics such as keeping a reserve force and creating a gauntlet. The attack might have been planned over several days. It was a classic tactic along the frontier to send a small party of men into a camp or a station as reconnaissance – to work out how many firearms there were, or what stores or goods could be raided. That ten men were followed by another ten the next day, and that the attack the day after included many more, follows such a pattern.[41]

The climate of fear that broke out among the stockworkers in the region cannot be understated. Patrick Drain was in the droving party that followed the advance group under Crossley. Drain later deposed that 15 miles on the other side of the Ovens River 'a stockman belonging to the first party, Thomas Thatcher', as Drain recalled, 'came up to us and told us that he had made his escape from the Blacks who had attacked them. We retreated to the Ovens River, and stopped there about three weeks'. During that time, Drain said he 'saw the blacks several times' but while they 'committed no violence', Drain and his companions 'were in dread of our lives'.[42]

John Conway Bourke, later described as 'Victoria's First Mailman',

The Battle of Broken River

was a convict who had been offered a pardon if he would deliver the mail between Port Phillip (Melbourne) and Yass for one year. In April 1838 (just after the Broken River battle) Bourke had stopped at Colonel Henry White's Ovens River station when one of Faithfull's men, John Todd, arrived from the cattle station seven miles away and 'gave information that the Blacks were expected to attack the cattle station that night'. According to postman Bourke, just a few days before, a squatter had arrived at Colonel White's who had come up from the Murray River, to 'give the darkies a drubbing'.

In fact, they arrived as part of a large party that had combined their herds and flocks to travel south. They were certainly well prepared to 'give the darkies a drubbing'. There were well over 10 000 sheep in the huge column. The group of squatters (and overseers working for squatters) included McKenzie, Dixon, Campbell, Snodgrass and Hughes. These men had joined forces for the journey, then, when they found the right moment, they would spread out across Aboriginal lands in a kind of blitzkrieg and stake their claims.

The vast column of men and sheep arrived into a scene of chaos and desperation at the Goulburn River. The ex-military man Colonel White hastily buried anything he couldn't carry in a hole in the ground and fled as swiftly as he could. Now, with a handful of men, the Colonel was cut off, deep inside Aboriginal lands with hundreds of warriors on the front foot from a victory over eighteen white men at Broken River. It seems he took his men to a hill where he might be able to see and defend against any approaching force. We can only imagine the terrifying few days and nights the ex-colonel, his young son and a few stockworkers spent on a hill near what was known as Mount Piper, near present-day Broadford.

White's rescuers were now at hand. Mckenzie and Dixon saw campfire smoke on a nearby ridge. They went to investigate and found Colonel White with his son Edward in a 'gunyah' [bark hut] on top of a hill, no doubt as some form of desperate defensive position. Apparently, the Colonel 'made them heartily welcome'. The Colonel now had McKenzie, Dixon, Campbell, Snodgrass and Hughes, their stockmen at hand all looking for grazing land to stop on.[43]

While the new arrivals dispersed their stock and claimed their runs, they seem to have vowed to work together to defend their new sheep stations. They were also well-armed. According to postman Bourke, 'every man' had both 'guns and horse pistols'. Vengeance for the deaths of seven fellow white men beckoned. A strong showing of armed force would also allow them to get on with the urgent tasks of fence, hut and stockyard building. We can only imagine the conversations between the new arrivals, but their energy over the next weeks showed they placed a priority on sorting out the situation with the local people, to settle the district by a show of force.[44]

When Faithfull, Snodgrass and twelve men headed to Faithfull's station on the Oxley Plains they found the stockmen in a state of sheer terror. They all now knew of the white deaths at Broken River. According to shepherd Patrick Drain, 'the next day the shepherds came running in from their sheep saying the blacks were after them'. Then, when Faithfull 'called for his horse', the shepherds believed they were being abandoned to their fate and they fled for their lives. Drain, a convict bonded to his employer, 'swam the Ovens River in company with four other men' and walked all the way to Yass before surrendering himself to the local watchman. He could easily plead that the reason he left his bonded employment was the desperate situation of the Aboriginal offensive at the Broken and Ovens Rivers.[45]

William Faithfull later suggested 'it must have been a desire of plunder which instigated them to commit so deadly a deed'. But the warriors did not in fact have any great need for the European goods on the drays – much of which they left scattered about after the attack anyway. Rather, they needed to halt the stockmen and cattle coming into their lands and to stop the violence against their people. The mobilisation of large numbers of Taungurung and Waywurru warriors and their oaths and shouts of 'white bastards' suggests this was much more than targeted payback or revenge. It was an attack against whites in general.[46]

*

Further details of John Brown's escape were written much later, in 1906, as told by his son Jim. Some details are mixed, but there are some elements that flesh out the court depositions by survivors of the battle. As Jim Brown related, his father and another man, Glenn (actually Walker), 'beat a retreat, but the latter snatched up a loaded gun before he ran. They went parallel with the river, but at some distance from it, as the reeds stood thick along its banks and formed an excellent cover for the aborigines'. They ran 'in a westerly direction towards Upoti-potpon' [Upotipotpon around 30 kilometres northwest of Benalla].[47]

Brown and Walker ran for their lives, believing that the warriors 'had made up their minds that none should escape'. 'One of the fleetest was rapidly gaining ... when Glenn [Walker] turned and shot him.' But the others continued the chase. There was no chance to reload a firearm – when one man threw a spear and missed Brown, he picked it up. With fear on their side, 'the two fugitives outlasted the aborigines'. They then took off their boots 'to make the task of tracking them more difficult'. It was as if they had been forced to fight and run like Aboriginal people themselves.

As Brown recalled from the war stories he had probably heard from his father around the fireplace, 'they continued running until they were almost blind from exhaustion' and found the warriors had stopped their pursuit. They turned east and

> crossed the North Winton Swamp, which was dry. A fire had been through the rushes that had grown in it, and when the men tried to cross the blackened soil they got their feet dreadfully cut. They camped that night in the ranges at a spot known as the Kangaroo Gap, near the swamp [present-day Taminick Gap].

It seems the 'cold, hunger and thirst' had seared Brown's recollection as his son recounted to the local historian Samuel Uren that he would 'have given a thousand pounds, had I it, for a drink of water'.

But when they reached Colonel White's camp at Three-mile Creek the next day they found the colonel had abandoned it and a group of Aboriginal people had occupied it. According to Brown's son, they 'called out to the white men, "Blackfellow been marm um (catch him)" and "Marm um again to-night"'. It was obvious these people already knew of what had happened at Broken River, were probably plundering the Colonel's camp, and that they thought more attacks would follow. William Faithfull admitted he could do little as he himself 'had but few men left [alive] to assist him' and was 'in hourly expectation of a renewed assault'.[48]

As Brown's luck would have it, 'five men shortly afterwards rode up, and the natives ran away'. As soon as the two men had been 'properly clothed and fed', the party of seven headed out to the Broken River to survey the scene. Here they apparently 'found the murdered white men, and buried the seven bodies in [what was in 1906 known as] the cockatoo paddock, close to the Goomaibee road'.[49]

'It would have been certain death to remain'

The Battle at Broken River swiftly became a crisis for the squatters and stockmen in the region. It was also a crisis for those who bankrolled them. As the journalist and early historian George Burnet Barton wrote, the report of seven white deaths in Sydney and Melbourne 'caused such an alarm among the stockowners that they looked upon squatting in Port Phillip as hopeless'. Indeed, Barton thought 'it had become a question whether any station beyond the Hume could be held against them'. In mid-1838, 'day after day letters were received in Sydney which revealed the terrible state of uneasiness existing at the outposts'.[50]

Especially poignant was one letter from 'the Hume', dated 15 May from an under-armed Dr George Mackay, who said 'it would have been certain death to remain' near Broken River:

> I have got back here after great labour. I brought away all the cattle and sheep and everything else of any value. I was very sorry to be obliged to leave my station, but it would have been certain death to remain with eight men and one musket, and no hut up. Faithfull and Bowman have left their cattle running about wild, and Colonel White buried his property in a hole dug in the ground. They fled and left me alone, after advising me to leave everything and fly too.

In June, the *Sydney Monitor* reported that:

> Every fresh arrival in Sydney adds to the melancholy list of outrages committed by the blacks, post after post we are furnished with harrowing tales of the waste of human life and the destruction of private property. Latterly the overland route has been virtually abandoned, and several of the more distant stations on the Hume and Goulburn have deemed it necessary, as a measure of precaution to return with their flocks and herds to the more thickly-populated districts for protection.

Within a few weeks after the battle, warriors had forced the abandonment of most stations in the Ovens River region. Goulburn Police Magistrate George Stewart arrived on the scene on 22 May and reported that Colonel White 'and other settlers had abandoned their stations'. The *Sydney Monitor* named at least five squatters who had fled and suggested there were more. Overlanders coming from the north were stopped in their tracks and massing at the Murray River, not moving south until it was safe to do so. Overlanders from the south joined forces for safety and formed massive convoys several miles long, all from fear of another attack like that at Broken River. The 'Ovens & Broken River tribes' had taken back a huge swathe of their Country.[51]

CHAPTER FOUR
Re-taking the Murrumbidgee River

'White devils ... were coming down'

As we proceeded, we noticed their bush telegraph, signalling to the tribes lower down the river, that white devils, as they called us, were coming down. This means of communication was effected by their setting fire to hollow trees, on the edges of the river or water courses, which sent up a column of black smoke, which could be seen at a long distance in this open and level country.

– Stockman John Phillips recalling overlanding west of Deniliquin in 1840.

Information travelled accurately, far and fast across Aboriginal lands. As Uncle Wayne Fossey notes, the 'colour, size and rapidity of smoke all meant different things'. There were many ways of making different signal meanings – as stockman Phillips noted, black smoke meant 'white devils'.[1]

In May 1836 Major Thomas Mitchell's party was wandering on a circuitous route through the Murray-Darling basin, searching for great rivers and expansive grasslands. When his party arrived at Benanee, 'a fine lake' near present-day Euston on the Murray River, Mitchell was 'not a little surprised' to come across his 'old adversaries from the Darling at a distance of nearly two hundred miles from their usual haunts'. Mitchell was astounded they had 'come across [as he was "afterwards told"] to fight us!'

If what Mitchell had heard was true, this was certainly a great march across more than 300 kilometres through neighbouring lands. Historians believe it was a march to avenge the deaths of seven Marra Waree men or the 'spitting tribe' as Mitchell called them, whom Mitchell's party

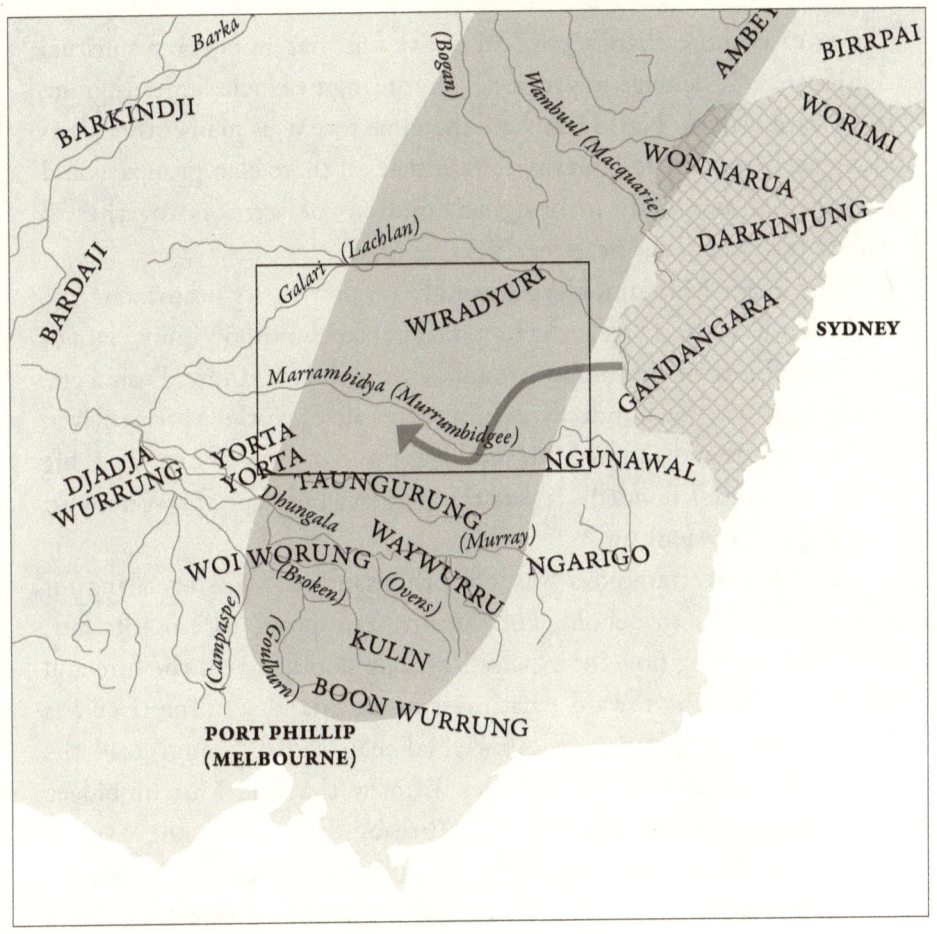

The Murrumbidgee River, 1830s
'Settled Districts' are indicated by hatching.
The movement of squatters, stockmen and stock marked with an arrow.

had shot on his earlier expedition along the Baaka-Darling. Mitchell was surprised by their journey to attack him, but also knew how the 'bush telegraph' worked; he had heard that people knew of Sturt's earlier party coming down the river well before Sturt arrived in their lands.[2]

Communication flowed up and down the riverways. Wiradyuri clans along the Murrumbidgee River from Wagga Wagga to Narrandera were traditionally aligned. For Wiradyuri people the river remains, as Uncle James Ingram notes, not so much a boundary, but a responsibility.

The river is more than a physical entity and has important spiritual significance. It belongs to everyone. According to Uncle James Ingram, the Lizard clan or 'Narin jera' had 'the same totem' as many other clans along the river. Uncle James is certain that all these clan groups would have united as a body in bringing hundreds of warriors together to defend the river at the heart of their Country.[3]

The upper Murrumbidgee River always flowed. Its headwaters rise in the wet heath and bog at the foot of Peppercorn Hill on Long Plain in the Fiery Range of the Snowy Mountains, north of Kiandra. From here, it winds its way for hundreds of kilometres along to the Murray River. More properly written as Marrambidya, the river was known as a 'big water' and 'often flooded'. It was the perfect landscape for Wiradyuri farming and aquaculture.[4]

The Bila Marrambidya was, after thousands of years of caring for Country, a sight to behold. For the first Europeans to cross its fast, westward-running flow interspersed by long pools, it held the lure and promise of heading toward what must be an inland sea. The river was known since 1820 when an Aboriginal man called 'Simon' told the pastoralist and land seeker Charles Throsby that the Murrumbidgee River 'communicates with the sea'. Throsby came across the river in 1821. Soon after, land seekers began to follow his tracks.[5]

At the same time, Governor Brisbane followed directions from London to open settlement west of the Blue Mountains. Brisbane created a land rush. Once the Bathurst Plains had come under control of the colonists after they defeated the northern Wiradyuri in 1824, bushmen with some capital, 'native born' sons of those made good by land grants after serving their prison sentence, or free men funded by wealthy pastoralists and investors, bought some sheep and cattle and headed beyond the 'limits of location'. They headed south, west and north from the inland hubs and staging posts of Bathurst and then Yass – bridgeheads for further occupation. They followed the reports of people like Throsby, Captain Currie and Major Ovens, who hit upon the Murrumbidgee River in 1823, and then Hamilton Hume and Captain William Hovell, who crossed a series of rivers to make it all the way to Port Phillip (Melbourne) in 1824.

After all these captains and majors led their expeditions, several years of dry conditions from 1827 to 1830 kept a check on overlanding ventures in their footsteps. When Captain Charles Sturt headed off looking for an inland sea in 1829, the last 'habitation' he passed was the lonely shepherd's hut at Henry O'Brien's station, Douro, at Jugiong, just past Yass. By 1831 the furthest stations (often merely a bark hut and a large chunk of land 'claimed' and stocked with sheep and cattle) had reached just to the west of present-day Gundagai.[6]

When the authorities in July 1831 ended the 'free land grant system' and set a minimum price of 5 shillings an acre on land sold at auction, those with less capital (often emancipists or sons of convicts whose stock numbers were growing and needed more land but had no capital) began to take their stock beyond the reach of government, outside the 'limits of location'. They claimed to be nomads, merely 'de-pasturing', moving sheep and cattle to where the grass was.

But the colonists were beginning to work out that dry and wet conditions come and go in swings and roundabouts. In the good times, squatters advanced. By 1832, with good water everywhere, there was what historian Bill Gammage called 'an extraordinary explosion of settlement' along the Murrumbidgee River from Oura (just east of present-day Wagga Wagga) to Darlington Point, a stretch of nearly 200 kilometres of fertile alluvial beds and regularly flooded river banks.

In the middle of this was the heartland of the Narrungdera Wiradyuri. The men who decided to take a few thousand acres of this land for their sheep and cattle graciously called the station on the north side of the river 'Narrandera', in a poor transcription of the Wiradyuri clan name. When those first squatters and stockmen travelled downstream along the Bila Marrambidya, they probably would not have noticed the boundary trees that defined Narrungdera homelands – trees that can still be seen just outside Narrandera to this day.[7]

Word of squatters heading south had undoubtedly arrived before them. Wiradyuri and others had gathered at Wagga Wagga or 'place of dancing' for thousands of years, often en route to the bogong moth feasts in the mountains and marriage gatherings to the north near present-day Canberra. At Wagga, the river is flanked by numerous billabongs that make for perfect campsites for hundreds of people at a time. As Uncle James Ingram notes, in times of flood, the lagoons would have been 'logged off' to trap fish and other resources for drier times or large gatherings. People from the Murray River would travel there, and others from the south and western plains. They would all then travel on toward the mountains to feast on the bogong moth. Undoubtedly, in the mid-1830s, they shared news of the squatters, and their sheep and cattle.[8]

'War by the Blacks'

By 1833 squatters had rolled in and taken up nearly the entire river frontage of the Narrungdera Wiradyuri. Many of them were so-called 'Airds Irish'. They were the 'native sons' of Irish people who had settled in the Airds and Appin districts southwest of Sydney and had used their parents' relatively small land grants as staging posts for their expeditions. Some of these families such as the Warbys were at Appin in 1816, when Dharawal and Gandangarra people were massacred by soldiers, and were very familiar with what happened when conflict broke out with warriors.

The climate and weather at first dictated how the influx of cattle and sheep affected the Narrungdera. By 1834, another drought meant that by 1836 several squatters had been forced to desert their new runs. Any Narrungdera people trying to work out what the future of squatting on their lands might be could have been forgiven for thinking it was untenable, at best perhaps always meant to be just a light touch on the land and river.[9]

But events in Sydney and a shift in the administration of the colony were to have huge ramifications for those people who were living in, or squatting on, lands along the Murrumbidgee River. Governor Bourke overturned the free land grant system that had been in operation since the early days of the colony. It had been used to provide incentives to convicts and rewards to others, but now the writing was on the wall for convict transportation. The only 'free' Aboriginal land available now was beyond the reach of government. In the late 1830s, the remoteness of land far from the eyes and ears of colonial authorities was, despite it being a dangerous and tenuous affair, an increasingly attractive proposition.[10]

After forty years of British arrivals, the colonists were still a mere pinprick in vast Aboriginal lands. In 1828 there were only 36 000 non-Aboriginal people in Australia. But from this point on, there was what historians have called 'a prodigious bout of explosive colonisation'. By 1841 there were 118 000 colonists. It was this period of boom and promise in the 1830s that also began to tip the military balance in favour of the colonists. Increasingly armed to the teeth for protection, they just kept on coming.[11]

The first signs of major conflict along the Murrumbidgee began in 1833. And it began, as it usually did everywhere, with Aboriginal people demanding a cut of the growing numbers of cattle and sheep on their lands. A letter to the *Sydney Herald* from a 'C. T.' (who we can safely say was the squatter Charles Thomson) in March that year was titled 'War by the Blacks'. Thomson, writing from his 'station on the Murrumbidgee below Wondibadgeree' (Wantabadgery, around 40 kilometres east of present-day Wagga Wagga) described how 'about the hour of midnight' on 26 February, 'the watchman of the folds at one of my sheep stations', Peter Carroll, 'was suddenly alarmed by the violent rushing of the sheep'. Carroll discovered that 'about 30 natives had surrounded the folds and were endeavouring to steal a sheep'. Carroll did not have a gun so tried a bluff, exclaiming to them, 'if they did not go away he would fire on them'.[12]

According to Thomson, Carroll then promptly 'received a jagged spear in his belly, which, fortunately taking an oblique direction towards the right side, did not penetrate the abdomen, but was withdrawn by himself, leaving however a considerable piece of the weapon in the wound'. Many more spears were thrown 'which did but little execution' before the warriors 'decamped taking with them one sheep and scattering the whole of the rest from the fold'. Thomson was livid – writing that 'this is the fifth sheep they have stolen from me within the short space of two months'. He was also concerned that 'they never used a spear before although they have threatened it', only 'prevented by the sight of a musket'.

Thomson was clear that 'success has so emboldened them' that they now 'threaten to annihilate property to a very serious extent'. At another of his stations, Bammen, [possibly Bomen Lagoon] 'the blacks endeavoured to kill the calves in the pen ... [took] one of the shepherd's pea coats, Carroll's bed, blanket, shirt, trowsers, and frock' and left his overseer and the stockmen cowering as they threatened to attack them that night. The overseer at Bammen wrote to Thomson that:

> They have done Mr. M—'s herd of cattle a great deal of injury, having killed and eat some – some they have speared, and many more (supposed about 60) they have driven quite away ... They have laid in ambush to surprise and cut off the man who is in charge, and he is in danger of his life. There is now (March 1) about a thousand of the blacks convenient to our stations and the shepherds are afraid to graze their sheep, or to watch them at night, lest the blacks should come on them by surprise.[13]

If 'Mr. M—' was overseer Anthony Marshall, who was in charge of the 'Berry Jerry' run for John Bray, he certainly was targeted. Apparently, 'the blacks, who were very ferocious, hunted him out'. Marshall moved to the 'Wagga Wagga run for R. H. [Robert Holt] Best', one of the first squatters to take Wiradyuri lands around Wagga. He was also one of the first to abandon a run: 'The blacks had speared so many of the cattle that Best's men abandoned the station' and all the land further down the river became vacant. According to local historian James Gormly: 'for the first year the blacks proved troublesome'. Frank Jenkins recalled later to Gormly that when he took up Best's abandoned run, he 'found that several of his cattle had been killed by the blacks'.[14]

James Gormly interviewed many squatters 'about the early days on the Murrumbidgee' in the early 1900s. Frank Jenkins (of Buckinbong Station) recalled to Gormly that 'the plan the black men adopted was to hide in the reeds that grew on the water's edge, and watch until the cattle went down the steep bank to drink. Then the blacks would range themselves along the top of the bank and spear the cattle that were below them'.[15]

Wiradyuri people were not merely killing sheep and cattle for food but were driving them away and attacking stockmen. Thomson noted that

Re-taking the Murrumbidgee River

'for some months past, the natives all along that [Murrumbidgee] River, from Warby's station [at the junction of the Tumut and Murrumbidgee Rivers] to 50 miles westward have evinced a mischievous disposition, by spearing and killing cattle'. Warriors were using the advantage of overwhelming numbers at this stage (possibly 1000 warriors compared to a few dozen armed Europeans in the area) threatening to kill, and trying to kill, stockmen.

In a response that was to echo down the Murrumbidgee River valley and beyond, Warby took matters into his own hands. Warby, one of the first squatters in the area in 1829, had some experience in frontier conflict. William used his father's land grant at Airds in Sydney to head south and join the land rush and set up a station he named 'Darbalara'. William and his brother Benjamin were sons of a man who had been through the warfare across the south of Sydney. They were born bushmen, as their father had become one before them. Ex-convict Bush Constable John Warby had been rewarded for guiding Governor Macquarie through the Cowpastures, for exploring Gandangarra and Dharawal land and for arresting Patrick Collins, a bushranger (with the help of a group of Darug men armed with spears) in 1814. He was again rewarded in 1816 for guiding soldiers who were pursuing warriors in Macquarie's campaign across the Sydney Basin that ended in the Appin Massacre. Soon after, in June 1816 he was granted 260 acres (105 hectares) at Campbelltown and built a house there that became the base for his sons to pursue squatting. Warby had worked closely with Aboriginal people, befriended them, learnt language and profited from his services as a negotiator with Aboriginal people by receiving grants of their land.[16]

Now it was his sons' turn to put their bush skills to use. William Warby went out with a party of his men and tracked people to 'where they killed a fat cow' and came upon 'the camp of the depredators ... in the act of roasting and feeding on the flesh'. One of Warby's men 'fired and wounded one of the tribe, who was suspected to be the ringleader'. Thomson matter-of-factly reported that this man had 'since died in consequence'. With no compunction and no thought to legal process, let alone the fact that shooting and killing a man for stealing a cow was a criminal act under British law, Warby's men could, and did, shoot and kill. And Thomson could openly write about it in the Sydney newspapers with no fear of punishment for Warby or his stockmen.

And he could justify it: 'Since that period they [Wiradyuri] do not appear to have molested Mr. Warby's station a second time'. Despite publicly describing a crime against British subjects, 'C. T.' did hope that this would not continue. He noted that

> the men generally employed at, and who occupy those distant stations, are people of a very low grade, who, if they possess the means of wrecking their vengeance on the savage tribes, by having fire-arms indiscriminately placed at their disposal, would not hesitate to do so; and the slaughter might be most sanguinary.

'C. T.' believed 'there are very many who would esteem it as much sport as a day's fowling [bird hunting], to be allowed legally to destroy half the native tribes in the Colony'.

'C. T.' was at this stage 'unwilling to yield to the urgent solicitations' of his men 'to allow them the indiscriminate use of fire-arms'. But he asked, 'should the Government not be able to extend sufficient protection to persons situated beyond the limits of colonization ... so as to awe into good order and subordination the native tribes of the remote stations' then 'those men take upon them indiscriminately to deal out vengeance on the blacks'. How, 'C. T.' asked, 'are proprietors of stock to act ... if they do not afford their servants some shew of protection in the wilderness [?]'.[17]

Killing and dispersing sheep and cattle in numbers that were obviously beyond what the warriors needed just for food was a sign of intent, a warning to the colonists. This form of economic sabotage had been a critical element in guerrilla warfare conducted by Aboriginal people working to push back or halt settlement and occupation of their lands since the Sydney Wars in the 1790s and around Bathurst in the 1820s.[18]

The threat these attacks posed in early 1833 was heightened by the fact they were conducted during night raids. The cover of darkness meant warriors could negate the range of muskets and could surprise unwary stockkeepers. It certainly spooked the colonists. As 'C. T.' noted, 'For, contrary to most other tribes, who appear to have a superstitious dread of darkness, these marauders commit their depredations during the night, which makes them the more dangerous'.

Just as had been the case in Bathurst at the height of the First Wiradyuri War in mid-1824, stockworkers were 'afraid to graze their sheep, or to watch them at night, lest the blacks should come on them by surprise'. 'C. T.' noted that the stockmen 'will not attend to the care of the stock they have in their charge, while under the dread of their lives from so artful an enemy'.

Isolated stockmen had often found comfort in the knowledge many Aboriginal people had 'a superstitious dread of darkness' and were reluctant to move from their camps and villages at night. But night raids in traditional warfare were not unknown, and in 1824 the Wiradyuri warrior Windradyne led a series of attacks to the north of Bathurst, killing seven stockmen, burning huts and destroying property and stock during a single night of terror.[19]

These attacks in 1833 might be seen as the first defence of the Murrumbidgee River. They occurred at least 50 miles (approximately 80 kilometres) along the river – a huge line that was also to be the scene of renewed attacks in coming years. The conflict in 1833 might have led to some kind of stand-off or understanding along this part of the frontier. There was no further reported conflict for several years. Perhaps the warriors believed they had halted the squatting push along the river. As historian Bill Gammage notes, during much of the early 1830s the Narrungdera had 'shown the white men the best camping places ... had pointed out the best building materials ... and allowed them to use the rich and varied resources of their country'. Now, they had also shown the squatters what might occur if these negotiations and understandings broke down.[20]

In fact, this early co-operation with the white newcomers could be most useful when conflict broke out. As the missionary Lancelot Threlkeld noted in 1837, the mode of surrounding a herd of cattle, the slaughtering of the beasts, the preserving of the flesh by smoke, and the plaiting of whips from the hides, were the lessons of a convict stockman; and under such tutors, so numerously scattered amongst the Tribes in the Interior, it is not marvellous that they become adept pupils in such arts.

Threlkeld was certain that Aboriginal people had picked up stock-handling skills that they were now using against the colonists. This would be seen right across the vast river country when warriors began to make stockyards and take cattle for their own herds.[21]

'War was going on on the Murrumbidgee frontier'

During the First Wiradyuri Homeland War from 1822 to 1824 around Bathurst, firearms were not the decisive factor in the British defeating Windradyne and his warriors. Wiradyuri leaders across the Central West had shown that numbers of warriors could defeat armed colonists and defy them in guerrilla warfare. It was not to be until percussion cap-fired rifles and then breechloading rapid-fire weapons predominated after the 1850s that firearms really came into their own. Before this, it was the combination of firearms and horses that was in fact the key. As Governor Brisbane had admitted in 1824, 'infantry have no chance of success' against warriors. During the Bathurst War there had been growing calls for a 'Colonial Cavalry' or some form of mounted military and by 1825, just a year after the end of the war, the first mounted police units had been formed.[22]

But the mounted police were few and far between. In 1837, Lord Glenelg informed Governor Bourke that 'the Settlers must not be led to depend on a Military Force for internal protection' but should 'provide as much as possible for their own defence'. Part of this broader strategy included inducements of 'advantages' to ex-army officers and land grants for soldiers along the exposed frontier districts. Another element was simply giving stockworkers a horse, a dog and a gun.

Now, 'C. T.' was to be proven correct – across the outstations, people with 'fire-arms indiscriminately placed at their disposal' would certainly 'not hesitate' to 'wreck their vengeance on the savage tribes'.[23]

...

In December 1838, a man who was later to become a Protector of Aborigines, a lieutenant governor in New Zealand and then governor in several British colonies in the West Indies, Edward John Eyre, was overlanding stock from Port Phillip to Adelaide. It was a good business proposition to kick start what was to be a rather tumultuous career – as Governor of Jamaica in 1865 he put down a rebellion and became known as 'the Monster of Jamaica'. Eyre's 1000 sheep and 600 cattle made a grand sum of £4000 in Adelaide, of which he netted half when he got there. On the way, Eyre's overlanding party passed through 'Ganmain' station (between Narrandera and Wagga Wagga). He remarked in his diary that 'the Stockkeepers were in the habit of making raids' against Aboriginal people. Indeed, Eyre was told that his hosts at 'Ganmain' had 'only recently returned from one of these expeditions'.[24]

By early 1839, after a period of stock raids and counter-attacks by colonists, it seems a determination to destroy the pastoral stations on Narrungdera Country was made. One of only a few historians to have looked at these events in detail, Bill Gammage, suggests that at this point Narrungdera Wiradyuri had decided 'to clear the invaders from the country' and that 'they had declared war'.

Gammage believes the Narrungdera would by now have had reports from 'all their trade routes and kin links north into New England and south into Victoria' that the number of whites and their cattle and sheep was constant and growing. They would have also undoubtedly heard of how other people were fighting back.[25]

The first major attack occurred in early January. Henry Williams, a 'Servant Overseer' to 'Mr. Robert Jenkins of Campelltown' wrote to magistrate Hardy at Yass in January to inform him that:

a Barbarous murder that took place at Mr. Jenkins' station on the Murumbidgie the Distance is about 95 miles from Gundigai – a man the name of Denis Denay assigned servant for life was murdered by the Blacks on the morning of the 8th of this month and the hut plundered of all contents and then set fire to [sic].

The stockman Matthew Donovan Holding a Ticket of Leave for the District of Yass returned on the same morning after coming from muster and found the Hut consumed and the man about 40 yards from the stock yard with 7 spears in him with several wounds about his head apparently to have been inflicted with a tomy hawk and the right eye knocked out of his head on the cheek the man was inspected by several free persons and then interred as the Distance is so far beyond the limits there was no other means of Keeping him over ground.[26]

The *Sydney Monitor* newspaper later suggested the killing of Denay was 'very coolly planned and perpetrated' and claimed the attackers had lain 'in ambush until the man went to milk his cows' before they killed him and plundered and then burned his property.[27]

The 'native born' squatter Frederick Anslow Thompson was a well-educated young man. His brother Charles was a poet and public servant who had written the first book of poetry by an Australian-born poet in 1826. Thompson rode from his station 'on the Morumbidgee about twenty miles from "Bangus"' all the way to Yass, to inform Magistrate John Richard Hardy of a murder. Hardy then wrote to the Colonial Secretary that he received a report from 'Mr. Thompson, managing the station of his Father Mr. Charles Thompson of Clydesdale near Windsor'. Thompson told Hardy that 'a well known Tribe of Blacks indigenous to that neighbourhood were known to have been on the spot on the morning of the murder as well as for several days previously'.

According to Thompson, 'amongst them was a very remarkable Black known by the name of "Brian Boru"'. Brian Boru was an historical figure familiar in British schoolboy education at the time as the chief who united Ireland, became 'High King' and halted the Viking invasions in 1014. Whether this name reflected his ability to unite disparate tribes or his military prowess, or both, may never be known. According to Thompson, Brian Boru had, 'amongst other peculiarities ... a foot of very great length (14 inches [about 36 centimetres] at least, and of proportionate breadth)'.[28]

Here was a man to take note of. Thompson suggested to Hardy the mounted police could easily find 'this Tribe [who] have not made their appearance since in the neighbourhood, but are known to have gone farther down the River'. With a 'great scarcity of water' at the time, there was nowhere else to go than 'down the river'. Thompson pointed out that 'the Tribe in question [were] certainly to be met with on its Banks, and at no great distance'. Thompson impressed on Hardy that 'cattle are frequently speared in that quarter'. Now the mounted police had evidence of Brian Boru's enormous footprint to find their man. According to Thompson 'the marks of this foot were distinctly seen on the ashes of the Hut and round about by several persons the same day the murder was committed'.[29]

Yet sending police to the area was difficult. If he wanted to investigate, Hardy had no police to accompany him at all. He said he would have 'at once have proceeded to Bangus to enquire into the matter' as had happened in 'the case of the murder of Mr. Faithful's men' in April 1838. Hardy hoped that Sergeant Rose of the Mounted Police at the Hume River might help. But he was concerned that 'there are few Policemen at Goulburn'. The protection for squatters and stockmen was almost nonexistent. Meanwhile at Buckinbong, squatter Michael Byrne soon chose discretion over valour and abandoned his run.[30]

'Not an open battle, but a regular guerrilla warfare'

In 1837, a young Scottish man, James Coutts Crawford, gave up his career as an officer in the Royal Navy for the seemingly boundless opportunities in the colonies. He discharged himself from the navy and sailed to New Zealand. In Sydney in 1839 he followed the money makers who were overlanding sheep and cattle. Coutts Crawford had the funds to purchase 700 head of cattle, employ an overseer and seven workers, and set off to sell the herd in Adelaide.

Coutts Crawford briefly observed in his diary that, 'at this time the beginning of 1839 War was going on on the Murrumbidgee frontier'. He made nothing further of it, as his overlanding party managed to avoid conflict. But it seems Crawford understood the situation well, saying it was 'not an open battle, but a regular guerrilla warfare'. Such an understanding of war was not uncommon among the many military and ex-military men who were involved in the great squatting boom of the 1830s. They knew war when they saw it. And they understood guerilla warfare as still war.[31]

Historian Bill Gammage suggests Brian Boru and his warriors 'brought allies from beyond both the Murray and the Lachlan' and that these alliances actually 'set forth to clear the invaders from their country'. The writer (later Dame) Mary Gilmore certainly noted the calling together of warriors along the river and beyond, taking down stories from her father from the 1840s. She had spent much time with Aboriginal people on the river as a child. Gilmore noted different language speakers communicated in various ways: 'sound (drums) and signs (smoke as well as message-sticks, and marks on trees and earth and shrubs)'. She noted there were 'interpreters', who 'in case of urgency ... were sent out either as runners, or followed runners with message-sticks, to whatever tribe information, warning or other matters had to be carried'. Gilmore added, 'when there were special things to be notified, it was compulsory for every tribe to have word sent them'. Gilmore recalled her father saying the reasons were those such as drought, flood, disease and 'possible attack'.[32]

Traditional Wiradyuri warfare was based in highly organised and structured systems. This meant that they generally resolved combats and disputes with minimal loss of life. Yet it also meant there was a level of organised military coherence – often missed or dismissed by historians – that they could readily adapt to fighting against armed squatters, stockmen and police. Wiradyuri warriors had what was effectively 'battle dress' of ochre paints and signs of rank or insignia such as eagle feathers. All warriors strictly followed any 'call to arms' when given, and traditionally their families did too, joining in any march to a ceremonial battle carrying provisions. One early colonist at Wagga Wagga recalled that 'the great chief of the Waradgery [Wiradyuri] tribe ... had five [eagle feathers] when I first saw him in a gathering of headmen and chiefs, two others had three or four, and several had two and one'. Wiradyuri fighting methods were underpinned by forms of rank, insignia and command that would have been at home in any European armed force.[33]

In 1839, the raids, attacks and killing of cattle and sheep followed a path – a path along the Murrumbidgee River. As Uncle James Ingram notes, 'from Narrandera to Gundagai ... the Riverine Red Gum was central to southern Wiradyuri people. It provided so much. The river and its richness was what the Wiradyuri wanted back'. The 'great scarcity of water' that Thompson had pointed out to Magistrate Hardy occurred at the same time Wiradyuri under Brian Boru began a significant series of raids. A dry spell was a perfect time to force any attack. It was a moment of weakness for the squatters during a heightened competition for water. By 1839, the squatting rush was at its peak and many squatters clung desperately to their runs, too scared to leave for fear of other squatters taking their place.[34]

Along the Murrumbidgee in early 1839, panic was setting in across the unprotected outstations. Soon after Denay's death, Police Magistrate Hardy received word that an employee of 'Mr. Baker' had 'also been murdered by the Blacks in that direction', but this was never confirmed and Hardy considered such reports to be 'generally untrue'. A missing stockman was always reason to blame 'the Blacks'.[35]

But the fear continued to grow. In February, squatter Michael Byrne at 'Buckinbong' sent his assigned servant John Williams out to look for a missing horse. Williams was later found by a stockman, Thomas Supple, when he saw carrion birds feasting on a body around a mile from Thomas Small's station. The mutilated body had one foot severed and 'in the back of his neck there was a hole' that Supple believed had 'been caused by a spear thrown by the Blacks'. Stockman John Tomkinson described how one of Williams's ears had been cut off, and that 'the whole of the flesh had been taken away except that which was on his face'. Perhaps leaving his face was a way to let the colonists know who the dead person was, and stripping his skin from his body a way to make a clear and gruesome warning to those who would find him. Whatever the case, this was a violence that shattered relations between the colonists and Wiradyuri. It was soon to become total war.[36]

Just a day after Williams was buried, four miles from where he had been killed, two of squatter James Thorn's 'ticket of leave men', Joseph Ferguson and John Tomkinson, were alerted by their dogs barking. A 'number of Blacks, about 150, armed with spears and boomerangs' were approaching their hut. In what was a classic moment of frontier warfare, the stockmen, with a musket each, took positions outside at both ends of the hut and awaited the onslaught until when, as Tomkinson later reported, 'the Blacks then commenced throwing spears'. At first the two men began 'dodging about' and managed to 'escape them [spears] for some time'. Soon enough however, Tomkinson was struck by a boomerang in the face and by 'a spear in the right hand, between the thumb and forefinger'. Their escape route to the river had been covered by warriors, so they retired into the hut, completely surrounded.

Their situation appeared hopeless. The hut was peppered with spears sticking in the roof – but they had only 'penetrated three inches through the bark'. Tomkinson found a corner of the hut where an 'open space of six inches between the slabs' meant they could see the warriors outside. The uninjured Ferguson 'discharged his musket through the slabs' and struck down one of the warriors, who apparently afterwards died from the wound. This only appeared to animate the warriors, who began to 'talk much louder, and quicker'. The two men believed they were about to 'rush the hut'. But when Ferguson managed to quickly fire again, the warriors left. Ferguson and Tomkinson had shown how the simple but effective defence of a bark-roofed and timber-slabbed hut, along with the firepower of two muskets, could be enough to withstand an attack by a large force of warriors.[37]

'The Blacks have ... struck so much terror into the minds of the settlers'

In 1839, the Narrungdera were killing stock with impunity. They were also taking cattle for their own herds, or simply driving them off into the bush. In February John Coutts Crawford saw for himself a bull with 'a broken spear right through his leg' and heard from two stockmen who had gone in search of a missing herd that 'all but 12 had been driven across the river by the blacks'.

In March, Michael Byrne reported taking 'six or seven spears out of different cattle' and finding 'several places in the Bush where the Blacks had looted Cattle'. At his Buckingbong station, stockworkers apparently 'watched helplessly while their cattle were ringed – driven round and round in a circle – and speared one after another by warriors surrounding them'.

It was a huge blow to squatters who had invested in cattle. Commissioner of Crown Lands Henry Cosby was the man in charge of all this and he had little to offer at this stage beyond observations. He noted how when cattle were 'rushed by the Blacks' they 'become wild and dispersed, and are also less valuable, because they are restless from alarm, and consequently do not settle to feed ... [which is] particularly injurious to breeding cattle'.[38]

If there was one way to halt British occupation of Narrungdera Country at this point, the rushing, herding and killing of hundreds of cattle was certainly a strategy that worked. The threat to the squatters was felt right back in Sydney. The *Sydney Herald* newspaper reported that 'the Blacks have again been killing cattle' on the Murrumbidgee. The reporter could only wonder at the fact that many animals had been speared 'apparently from mere wantonness, as in several instances they have not removed the meat after killing the beasts'.[39]

Along the river however, colonists were beginning to understand that this was far from 'mere wantonness'. According to Commissioner Cosby, at six stations along the lower Murrumbidgee, Wiradyuri had speared a total of 479 head of cattle by mid-May, of which eighty-five were confirmed to have been killed. The number that had been 'rushed', and were still missing, was between 482 and 532.

Clearly, the strategy was one of economic sabotage, and clearly, the Wiradyuri were on the offensive. In early July, they were reported to have 'rushed a herd of cattle ... consisting of one thousand two hundred head, and speared a great many of them'. This was the height of guerrilla warfare. Of the 1200 cattle, stockmen 'were only able to muster two hundred and fifty'. Fifty more were found dead, and another fifty 'with spears sticking in various parts of their bodies'. Eight hundred and fifty remained unaccounted for.[40]

This was a massive blow. Yet there were more to come. Before burning Denay's hut to the ground Wiradyuri had plundered it of all its contents, among which were '3 stands of arms'. The Wiradyuri now had firearms in their possession as well as herds of cattle. The stockmen in the district now did not dare 'to go out even the shortest distance from their huts, except in parties of two or more, well armed'.[41]

On 24 May, the *Sydney Herald* noted that squatting parties travelling the lower Murrumbidgee were now ensuring 'watches at night to prevent a surprise from the blacks' and urged 'utmost vigilance on this point'. Meanwhile, Tomkinson and Fergusson had been 'so much alarmed' by the attack on their run that they 'did not dare to remain and abandoned the station in consequence'. Commissioner Cosby emphasised that 'the Blacks have gone so far, and struck so much terror into the minds of the settlers, that the white inhabitants will be compelled to abandon at least 50 miles of the river'. Over the next months, Cosby's assessment proved correct and he reported how several squatters had 'been obliged to desert their lower or most remote stations, in consequence of the hostility displayed by the blacks'.[42]

In May 1839, warriors had taken back a huge stretch of their river. Perhaps one of the reasons we have little understanding of these events today is that only a handful of white people were recorded as losing their lives during the sustained conflict of the first half of 1839. It doesn't feel like a 'real war' in the context of other wars of empire. But this warfare was largely directed at the colonists' infrastructure – their property and stock. In this, the Wiradyuri attacks were incredibly successful, and one of the most successful pound for pound across the entire colony. Importantly, it was also a form of warfare that aligned with traditional Wiradyuri methods. In this, as any successful guerrilla warfare campaign, killing people can be counter-productive, often creating a disproportionate response or increased military mobilisation. Destroying infrastructure is often far more effective, and a far better use of available military resources. And it cost the investors in sheep and cattle runs thousands of pounds – in 1839 cattle were selling for between £6 and £10 per head. While it is unclear how many he purchased and how many were bred, Michael Byrne's loss of nearly 1000 cattle cost him dearly, and £10 000 in profit evaporated overnight.[43]

How suddenly things had changed across southern Wiradyuri Country. In 1838, squatters and stockmen were carrying arms to attack any warriors who attempted to spear cattle or raid huts. In 1839, they were carrying arms to defend themselves and were abandoning their stations. The Narrungdera and other Wiradyuri warriors had not only halted the seemingly inexorable push of squatters into their lands, but forced them to retreat.[44]

CHAPTER FIVE

The Battle of Meewah

'The finest meadow pasture I have seen'

In the 1830s, Moreton Bay in present-day southeast Queensland was an outpost of secondary punishment for convicts who had committed serious offences. It was one of the most isolated places in the British empire. At first, after moving from Redcliff on the coast after constant conflict with the Ningy Ningy people further up the Brisbane River, the settlement with strict military and administrative control posed little threat to the Yaggara, Yuggarapul, Giabal, Turrbal, Nunukul, Quandamooka, Kabi Kabi, Jarowair and Western Wakka Wakka peoples who had lived across the region for tens of thousands of years. There were around 8–10 000 Aboriginal people across southeast Queensland. At the height of the Moreton Bay penal settlement in 1829 there were only 1292 British, mostly convicts. Moreton Bay was hardly a threat to the traditional owners. The only way in and out of Moreton Bay at this time for the white population was by boat.[1]

But it was a bridgehead for the inevitable colonial expansion that was at some point bound to follow. Settlers in search of grazing lands soon tracked out the way through Aboriginal lands to the west of Moreton Bay. In 1827, the botanist Alan Cunningham had travelled across the Peel and Dumaresq Rivers, and waxed lyrical about the grazing potential of the Darling Downs around present-day Toowoomba. He called it 'the finest meadow pasture I have seen in New South Wales'.

But Cunningham had not marked out a feasible route for bringing cattle and sheep overland from the New England region in northern New South Wales.

By the 1830s, squatters in the New England region in current northern inland New South Wales were competing with each other for new runs and pushing each other further north as they followed their

The Battle of Meewah

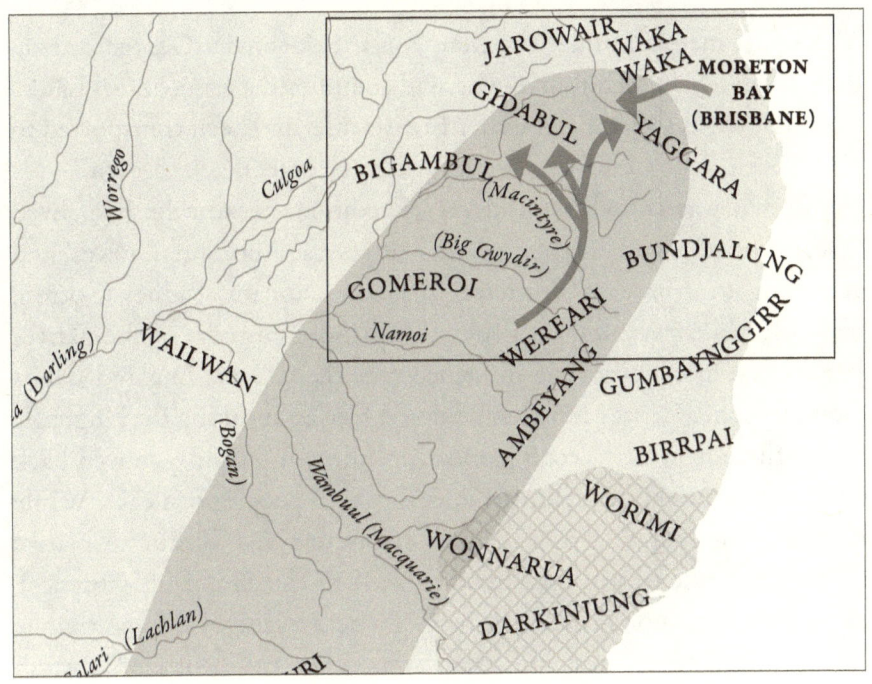

Southeast Queensland, late 1830s and early 1840s
'Settled Districts' are indicated by hatching.
The movement of squatters, stockmen and stock marked with arrows.

noses along the riverways of the giant Murray-Darling river system that came down from what we know today as southern and central Queensland.

By 1839, the penal colony at Moreton Bay had served its purpose as calls to end convict transportation were growing. The settlement was to be dismantled and free settlement opened up to those who could get their sheep and cattle into the downs. The outgoing administrator Commandant Gorman decided to pave the way for the New England squatters and sent out a small party to find an inland route.

Gorman received a report that an escaped convict named Pawson had been 'in the habit of telling other Prisoners that he could easily make his way to the settled districts' in the New England region via the 'Gap in the dividing range of mountains to the South west of this Settlement'. At this, Gorman cobbled together a group of three constables and three

Aboriginal men, all under the charge of the ex-convict George Brown. Brown was a Sri Lankan man who had committed a crime in Sri Lanka (then known as Ceylon and under British rule) and been transported to New South Wales. He was often known as George 'Black' Brown.[2]

Brown was chosen to lead the expedition, because he had 'lived 7 years entirely with the blacks', he had several Aboriginal 'wives' and according to a previous Moreton Bay commandant, Sydney Cotton, had become 'conversant with the meaning and customs of the natives [and] has a most incredible influence over them'. New England Lands Commissioner George Macdonald noted him as 'speaking the language' of the three men who accompanied him. Brown certainly moved back and forth between the colonists and Yaggarah people with ease. While Gorman saw him as a useful 'Bush Constable and Visitor to Native Tribes' (the title he was appointed in 1838 at the end of his sentence), suspicions were soon raised 'that he might act treacherously' and that he had no allegiance to the colonists, but was in fact an ally of the Yaggarah people he had lived with.[3]

On 27 August 1839, the eclectic mix of a Sri Lankan convict, bush constables and Yaggarah men left Moreton Bay and headed south, 'to test the probability of a communication between that place and the stations about New England'. According to a later report in the *Sydney Gazette*, they initially found 'the country interspersed with fine forest land and rich grass tracts' and then a few days later, they reached 'fertile valleys opening to the west-ward'. By early September, they had passed forests, seen 'many hundreds of kangaroos' and 'crossed some beautiful plains of good alluvial soil, and finely watered'. They then steered southward, the country 'getting less wooded, and emus abundant'. While they did cross some 'rugged ranges', these 'were considered perfectly safe for cattle to travel, [with] feed and water in abundance'.[4]

Within two weeks, just as the escaped convict Pawson had said, they 'arrived at one of Mr. P. M'Intyre's stations in the district of New England, by that means proving the perfect practicability of the route'. George Brown did show his true colours, deserting his party and taking his provisions and a firearm with him. The other bush constables made it back and their report was published in newspapers in November 1839. Just a few months later, the overland march of men, sheep and cattle northwards from the New England region to the Darling Downs began.[5]

In March 1840, a young man from a wealthy Scottish family, Patrick Leslie, packed up and left the station he had established on the Mooki River near present-day Tamworth and headed north. After passing the furthermost stations near the Severn River, he began marking the trees for his brother to follow. With him was a well-provisioned column of '4000 breeding ewes, 100 ewe hoggets, 1000 wether hoggets, 100 rams, 500 wether ewes, 2 bullock teams and drays and 22 ticket of leave convicts'. For protection the party had more than enough firepower with thirty firearms among them.[6]

Near present-day Warwick he chose a large slice of Gnarabal and Gidhabal peoples' land on what was to be called the 'Southern Downs'. Leslie had lucked out by moving into the scene of a long-standing conflict between the Gidhabal people and the Gomeroi of the MacIntyre River area. He called the Gidhabal the 'Blucher Tribe' because, like the Prussian general at the 1815 Battle of Waterloo, they came to his aid. Other squatters soon followed and formed stations on and around what was to become known as the Darling Downs. They all followed what they called 'Leslie's Marked Tree Line'.[7]

It was well that Leslie had a good stock of firearms. At one point on his journey, Leslie and his companion Peter Murphy woke up in their camp to find themselves surrounded by Aboriginal people. They apparently stood back to back and fired their guns in the air, and the warriors left. Another squatter at this time, Thomas Archer, later recalled that when travelling with his stock he was 'armed with a couple of guns and a brace of pistols'. When they made camp the stockmen all placed their saddles in front of their sleeping heads 'to fend off any missiles' while keeping a 'weather eye tolerably open'.[8]

While Leslie had protection from his so-called 'Blucher Tribe', others were not so fortunate. Many squatters made their campsites on new runs 'better calculated for resistance' and were quick to set up defensive positions. By the 1830s they were like well-drilled military units. As the self-styled adventurer William Frederick de Brébant Cooper recalled, when his party looking to establish a station near the MacIntyre River heard a 'cooey' in the distance:

> This had the effect of rousing us instantly, and sending a horseman to round up the herd we threw the saddles on the remaining horses, and started for a camping place better calculated for resistance. This we found. The summit of a small hillock afforded a good view round, and in half an hour a sufficient number of logs were cut for defences, from behind which we could fire. After placing the cattle in the hollow immediately between us and the river, and tying the dogs at convenient spots around them we lay down, leaving as usual one 'hand' on the 'look out'.

Another squatter recalled how 'stations were separated about ten miles from each other, for it was the custom to form ... homesteads close together for protection for one another from the attacks of the blacks, which people were very numerous'. Even with the co-operation of the 'Blucher Tribe', Leslie set up his runs in a defensive fashion, noting that 'for the protection of men and stock, [we] made one station on the north bank of the river, and two others opposite – one on either side of Sandy Creek, thus giving mutual protection'.[9]

*

Between 1824 and 1839, the penal settlement at Moreton Bay had not been immune to conflict with Aboriginal people. On Moreton and Stradbroke Islands there was a series of killings and reprisals in 1831 and 1832, as well as a 'genuine stand-up fight ... west of the Big Hill on Stradbroke, where the blacks were badly beaten' according to a later account by George Watkins. Outside Moreton Bay there had been a series of skirmishes on North Stradbroke Island during 1830–31, which have been collectively described as the Battle of Narawai.

In the late 1820s, one of the most bizarre efforts to defend European farmlands in Australian history occurred at Moreton Bay. Settlers had cleared land around the south bank of the Brisbane River and at Kangaroo Point to grow crops to feed the penal settlement. During what has been called the 'cornfield raids', raids that were not only for food but also aimed to 'destroy portions of the second maize crop' threatened the settlement.[10]

Between 1827 and 1828, large groups of warriors from Woolloongabba and South Brisbane carried out such regular raids that the Commandant Captain Logan established a system of guards for the fields. He set up trusted convicts in platforms in trees and tasked them with shooting at anyone taking or destroying crops. Their gunfire would also alert the soldiers if needed.

The convict guards were called 'crow minders'. The South Bank 'crow minders' shot and killed at least one warrior, and probably wounded many. According to an early Moreton Bay colonist, Tom Petrie, writing in 1904, 'one was shot and skinned, then stuffed and put up among the corn to frighten the rest'.[11]

As New South Wales was slowly moving away from penal settlements and reconsidering convict transportation altogether, the Moreton Bay establishment went into decline from 1832. In the 1830s, it might well have seemed to Aboriginal people around what was to become Brisbane that the colonists might just remain in a small and manageable area. They might remain useful suppliers of goods, or even soon leave for good. But by the late 1830s the government was making moves to open the area to free settlers. Governor Gipps sent a new commandant – a military man, Lieutenant Owen Gorman of the 80th Leicestershire Regiment – to oversee the process.[12]

Meanwhile, overlanders from the New England and Liverpool Plains areas arrived in the Darling Downs with the experience of battle-hardened veterans. Squatter Pemberton Hodgson came to the Downs in 1840. In 1846 he recalled that when squatters first arrived on a new run, they ensured that people knew the effect of firearms and actually rode around firing warning shots announcing their presence and showing off their firepower. Some squatters went even further, simply riding into Aboriginal camps and 'clearing' them from their chosen run by shooting indiscriminately.

The history of squatting in Australia has rather deceptively described the process of occupying Aboriginal land as 'taking up runs'. We still describe it that way – 'such and such took up a run'. Across the Downs, a blitzkrieg would be a better description. Here they used all the weapons they had to hand – including their animals. As the long columns of hungry, well-travelled sheep and cattle spewed forth onto the massive plains of the Downs, squatter Christopher Pemberton Hodgson admitted to using guns, horses and herds of cattle to shock and awe the locals into what he hoped was submission, 'dispersing' any villages or campsites. Hodgson recalled that 'the earliest ... inroads of the settlers, were marked with blood, the forests were ruthlessly seized, and the native tenants hunted down like their native dogs'.[13]

By 1841, even the Leslie brothers' tune had changed remarkably from the initial warmth they showed to their 'Blucher Tribe'. George Leslie wrote to his family in England in August that year: 'we never allow them to come about the station or hold any communication with them except it be with a gun or sword'. He also noted in November that year that when sixty sheep were taken, the Leslie brothers and their stockworkers gave the local Aboriginal people 'what they will not forget in a hurry'.[14]

'Attacked by a large body of blacks'

Prior to 1840, there were no sheep on the Darling Downs. Ten years later, there were over 600 000. Some Aboriginal people seem to have moved away from the storm of sheep, cattle and guns and joined neighbouring groups. The Gooneburra fought back. They had tended their lands with tall, thick grasses for millennia and were known as the 'fire people'. Commandant Gorman noted in November 1840 that 'from all the information I was able to obtain, it appeared that the Blacks tried to burn the whole of the grass on the Darling Downs and Peels Plains'.[15]

But the 'fire people' could not outrun the gangs of mounted stockmen. There were some places with terrain that made for a more level playing field, and these places were defended, or became like 'bastions' or natural fortresses. A heavily forested mountain on the edge of the

Darling Downs was one. They followed regular attacks on stock with retreats to the mountain where horses struggled to follow. According to local memory, the stockmen 'learnt to be ever alert for the black rascals and named their mountain Mt Rascal'. The name remains a locality today, just south of present-day Toowoomba.[16]

It was clear that Aboriginal people across the region had begun to push back. The authorities issued 'repeated cautions of the Consequences likely to ensue' of 'taking up runs' in 1841. A 'Return of the number of White people killed' that year noted that it was not 'possible for the Government to protect persons who had voluntarily gone into so remote a District'.[17]

It seems that from mid-1841, Aboriginal people across southeast Queensland had made a combined decision to attack the increasing numbers of settlers, firstly by driving off their sheep. There had been a large 'pullen pullen' or traditional combat in August between the Yaggara people and the 'Yanmonday natives' (Kabi Kabi) at Toorbul near Bribie Island. Several missionaries who witnessed the combat were astonished to see about 2000 people gathered, including women and children. At large gatherings such as these, neighbouring groups must surely have discussed the increasing numbers of sheep, cattle and colonists arriving in the area. Perhaps too they talked about the effects of diseases such as smallpox and syphilis, which the Europeans introduced. In 1836, Quaker missionary James Backhouse noted the 'scourge' venereal disease had become to the 'Moreton Bay blacks'.[18]

Yaggara people had lived in the 'gateway' to the Darling Downs, from Ipswich to Toowoomba, for millennia. Their lands encompassed the striking mountains, the forests, rivers and grasslands above and below the escarpment that overlooked the mouth of the river on the coast. They were custodians of mineral water springs at Helidon and called their mountains 'cloud catchers'. They were known to the colonists as 'Moppy's Tribe' after the important figure Moppy (Mope or Mappi) who was reported to be a towering, strong man and the leader of hundreds of warriors. One squatter said he had never seen 'a more formidable looking fellow … upwards of seven feet high, beautifully proportioned, and the muscles of his upper arms reminded me of the gnarled trunk of an oak'.[19]

Between 1839 and 1841, Moppy had worked with Commandant Gorman, assisting in the capture of two men, Mullan and Ningavil, who were part of a group of warriors wanted for killing the surveyor Granville Stapylton and his assistant William Tuck. Despite almost certainly being innocent of the killings, the frenzy of vengeance over Stapylton's death demanded some Aboriginal deaths and the two men were hanged at Windmill Hill, watched by several hundred Aboriginal people. Other Yaggara had also worked with the colonists as guides and helped with the first track for bullock teams across Cunningham's Gap – a route that settlers first saw as the way from New England to the Downs and then for taking wool over the ranges to ships at the Brisbane River.[20]

Gorman presented him with a breastplate inscribed 'Moppy, King of the Upper Brisbane Tribe'. Moppy might well have expected some assistance from Gorman in dealing with the growing numbers of squatters and their sheep on the Darling Downs. But Gorman could hardly restrain squatters who complained to him that 'the blacks' were trying to 'burn them out' of their runs and were constantly harassing stations.[21]

When the Yaggara returned to the Lockyer Valley after the Bunya Gathering in September 1841, several squatters had 'taken up runs' in their homelands. It seems now, Moppy and his warriors had no choice but to fight them.

'Able and ready to resist 1500 blacks'

The first attacks came, however, from other warriors to the north who would also have attended the Bunya Gathering. In September, a force of 'Mary River blacks' of 300–500 warriors attacked the stockworkers at John and Robert Balfour's run 'Colinton', just west of present-day Kilcoy, scattering over a thousand sheep into the bush. Balfour said he

> took possession on the 19th of August with my drays and stock of the run on the upper Brisbane River [and] continued to remain on friendly terms with the native blacks. But on the 27th one of my

stations was attacked by a large body of blacks from about 3–500 who not only attempted my men's lives but succeeded before their eyes in carrying off a flock of 1100 ewes.

Balfour said they seemed 'fearless of firearms'.[22]

In a sweeping series of attacks the next day, the warriors raided Evan Mackenzie's nearby 'Kilcoy' station, and killed and scattered more sheep. Two days later, they attacked 'Colinton' again. Balfour's men refused to stay and abandoned the run. The Balfour brothers retreated to the neighbouring Kilcoy station and then rode to Moreton Bay to request military protection from Commandant Gorman. On their return to the Mary River, the warriors raided more stations and wounded a shepherd.[23]

The 'Mary River blacks' had struck an important victory. They had terrified shepherds, forced squatters to abandon their runs and scattered, stolen and undoubtedly feasted on numbers of sheep. But the squatters, often in competition with each other for pasture, were united in defence and rallied their men. At Cressbrook in November, they had formed what in effect was a fighting unit. David McConnel with his workers, combined with 'Balfour and 5 or 6 men and Mr Mackenzie with about 12 men' at Cressbrook and as McConnell wrote, they were 'now together, able and ready to resist 1500 blacks'.[24]

Wooninambi's stand – from battle to massacre

These victories either inspired warriors in the Lockyer Valley or were part of a co-ordinated campaign. Shortly after the attacks in the north, in October, around 500 warriors from across the Lockyer and Brisbane River valleys to the south were reported to be on a spree of attacking stations and stock. The hills and passes of the main range at the head of the Lockyer Valley were perfect terrain from which to base raids on stock, but also to conduct attacks on the colonists themselves as they wound their way along roads in long trains of carts, drays, horses, sheep and cattle. The thick bush of the Rosewood Scrub below the range was a perfect refuge or retreating ground. It was also on the route that was a thin umbilical cord to the Darling Downs squatters' economic survival, the coast.[25]

Over a period of four days, a series of raids occurred – all reportedly under Moppy's leadership. Warriors plundered outstations; killed, stole and herded away sheep; and killed one shepherd. James 'Cocky' Rogers was the manager at George Mocatta's station, 'Grantham'. Many of the first stations or pastoral runs in a region were the origin of towns today. 'Grantham' near Gatton on the Warrego Highway west of Brisbane is one. Rogers had never had good relations with his neighbours, the Yaggara. His tiny outstation with just a few stockmen was vastly outnumbered by Yaggara people, who had one of their camps at a waterhole at a place known to the stockmen as 'Humpy Flat'. Rogers's tactic to ensure his security was intimidation – and collecting as many firearms as he could muster.

It seems Rogers got his nickname 'Cocky' because he was swaggeringly confident (at least with firearms in hand). Earlier, he had denuded the Humpy Flat camp of the then-empty Yaggara bark huts for his own use and shot Yaggara hunting dogs. With the attacks escalating, the isolated Rogers (and perhaps feeling a possible target himself) decided, he later said, to 'capture' some of those responsible for the raids in the area. Such a citizen's arrest – as the Attorney General for the Colony of New South Wales Roger Therry later pointed out – was invalid, as it actually required some sort of authority.

But this did not deter 'Cocky' Rogers. He gathered men from nearby Sommerville station. Rogers himself was armed in classic frontier fashion with a double-barrelled long arm, a brace of pistols and a sword. Along with George Sommerville, whose station had also been attacked, they set off after the Yaggara people, almost certainly knowing that they would be back at their Humpy Flat camp some time soon.[26]

Rogers and Sommerville approached at night and found the Yaggara were there. But then they heard a gunshot ring out. This was a concerning turn of events, even for 'Cocky' Rogers. It seems that the Yaggara warriors had firearms. The two station managers returned to Grantham and Sommerville to gather more armed men and went back to the camp the next day. Unknown to Rogers, George 'Black' Brown was at the camp, armed with a pistol that he had fired off that night, it seems to show the Yaggara he could protect them.

What happened next remains unclear, and difficult to unravel in the murky testimony of armed white men. If we are to believe anything of the later (and inconsistent) statements by Rogers and others involved, a massacre might have begun after a bold defence of the Yaggara camp. Rogers and his fourteen armed (seven mounted) men halted on the opposite side of a dry creek bed just 200 metres from the camp. Whether they had hoped to surprise the Yaggara or not, they had been seen. According to Rogers, Moppy was not at the camp and their leader was Wooninambi, who seems to have been one of Moppy's sons. Wooninambi apparently arranged his warriors into a traditional battle line in front of the camp, with the creek bed between the two forces.[27]

According to Rogers' deposition of events to Lieutenant Gorman, when Wooninambi moved forward ahead of his line, Rogers ordered stockmen Peter Pigott and Charlie Campbell to ride forward and capture him. When the riders plunged their horses down the creek bank, Wooninambi deftly speared first Pigott in the groin, and then Campbell. At the spearing of the two men, Rogers and the rest of the horsemen galloped across the creek bed and into the Yaggara camp.

Despite Commandant Gorman's suspicion that George Brown was 'likely to lead the natives astray instead of setting a Good Example to them', he seems to have been the most reliable (recorded) witness of what happened next. After guiding the expedition to New England and then absconding again with supplies, Brown had been dismissed in August 1840 as a bush constable by Commandant Gorman and sent to Sydney. But he was now back with the Yaggara people. He was captured by the armed party, and seems to have escaped being shot by telling them he was a Christian. He later told Magistrate Hodgson that the Yaggara were retreating, 'jabbing their spears at them' as the 'horsemen were riding after them'. Brown said that 'firing was continued about half an hour' but he could 'not say the numbers that were killed'.[28]

On 23 December the Attorney General Roger Therry wrote to Commandant Gorman that he had suspicions about 'the occurrences of the 21st of October'. For Therry it was 'manifest these depositions do not disclose the whole of what took place on that occasion'. (Therry was the junior to Attorney General Plunkett in the trial of the eleven colonists for the Myall Creek Massacre in 1838, so he had some experience in investigating such matters, and perhaps good reason for suspicion.) He wrote to Gorman: 'Mr. Roger's deposition that "He regrets to add that he has reason to believe that several men were severely wounded" falls very short indeed of what might be disclosed as to the effect of the firing that took place'. Therry observed that

> the wounds inflicted on the members of his party are detailed with great minuteness, but a general and vague expression is deemed sufficient to describe and comprehend the extent of the injury done to the party which Mr. Rogers and his armed assistants endeavoured I know not on what authority to capture.

Not only did Therry doubt the validity of the reported casualties but he questioned the authority of their actions.[29]

Therry wanted to know more, demanding that Gorman investigate whether Brown

> had made no disclosure on the subject? How many shots were fired? How many / if any / of the Native Tribe were Killed? Of how many did Mr. Rogers' party consist of and of them how many were armed? Was the Gun found with Brown loaded or did it appear to have been fired off recently? Did any person in Mr. Rogers' party, either see Brown fire a gun or see him at all until he was apprehended in the Camp? How long had Brown been with the Native Tribe? When and where had Brown been last seen before he was apprehended at the Native Camp?'

Whether this reprimand from Sydney sparked him or if it was the fact Gorman knew why Rogers was known as 'Cocky' Rogers and had indeed massacred people, Gorman later viciously pummelled a drunken Rogers, who was abusing him on his verandah. As historian Raymond Evans eloquently puts it:

even after Gorman had knocked Rogers down he fell upon him, 'held him by the throat and with the whole weight of his body, continued to strike him on the chest'. Behind the vehemence of this encounter, as Gorman himself attested, lay the bitterness arising from Rogers' farcical trial of the previous month, 'when … it was understood that he had with an armed party assailed and shot a number of Aboriginal natives near the station of George Mocata, his employer'. It does not require too extensive a stretch of imagination to interpret this little fracas between the last penal commandant and an aggressive representative of the new land-takers as a meaningful symbol of the 'changing of the guard' in the Moreton Bay region, now more expansively referred to as Northern New South Wales.[30]

The isolated convict shepherds on the frontier have often been held to account for much of the conflict and violence. But as Evans notes, 'gentleman squatters could be at least as forceful in defence of their extensive interests as desperate convicts or combative soldiers'. In November, the warrior Wooninambi who had escaped the Grantham aftermath was 'killed while resisting arrest' by Richard Somerville. Magistrate Hodgson later ruled the killing as self-defence by Somerville.

Around the same time, the fearsome warrior Moppy was killed, it seems murdered, by the ever 'Cocky' Rogers. Rogers and Sommerville were certainly 'shoot first and ask questions later' frontiersmen. Yet as historians Ray Kerkhove and Frank Uhr note, the two Yaggara leaders' deaths 'ushered in a new leader, Multuggerah, who was to prove even more troublesome to squatters and government alike over the next four years'.[31]

CHAPTER SIX

'These Tribes vowed vengeance'

'About fifty or sixty Aboriginal people had been poisoned'

Attacks escalated across the region of present-day south-east Queensland in early 1842. When a large group of 'Mary River blacks' killed two shepherds to the north of Kilcoy, all the stockmen at the outstation at Kilcoy Creek were certainly spooked. They fled to the head station of Evan and Colin Mackenzie, 'Kilcoy', likely named in celebration of their father's title 'Baronet of Kilcoy' in the County of Ross in Scotland. It seems that the terrified stockworkers then resorted to a horrific action, uninstructed by the Mackenzies, who were away at the time. When they fled their station, they had left behind a deadly concoction of food laced with arsenic.[1]

On a trip to the Wide Bay district in June 1842, Aboriginal guides told a German missionary, the Reverend Karl Wilhelm Edward Schmidt, that 'about fifty or sixty Aboriginal people had been poisoned at one of the squatters stations'. Other missionaries reported similar stories and it was clear that a terrible massacre had occurred at Mackenzie's Kilcoy station.[2]

In May 1842, Dr Stephen Simpson had been appointed to three roles in the newly created 'Moreton Bay District' – Magistrate, Commissioner of Crown Lands, and Protector of Aborigines. Simpson was the senior government official in the district until the arrival of John Clements Wickham in January 1843. His position as Protector required him to 'communicate' with Aboriginal people as well as to 'repress the predatory attacks of the natives'. He was also to 'keep order among all the classes'. Simpson's role was far greater than sorting out who could take what land and where – he was to police the entire expanding frontier around Moreton Bay, an area that the missionary Handt noted

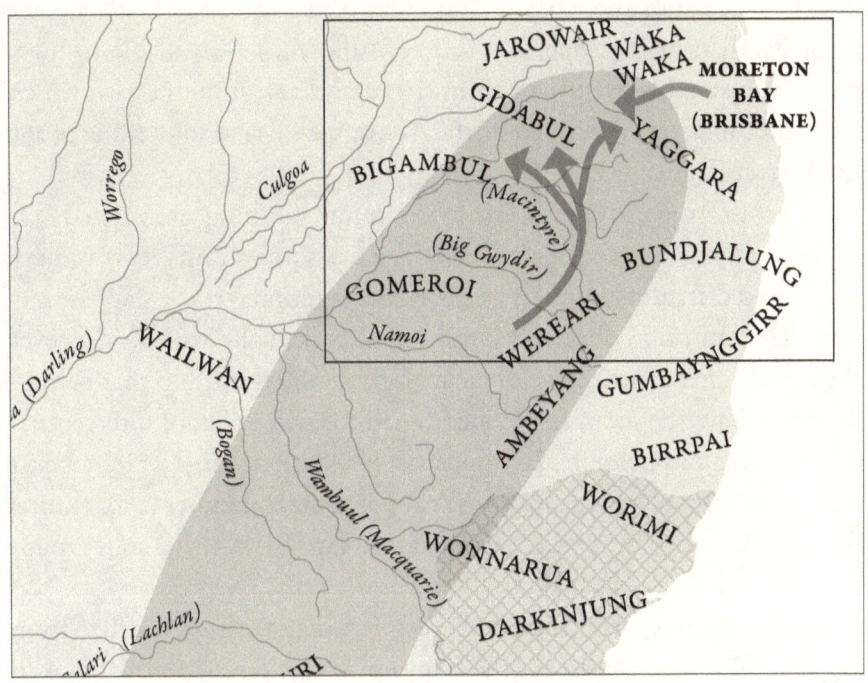

Southeast Queensland, late 1830s and early 1840s

in 1842 within 'fifty miles circuit [radius]' around Moreton Bay had an Aboriginal population of 'from about One Thousand to One Thousand and Five Hundred'.³

Simpson was eminently suitable for such a role. He began his career as a young man in the Napoleonic Wars. In 1813 Simpson enlisted in the 6th Warwickshire Regiment of Foot as an ensign and by 1814 he was promoted to cornet in the 1st (or Royal) Regiment of Dragoons, then he was promoted to lieutenant in the 14th (or Duchess of York's Own) Regiment of Light Dragoons. Serving in the British Dragoons (cavalry) certainly meant he knew very well how to ride and shoot.⁴

After his military career Simpson became a surgeon and authored the 1836 book *A Practical View of Homeopathy*. Simpson was well placed to comment on the deaths at Kilcoy. He wrote to the Colonial Secretary that 'a very extraordinary statement' was circulating that was 'first brought here by the Limestone Blacks & since repeated on all hands'. The 'Dallambarah and Coccombraral tribes' reported it to him, but 'the Giggabarah tribe, the one said to have suffered, I was unable to meet with'. Simpson believed that 'from the remarkable minutia with which the symptoms were described by the Aborigines ... that something of the kind has really occurred'.[5]

Despite some investigation by Simpson, nothing eventuated. Or nothing from the colonists, at least. The mass poisoning seems to have galvanised different groups of warriors into a counterattack – apparently 'the neighbouring tribes had determined to kill the whites whenever they might meet with any of them'. Simpson noted in 1843 that behind Moreton Bay, 'the mountain tribes ... had formed a plan of intercepting all (our) communication'. In Simpson's estimation, these were not just one 'tribe' but several groups consisting of 'a great number ... extending from Wide Bay to beyond Cunningham's Gap'. By 1843, various groups had certainly formed a major alliance.[6]

These groups were in fact all very familiar with each other from the great Bunya Gatherings. The bunya pine tree forests in the Blackall Ranges were a valuable resource. The majestic trees produce huge cones of around sixty edible seeds in each cone. The seeds taste similar to chestnuts and could be roasted, boiled or ground into a flour to make a sweet bread.[7]

Lands Commissioner Simpson described the gatherings in 1842:

> The great Bunya Scrub, called Boorum by the Natives, from an open space in the middle of it, where they hold their great meetings, extends in a direction from S.E. to N.W., perhaps for 50 miles in length. Here the Bunya are very plentiful & in the month of January the Blacks assemble for hundreds of miles round to partake of the fruit & often dispute the possession of particular spots with great acrimony.[8]

While some groups collected bunya seeds every year, the bunya cycle meant that every three or four years there was a rich crop. Messengers were sent out sometimes several months before the event with message sticks. It was possible to signal by smoke from peaks near the Tweed River to Gowrie Mountain near Dalby and the Bunya Mountains. As Uncle Wayne Fossey notes, communications were sent to the Kabi Kabi on the coast and right up to present-day Bundaberg and even further north to Rockhampton. To the south, Bundjalung, Yaegl and Gumbaynggirr people came from the north coast of present-day New South Wales, and the Gomeroi travelled from the south-west.[9]

Many people today recall the long routes south to the Bunya Gatherings. As Yiman man Marshall Bell notes, 'I was told the Kamilaroi [Gomeroi] people came up to the Bunyas up past Kogan' (west of Dalby, north of Bogabilla). Gomeroi man Bill Priestley describes how

> a Songline comes up this way (the western Darling Downs). Our family talked of the track up here – the songline – it had to do with bora (ceremony). Lots of people came. We used to often travel through one another's country ... We went up (to the Bunyas) to talk to one another, and obtain wives.

Uncle Wayne Fossey describes a 'dreaming path' that at the escarpment at Toowoomba was a 'central joining point'. Gomeroi man Boe Spearim notes that 'this mob would meet up with that mob and they would have had small ceremony each on the way up'. The northern Gomeroi would have come to the Bunya through present-day St George, and 'caught up with Waka Waka and Gabi Gabi' and 'they came up on songlines'. Importantly, Boe notes that traditional enmities were often put aside: 'the Gomeroi and Bunjalung would go to war all the time, then [come together and] do ceremony'.[10]

From the Burnett River valley in central Queensland and as far as present-day Dubbo and Bourke in central and western New South Wales, people flocked to the Great Bunya Gatherings. Even the colonial authorities realised their importance. A government order was issued in April 1842 that sought to keep it from the hands of squatters and timber getters:

> It having been represented to the Governor that a district exists to the northward of Moreton bay, in which a fruit-bearing tree abounds, called Bunya, or Banya Bunya, and that the Aborigines from considerable distances resort at certain times of the year to this district for the purpose of eating the fruit of the said tree: His Excellency is pleased to direct that no license be granted for the occupation of any lands within the said district in which the Bunya or Banya Bunya tree is found ... His Excellency has also directed that no licenses to cut timber be granted within the said districts.

Much of the present-day Sunshine Coast was included in the reserve, which stretched from Eumundi (North Maroochy River) south to Beerwah and west to the Bunya Mountains.[11]

Gatherings such as this were times of great social interaction, of family reunion, trade, negotiation and ceremony. People shared dances and songs, and settled disputes. They were also known as a time of collective decision making among various groups that has been seen as a kind of regional system of governance. As Uncle Wayne Fossey notes, 'councils of Elders made decisions in consensus' and only then 'head warriors worked in line with these decisions'. Such gatherings were a time of telling news about far-off events – often in the form of a kind of re-enacted performance of what had occurred.[12]

White men who had been living with Aboriginal people for several years provided Commissioner Simpson with first-hand accounts of what had happened at Kilcoy. In May 1842, an expedition led by the Scottish builder, architect and part-time explorer Andrew Petrie came across two escaped convicts near present-day Hervey Bay. One, James Davis, informed the party that they were 'in great danger' because, according to Petrie, of a 'great gathering of tribes and fighting men'.

Davis, who had been taken into Aboriginal society and given the name 'Duramboi', explained the reason for their anger: 'all the scenes of the deaths of some fifty or sixty blacks', including 'the increasing agonies; the crawling to water; the insatiable burning thirst; then – death' were enacted out by people telling the story of their countrymen's deaths. As Uncle Wayne Fossey notes, even the 'crushed bark of the handwashing tree was used to show the frothing at the mouth as part of the performance of the Kilcoy poisonings'.[13]

In May, Commissioner Simpson reported that there had been 'a great meeting of the Native Tribes, 13 or 14 in number, called a "Toor" (Ring) by the blacks, from the circumstance of a great circular ditch being dug out by the Women for that ceremony'. He continued:

> To this meeting a party of blacks from the S. W. the district of the Bunya called the (Inwarrahs) and the (Tombaraha) made mention of a great number of blacks, at least 30 in number, belonging to different Tribes but principally the (Wooganbarahs) having died in consequence of food given to them by white men, at a Station, where there were Sheep, horses & a tent : they described the symptoms, swelling of the head, foaming at the mouth, violent retching & thirst – trembling of the members & sudden prostration. These Tribes vowed vengeance & said they had had some already but would have more. The Blacks at the Toor were much infuriated at this report ...[14]

A traditional bunya gathering had formed into a military alliance. And it seems to have galvanised groups far and wide. In effect, war had been declared upon the white man. The Kilcoy Massacre, as Raymond Evans notes, 'was an enormity alongside which virtually all that had happened between Aborigines and penal personnel over the past eighteen years seemed to pale'. It brutally ushered into southern Queensland what was for many years after recalled as 'The Black Rising'.[15]

'Plunder does not appear to be so much their object as the destruction of life'

From mid-1842, the confederacy or alliance of 'tribes' from across southern Queensland went on the offensive. A factor in the Yaggara warriors' prominence was undoubtedly the new leadership role taken up by the man the squatter at 'Cressbrook', Frederic McConnell, called a 'handsome young fellow', Multuggerah. According to McConnell, Multuggerah had 'threatened to kill six white men in revenge' for the death of his father Moppy. Other threats had been made to 'kill whites whenever they meet them'.[16]

By July, Commissioner Simpson was certain the increasing attacks on the colonists were more than raids for food or revenge. He wrote to the Colonial Secretary Edward Deas Thomson that 'the Stations to the North of the Brisbane [River] are suffering considerably from the hostile proceedings of the Aborigines'. Simpson was clear they were 'carrying out their vengeance in a very insidious manner by attacking any defenceless individual that may fall in their way'. In a critical observation, Simpson wrote that 'in fact plunder does not appear to be so much their object as the destruction of life, which they effect by proceeding in small bodies without giving the least warning of their approach'.[17]

In the upper Brisbane River area in June and July, warriors sent the colonists a strong message. Hutkeeper James Robertson was killed at Colinton and a few days later at Mount Brisbane a shepherd, Barney Goldriche, was also killed. Robertson's body was 'mangled' and thrown into a waterhole. Frederic McConnell's response to the deaths of the two shepherds was to gather up a party of armed men, ride out and shoot the 'set of treacherous, cruel savages'. In what he described as a 'battle', he killed the warrior known as 'Commandant', a man he described as 'a fellow 6 ft 3ins high and strong in proportion' and wounded two other men. McConnell had sent an unambiguous reply to the warriors' killings and mutilations.[18]

*

When an ex-convict, Tom Dowse, arrived at Moreton Bay in 1842 to become a news correspondent he was shocked that it was unsafe for whites to venture any distance from the township 'unless in company and well armed', as the surrounding bushlands swarmed with what he called 'wild Aboriginal savages'. In August 1842, squatter McConnell wrote that 'every man is obliged to be armed and never thinks himself perfectly safe'. In fact, he was quite clear that 'actually we are in a state of silent warfare in all new districts'.[19]

Commissioner Simpson had a plan 'to remedy this state of insecurity'. He informed the Colonial Secretary that 'the squatters themselves are ready to make any sacrifice & should it meet with his Excellency's approbation, would be willing to furnish a man mounted and armed at every Station to accompany the Commissioner, when called upon in cases of emergency'. Simpson was keen to enlist a sanctioned militia force. He hoped that with 'the assistance of the Police' these 'mounted and armed' men 'might suffice to keep them [warriors] in check'.[20]

In August warriors killed another two shepherds and colonists found the bodies of two more who had been killed earlier. Simpson prepared for action in September, purchasing 'four strong Horses for the Police' from the Darling Downs squatter Patrick Leslie, of 'Leslie's Marked Tree Line' fame. Soon after, he applied to 'form my Border Police Station at Woogaroo' near present-day Wacol, strategically located between Moreton Bay and the upper Brisbane River Valley. Simpson was so keen for such a force he let the nascent police unit camp on his own property, making this in effect the first unofficial barracks of what would later become the feared Queensland Native Mounted Police.

Simpson now had his own small armed force – the standing orders for the border police were that 'every individual employed in the Border Police is expected to pay implicit obedience to the orders of the Commissioner, in the same way as troopers of the Mounted Police or soldiers in any Regiment of the Line'.[21]

In November the *Sydney Herald* rather matter-of-factly noted in its report on Moreton Bay that 'the blacks still continue troublesome about the Darling Downs, making it very un-safe travelling, unless in company and well armed'. In March, four shepherds were killed in an attack. Assistant Commissioner Rolleston later found they had 'forcibly abused a Black woman'.[22]

The *Sydney Morning Herald* gave further details of the attack. The shepherds apparently:

> ... fired to intimidate them, when the whole body rushed on them: four out of the five at the hut were immediately knocked down, and their sculls beat to pieces with waddies; the fifth man made his escape to another hut, above five miles off, where two other men resided; the three were again surrounded in the building by two to three hundred blacks, and there kept bailed up for eight days, until they were released by a party dispatched from the head station ...

The sheep under these men's charge were 'slaughtered by scores' and the *Herald* correspondent noted that 'it will be some time before any man can be found courageous enough to venture out with them again'. Warriors were massing across the region, 'as they are collecting in the vicinity of Wide Bay from all parts of the northern coast' and 'from six to seven hundred blacks were assembled on Frazier's Island'.[23]

In August 1843, a shepherd, Richard White, was found with '30 to 40 spear wounds in different parts of the body and had been horribly mutilated by tomahawks or waddies'. In early September, 'the blacks attacked a station of Mr. McConnell, killed a man, and drove off a flock of sheep, but being hotly pursued by an armed force, they were compelled to abandon their prize after killing sixteen fat wethers ...'[24]

'Open rebellion'

In mid-August, Sydney's *Colonial Observer* newspaper correspondent in Moreton Bay reported that:

> The blacks, I am sorry to say, still continue their murdering and plundering practices. Since my last, a shepherd in the service of Sibley and King, on the Darling Downs, has been murdered, and a flock of 1300 sheep driven away, 500 of which have only as yet been recovered. The whole of the settlers on the Downs are in a state of great excitement, compelled to keep their servants constantly armed and on the alert for fear of an attack.[25]

Attacks occurred on both side of the main range. In an offensive on two fronts, in early September, the eastern areas of the Lockyer Valley – across the stations that are today the Brisbane suburbs of Tenthill, Grantham and Helidon – attacks on sheep and shepherds were occurring almost daily. To the west, on the Downs, an Eton Vale stockman, John Hills, was caught alone with his cattle, hit with a waddy and speared in the back. Hills was the station overseer – one of what Aboriginal people called the 'Commandants'. His gravestone, marked 'Killed by the blacks', can be seen today at the old Toowoomba Cemetery.[26]

One of Assistant Lands Commissioner Rolleston's perhaps unexpected duties was to prepare returns on 'the number of White men killed and wounded by the Aborigines in the District of Moreton Bay' as well as the Darling Downs District. By October 1843, seven white men and a female child had been killed and two men wounded across Moreton Bay (and six men had been killed in 1841–1842). Another five men had been killed in the Darling Downs up to September (five had been killed in the previous year). Rolleston noted in the margins of his return that 'upon the report of these Outrages which took place in the vicinity of the Dividing Range, the Commissioner promptly hastened to the spot' and found 'that the Blacks had assumed a formidable attitude'.[27]

In fact, warriors led by Multuggerah had declared war. In August, according to John 'Tinker' Campbell, he received a message from Multuggerah, who he knew well and who had exchanged names with him. This was a widespread Aboriginal practice showing respect and a kind of reciprocal alliance. Multuggerah was now also known as 'Campbell'. As John Campbell later recalled he received:

> ... a messenger sent by Multuggerah to tell me that it was to be war, now in earnest – that their intention was to spear all the commandants [squatters], then fence up the roads and stop the drays ... [and] starve the Jackaroos.[28]

Multuggerah's plan to 'starve the Jackaroos' might have been in response to how the pastoralists and their sheep and cattle were starving out his people. It was also a very well-considered military strategy.

Uprising

*

On 27 September, 'The Squatter's Friend' wrote to the *Sydney Morning Herald* from Moreton Bay about 'the very unpleasant occurrences that have taken place between the aborigines and the squatters of this district'. The writer was clear that 'the blacks are in open rebellion' and that they were 'determined, from their well-devised proceedings, to drive the settlers from that district'. Their 'well-devised proceedings' included 'having folds [pens or yards] in the scrubs prepared for the reception of the captured flocks'.[29]

The attacks were indeed 'well-devised'. Communication between the Downs and the Moreton Bay area had effectively been cut off. As the Moreton Bay news correspondent Thomas Dowse was to note in early October: 'the last few weeks have shown us, that a regular systematic plan of plundering operations has been organized amongst them'. Dowse was so surprised by the 'talented' execution of the plan that he could only suspect that 'some pale faces were at work amongst them', but there were no reports of Europeans assisting these attacks.[30]

Dowse noted that at 'Mr. McDougall's sheep station, only a few miles from Limestone ... they assembled in the neighbourhood to the amount of some scores, and then went in a body to the head station, and ordered the occupants of the huts to be off, as it was their ground'. Dowse was reporting what Aboriginal people had said to the men at McDougall's station – that this was their 'ground', their Country and they would do as they pleased.

The warriors 'then commenced plundering the huts, carrying off about 15 cwt. of flour, and stores and valuables of every description, and what they could not take away they destroyed'. Clearly, this was all-out war against the colonisers. Dowse was alarmed that 'the various tribes of aboriginals throughout the district are assembling at all quarters for a great pullen pullen (fight) ... but whether the white population are the party to be attacked, a short time will show'.[31]

Commissioner Simpson was also concerned that the attacks would escalate. In a report to the Colonial Secretary he outlined a list of attacks that had occurred almost daily in the first two weeks of September:

On the 1st September they attacked Mr. Jones' Station on Laidley Cr. & took away about 150 sheep & injured many more –

On the 5th they again attacked the same Station but were driven off with the loss of one Sheep only –

On the 6th they came in a large body to the Shepherd at the same Station & would have murdered him but for the timely aid of a party of Horsemen –

On the 7th they attacked a shepherd of Mr. Brown and took part of his flock – the man however escaped from the barking of his dog at one of the Aborigines who were in the act of Spearing him –

On the 8th they killed a horse, a Cow & two bullocks belonging to Mr. Uhr at Tenthill
On the 9th they attacked Mr. Hicks & Mr. Campbell on the high Road to Darling Downs & speared the former Gentleman's horse –

On the 10th they killed a Shepherd in the employ of Mr. Pearce of Hellidon & another had a narrow escape for his life –

On the 11th they attacked another flock at Hellidon, but were driven off.[32]

This constant series of raids and attacks by Multuggerah and his warriors not only targeted sheep and cattle, but stockmen, their horses, their huts and supplies. It was a furious assault clearly designed to drive the squatters and stockmen out. It also showed just how powerful a large force of warriors could really be, moving swiftly across various locations and striking targets of their choosing.

The Battle of Meewah (One Tree Hill)

The next conflict was to be one of the greatest moments of any Aboriginal resistance campaign in Australian history. The squatters were desperate. They decided to force the passage between the Darling Downs and the coast by pushing a convoy of supplies across the range. In his message to Campbell, Multuggerah had declared he would 'cut the roads'. This would show him.

According to Thomas Dowse, 'three drays loaded with shearing supplies for the stations of Messrs. Hodgson, Dennison, and Marsh' were sent to the Downs, protected by 'fourteen to seventeen' armed men. Such convoys were the lifeblood of the isolated squatters and stockmen on the Downs. They carried supplies in, and then returned laden with wool for Moreton Bay and overseas markets. The convoy and its escort were to proceed along the track that wound its way up the edge of the escarpment before the Downs, nowadays easily bypassed along the Toowoomba Connection Road.[33]

In 1843 the track to the Downs ran alongside Monkey Water Holes Creek, passing between two peaks, Davidson and Table Top, known to Jaggara and other people as Meewah or 'Place of Eyes'. Today, the roads over the escarpment pass scenic lookouts with sweeping views of the Lockyer and Brisbane River valleys. Any convoy of drays with probably eighteen bullocks pulling each dray, along with several bullock drivers and a group of armed men – all only managing around 8 miles (around 13 kilometres) travel per day – would have been very easy to spot from any one of these peaks. The view from the Tobruk lookout east of Toowoomba, named after the famous Second World War siege, is dominated by a very different battlefield.[34]

On 12 September, the convoy entered the Helidon scrub, just west of present-day Helidon Spa. James Campbell recalled what happened next:

> Three bullock teams belonging to Messrs. Francis and David Forbes, of Clifton, were passing up [the range] loaded with shearing supplies. They were accompanied by a number of men ... eighteen

altogether, and all said to be armed. Upon arriving at the scrub they found several logs fallen across the road, those the bullock-drivers drove over. Before, however, getting through the scrub they found saplings triced up to the trees on each side of the road, and thus the road was completely fenced. Of course, the bullock-drivers had to stop ... the road was so extremely narrow that there was no turning out.

Lands Commissioner Simpson later wrote:

> I found they had actually attempted to barricade the Road by cutting down trees & throwing them across the Road at a point where it traverses a Scrub & is not above 8 feet wide – here they lie in wait & a shower of spears is the first indication of their presence.

The supply convoy had arrived into a perfect ambush. 'Palisades' or 'fences' were certainly not unknown to Aboriginal people across southeast Queensland. They were used to corral kangaroos (and then cattle and sheep) into pens and traps. In fact, they were part of Aboriginal architecture. 'Palisaded rings' were recorded from Maryborough to the Darling Downs. They were used for ritual fights associated with initiation ceremonies. Matthew Flinders in 1799 and John Oxley in 1823 both reported buildings on Bribie Island made from slender wattles and vines, intricately interwoven with 'strong, wiry grass' and roofed over with ti-tree bark, 'compactly laid in, as to keep out wind and rain'. They were 'solid, semi-permanent constructions sometimes individually extending upwards of eighty feet [in length] and covering a considerable space of ground'. The naturalist Frederick Strange reported one building that was

> in the form of a passage, with two apartments at the end. The arches were beautifully turned, and executed with a degree of skill which would not have disgraced an [sic] European architect. In one of these apartments the chief of the family resides; in the other the married people, and the young men claim the passage as their proper dormitory. These habitations ... serve their purpose admirably.[35]

The road-block and fencing were a complete success. The moment the convoy halted to clear the logs, 'they were attacked by upwards of 100 black fellows'. The warriors were in the cover of dense bush, making musket targets near impossible. It was a frightful situation. According to Campbell, 'the moment the drays stopped the blacks gave a tremendous shout and the croppies [stockmen] all ran away'. The warriors then 'robbed the drays of everything they could carry away – flour, sugar, sheep-shears (the latter they broke, and armed the point of their spears with them). They also broke open boxes and took several watches ... in fact, whatever suited them best'. The stockmen and drivers were 'compelled to beat a retreat, leaving the drays and their contents to their fate'. Simpson noted that 'on the 12th they stopped three Bullock-Drays on the Road to the Downs & carried off a large amount of property – having driven off fourteen men sent to protect them & speared one of the bullocks'.[36]

Multuggerah and his warriors had not only captured supplies and effectively blocked the road to the Downs, they also sent a powerful message and spread fear from the Darling Downs to Moreton Bay. Campbell was clear that the message he had received earlier about Multuggerah going to war had proven correct: 'Thus, within three months of young Moppy [Multuggerah] sending me the message, the blacks had carried out their programme'.[37]

Campbell recalled how the fleeing stockmen headed several miles back to where 'a party of squatters [were] at camp' and 'they were quickly in the saddle, and arrived at the drays within two hours after the attack; but the birds had flown'. Thomas Dowse reported that 'upon obtaining a reinforcement, and returning to the spot, the whole of the lading of the teams were found scattered about, and a quantity of flour, tea, sugar, tobacco, wine, sheep shears, wool-bags, &c. taken away into the scrub'.

The squatters who had gathered at the Half Way House inn headed the 'reinforcement', and gathered 'all the hands they could muster'. It is unclear exactly how many, but somewhere between twenty and fifty armed men arrived at the ambush site.[38]

According to Campbell, although they had a black tracker with them, they 'did not follow the [warriors'] tracks up a spur, but attempted to scale the mountain on the side next to road'. Campbell described how:

> The blacks took up a position above them, and rolling down stones upon them, fairly drove them back. Several of them were hurt more or less severely, some guns broken, etc., so they returned and camped at the drays which had been robbed, and this was what was known as the battle of the One-tree Hill.[39]

According to Commissioner Simpson, the 'party of Squatters having proceeded to the rescue of the drays the Aborigines took up a strong position on a hill in the vicinity & actually repulsed them, two of the party being wounded by pieces of Rock rolled down on them'.[40]

We can only imagine the victory shouts echoing around the valleys from the top of Meewah. It might also have been made all the more poignant for the Yaggarah warriors as Meewah was a ceremonial site, with a pathway and stone arrangement on the flat 'table top'. Campbell and Simpson's brief, perhaps embarrassed, reports are all the historical records of one of the most skilled and energetic of all the Aboriginal victories in the Australian Wars.

While Meewah (Mount Table Top) is still to this day strewn with boulders, there might well also have been a stockpile of rocks prepared in a defensive position. There are many examples of such tactics; in 1830, Captain Patrick Logan on an expedition between Esk and Wivenhoe reported 'upwards of 200 blacks ... began throwing and rolling down large stones on the party'. Thomas Mitchell reported in 1831 a group at Wollombi who 'took up a strong position and rolled down rocks'. At the Razorback Range in north Queensland, police were confronted by warriors who 'showed their hostility by rolling large stones down'. From Battle Mountain near Cloncurry in Queensland to the Razorback Range in southern Sydney, prepared positions of stockpiled rocks – as well as spears – on the top of a hillside were reported. It was a widespread and highly successful tactic.[41]

The 'party of Squatters' retreated to the Half Way House. Such a strong group of armed men must have been supremely confident even trudging up a hill in an exposed position – the combined firepower of over twenty muskets might have seemed a strong force against ten times that number of warriors with traditional weapons. Yet they had been beaten.

Commissioner Simpson soon learned that this was part of a larger plan:

> By an intelligent Aborigine, named Toby, recently attached to my Party I am informed that the Range Blacks have a plan of intercepting all communication by the Road to Darling Downs.

There were perhaps one hundred armed squatters and stockworkers in the surrounding districts who the squatters could potentially have mustered at this point. Multuggerah could call upon over 1000 warriors across the region. At this stage the scales were certainly evenly balanced, and with a supply and terrain advantage, Multuggerah was on the front foot and his plans to conduct a long campaign were in place.[42]

PART TWO
The Counteroffensive

It is notorious that in many distant stations some of the settlers destroy the natives, with as little compunction as the native dogs; many cold blooded murders of this description take place unrecorded by any human being ...

— *Australian*, 12 July 1836

The act of massacre is not so much an expression of power by a strong regime or a strong group of people but an expression of a position of weakness.

— Lyndall Ryan, 2010[1]

CHAPTER SEVEN
'This deed of blood'

'I am speared, I am speared!'

On 26 January 1838, Foundation Day in the Colony of New South Wales (called Australia Day after 1935), Major Nunn's expedition to stop 1000 warriors from invading the settled districts had itself been stopped in its tracks. As we have seen, after several weeks criss-crossing Big River country, Nunn's party in search of warriors who had been terrorising the squatting runs across the region had eventually been guided to Snodgrass Lagoon just south of present-day Moree. Here they found a large group of warriors. As soon as the mounted police moved on them, the warriors attacked.

The battle at Waterloo Creek was a confusing engagement, according to the mounted police who were much later forced to testify in court about what had occurred. By the time they recounted what happened, white men had been tried and hanged for the murders at Myall Creek. The police had to be careful about what they said.

Lieutenant Cobban believed he was about to capture people just by rounding them up with his sword. But there was little chance of that happening. Confronted by a party of 'soldiers', as the police were called, along with armed stockmen riding into their camp, warriors did as warriors would – they fought back.

Corporal Hannan was certain that 'no shot was fired until I was speared'. The light scrub made it difficult for the mounted police, but not impossible. Sergeant Lee heard Hannan cry out and try to break the spear shaft from his leg. He galloped toward Hannan and shot the man who had speared him, according to Hannan, 'just as he was in the act of throwing a second spear at myself' only 'nine yards' (about 8 metres) away.

The Counteroffensive

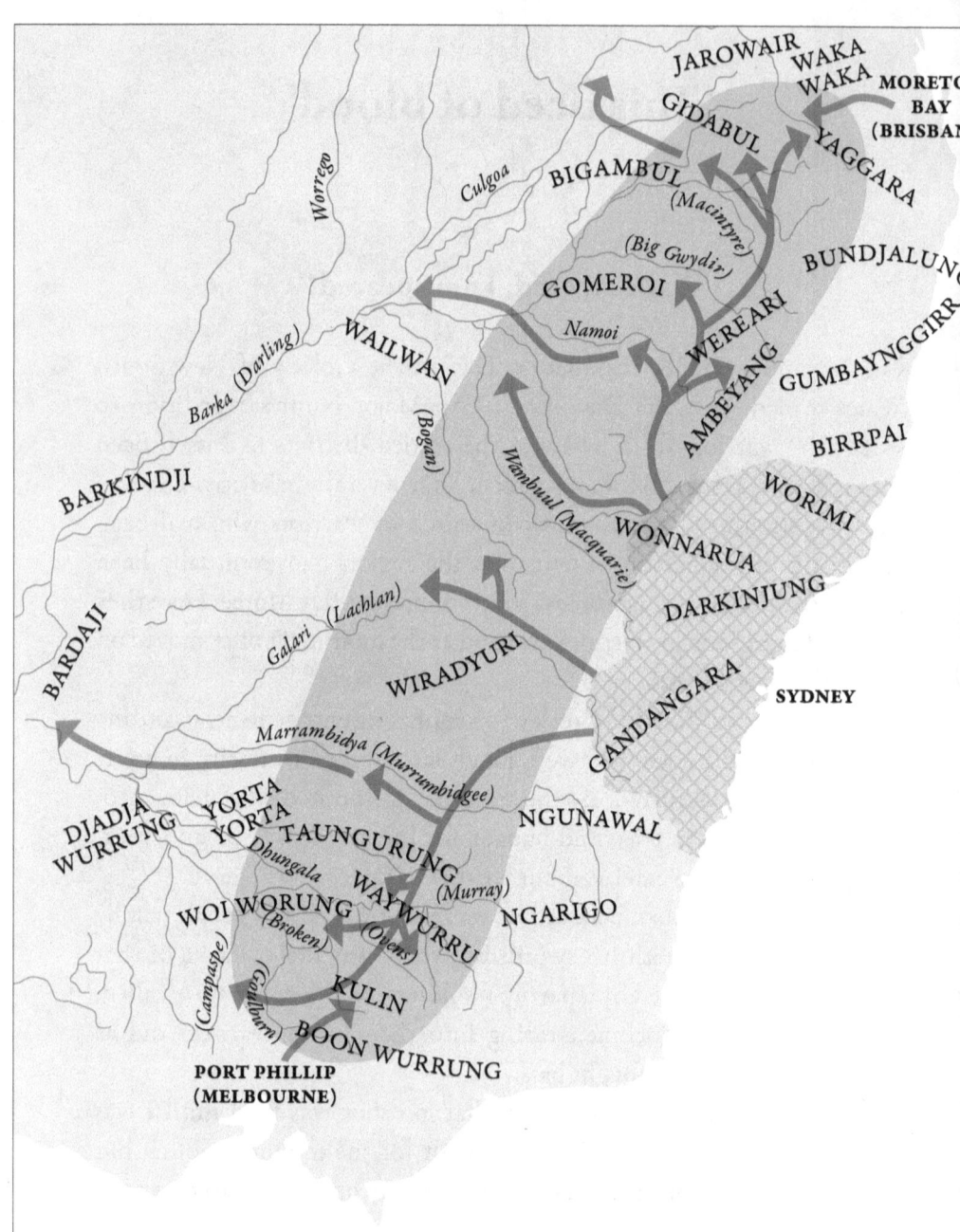

The Counteroffensive, early 1840s
'Settled Districts' are indicated by hatching.
The movement of squatters, stockmen and stock marked with arrows.

According to Lee and Hannan, a general firing was 'taken up by the rest of the party and continued for some time', until the warriors broke off through the bush. Nunn saw 'Corporal Hannan returning from the front' (Nunn believed it to be a battle) wounded, and crying out 'I am speared, I am speared!'

Nunn said he then heard several shots in rapid succession. The tactics were on a small scale, but the military training of the police – soldiers one and all – kicked in. Nunn later admitted he was 'perfectly unable' to reign in the troopers. Nunn said that once the warriors had speared one of the police, they showed 'evident intentions of spearing many more'. When warriors put up such a defence against cavalry it could only mean one response: Nunn's typically understated British military euphemism for it was that he had to resort to 'sharp measures'. He ordered whoever could hear him to open fire.[1]

Nunn said he regretted that some people 'fell in consequence' of the firing at Snodgrass Lagoon. He was 'positive' that he only saw four bodies. But the day was not over. The police regrouped, and extracted the spear in Hannan's leg with 'the assistance of a black man'. They found some Gomeroi women hiding in the bush and learnt that this was only a 'small detachment' of the main tribe. The police were told the rest of the 'formidable' tribe were but a 'short distance' along the 'same Creek'. With their dander up and their horses rested, and with some women who, for reasons we may never know, promised to guide them to the rest of their 'tribe', Nunn and his team moved out.

Cobban set off with a detachment on one side of the creek and said he would fire a warning shot if they made contact with the enemy. They had only travelled a short distance when a shot rang out; Cobban had seen two men and he apparently, almost farcically in the circumstances, called on them to halt. But they plunged down the steep creek bank where the horses could not follow. The soldiers fired at them. Cobban believed they missed the mark. He ordered his detachment onwards.

Soon after, in what might have been the critical moment of the entire engagement, Sergeant Dean came across the main camp. He found 'three or four hundred spears and other weapons'. Fortunately for Dean, he found them just before the warriors ran in to 'seize' their arms. Dean said he then 'opened fire on them and they retreated'.

The horse was a critical element in conflict across the frontier. Horses meant police and armed parties could catch up with fleet-footed warriors. The horse provided a height and power advantage. Importantly, with a horse, a soldier or stockman could carry extra ammunition in their saddle bags. Warriors and women carried extra weapons but stockpiled them in their camps until required.

As Richard Flanagan described in 1853:

> When a tribe of aborigines encamp in any locality, an armoury is formed, in which the whole of the weapons belonging to the warriors are deposited. The site chosen is generally the shade of some gigantic gumtree, or other towering lord of the forest, round the trunk of which, in a standing position, and with a due regard to regularity, are placed the spears, while the boomerangs, clubs, shields, and other smaller weapons are arranged with equal care on the turf at the base of the tree.

The horse also added the critical element of surprise. Now, with their armoury captured, the warriors were forced to retreat.[2]

But the police did not stop shooting. According to Cobban, a 'straggling fire' further back resulted in the 'one or two' casualties to the warriors. The police and their auxiliaries were widely scattered and firing was 'very desultory'; there was 'nothing like a regular firing'. Although he 'rode over a great deal of ground' Cobban said he 'saw only three or four bodies'.

It was Sergeant Lee who provided what must be the most honest account of the casualties at Waterloo Creek. Lee deposed that the 'scrub was so thick' and the 'confusion was so great' that no one could put a stop to the firing. He said, 'from what I saw myself ... from forty to fifty blacks were killed when the second firing took place'. In 1849 the outspoken lawyer and executive council member George Nichols told the council that 'Gentlemen who visited that place [Waterloo Creek] some time afterwards, reported that some 60 or 70 of the blacks were killed – that some of them were shot like crows in the trees'. Ever quick to pen commentary on conflict with Aboriginal people, the Reverend Threlkeld said he was told 'upwards of 120 were destroyed', and later suggested it was 'two or three hundred'.[3]

Threlkeld, consistent with the police depositions, also noted that 'the blacks stood battle' before they were 'destroyed by the police in a swamp where they were surrounded, or into which they were driven'. While it is almost certain there was an indiscriminate killing spree, we should not forget that all reports on Waterloo Creek agree that it began as a fight. Gomeroi people died defending their Country from 'soldiers'.[4]

*

After a whirlwind campaign, Nunn returned to Jerry's Plains in the Hunter Valley on 21 February 1838. His detachment had spent fifty-three days in the saddle. Nunn's expedition had struck 'terror' among the 'natives' and had stiffened the defences of the outstations. The 'thousand blacks' that so worried Lieutenant Colonel Snodgrass were surely defeated. Now the squatters could truly consolidate their foothold in Big River Country and even begin to move beyond it.[5]

In April, Governor Gipps duly reported to London that an investigation would take place 'into all the circumstances of the case' before the police magistrate and bench of justices at Invermein, the nearest outpost to the distant Big River. Gipps vowed he would demand investigations of all such 'incidents' – and informed the Secretary for the Colonies he would soon issue a 'Government Notice declaring that, in all cases where any of the Aboriginal Inhabitants of this Territory shall lose their lives in consequence of a quarrel or collision with white men, an Inquest or Inquiry shall be held' in the same manner as 'when a white man comes to a violent or sudden death'. Why this had not been the case before was not mentioned. At the same time, Gipps decided that the commissioners of Crown lands who were beyond the Boundaries of Location were 'to be charged with the duty of protecting the Native Blacks'.[6]

Governor Gipps was just getting started. In early April of 1838 he was about to push through a raft of humanitarian proclamations and policies that could re-shape relations between Aboriginal people and colonists. But in a hasty postscript to his flurry of correspondence to Lord Glenelg, the governor changed his mind. News of the deaths of a group of overlanders at Broken River in the south had just landed on his desk and it made him hesitate. Gipps believed that his proclamation and inquests could 'exasperate the public mind against the Blacks'. He thought it best to 'defer the publication of these Notices for a few weeks'. In fact, it took over a year.[7]

'Both from the North and the South'

In April 1838, the colony of New South Wales was under attack left, right and centre. Governor Gipps had received reports that 'to the North, and in the neighbourhood of Major Nunn's late operations' more white people were dead. Warriors were slaughtering cattle in numbers. What was even worse, 'from the South', the governor had received accounts 'of a large Convoy of Sheep and Cattle, belonging to a gentleman of the name of Faithfull, having been attacked on the 13th ultimo on their way to Port Phillip, and eight men killed out of eighteen, who formed Mr. Faithfull's party'. Gipps noted they were attacked by 'a party of 300 Blacks'. He wrote to Lord Glenelg in April saying the 'collisions' between colonists and Aboriginal people were occurring 'at a great many different points' across the colony. Gipps said he would have to suspend the inquiry into Major Nunn's 'skirmish' (Waterloo Creek) because the 'continuance of similar outrages' meant the 'services of the Mounted Police have been so constant'.[8]

Whether Waterloo Creek was a massacre, a battle, or more likely both, Nunn had gotten away with it. Eventually, when Downing Street had been sent the reasons for the delays in investigating Nunn's actions at Waterloo Creek, the new Secretary of State for War and the Colonies, Lord John Russell, reluctantly agreed to let it pass. The condition was that Governor Gipps was to 'make every practicable exertion for the prevention of similar calamities in future'.

But Russell, a renowned reformer in England, had a rather novel suggestion – he asked Gipps 'how far it is necessary that the Force employed upon similar service should be always entrusted with the use of Fire Arms?' He thought the 'object of capturing Offenders was entirely lost sight of, and shots were fired at men, who were apparently only guilty of jumping into the water to escape from an armed pursuit'. Lord Russell certainly had an eye for a more humane form of policing and justice.

In fact, Russell's suggestion was an unthinkable, radical one – to have mounted police without guns. The protests would have come thick and fast from people who believed not just police, but every single white man on the frontier should have a gun, or preferably a brace of pistols and a rifle. And they were correct; warriors would have made mincemeat of mounted police who were armed only with sabres and batons.[9]

'This deed of blood'

Henry Dangar ended up with a sheep station at the far reaches of the squatting districts in unusual circumstances. He arrived in the colony as a surveyor and after mapping out much of the Hunter Valley area for settlement in the early 1820s, wanted some land for himself. After a dispute over the parcel he chose he returned to England, but his survey work had attracted attention and he was soon employed by the newly established Australian Agricultural Company. He went back to New South Wales, staked out a huge claim for the company and then began establishing himself as one of the largest land holders in the colony.

From his base in the Hunter Valley, Dangar set about controlling a huge grazing empire. One of his stations was at a place the Europeans called Myall Creek. In 1838, the station was isolated, away from the main traffic passing through what would become Bingara township. Like many station owners with vast pastoral interests, Dangar himself had visited but once, and left an overseer and three assigned convict stockmen stationed there.

Dangar's 'Myall Creek' station was deep in Aboriginal land, the home of the Wirrayaraay. The stockmen all wore a 'brace of pistols'

The Counteroffensive

whenever they went out from the huts. At nearby Newton's station, overseer Thomas Foster considered it customary 'to carry pistols in the bush'. The overseer at Myall Creek, free immigrant William Hobbs, said the stockmen were 'always mounted ... in consequence of the danger ensured by meeting the blacks'. He said the assigned convict stockman 'Kilmaister had a brace of pistols at his command, and he rarely went without them' and that he, too, 'never went out without a brace'.[10]

But there had been no trouble of late at this end of the Big River region. Major Nunn's expedition seems to have inspired a similar sweep of Big River Country, but by armed stockmen in some sort of mopping-up operation. Between February and June 1838, in what was locally remembered as a 'Drive' or the 'Big Bushwack' possibly hundreds of Gomeroi people were killed. On 31 July 1838 Magistrate Edward Denny Day wrote to Colonial Secretary Thomson that Aboriginal people had 'been repeatedly pursued by parties of mounted men and armed stockmen, assembled for the purpose, and that great numbers of them had been killed at various spots, particularly at Vinegar Hill, Slaughter-house Creek and Gravesend, so called by the stockmen, in commemoration of the deeds enacted there'.[11]

By mid-1838, survivors seem to have been drawn toward friendlier stations. According to testimony at the trial, the Wirrayaraay people in the area were moving 'backwards and forwards from one station to another' and were known to be 'very peaceable'. At a nearby station, stockman Andrew Eaton said after initial problems with cattle being rushed, around forty or fifty people 'were on friendly terms with me'. In May, a group of Wirrayaraay had set up camp at Dangar's station and according to superintendent Hobbs, were 'perfectly quiet'. Perhaps they were welcomed by stockmen who were interested in the women. It seems that for a few weeks in May and early June 1838, the four men at Dangar's station got along well with the 'upwards of twenty' but 'not forty' people encamped there about the stockmen's bark huts.[12]

On the night of 7 June, a number of stockmen had gathered at Bell's station on the Big River, around 60 kilometres away from Dangar's. According to one of Dangar's assigned convict workers, Andrew Burrowes, they all talked about how the 'blacks' were 'rushing' cattle

'This deed of blood'

and spearing sheep. A horse was also said to have been speared. The men gathered there had been out looking for the culprits. They were hoping to find more stockmen at Bell's station to join and continue the hunt.

They were in luck, as over the next two days, other men who were also out 'after the blacks' joined them. One, John Fleming, the 22-year-old 'master of Mungie Bundie' station, rode in with a sword in his belt and a rifle slung on his saddle. The hunters were told of the group of Wirrayaraay camped at Dangar's station. With no other reports of Aboriginal people in the area to go by, on Saturday 8 June, with the sword-wielding Fleming at their head, they decided to ride over to Myall Creek.[13]

Meanwhile, at Dangar's station on Myall Creek, the overseer from the neighbouring Newton's station, Thomas Foster, turned up and asked for some of the Wirrayaraay men to come and help cut bark on his station. He said he 'only wanted three boys' but ten men turned up, possibly buoyed by the past few weeks of reportedly 'friendly terms' in the area and the promise of flour and tobacco. Foster duly set off with the ten men, headed by an Elder known as 'King Sandy'.

Then, at Newton's station that afternoon they learned there was 'a party out after the blacks'. Foster quickly summed up the situation and told Sandy and the men they should head straight back to Dangar's station and warn their families to escape as quickly as possible.

But it was too late. Fleming and his followers had obviously decided that any 'blacks' would do and should be killed as a lesson to terrify them all and stop the rushing and killing of sheep and cattle. Ten heavily armed and mounted men rode up to the huts at Dangar's Myall Creek station. It was instantly obvious to all there they were intent on killing Aboriginal people. Two young boys fled to the creek while mothers grabbed their children. The stockmen gathered all who were there and tied them together with a rope and handcuffs. When the station hand Anderson asked what was going to be done, John Russell, the overseer from Bell's station, said they were going to take them 'over the back of the range' and 'frighten them'.[14]

As they led the crying women and children away, one small boy who had been hiding in a hut tried to run after his mother. Anderson grabbed him and thrust him back inside. No one noticed, or cared. Kilmeister went with the stockmen. Anderson stood at the hut with two young Gomeroi stockmen from the Peel River, Billy and Davey, who were at the station. They watched helplessly in the fading winter afternoon sun as around thirty mostly women and children were led away. Davey and then Anderson asked if they could each take a woman. The stockmen obliged. They still had around thirty people roped up, ready to be 'frightened'.

The terrible column was led away. After about 15–20 minutes two gunshots rang out in the distance. There were no young men in the group. Perhaps the Wirrayaraay Elder known as 'Daddy' had tried to resist and was shot and that was the call to kill the rest – using swords and cutlasses. None of the men who were later tried and sentenced for the killings gave any description of events. One, John Blake, kept a woman for himself. All the others were decapitated.

Davey went out from the hut to check what had happened and returned to tell Anderson he saw 'some of the blacks dead up there where they went'. Around ten o'clock that night, Sandy and the other men returned. Anderson managed to persuade them to leave and hide lest the stockmen return.

The next morning the killers went in search of King Sandy and the men. At Newton's they asked Foster where they were. Foster showed some courage and empathy – he lied and said, 'God knows where they are now'. The murderers then returned to Dangar's, where Anderson told them he had sent the survivors on to McIntyre's. The next day they returned to the site of the killings and burned the bodies. Fleming led the men off and left Kilmeister behind to tend the fire. Anderson said he saw smoke rising from the hillside all day long. But Kilmeister failed miserably at his job of destroying the evidence. When Hobbs returned to the site he found 'a great number of human heads' obviously cut off from the mass of bodies 'thrown together' in a pile, some not even scorched by fire. He struggled to count the number of dead due to the incredible stench of human flesh. Perhaps there were twenty, perhaps thirty.[15]

'The Public mind continues to be exasperated against the Blacks'

This was far from the end of the killings. Over the next few days it seems Fleming's men carried on regardless and committed other atrocities before they were satisfied. Governor Gipps later noted that the stockmen 'scoured the Country on horseback, endeavouring to find ten or twelve of the Blacks who having left Dangar's station on the morning of the 10th, had escaped the massacre'. He felt they may have been 'overtaken and murdered also'.

By October, the governor had more than enough information about what had occurred. Gipps noted in his correspondence to his superiors in London that 'Magistrate Denny Day and a party of Mounted Police had been out for 53 days' and had captured those 'who were known to have taken part in the massacre' and who had taken 'great pains to destroy the whole remains of the slaughtered Blacks by fire'. He wrote, they had 'succeeded in taking eleven out of twelve of the persons who were known to have been concerned in this deed of blood'.

The ringleader, the swaggering, sword-wielding Fleming, however, was never brought to justice. He lay low in the upper Hawkesbury River region for several years but from the 1840s until his death in 1894, he lived a free and public life. He continued running sheep and cattle in southern Queensland and became an esteemed member of the community, signing petitions, subscribing to relief efforts, working as a committee member for the construction of a church at Sackville Reach, as well as a trustee of land at Wilberforce for a burial ground and at St Albans for a church. Perhaps out of some kind of contrition he paid for a stained-glass window and was a member of the Hawkesbury Benevolent Society. The final irony was that in 1882, despite a protest that 'a warrant for murder had at one time been issued' against him, Fleming was made a magistrate. His obituary described him as 'an old ... respected resident of Wilberforce' who would be 'missed for his kindness ... and generosity'. The Myall Creek Massacre quietly slipped into 'stirring stories of the early days ... and the trouble he had with the Blacks'.[16]

People had been warned back in 1836 that 'the promptest measures will be taken by me to cause Persons who may be guilty of any Outrage against the ABORIGINAL NATIVES, or of any breach of the said LAWS, to be brought to Trial before the Supreme Court of New South Wales, and Punished accordingly'. But beyond the eyes and ears of the authorities such proclamations had mattered little. Until now. Gipps reported to Lord Glenelg in December that it was his 'painful duty' to inform him that 'seven of the perpetrators of this atrocious deed, having been convicted on the clearest evidence, suffered yesterday morning the extreme penalty which the law awards for the crime of murder'. Finally, it appeared black lives were being treated as equal to white lives.[17]

Many colonists had a very different view. Gipps noted that a large number of people 'thought it extremely hard that white men should be put to trial for killing Blacks'. If the murderers' deathbed confessions were true, the seven men believed they were not 'violating the law' but merely defending 'their masters' property'.[18]

'Silently and surely they laid their plans'

As historian Roger Milliss notes, 'it will never be known exactly how many people were killed in the pogrom of which Myall Creek clearly formed only a part'. It was certainly only 'a part'. Governor Gipps was clearly exasperated. He had to deal with what he called 'very great irritations ... in consequence of the collisions between the settlers and the Natives in distant parts of the Country'. In 1838, it was not just at Myall Creek, but right across all the lands along the riverways where squatters had staked out their huts, yards and grazing runs.[19]

While the attacks by warriors across the colonial frontier during the Uprising continued, the colonial counteroffensive was, despite the justice meted out over Myall Creek, moving into a different gear. The squatters, stockmen and their overseers wanted Aboriginal land, workers and women. Now, they also wanted revenge.

But we must also remember that it sparked Aboriginal revenge as well. And it was not just the Bigumbal, Gomeroi and others in the northern inland who wanted revenge. By the end of 1838, across a huge swathe of Country, warriors conducted many successful operations that forced squatters to abandon their runs, destroyed thousands of stock and generated fear across the frontier.

Between 1838 and 1840, on the present-day Central Coast, the mid-north coast and inland around the upper Williams River and Barrington Rivers, squatters responded to numerous raids and attacks on stock and stockmen with massacres. Some warriors obtained firearms. In November 1840 in the Dungog to Gloucester area 'a band of mounted and armed bushrangers' was causing havoc and the local authorities armed two Aboriginal men with muskets, who then promptly 'made off to join the bushrangers'. Orders were issued to disarm all the Aboriginal people in the 'Dungog and Gloucester' area.[20]

But by the mid-1840s, the struggle for control of the mid-north coast and ranges had effectively been won. The armed might, horses and growing bush skills of the squatters and their stockworkers gave them the ability to hunt and destroy Aboriginal people in the most rugged terrain. These one-sided battles and massacres clearly showed what would happen to those who killed white people, even if it was in retaliation for the massacre of black people. White man's 'payback' generally came along with attempted annihilation.

Further north, similar work remained to be done. One early colonist along the Macintyre River later suggested that it was 'the blacks' method of warfare' that meant the settlers were forced to take their own forms of military action against them. According to an 'early settler of the Lockyer and MacIntyre', William Gray, 'these battles have principally been with the settlers; it is very seldom that soldiers or police have been brought into action'. Gray argued this was precisely because of 'the blacks' method of warfare' and had high praise for warriors' guerrilla warfare tactics. He believed the first squatters and stockmen were 'in a state of silent warfare in all new districts'. He wrote, 'every man here is obliged to be armed, and never thinks himself perfectly safe unless he is'. Early squatters on the Big, Macintyre and Severn Rivers formed their stations 'close together for protection for one another from attacks of the blacks ...'

Gray described the process that the squatters and stockmen across the region deployed:

> Whenever the blacks committed any murder or killed any cattle, there was word passed along from station to station, and the stockmen would collect at some appointed place, and follow up the tracks of the miscreants until they came up with them, and then the blacks were killed without mercy ... They came upon them in their camp within about five miles ... and at daylight the next morning they opened fire, and killed every one they could get a shot at, whether man, woman, or child. They let none escape that it was possible to get a shot at.[21]

'They fell in with a tribe of the natives, who evinced a desire of determined resistance'

Colonial authorities declared the Bogan River a no-go zone after squatters had been pushed out of the area in the late 1830s. In 1841, William Lee and a 'Mr. Moulder' tried their luck and decided to take stock down the lower Macquarie River. When they did, three of their stockmen were killed. The so-called 'Bogan Blacks' were still defiant, still spearing cattle and still killing stockmen.

A party of mounted police from Bathurst went out 'in search of the murderers'. The police force, according to a report in the *Colonial Observer*, 'consisted of seven troopers and the corporal'. As was typical of policing the frontier, they had no qualms about getting back-up from locals and were 'joined by eight or nine settlers'. The now-strong force:

> proceeded direct to the spot where the murders had been committed. On arrival at the Bogan country they fell in with a tribe of the natives, who evinced a desire of determined resistance; as however none of the tribe could be identified as being concerned with the murders, the party fired over the heads of the natives' and went on.

The report from 'W. T. T.' fails to explain how the troopers knew who were the 'tribe who had been guilty of the atrocious murders', but somehow soon after, probably with the assistance of a guide, the police came upon them. The warriors at first gained the upper hand. They 'retired into a thick scrub, from whence they attacked the party with their spears and wommeras, which caused the party to retreat'. The warriors then boldly pressed their advantage and 'left the scrub and advanced into an open plain in a dense body to continue the attack'. It was in the open terrain where the firepower of around twenty muskets came into play. 'W. T. T.' briefly related that 'the party returning fired upon the natives ... very many fell'.

Apparently the police had 'left Bathurst in such a hurry they forgot to take their swords with them'. It seems that en route the forgetful troopers fashioned 'large headed [wooden] clubs' and then 'charged ... and succeeded in taking prisoner three natives who were pointed out as being concerned in the murder of the Europeans'. The account in the *Colonial Observer* continued:

> The number of the natives killed is variously stated, and it is quite impossible to come at the truth – some say fifteen, others thirty – but it is evident a great many were killed.

Even with such casualties, warriors along the Bogan River remained defiant. Land Commissioner Allman and Captain Nicholson had been dealing with 'the pursuit of two parties of bushrangers who had been committing depredations in his district'. When, 'with part of the Wellington police force', Allman and Nicholson arrived on the scene, they were 'challenged out to fight' by a group of warriors. Allman refused combat and collected stray cattle instead. 'W. T. T.' believed that more punishment was needed: 'Without it, they [warriors] entertain the idea that we either have not the power or the will to punish crime among the natives'.[22]

Governor Gipps revoked William Lee's squatting licence as he viewed Lee's disregard of instructions not to occupy the lower Macquarie and Bogan rivers as the reason for the conflict. Lee's case soon became a rally cry among squatters opposed to Gipps's sympathy for the people whose lands were being occupied. Still, the ban on occupying the Bogan River area remained until the 1850s, a testament to its active defence.[23]

'Left at the mercy of lawless blacks, and bushrangers'

Despite the apparent threat after the Myall Creek trials that white people could actually hang for killing black people, in April 1839 the *Gazette* and the *Australian* newspapers reported more massacres. After two shepherds in the New England region had been killed, and another at Byron Plains near present-day Inverell had been found with his body 'terribly mutilated', an armed party had 'gone out in search of the blacks'. They were successful and nine people were 'butchered in cold blood'.

The Myall Creek trials did not stop the killings. Many went underground. But incredibly, many were also recorded – some published widely in newspapers at the time. Often the reports were intended to show how terrible the 'outrages' by warriors on stockmen were. Others were merely including mass killings in their daily reporting. In April 1839, the *Sydney Gazette* noted 'Another Black Massacre' near the 'Big River' as a 'second edition' of the 'Liverpool Plains Massacre' in November 1838. Even the perpetrators were well known. According to the *Gazette*, 'a person of some respectability' a 'superintendent on the estate of a gentleman in the neighbourhood' was said to be responsible for killing nine people 'butchered in cold blood'. The *Australian* newspaper followed suit, describing 'More Black Murders ... at the Big River'. It would not have been difficult for the authorities to work out who the offending 'superintendent' at Big River was. No one was brought to trial.[24]

In 1839, newly appointed Commissioner for Crown Lands for New England George James Macdonald had his hands full. As was often the case, where a commissioner set up camp in a district, a small settlement began to grow – in this case, Macdonald grandly named it Armidale after a castle on the Isle of Skye in Scotland. With a small troop of eight border police for assistance, Macdonald was magistrate, squatting licence fee collector, settler of boundary disputes, and punisher of bushrangers and absconders. He was also Protector of Aborigines.

Macdonald had no small experience with Aboriginal people from his time as a clerk at Port Macquarie, even learning the local language. He published a poem in the *Sydney Gazette* that gave high praise to the local 'Birpai' (Biripi/Birrpai) people who had become 'attached to him'. Macdonald had a hunched back and this apparently reminded the Birrpai of one of their people who had passed away. Macdonald's 1831 poem recalled how he made 'friends with that fierce race' and that he was 'loved, adored, revered by savages the white man feared'. But the tension between the two arms of his job as Protector and police was great. Right across the New England region from late 1838, attacks against the squatters and stockmen and the killing of cattle and sheep increased.[25]

There were some remarkable successes, forcing squatters to retreat, away from the New England Tableland of the Ambēyang people. In early 1839 an Australian Agricultural Company overseer, Patrick Brennan, drove 7000 sheep to the coast at Port Stephens 'to have them shorn', and then return to the Peel River, near present-day Tamworth. But Brennan delayed his return to the Peel. According to 'A Bushman' who sent a letter to the *Sydney Herald* outlining Brennan's tale of woes in early 1839, the overseer 'determined upon keeping the sheep on the [New England] Table Land, on the dividing range, until rain should set in'. He 'pitched upon a spot called the "Rocky Springs", about five miles from the head or Little's Creek, and about sixteen from "Inclebar" stockyard'.

Then, 'On the morning of the 7th of February, eight blacks ... ransacked the hut, taking away provisions of every description'. Stockman Thomas Casey 'did not come in' and 'ninety-six [sheep] were deficient ... the blacks had been at work amongst them'. Brennan and a stockman rode out and found 'nearly one hundred of these savages, men, women, and children, busy round several fires'. Here Brennan 'found eleven sheep cut up in quarters, and roasting and close by, a fold, where the remainder had been kept all night ready for their next repast'.

Then 'poor Casey's dog, which had been keeping watch all night by the body of his murdered master' led them to the 'mangled and bloody corpse' that lay in the creek, 'a ghastly spectacle'. The mutilation of

Casey certainly did the trick. Brennan's shepherds all 'positively refused to go out with the sheep at that place, [so] the station was vacated, and Brennan moved down with his sheep to the Peel'. The warriors of the New England Tableland sent Brennan's party and their 7000 sheep (minus a few) packing, back to the comparative safety of other stations around the Peel River.

The 'bushman' who related the tale, no doubt a local squatter or overseer, joined the chorus of growing complaints that the government was doing little and that 'the whole of this district, Peel's River and New England' had been 'left at the mercy of lawless blacks, and bushrangers'.[26]

Many squatters and stockmen acted as if they were military units in a war zone, seamlessly transposing their working lives into military terms. In July 1840, the Everett brothers at their 'Ollera' station 40 miles northwest of Armidale set out to recover some sheep they believed had been taken by Ambēyang people. George wrote in a letter home to his family in England that he had to leave some men behind 'to defend the garrison during our absence in case of attack'. Across the region, stockmen were mobilising in attack as well. George's brother John wrote to their brother William in June 1841 that after a stockman on a nearby station had been killed, his killers had been 'made to repent it, numbers of their tribe having been shot by parties who went out in pursuit'.[27]

Squatters complained to the newspapers asking where Commissioner Macdonald was in all this? Meanwhile, they took it upon themselves to get rid of these 'lawless blacks'. In March 1840, the *Sydney Herald* published a letter from 'New England' from an overseer to his employer. He wrote:

> It becomes my painful and unpleasant duty to inform you that on Thursday the 17th a shepherd in charge of your sheep was murdered by the blacks and that fourteen of your sheep were slaughtered by them. On the shepherd not making his appearance as usual at sundown, my younger brother and I with all the men we could muster went in search the whole night, and at sunrise the following morning we came on an encampment of blacks on the falls of the McLeay River, into which they made their escape, leaving the

heads and skins of fourteen sheep. I immediately reported the circumstance to Mr. McDonald the commissioner whom I daily expect here, with his Mounted Police to drive these murderous savages from this quarter and I trust he will if possible make an example of some of them.[28]

It seems the man who had waxed lyrical in poetry about his empathy with Aboriginal people, Commissioner Macdonald, had either finally snapped due to all the violence and conflict swirling around his vast domain, or he succumbed to the public taunts and criticisms of inaction. In 1841, after a raid on Dr John Dobie's 'Ramornie' station, he led his border police against Bundjalung people on the Clarence River near present-day Grafton. His troopers certainly made 'an example of some of them' – bodies were apparently seen floating downstream from the riverbanks at the 'Settlement', later called South Grafton.

According to a much later account from 1935, 'a cordon was formed during the night, hemming the camp in with the river behind it. At a given signal at daybreak in the morning the camp was rushed, and men, women and children were shot down indiscriminately. Some took to the river, and were shot as they swam'. The commissioner, known in his district as 'Humpy', failed to report to his superiors very much of anything that occurred on his watch; merely that by July 1842, 'the outrages formerly of such frequent occurrence in the colony from shepherds and stockmen taking the law into their own hands and making indiscriminate reprisals on the natives for cattle scattered and flocks driven off, have in this district entirely ceased'. 'Humpy' Macdonald's empathy for Aboriginal people had its limits.[29]

'They shall kill them as long as a head remains on the Big River'

Further north, on the Macintyre River in May 1840, a young Scotsman whose father had given him £500 to emigrate and establish a sheep station, Robert Muir, prosaically wrote an entry in his diary:

The Counteroffensive

> 23rd Saturday. Was out on the run after some of the working bullocks. Tom Hewitt was here last night. He lately shot 16 Blacks who were stealing sheep, etc.

There is no reason not to believe Muir's private account of Hewitt's actions. There is however reason to wonder at what happened to Tom Hewitt, noted in the *People Australia* biographical entry as a 'Pastoralist and Businessman' who had a large family and died in 1876. His obituary recorded him as one of 'the earliest pioneers of these northern districts' who became a wealthy businessman in steamships in Grafton. Hewitt certainly had no repercussions in later life from shooting '16 Blacks'.[30]

Despite such atrocities, warriors across the northern inland area continued their attacks on sheep cattle stations into the early 1840s. Across the New England region and the surrounding plains, Ambēyang, Gomeroi and others were described as 'prowling about the country, plundering, murdering and carrying off flocks and herds wholesale'. In November 1841 it was reported that right across 'the country on the Big River, the Boomi, the Macintyre, Frazer's Creek, and the Severn, also the Bundara country and the northern part of New England ... the blacks ... destroy both cattle and sheep with perfect impunity'. The correspondent to the *Sydney Monitor* newspaper, writing from 'Peel's River', noted that warriors had been so brazen 'they have been heard to say (for most of them can now talk a little English) they shall kill them [stock] as long as a head remains on the Big River'. The message to pastoralists could not have been clearer.[31]

In October 1842, the overseer for 'Mr C. M. Doyle Esq.' at Mooney Creek on the Liverpool Plains reported an attack where warriors killed one stockman, speared another, took firearms, and besieged the wounded stockman in his hut for ten hours before help arrived. The overseer abandoned the run. A few days later from the safety of a nearby station he wrote in desperation to Doyle:

> The sooner you send me help the better. My horses are both unable to work; the quicker the cattle are taken away the better. The blacks have taken the rations. I expect Hunt will not live one moment.[32]

Soon after, the editor of the *Sydney Morning Herald* was taken aback that the attacks were not on new stations but on 'the old established stations on Gwyder [Big], Namoi and Barwon rivers'. According to the editor, 'The blacks are in the habit, all over the district, of bailing up the hut-keepers, plundering the huts of all provisions, clothing, &c'. Even more concerning was that 'most of these depredations are committed by blacks who have been reared by the whites'. How was it possible that Aboriginal men who had worked for pastoralists then turned against them?[33]

After 1842, the uprising across today's northern and northwestern New South Wales shifted in both intensity and ferocity. With the increasing numbers of arms and men flowing onto the stations, it was becoming more difficult for warriors to escape the wrath of armed settlers. Attacks by warriors became more irregular, and with swift retreats into rugged terrain to avoid reprisals. They also became more deadly. Warriors were obtaining firearms and using them. At a station 'Ward's Mistake' northeast of Armidale in April 1842, it was reported in the *Hunter River Gazette* that 'the savages were in large force, and carried a number of muskets'. They 'took several stand of arms', killed three men, and drove off horses that belonged to the Mounted Police. On top of all this, they 'speared and dispersed various herds of cattle'.[34]

In January 1843, Commissioner Macdonald wrote his second annual report to the Colonial Secretary on the 'condition and prospects of the Aboriginal Tribes frequenting the District of New England'. Macdonald believed that over his vast domain, there had been a 'diminution of hostile feeling and outrage' on both the part of the 'Shepherds and Stockmen' and Ambēyang people. He outlined two principal causes of conflict: revenge and retaliation for 'outrages' and that whenever a new station was established, the Europeans were looked upon as 'intruders and enemies'. Macdonald clearly understood warriors were still trying to defend their Country.[35]

And they were resorting to more desperate measures and defensible terrain. In early 1843, prospective squatters HG Hamilton and Henry Denison set out on a 'tour northward in search of a cattle station'. After a nine-week-long trip around northern New South Wales trying to find a piece of Aboriginal land that was suitable for cattle but not yet occupied by pastoralists, Hamilton made an assessment of the 'very broken country' on the edge of the New England tablelands. This was the landscape of today's scenic tourist drive, the Waterfall Way. It was – and still is – dramatic, rugged country cut by rainforest and waterfalls. Hamilton thought it rather romantic, 'as fine as anything [he] had seen in Switzerland'. He also believed it would be 'left for many years to come in the hands of the blacks'.

Hamilton was correct. As Ambēyang historian Callum Clayton-Dixon has pointed out, resistance continued across the eastern edge of the tablelands for two decades from the 1830s. It was not finally under colonial control until the 1860s, when groups of warriors with firearms held out in rugged terrain and fought gun battles with police.

So too, Gomeroi resistance continued over a 20-year period. According to historian Roger Milliss, there were 'periodic uprisings' that ultimately culminated in 'a valiant last stand on the Macintyre River in 1848–9'. The year 1844 was arguably the end of a string of major uprisings along the entire squatted edge of the colony of New South Wales. It was not the end of the wars, nor what military historians rather off-handedly call 'mopping-up operations' by the ultimate victors.[36]

CHAPTER EIGHT
Murdering Island and Poison Waterholes Creek

'Mounted Policemen and constables are much wanted'

In 1839, along the southern reaches of squatted lands colonists were clamouring for military assistance. They were under serious threat of being repulsed entirely from their runs. Reinforcements of mounted police were sent to the Goulburn and Hume (Murray) rivers. The *Sydney Monitor* conveyed the gratitude of 'the respectable Squatters betwixt the Murrumbidgee and Port Phillip'.

However, the lower Murrumbidgee remained beyond the reach of these detachments. The *Sydney Monitor* noted that 'a Police Magistrate, and a few Mounted Policemen and constables are much wanted on the Murrumbidgee River ... at least 80 or 90 miles beyond Yass, where both blacks and whites require to be placed under more control'. As we have seen, Magistrate Hardy, based in Yass, could not investigate Denay's death 'in the absence of any Mounted Police'. He appealed to his superiors for reinforcements.[1]

Meanwhile, Commissioner of Crown Lands Cosby decided to investigate and made two trips to the Murrumbidgee. The commissioner came prepared and was escorted by 'a troop of Mounted Police'. He seemed to relish his role as leader of a military force, seeking enemy warriors. When Cosby heard 'several Blacks were supposed to be lurking in the Ranges' north of the Murrumbidgee, he resorted to the now well-understood British practice of bolstering a military force with auxiliaries of armed colonists who knew the terrain. He reinforced his detachment of mounted police with 'six stockmen with mounts' and headed into the ranges.

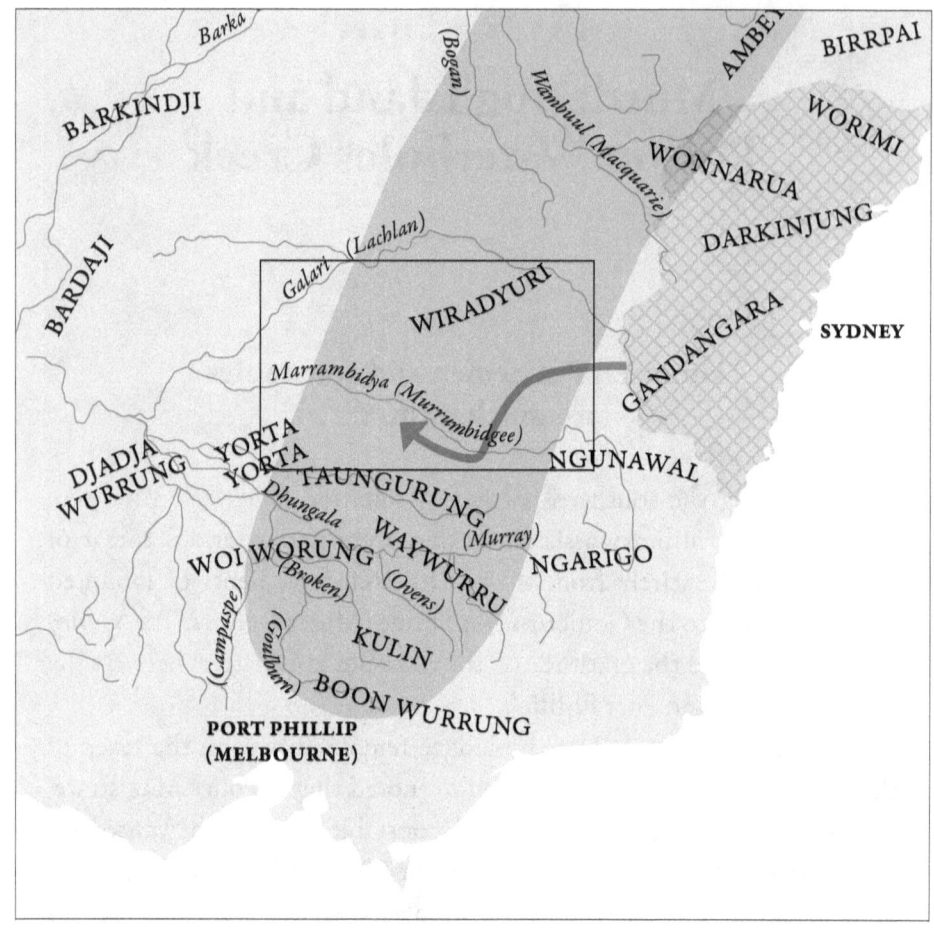

The Murrumbidgee River, 1830s

Cosby and his now-strong force were no target for warriors. Cosby scoured the bush but 'did not see a Black the last 60 miles'. Some stockmen then informed Cosby the Wiradyuri had probably 'taken their departure for a short time, and gone towards the Murray'. Cosby did come across a deserted Wiradyuri camp. Here, evidence of how destructive the Wiradyuri cattle raids had been was plain to see. Cosby noted that the ground 'for the distance of several miles [was] strewed with the bones of the cattle they had killed [sic]'.[2]

After two tours of the region, Cosby came to a view that 'the hostile feeling displayed by the Blacks proceeds from their not wishing any more stations to be formed down river'. People he met in his travels might have told him this. Cosby had certainly gathered an appreciation of the impact of squatting: 'the interference which the formation of stations necessarily occasions with respect to the hunting grounds of the Aborigines' was, he felt, at the heart of this 'hostile feeling'.[3]

The idea of 'an additional force to the Mounted Police' had been floated at least since September 1838. It came in response to the conflict occurring from Port Phillip in the south to the Big River in the north. The *Sydney Gazette* suggested 'the establishment of an Interior Police from a revenue to be derived from a rent on Lands held under Lease'. By February 1839, Governor Gipps had heeded these calls and introduced further regulations around the occupation of Crown lands.

The Act proposed the recruitment of 'so many men mounted, armed, and accoutred, in such manner as shall be appointed by the Governor, as and for a Border Police Force'. The idea of a 'border' police suggested there was indeed a border to police. There was no 'border' between nation states. Or not one admitted by the colonial government, at least. And defining any such border was all but impossible as squatters kept moving into more and more Aboriginal lands.

The Act had other important elements. It gave commissioners the power to call upon 'persons within his district, and mounted and armed in such manner as he shall desire ... in the prevention or suppression of any attack or aggression'. In effect, this legislated past practices of recruiting informal militias to assist in policing operations. Some squatters felt they would be 'attended with very great inconvenience and loss' if they had to supply men to defend their runs. But the idea of a border police force for the frontier districts was more acceptable. The role of land commissioners was increasingly bound up with the military defence of colonists on the frontier.[4]

The timely arrival of a number of military convicts arrested for desertion in the Cape Colony of South Africa gave the Commissioner of Crown Lands for the Gwydir, Edward Mayne, a bright idea. He suggested that transported prisoners with prior service in the army should be enlisted into the border police. Henry Fyshe Gisborne, Commissioner for the Port Phillip District, agreed and suggested that 'the whole corps should be selected from prisoners at Hyde Park Barracks, having regard to good conduct, upon a system of reward by mitigation of sentence' and even suggested that 'men might be kept in training at Hyde Park, to keep up this force'.[5]

Historians have generally seen the border police as incompetent, a failed policy at best. Yet in times of need the overstretched British empire consistently resorted to trying to reform military prisoners and giving incentives to soldiers to become settlers as a way of stiffening defences. As an emergency military stopgap measure, the border police were in no way a complete failure. It was more the case that ever-increasing numbers of them were needed.[6]

'A perpetual state of warfare'

In 1839 the self-described 'wanderer' James Byrne joined an overlanding party with 1000 head of cattle and other stock heading from Yass to Adelaide. The young man with some money behind him to try his luck in the colonies arrived at the 'Berembed' head station on the Murrumbidgee in August 1839. He later recalled in his *Twelve Years Wandering in the British Colonies from 1835 to 1847* that two nearby outstations 'had been both deserted a short time before, in consequence of the men at one of them having been murdered, and numbers of the cattle speared'. Byrne said the area was in 'a perpetual state of warfare ... deaths on either side being not uncommon'.[7]

Guerrilla warfare relies heavily on favourable terrain. In the Sydney Wars between 1788 and 1816, the 'advantageous retreating grounds' of the Blue Mountains and the rugged reaches of the Georges River were key factors in resistance warfare. At Bathurst too, Wiradyuri could retire into the 'deep dells of the Capertee Valley'. But in the flat, expansive lands in southwestern New South Wales, there were few such rugged ranges. In this open terrain, horses were a significant advantage.

But mounted forces were not invulnerable in this river country. In the soft ground around wetlands, billabongs and marshes, horses could become a liability rather than an asset. In such ground, reeds as tall as a person meant any colonist who dismounted to follow retiring warriors could become a sitting duck. The great river system of the Murray-Darling Basin offered squatters a pathway to new grazing lands. It also offered warriors a unique form of defence.[8]

In dry times, reeds and grass could be burned. Stockworker John Phillips recalled in 1893 when he was with a party moving sheep near the junction of the Murray and Edward Rivers in 1840, 'the land on either side had been recently burnt by the Aborigines'. Phillips had heard it was done 'to prevent the occupation of their country by the white fellows, as was said'.

While it might also have been burned as part of regular land maintenance, Phillips and his men were taking no chances. He said 'we formed our camp in such a manner as to make our drays act as outworks, camping our sheep and stock between, so as to protect them from the wild dogs as well as the natives'.[9]

Phillips was part of an overlanding party heading downstream to take up Aboriginal land around 'Warbreccan country', as he called it, near present-day Deniliquin. Phillips recalled an attack south of the Edwards River on the Gwynne brothers' hut, on what he called 'Baratta country'. After spearing cattle, warriors laid siege to the hut, then approached it 'with firebrands attached to the ends of their spears ... intending to thus burn them out'. At this point and when 'reduced to their last round of ammunition', a detachment of mounted police arrived on the scene. The troopers opened fire on what Phillips was told was 'upwards of 200' warriors attacking the hut. The cavalry had saved the day. According to Phillips, the warriors 'dispersed, making for the reed-beds and the river'.

At the time, Phillips was at a neighbouring station, so his account seems reliable. In a turn of events, the stockmen and police followed the warriors and found they had more than 200 head of cattle with them. What came next was certainly a surprise to Phillips, who recalled 'the natives having formed a kind of rampart, or wall, of masses and junks of beef, cut from those they had slaughtered, thinking it would afford them some protection in the event of a surprise'.

The police and stockmen caught them at early dawn and a battle commenced. According to Phillips, the troopers' surprise arrival meant they secured 'a large bundle of spears'. They took the warriors' stockpile of arms. Phillips called the battle a 'general scrimmage' with 'the whites using their firearms and the natives, nothing daunted at being taken so unawares, fought with their weapons, spears, boomerangs and tomahawks, inside their barricades of beef'. In a twist of fate, the captured cattle stampeded through the camp, forcing the warriors to retreat. The warriors held their makeshift fortification against an attack by firearms, only to be beaten by a stampede of cattle. Yet they retired in good order 'to their stronghold the reed-beds, taking the most intricate line of country, knowing they could not be followed by the horsemen'.[10]

'The Blacks ... are committing numerous outrages'

In late 1839, the flow of squatters and their workers into the southern districts was incessant. The north bank of the Murrumbidgee was a highway for stock. It had become the preferred route for overlanding sheep and cattle to the colony of South Australia. One such expedition led by Ephraim Howe travelled through the lower Murrumbidgee stations in early November and was reported as being 'well armed'. The *Adelaide Chronicle* newspaper said Howe's party was unmolested for 'the first 110 miles below the stations on the Murrumbidgee' because Aboriginal people now knew of 'the great superiority of our weapons'.[11]

In late 1839 the situation around the lower Murrumbidgee was tense. The Yonco and Berembed stations had been abandoned in October, and another 'hut which Mr. Small had intended to have formed into a station' was, according to the *Adelaide Chronicle*, in ruins 'on account of the hostility shown by the natives'. So too 'at least two stockmen had been killed' at 'Ganmain' station. In July 1839 Commissioner of Crown Lands Henry Cosby reported that the only station occupied west of Ganmain was Yonco – all others had been driven off. James Devlin abandoned his Ulong station at this point and James Thorn abandoned his station west of Brillinball. The southern Wiradyuri were still in control of their Country.[12]

In December, Commissioner Cosby was informed by a concerned squatter at 'Harrington' on the lower Murrumbidgee that stockmen were 'furnishing themselves with fire arms and ammunition'. The unknown correspondent to the commissioner thought it likely that 'blood will be shed on both sides' and pleaded him to 'afford such protection as may be in your power' to his district.[13]

In fact, Commissioner Cosby had had enough. In May 1840, he wrote that the 'Blacks encamped in the neighbourhood' were still 'committing numerous outrages' and Cosby decided to 'proceed far into the Interior to tranquilise' the disturbed regions on the lower Murrumbidgee.

With a mere three policemen, Cosby ventured 'beyond the furthest stations' and managed to capture three men. While this might have been regarded as an unsuccessful campaign, in June, Cosby reported favourably on the performance of the border police and the subsequent 'tranquillity' in the district of Lachlan. The sweep through Country of an armed force often produced results that were not calculated in numbers of casualties, but in displaying the potential of military or police power.[14]

The Battle of Hulong Sandhill and Murdering Island

The details of just how the resistance of Narrungdera people was quashed are vague. At some point in 1840, according to a much later newspaper report, 'a pitched battle between the pioneers and the blacks was fought' during which 'quite a number of the dusky warriors bit the dust, and were buried in the sand'. There are few other details of what was said to have taken place on the sandhills at Hulong near present-day Narrandera. If the Wiradyuri had gained confidence and chosen to fight an open battle, shifting their tactics from the previously successful guerrilla warfare, the increasing flow of firearms into the hands of all colonists in the area might have meant this strategy could not succeed. Whatever the case, after the battle, it was the colonists who went on the offensive.[15]

According to James Bayliss, a Narrandera local historian writing in 1914, 'the settlers on both sides of the river chased them [Wiradyuri] on to an island in the river just below Bucking Bong homestead, where several were shot'. A report in the *Bendigo Independent* in 1911 claimed the colonists set fire to the dry reeds to 'flush out' the people on the island. Apparently only one person escaped alive, a man named 'Mungo', who lost an eye in the massacre. Uncle Robert Carroll says hollow reeds were used as a kind of snorkel to survive underwater – a well-known hunting practice to sneak up on birdlife. Uncle Robert took me to see the island in the river – still known today as 'Murdering Island'.[16]

In 1832, Arthur Jenkins and his two sons John and Frank had taken Wiradyuri land along the Murrumbidgee River and, as was common, used local language to give names to their stations. They called their station 'Tooyal'. Apparently it was first known as 'Toyeo', which means the 'jag of a spear' (barbs cut into the wood). In 1839, the Jenkins sons branched out and John and Frank took over Buckingong station from Robert Holt Best, who had previously taken over from Michael Byrne when Byrne abandoned it due to constant Wiradyuri attacks during 1838.

Buckingong was originally named 'Boganbong' – bogan (rushes) and bong (dry). According to local historian Geoff Burch, there are plenty of dry reeds 'in the big swamp near Buckingong homestead'. All along the river today dry reeds can be seen. From the Naranderra Road, a glimpse of Murdering Island through the trees shows it still is thickly covered in dry reeds.[17]

In the 1990s, Wiradyuri Elder Ossie Ingram recalled an account given to him in the 1930s, 'by one of the old people'. In this account, people were poisoned ('six hundred of them') and survivors went to Duck Bend (which is like an island) and there were shot except for one man who escaped in the water using a reed as a snorkel. He later became a Karadji (Shaman or Medicine Man).[18]

The *Freeman's Journal* in 1895 and the *Bendigo Independent* in 1911 claimed that 300 people were slain. In 1926, the writer and political activist Mary Gilmore (later Dame), who had grown up near Wagga during the late 1800s, gave another death toll. Gilmore claimed to 'know for a fact' that there were '70 natives killed' in what she called the 'Narrandera Massacre'.

The Wiradyuri had used the reeds and islands of the rivers successfully over the previous two years of warfare. The location surrounded by dry reeds might well have been a defensive decision, providing a ready supply of dyiriil or reed spears. But as had happened in other areas of the colony, when colonists were in numbers, could outflank warriors or cover a retreat and were well-armed, favourable guerrilla warfare terrain could also turn into a death trap.[19]

Historian Bill Gammage has suggested the colonial authorities 'turned a blind eye to the solution the squatters found'. This would explain the lack of a report on the matter. The authorities were certainly demanding squatters look to their own defence. In June 1840 Cosby had been informed 'that several Head of Cattle have been speared by the aborigines in consequence of Cattle having been left unprotected on a station at the Lower Morumbidgee [sic]', but nothing further transpired.

In 1839, Governor Gipps had proclaimed that any squatter 'abandoning a station should be deprived of his License'. Now, squatters could not just leave a run and move to another one if it was destroyed by warriors. With questions being raised about the border police's inactivity – the *Sydney Herald* claimed that 'the Border Police ... don't fight' – armed colonists themselves were undertaking the growing offensive against the Wiradyuri. As historian Jack Clear notes, now that they could no longer withdraw from a run and find another one without being deprived of a squatting licence, the pressure mounted on colonists to 'resort to massacre as a means of depopulating and demoralising their Wiradjuri adversaries'.[20]

End of the war?

The Narrandera Massacre at Murdering Island seems to have brought an end to the southern Wiradyuri resistance. It was, and still largely is, remembered that way in the broader community – expressed in local histories as 'the squatters were left more or less in peace' or that the massacres had 'lessened the troubles of the settlers'. But we now need to remember it differently. As Bill Gammage wrote, 'the Wiradjuri around

Narrandera declared war on the white men' and 'they fought bravely and successfully for well over a year, temporarily recapturing sixty miles of their country from the enemy'.[21]

Despite the beginning of an economic downturn in 1840, the squatters and their cattle and sheep kept coming. In 1838, the white population of New South Wales was 97 912. In 1845 it was 181 556. The land under cultivation in 1838 was recorded as 92 912 acres and in 1845 it was 163 979. Horses had increased in this period from 56 585 to 82 303; cattle from 897 219 to 1 348 022 and sheep from over 4 million to over 6 million.[22]

While the squatters along the Murrumbidgee River might have been 'more or less' left in peace or found that their troubles were 'lessened', they weren't over. If they wanted to sell their stock, the overland route to Adelaide continued to be a dangerous proposition. It wasn't until in 1841 that the government deployed an expeditionary force from Adelaide to bring the route under control. As Edward Eyre wrote, around Moorundie north-east of Adelaide on the Murray River, 'frightful scenes of bloodshed, rapine and hostility between the Natives and Parties coming overland with Stock had been of very frequent occurrence'.[23]

The ending of Wiradyuri resistance along the Murrumbidgee is shrouded in a mixture of denial and bold claims. In 1840, it was best for those who went out with massacre parties to keep quiet. By the 1880s, it had become a source of pride for 'pioneers' in the district, a sign of how dangerous it was in the 'early days'. While this conflict was recorded as part of reminiscences, the details and potentially incriminating locations were not.

Uncle Robert Carroll heard stories from his father who spoke fluent Wiradyuri and was a drover who worked across New South Wales and Queensland. He was told stories by other Aboriginal stockmen and shearers about how squatters murdered people by shooting and poisoning water and flour. As Robert recalls, 'children's heads and bodies were smashed against trees and rocks like they were rabbits or vermin and bigger children were buried in the sand with their heads protruding so that horses could smash them in with their hooves or were smashed in by squatters with wooden clubs like polo players!'.[24]

At Narrandera, there is not a lot of information about Poison Waterholes Creek. Uncle Robert is clear that a local squatter or stockman laced the waterholes with arsenic when there was a dry period and they knew people would come to drink from them. It is not clear if this occurred around 1840 or later, or indeed which particular waterholes. Whatever the case, when you drive into Narrandera from Wagga Wagga today, the last road sign you see before entering town is 'Poison Waterholes Creek'. When the local council suggested changing the name, the Local Aboriginal Land Council defiantly resisted the change.

CHAPTER NINE

'A commission to wage war against the aboriginal natives'

'I much fear that should they encounter the natives there will be great slaughter'

In May 1838, a month after the Battle at Broken River, William Faithfull wrote to the Colonial Secretary in May for 'the information of His Excellency the Governor the further particulars' of what had happened at the 'Winding Swamp or Swampy River'. He said that:

> the Blacks attacked the Party between 10 and 11 o'clock of Wednesday the 11th April by first commencing to throw spears at the Shepherds, that on their retreat to the Drays one of the Deceased men (Bentley) fired in the air, wishing to intimidate them, but finding this ineffectual he fired with Ball and shot one of the natives dead, they immediately rushed upon him and Killed him :– The party becoming intimidated fled, when seven men named in the margin were murdered – The Blacks have taken away from the Drays goods to the value of £150 – besides the loss of 103 sheep which are irrecoverable, there are also 150 head of Cattle astray which possibly may be recovered – There was not the slightest provocation given for this outrage, but on the reverse every means were taken to keep on friendly terms with them, and it must have been a desire of plunder, which instigated them to commit so deadly a deed.

Faithfull believed that 'the Blacks are so numerous that it is supposed a very strong force will be required to keep them quiet'.[1]

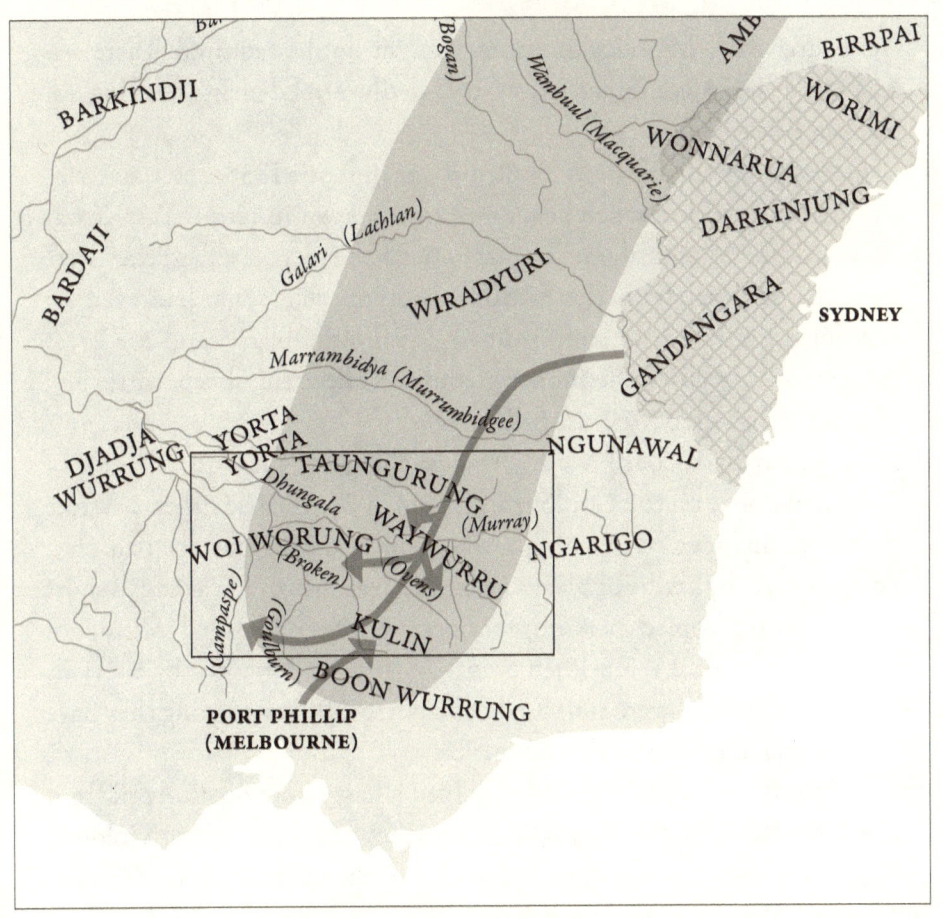

Northeast Victoria, late 1830s

The *Sydney Gazette* soon echoed what everyone was demanding – military intervention:

> To protect the travellers by land to and from Port Phillip, it has now become a matter of absolute necessity, that stockades, manned by an adequate military force, should be stationed at regular distances along the route; until that is done there can be no safety for the traveller, and all communication by land must necessarily cease.

Yet a large force of police or military might not be required. There was already a 'large combined party of heavily armed men' heading for Broken River.²

Soon after the Battle at Broken River in April 1838, the vengeance of squatters and stockmen began in earnest. Even in far-off Yass, it was reported 'the settlers about this part are on the alert'. In fact, they were in such solidarity with the Faithfull brothers that some had even set out 'with the Police to endeavour to capture the blacks and use every endeavour to recover the property, and to collect the sheep, cattle and horses belonging to Mr Faithfull'.³

Lieutenant Richard Waddy was in charge of the 2nd Division of Mounted Police on the Goulburn Plains. On 25 April he urgently wrote to his commander, Major Nunn, that 'a most daring outrage had been committed ... by a tribe of Blacks near the River "Murray"'. Waddy's short note to Nunn (copied by Nunn for his superiors and headed 'Murder of 8 Men by the Blacks') outlined events and was underscored by a serious threat: 'The Blacks were supposed to be nearly 200 men strong they have taken some of the arms & ammunition'.⁴

Colonel Henry White had scribbled a hasty note on 15 April from the 'Left Bank of the Ovens' that somehow made it to the Colonial Secretary's Office, possibly in the satchel of the postman, John Conway Bourke, 'Victoria's First Mailman'. White claimed 'a most furious attack' had been conducted by 'about 300 of the Aboriginal Natives'. He said that George Faithfull told him he had come across one corpse (John Bass) that had been 'mangled' and a wounded man 'so dreadfully lacerated' he was not expected to live.⁵

With such horrific news, the 'settlers' mobilised well before the Yass police. But not before the military from Port Phillip. The once-confident overseer James Crossley, who thought 'one shot fired over the heads of a thousand blacks would cause them all to flee in terror', rushed to Melbourne to report the attack. The commandant at Port Phillip, Captain William Lonsdale, ordered Lieutenant George Brunswick Smyth of the 80th Regiment to the scene.

As we have seen, Smyth was familiar with the route – he had only recently overlanded with his fellow lieutenant, Alfred Miller Mundy.

Perhaps Smyth had the chance to play a game or two of cricket between arriving in Port Phillip and being sent back to investigate events at Broken River – he certainly played in the first Melbourne Cricket Club match in November that year. He also seems to have had some small investment in a station in the area with the brothers Alfred and Charles Mundy. At this point, Smyth might not have known about how one of the Mundy brothers (locally known as 'Colonel Mundy') had 'rode down upon' people and shot dead 'men, women and children'.[6]

Smyth and 'a policeman' went firstly to Clarke's station, and then on to 'Winding Swamp'. Smyth wrote to Lonsdale that when he reached the 'Swampy River' on 21 April, he 'found only some flour and tobacco lying about. The shed under which the men had slept in was standing but no particular evidence of any affray'. Smyth then 'fell in with some eight or ten blacks armed with spears and quite naked' who said they were 'on their way to the Murrumbidgee'. Smyth 'ordered them to lay down their spears', upon which 'one of them did so but the others remained in threatening attitude'. Smyth and his sole companion chose discretion over valour and proceeded to Colonel Henry White's station, where Smyth was able to take down statements from some of the survivors of Faithfull's party.

Here Smyth wrote a hasty note to Commandant Lonsdale. He was concerned that 'a large combined party of heavily armed men will reach here tonight, but they are well prepared. The settlers in this part are in great consternation and highly exasperated. I much fear that should they encounter the natives there will be great slaughter'.[7]

'Every man who attacked them was armed with guns and horse pistols'

Postman John Conway Bourke recalled some years later that around ten days after the Battle at Broken River, as he was carrying the mail from Port Phillip, he met the Murray River squatter Peter Snodgrass, who had arrived at Colonel White's run with a group of around twenty mounted and well-armed men. Bourke believed they were seeking vengeance for the attack on Faithfull's party. He recalled that 'Peter Snodgrass was at the Murray [and] he waited for others and wended his way towards the scene of those atrocities'.

When Bourke with his satchel of letters for Sydney arrived at the Ovens River, he said it was 'a sight to see and a number of people were collected there with long lances and sharp instruments'. Like a troop of light dragoons or lancer cavalry, these men were all 'armed with guns and horse pistols' as well as swords and, it seems, home-made lances. Many of the squatters such as Colonel White had military training or some experience of war. Peter Snodgrass came from a military family – his father Kenneth served in the Peninsular Campaign before settling in New South Wales (at one point serving as acting governor of the colony between Governor Bourke's departure and Gipps's arrival in early 1838, perhaps adding to Peter Snodgrass's apparently self-appointed role as leader).

When the armed party gathered at the Ovens River, one can just imagine White and Snodgrass giving hasty drill sessions to stockworkers in the technique of using a lance or a sword on horseback. Perhaps they conducted demonstrations galloping against a target. Edged weapons could save on ammunition. They were also back-up if a rider had no time to reload his firearms. It seems the group of faux-lancers were well prepared to shoot, then ride down and lance and slash warriors, reminiscent of a Napoleonic cavalry charge.[8]

Bourke noted that 'the weather had become very rainy and the blacks with their swags of plunder took to the King River hills of mountains'. In such weather, foot tracks were much easier to follow. Bourke, as postmen did, seems to have talked to everyone on his lonely route. His recollections ring true: 'when they approached the King River they plunged in at once and many of them never reached the opposite bank for they were shot dead'.

It seems Snodgrass's killing party had been ranging the countryside, found their tracks in the wet ground and managed to beat them to the river. According to Bourke, Snodgrass and his men 'galloped furiously towards them [Aboriginal people] ... [and] they crowded together for what they thought was protection and they got well riddled. Many of them jumped into the King River [and] very few escaped ... for every man who attacked them was armed with guns and horse pistols'. Snodgrass's massacre party 'dispatched several of them including Wellington and the ringleaders of the Faithfull slaughter'.

Bourke also noted that some of the Faithfulls' stockmen were with Snodgrass so 'it can easily be imagined they would not show much mercy to the savages'. According to the mailman, some people who escaped the slaughter sought shelter in a stockman's hut. Here Snodgrass apparently lectured the terrified people on what would happen if they did anything to harm white men or their stock ever again, saying 'they would be shot like dogs'.[9]

'That dreary road to the southward'

Somewhere during the attacks and while squatters were abandoning their runs, furiously riding between stations and gathering stockmen, and while the military and police were criss-crossing the area, the commissioner for Crown lands was conducting a tour. The wonderfully named Evelyn Pitfield Shirley Sturt, brother of the inland adventurer Charles Sturt, was camped by the Ovens River. Evelyn was born into a soldiering family, but after leaving Sandhurst Military College in 1836 he set out for adventures like his brother's in New South Wales. At just 20 years of age, the well-connected younger Sturt was instantly appointed a commissioner of Crown lands at Yass and was known as 'the boy commissioner'.

One of the survivors of the Battle at Broken River straggled into his camp near the Ovens River and alerted him to events. Commissioners were the highest form of authority in their areas. But there was no sign of Sturt in all this – no reports, nothing. Perhaps, as he later reflected, he just wanted to continue camping by the river. He later wrote to Lieutenant-Governor La Trobe:

> It has often been a source of regret to me that all the charms attending the traversing of a new country must give way to the

march of civilization ... I look back to those days as to some joyous scene of school-boy holidays.¹⁰

The news of the Broken River attack reached Yass on 23 April and was published in the *Sydney Monitor* on 27 April. The 'distressing intelligence' brought by the last Port Phillip post (via that hardy postman John Conway Bourke) was that 'a party of the Aborigines, in number about 300' had 'lately attacked Mr. Faithful's party—viz :—An overseer and eight men, who were in charge of 4000 sheep, three drays laden with property to a considerable amount, and several horses, &c'.

According to the wild first reports by the Yass correspondent for the *Sydney Monitor*, 'the over-seer and all the men were murdered, the drays plundered, (part of the load was two tons of flour) and a vast portion of the goods wantonly destroyed—the sheep, oxen, and horses are scattered through the bush, and it is not likely the whole of the sheep will be recovered'.

The Yass correspondent noted that all 'the settlers about this part are on the alert, and some few have started with the Police to endeavour to capture the blacks, and use every exertion to recover the property, and collect the sheep, cattle and horses belonging to Mr. Faithful'. He continued:

> Surely after this unprovoked outrage, Her Majesty's Government will now augment the Police force up here. There are but two constables to perform the duties of this very extensive district. A police station ought to be formed at the 'Murray'; it would be a protection to travellers passing to and from Port Phillip. At all events something must be done, as it is now pretty evident that the lives and property of Her Majesty's subjects are in imminent peril while journeying along that dreary road to the southward.[11]

Calls for protection along 'that dreary road to the southward' were in all the newspapers. As the *Sydney Monitor* wrote in May, 'as so many settlers are now travelling the Port Phillip Road, would it not be advisable to establish military stations along its line?'[12]

'Sheer terror of the blacks'

The Europeans almost always referred to the Waywurru and Taungurung people as 'The Ovens and Broken River tribes' or the 'Goulburn River blacks' or similar. Fed fearsome stories of the white deaths at Broken River only a year before, Dr Hobson, who travelled with Lady Jane Franklin through the area in 1839, described the 'Goulburn River' people as 'the most sanguinary and cruel of any natives in New Holland'. Hobson was also keen to note as a sign of their ferocity that 'they also move at night, which is a sign of their character, marking at once their superior courage'. Lady Jane Franklin also noted their skill:

> they twist round trees, hide & very slowly move, stand motionless like a stump. The district in which we were now entering between the Goulburn & Murray [rivers] is said to be most frequented by them.[13]

Not a great deal is known about the victorious warriors at Broken River. Europeans never recorded their stories, other than what the Protectors of Aborigines gleaned. Several men have been identified as involved: 'Wellington', 'Big Micky', 'Charlie' and Merriman. In 1841, Protector George Augustus Robinson was told by a Pallangan-middang man, Mul.lo.nin.ner (aka 'Joe'), who Robinson regarded as a most reliable informant, that 'Wool-gid-yer-dow-well [Wul-kidja-duwil] alias Big Micky killed Faithfull's men'.[14]

Wulkidjaduwil (Michie, Micky) and Merriman were also held responsible for killing a station hand near Wangaratta in mid-1842. This was one of a number of attacks and conflicts that occurred throughout the Ovens and Broken River valleys over several years after the Battle at Broken River, part of what Benalla local historian Hamish McPherson notes as 'a rising cycle of conflict across the expanding frontier in central and north east Victoria'. In September 1842, the *Port Phillip Patriot and Melbourne Advertiser* held that 'Old man Micky ... has been the ringleader in all the depredations committed on the whites in that quarter for several years back'.[15]

Megan Carter is the fourth great-granddaughter of 'King Brangy of the Ovens River'. Brangy (Brandy, Frank) was a contemporary of Merriman and brother-in-law of 'Big Micky'. Megan believes these men led the attack at Broken River because of both the disrespect and harm done to Aboriginal women and they despaired at the numbers of white people coming into their Country. When the first overlanders arrived, Merriman had ferried people across the river in his bark canoe. By 1838, Megan is clear they had 'made a decision to resist any more white men and their stock entering their Country'.[16]

For several hundred warriors to be involved there must have been an alliance of several groups across central and north-eastern Victoria. Megan also notes that 'Waveroo [Waywurru] and Taungurung men came together and all the kinship groups were uniting'.[17]

Such an all-out attack on an overlanding party could not have been made lightly. Kulin clans, like all Aboriginal groups, were governed by Elders making collective decisions. Each of the Kulin clans had one or two clan-heads or Ngurungaeta, who provided leadership and represented the clan in meetings with other groups.[18]

The overlanders and stockworkers well knew Aboriginal warriors could co-ordinate their attacks. As the *Sydney Monitor* reported in May 1838, 'an alarming outbreak' of attacks on the outstations of Port Phillip had seen 'hordes exceeding 300 in number, but coming from different directions ... evidently acting in concert'.[19]

Squatter Edward Curr was in northern Victoria in the early 1840s. He noted that there were designated messengers who were highly valued, carrying news from other tribes and helping arrange meetings and corroborees. Curr understood the 'Bangerang' in northern central Victoria to have their own version of the intrepid John Conway Bourke – what he called 'postmen':

> Like other tribes with which I have been acquainted, the Bangerang used to have messengers who went from one tribe to another to arrange the times and places of meetings and corroborees, and also to gather news. These men we used to

call postmen. They were personages of no little importance amongst the tribes, and welcomed accordingly ... [and] each blackfellow would make a point of hearing the news direct from the postman, never being satisfied with the relation at second hand.[20]

In 1839, Assistant Protector of Aborigines William Thomas noted that at the 'settlement' he was trying to establish in Boonwurrung and Woiwurrung Country in the area of the Mornington Peninsula, an Aboriginal messenger arrived 'with a report that all Blackfellows come to Melbourne which creates some excitement'. The next day, Thomas was 'much vexed', as almost all the people he had gathered together at his 'settlement' had up and left for Melbourne.[21]

Whether Bangerang, Taungurung and Waywurru 'postmen' had brought together several hundred warriors or not, the attack on the Faithfull party was certainly co-ordinated. It must also be seen as part of an effort to push the stock and stockmen out of Country – a push that had been building ever since 'Pioneer Piper' shot at a tree at Broken River.

'We dare not move ... without a gun'

By June 1838, not only had the Faithull overlanding party been decimated and a string of other raids and attacks in the area occurred, but many squatters were abandoning their runs 'due to the aborigines'. While he was investigating the attack at Broken River, Police Magistrate Richard Hardy received a letter 'addressed by Dr. Mackie [Mackay], late of Yass and now a Squatter outside the limits' regarding 'the circumstance of his being compelled to abandon his station on the Hume [Murray] River, from fear of attack by the Aborigines'.[22]

The Broken River attack sparked more raids. During 1838, right across northeast Victoria, the raids were forcing squatters to give up their stations. As a mounted policeman told Lady Jane Franklin when she passed through Broken River on her travels in 1839, George Faithfull was 'now at [his] 3rd station' since the attack and 'is going to shift again on account of the Blacks'.[23]

Rather than being targeted, George Faithfull believed he suffered most for no other reason than that he was one of the few who stuck it out against the counteroffensive in northeast Victoria at the time. He later wrote that 'the country was left to us for some years in consequence of the hostility of the blacks'. He recalled that he and his men 'were kept for some years in a perpetual state of alarm. We dare not move to supply our huts with wood and water without a gun'. Many of his men absconded and threw away their firearms. When they did this, 'in some cases destroying the locks and making them wholly useless', no doubt so warriors could not use the weapons against them. They did all of this, Faithfull said, 'from sheer terror of the blacks'.[24]

In 1838, squatters and their stockworkers across the region were under a state of siege. They soon resorted to inhumane tactics to defend what they saw as their property. Assistant Protector of Aborigines in the Western District (around present-day Geelong), Charles Wightman Sievwright, reported to Protector William Thomas on 'the awful state of society towards the Aborigines in the interior districts'. Sievwright, an ex-military Scotsman, annoyed many of his fellow Protectors and others. He was known for telling the truth about what was happening to Aboriginal people. Indeed, Sievwright later began what would become a lengthy series of investigations into massacres and was determined to seek prosecutions for mass murder – in one case of up to eighty people.

This made Sievwright, according to some, 'the most unpopular man that ever breathed' in the Colony of New South Wales. The authorities met his efforts with inaction. Even the two most senior men in the colony, Superintendent Charles La Trobe and Governor Sir George Gipps, detested him. On a tour of his western district in April 1839, Sievwright visited two stations where, as he said, he 'found the skulls of Aborigines placed over the doors of the huts as if to warn the lawful owners of the land at their peril to approach'.[25]

'Levy war against the blacks, or sanction the enrolment of a militia'

When in late April 1838 accounts of the Battle at Broken River landed on the desks of colonial authorities such as Colonial Secretary Edward Deas Thomson, it was significant news. This was the largest number of white deaths in one frontier conflict since the colony began in 1788. Rather than being a celebration of fifty years since the arrival of the British in Australia, 1838 was increasingly becoming a headache for Governor Gipps, the Legislative Council, the military and the police. Gipps was still trying to begin an investigation into accounts of a massacre at Waterloo Creek in north-west New South Wales by Major Nunn – who was now attempting to sort out what happened at Broken River. The investigation into Nunn at Waterloo Creek would have to wait.

When the news reached the Sydney press, all hell broke loose. The *Australian* said 'the tribes from Port Phillip to the Hume [Murray] have organised a regular system of plunder and outrage, and threaten to annihilate every white man in that portion of the colony'. The *Gazette* received a report from 'a gentleman who arrived overland from Port Phillip' that stressed 'the murder of so many of Mr. Faithful's men by the blacks on their route to Port Phillip has spread great consternation over the settlement, where it is looked on as amounting to an actual prohibition of all intercourse by land with the parent Colony'. At this point, Port Phillip and Sydney were cut off. The report the *Gazette* received from 'a gentleman' suggested the attack was 'a deliberately formed scheme, which had been in contemplation for some time previously'.[26]

All the newspapers were urging the government to establish a military presence. The *Gazette* urged: 'to protect the travellers by land to and from Port Phillip' as 'it has now become a matter of absolute necessity, that stockades, manned by an adequate military force, should be stationed at regular distances along the route' and 'until that is done there can be no safety for the traveller, and all communication by land must necessarily cease'.

The *Monitor* had a more sinister warning: 'should the different tribes again unite to attack the stations, they [colonists] will use their best exertions to shoot every black they meet in open warfare'. While the Sydney press were certainly animated, they were surprisingly well informed and clear about what should happen – 'tribes' were uniting, threatening, had cut the communications between Sydney and Melbourne and now should be met in 'open warfare'.[27]

'A punitive war against the blacks'

In June 1838, the squatters, pastoralists and their financiers – the people in the colony with huge investments and large sums of money but no formal political power – decided to push the governor along. They circulated a petition among themselves demanding 'coercive measures' against these 'hostile tribes' who had 'committed many murders and outrages' and were 'assembled in large numbers armed and attacking such persons who are most unprotected'. It was devastating to these petitioners that many of their fellow squatters had 'been obliged to abandon their stations leaving in some cases their flocks and herds at the mercy of hostile tribes'. What's more, travelling the Port Phillip Road had become a journey 'of imminent danger to life and property'.

The petitioners actually wanted the governor to declare war. And if he would not do so, they suggested the government create a militia force that could conduct the desired 'punitive war against the blacks'. They called on him to 'take such energetic and effectual steps as will for the present repress and for the future prevent the aggression of these hostile tribes, and protect the lives and properties of Her Majesty's subjects'.

These gentlemen in Port Phillip and others in Sydney were so concerned that some of them actually collared, or 'waited upon', Governor Gipps after a meeting to personally request that he should 'levy war against the Blacks'. And if he would not do that, then he should sanction 'the enrolment of a Militia for that purpose and allow them to be supplied with Arms and Munitions of War from Her Majesty's stores'. These concerned citizens were quite clear that this was now war, and that if the military could not be deployed, they could step in.[28]

The roll-call was impressive. Headed by two members of the

Executive Council itself, Sir John Jamison and John Blaxland, it included the names Donaldson, Dutton, Icely, Eales, Lethbridge, Bell, Walker, McFarlane, Hovell, Hume, and King. Eighty-two 'gentlemen', who grandly called themselves 'pioneers of civilisation', wanted total war – either via formal military intervention or a sanctioned militia. And they threatened that if 'adequate protection be not afforded by the Government', the settlers would not 'remain quietly looking on whilst their property is being destroyed and their Servants murdered'.

Gipps neither declared war nor established a militia. The governor was incensed by the petition and railed back at the eighty-two men that he would not 'give sanction to any measures of indiscriminate retaliation'. He reminded them it was his duty to 'treat the Aboriginal Natives as subjects of her Majesty' and that this had been made clear in 'late years, that the British Public has been awakened to a knowledge of what is owing these ignorant barbarians'. He directed their attention to the House of Commons report of 1834 and gave the warmongers a dressing-down they would not quickly forget. It was arguably Gipps's finest hour.

But the governor had one more sting in his tail, squarely aimed at the squatters' reliance on convict workers. In July, he wrote to Lord Glenelg about the:

> attack ... made on Mr. Faithfull's Convoy of sheep and Cattle on the 11th April last, in which seven of his men were killed, and all the rest dispersed. These men (who were chiefly convicts) did not defend themselves, but ran at the first appearance of their assailants, though, as there were 15 of them with fire arms in their hands, they ought to have beaten off any numbers however great of naked savages.

Gipps was quite clear – this was an attack by warriors against an armed party of cowards.[29]

Still, the governor could not ignore the situation. He informed the Legislative Council that a 'party of the Mounted Police with a Stipendiary Magistrate' had been sent 'to the spot, where eight white men were murdered'. He had given Commandant Lonsdale 'a discretionary power' to 'cause parties of infantry to advance, if necessary, into the interior'. Importantly, he also decided to establish 'Military Posts on the road' at places 'where the road crosses the following streams on the way, vizt., the Murray, the Ovens, the Violet Creek, and the Goulburn'. With that, the matter was over. In a final note of chastisement, Gipps told the petitioners, 'every wanderer in Search of pasture cannot be attended a military Force'.[30]

'For the protection of the immense tract of Country ... from Port Phillip ... to Moreton Bay'

Governor Gipps had served as an officer in the Peninsular Campaign during the Napoleonic Wars. He would have well understood the importance of the threat to, as he called it, 'the line of our communication with Port Phillip' that had by all accounts been cut off. 'Outrages', as he called them, had taken place 'over two or three hundred miles to the North of Sydney, others at more than 500 miles to the South, and some (at Geelong, the Western limit of Port Phillip) at still greater distance'. The entire 800-mile (around 1288 kilometres) long, overstretched and vulnerable frontier of the colony was under attack.[31]

Even the nascent colonial navy had been drawn into action over the threat. The need to obtain a 'Government Steam Vessel' for 'the purposes of maintaining the required Communication between the seat of Government and the out Stations' became a priority. The vessel was to be specifically constructed to 'give the greatest possible facility for the conveyance of Troops'.[32]

By July, the wheels of the colonial administration were moving into gear. The Assistant Military Secretary's Office had received the Colonial Secretary's letter of 29 June directing it to construct military garrisons. The office approved the locations to be 'well chosen for the general protection of the road from Yass to Port Philip [sic]'.

British infantry were at a premium in the ever-expanding colony. Someone soon realised that the highly mobile mounted police would be of much better service than the infantry Gipps suggested. At any rate, the mounted police were at this time soldiers on secondment from the British regiments garrisoned in the colony. In September 1838, Major James Nunn of the 80th Regiment and Commander of the Mounted Police was tasked with supervising the construction of the posts. Luckily for Nunn, his services were in demand. The investigation into his conduct at Waterloo Creek earlier in the year was now held over. Ever cost-cutting, the administration decided to build three rather than the initial five outposts – at the Murray, Broken and Goulburn Rivers (but not the Ovens River and Violet Creek). Still, this was to be the most significant military presence on the frontier prior to the gold rush period of the 1850s.[33]

'The Poor Blacks'

To allay the squatters' concerns even further, a new form of police force was to be established. It was specifically formed to operate in conflict zones where the squatters were taking lands beyond the limits of location. Rather than having mounted police ride out from Yass or Port Phillip several days after a battle or raid, a new 'Border Police' would be tasked with patrolling the frontier – perhaps unwittingly, but more aptly, called a border.

Gipps proposed the 'levying of a tax or assessment on Cattle depastured beyond the Boundaries to defray in part the expenses which must be incurred for the maintenance of the Police'. While 1 shilling for 'every head of horned cattle' and 6 shillings for every horse was, Gipps admitted, never going to cover the cost 'for the protection of the immense tract of Country extending from Port Phillip almost to Moreton Bay', he felt he could not ask for more tax than that.[34]

Gipps well knew the problem: 'It is too late to calculate the evils of dispersion in New South Wales. All the power of Government, aided even by a Military force ten times greater than that which is maintained in the Colony, would not suffice to bring back within the limits of our twenty counties the Flocks and Herd, which now stray hundreds of miles beyond them'. For Gipps, the only question was 'whether to abandon all control over these distant regions' or 'preserve order amongst all classes'. Abandoning them meant leaving the 'occupiers ... unrestrained in their lawless aggression upon each other and upon the Aborigines'.[35]

Gipps was not surprised that 'the Natives' would attack the overlanding parties driving sheep and cattle through their lands. He saw it as a manpower problem; the overlanders had 'a very insufficient number of people to guard them, often not more than the proportion of one man to several hundred sheep'. The governor realised that it was impossible to 'keep Military parties always in advance of persons who are migrating in search of pasturage' as the 'resources of Government would be quite insufficient'. As the opinionated letter writer JH Wedge was to inform Lord Glenelg in April 1839, 'if the whole Military and Police force were applied to prevent the aggressions of the Stockeepers on the one side, and the attacks of the Natives on the other, that it would fail in attaining that object'. Gipps noted in a report to Lord Glenelg that 'in the case of Port Phillip' squatters had gone beyond the 'former limits between three and four hundred miles in the last three years'. Gipps was clear: these overlanders and squatters ran a risk and it was a risk that government could – without more money – do very little about.[36]

Gipps likened the risk of grazing beyond the limits of location as driving 'their sheep into a Country infested with wolves'. He bemoaned that if only Aboriginal people were indeed wolves, then the government could 'encourage the shepherds to combine and destroy them'. But they were 'poor savage fellow creatures' and their voices were 'too feeble to be heard at such a distance' beyond the reach of government. Still, the colonial government, Gipps grandly pronounced, would 'raise, in the name of Justice and Humanity, a voice in favour' of them.

The governor had the humanitarians in London on his back. Lord Glenelg stressed to him that it was important 'to atone to that injured race for the wrongs which we have inflicted on them'. Now, there was to be a new system. Glenelg instructed Gipps that 'Protectors of Aborigines' would be established. And now the squatters would believe their government had completely deserted them in favour of the 'Poor Blacks', as the newspapers repeatedly and patronisingly headlined their articles.[37]

'Protectors of the Natives'

In 1838 Governor Gipps was juggling squatters' calls for all-out war and the condemnation of the colony's treatment of Aboriginal people by the British government. Gipps attempted to allay both. He outlined the establishment of a border police, which would operate 'for the purpose of putting a stop to the atrocities which have been committed both on them [Aboriginal people] and by them'. And with no sense of irony, it seems, he would turn commissioners of Crown lands into 'Protectors of Aborigines'.[38]

In March 1838, the governor had doggedly managed to gain Executive Council agreement on a public notice to ensure that colonists understood that Aboriginal people were British subjects and had the same rights under law as any other British person. By May, after some adjustments to wording reflecting the awkward situation of Aboriginal people's sovereign status and their 'belligerence' (which was not to be seen as if it was war by a foreign nation), he had the proclamation published. It commanded 'the Colonists', as the *Sydney Gazette* reported:

> to abstain from any hostile measures whatever against the aborigines; and especially not to use or threaten to use fire-arms; but to remember at all times that, the native population are under equal protection of the laws, and are to be regarded and treated, and are liable to the same punishment in all respects, as her Majesty's other subjects.

Following the directions of the select committee (via Lord Glenelg), Gipps also convinced the Executive Council to direct that commissioners of Crown lands take on additional duties as 'Protectors of the Natives' (soon changed to 'Aborigines' to avoid any confusion with 'native-born' whites). Apart from cultivating 'an amicable intercourse' with Aboriginal people and giving them 'occasional presents', the Protectors were to investigate and report on all cases of Aboriginal people 'being killed by any white person'. Colonists were also directed, whenever they witnessed an instance of 'an aborigine committing a fault or any act of impropriety, to report the circum-stance to the Protector of the Aborigines, in order that measures may be taken to prevent repetitions of such conduct, by an uniform system of punishment'.

But would it be heard in the distant stock runs and outstations? Gipps himself had little hope the proclamation would do anything to 'check the outrages [which are] of frequent occurrence beyond the boundaries of Location'. Even before the infamous Myall Creek Massacre of June 1838, Gipps knew that settler reprisals were widespread in the squatting runs across the frontier.[39]

In mid-1838 it seemed that the colonial authorities were making steps to defend the rights of Aboriginal people, as a colonised people. But at the last minute the proclamation didn't make it to official public notices. An advance copy was partially published on 1 May in the *Sydney Gazette*. Shortly after this, the governor felt it better to 'defer the publication of these Notices for a few weeks'. After the Battle at Broken River, and with reports of incidents 'both from the North and South', in a bizarre contradiction Gipps now thought it would 'exasperate the public mind against the Blacks' if he ordered 'an uniform system of punishment'.

In fact, the proclamation, and the investigation of Major Nunn at Waterloo Creek, would wait until after the border police had been established. Measures to enforce 'the just and humane treatment of the Aborigines of this country' beyond the 'Settled Limits' were deferred for nearly a year. The trial of the Myall Creek Massacre perpetrators in late 1838 turned the clamour into a crescendo. In one of the many tragic episodes of the period of the uprising, a colonial outrage over white deaths and stock losses forced Governor Gipps to set aside any idea of pursuing Aboriginal rights and equality before the law.[40]

CHAPTER TEN

'Come on you white buggers!'

'It was then that the destruction of the natives really did take place'

In 1838, the large number of white deaths at the 'Fight of the Broken River' generated such fear among stockworkers and such a threat to squatters' runs that what can only be described as a frenzy of armed violence began across north-eastern Victoria. In 1853, George Faithfull himself recalled that after a period of protracted raids and counter-raids in 1838, 'people formed themselves into bands ... and then it was that the destruction of the natives really did take place'. At the time, Scottish squatter Niel Black, who took 43 000 acres of land near Terang and called it Glenormiston, wrote in his journal in December 1839: 'the best way to procure a run is to go outside and take up a new run, provided the conscience of the party is sufficiently seared to enable him without remorse to slaughter natives left and right'.[1]

In 1838 the 'Goulburn River Tribe' had struck terror into the small and isolated white population in the region. Now the whites struck back. Between 1838 and 1841 the Taungurung and Ngurai Illum Wurrung were the focus of attacks led by Colonel White, George Faithfull and Peter Snodgrass. 'Colonel' Mundy attacked the Taungurung and Djadja Wurrung people, while squatters Ebden, Yaldwyn, Hutton and Munro hunted down various clan groups on the Coliban and Campaspe rivers.[2]

Samuel Faloon was an Irish convict who had been transported in 1833 and by 1838 was assigned to William Hutchinson and 'employed as Shepherd to one of his flocks near Mount Macedon'. Faloon later made a deposition about events in May that year. He said that on 19 May 'another shepherd named Thomas Jones was missing, his flock came home in the evening without him, the next morning the overseer Mr. Robert Bell went out with some men to look for him'. Faloon was

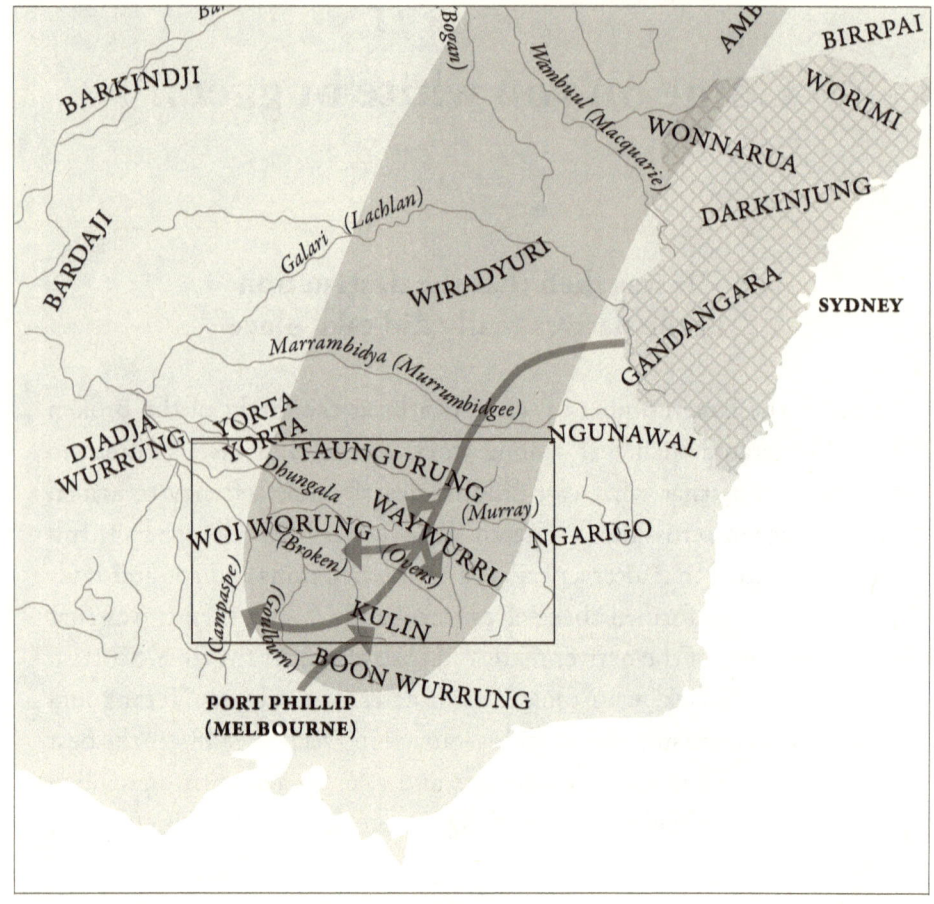

Northeast Victoria, late 1830s

with the party and 'about half a mile from the hut' they found Jones lying dead with 'two large spears sticking in his body, and his stomach cut open and the inside taken away'.

Faloon had 'no doubt but Jones was killed by the blacks', as they saw two men lurking about the station. He noted that 'the blacks have been very troublesome lately, the day before the murder was committed they took a flock away from one of the shepherds and when the flock was found the day following there were four sheep short, also on the same day several blacks came to one of the huts and took the bedding and a sheep which was left at the door for killing'. The sheep belonged to the adjoining station of William Yaldwyn.[3]

Disembowelment was known elsewhere as a message to those who would find the body. It could also be part of a process of gaining power over others. As Waywurru woman Megan Carter understands, this practice of evisceration 'was a specific act of absorbing the power of the person'. As Megan notes, it was often reported as disembowelment, but 'the actual act was the removal of caul fat around the kidneys, often whilst the victim was still alive'. Waywurru believed that this fat that 'held a person's vitality, strength and power. It was consumed and rubbed on the body as a way to absorb the victim's strength.' Importantly, Megan notes that 'by attacking a hut keeper or a shepherd in this way, the belief was that the sorcery transpired to those who occupied the squatting run in its entirety'. Such a practice, Megan suggests, undoubtedly added further reason for squatters to go on 'killing sprees such as on the Oxley Plains in the 18 months that followed Broken River'.[4]

After receiving Faloon's deposition about finding the dead and disembowelled body of Thomas Jones, the 'Chief Agent of Government', Commandant and Police Magistrate at Port Phillip Captain William Lonsdale wrote to the Colonial Secretary that 'Mr Bowman's overseer has reported to me that this unfortunate circumstance has caused much fear among his men'. Lonsdale's response was to send 'a party of the Mounted Police to shew themselves thereabouts for a short time in order to inspire confidence and to alarm the blacks'.[5]

In May and June 1838, attacks on stock and stations in the area continued. Indeed, Aboriginal people actually began telling the squatters to their faces that they were no longer welcome. A senior Djadja Wurrung man told one of the first pastoralists to move into the area, Charles Hutton, that the land and waters were his, and that Hutton should not remain there.[6]

The mounted police patrol sent to the area built a mud hut headquarters on the Campaspe River, in the midst of the wide expanse of the Campaspe Plains, where 'millions of murrnong' once were, but had now gone, eaten and trampled by sheep and cattle. However, the squatters and their stockmen had become well versed in setting out after Aboriginal people without the aid of mounted police or permission from any authority.

When some sheep were stolen from William Henry Yaldwyn's Barfold station on the Coliban River on the Campaspe Plains, Yaldwyn's overseer, John Coppock, 'assembled and armed three men' who were joined by 'four or five' of nearby station owner William Bowman's men. The party followed the sheep tracks and found a camp of around fifty Aboriginal people where, according to Protector of Aborigines George Augustus Robinson, they had actually corralled the sheep. Robinson, who visited the area later, was also told that when one man fired a shot, the warriors dared the whites to approach, shouting 'come on you white buggers or come on white fellows'.7

According to Coppock's later testimony, when the armed party reached the camp 'a shot was fired' and the Aboriginal men 'immediately manned their spears and gave another shout and instantly began throwing them at us. These spears dropped by us and passed and we were obliged to shelter ourselves behind trees'.

This was a defiant stand by a large group of warriors against eight or nine armed stockmen. A classic confrontation of bush warfare followed as both sides sheltered behind trees and attempted to spear or shoot anyone who broke their cover. Coppock recounted that they 'fired upon the blacks and there was a regular engagement for about three-quarters of an hour'. Assistant Protector of Aborigines Edward Parker was informed later that the men fired more than ninety rounds.

The warriors had stood their ground, but as night approached Coppock decided that it was time to force the engagement, and the party 'rushed up to the fires to take possession of the place'. But the warriors had left. Coppock said 'when we got to the fires the blacks had deserted them, but we saw them about one or two hundred yards off still in possession of the sheep'. Not only had the warriors held off the stockmen but they withdrew in good order and with the sheep still in their possession. Coppock recounted that 'it was at this time quite dark and we were afraid to make any further attempt to take the sheep. We therefore went home'.

But not before they discovered the effect of their firepower. Coppock noted that 'At the place where the blacks stood during the engagement we found seven or eight blacks dead'. If Coppock's testimony is to be believed, the warriors had continued to fight despite such a number – seven or eight out of fifty – being killed (and no doubt others wounded).

There are some suspicions around the limited account of the battle. Coppock and six stockmen returned to the camp the next day, and 'found the bodies of the blacks who had been killed had been put upon the fire and were partly consumed'. Unless Coppock's men had done this, it seems unlikely the warriors would have thrown their dead on the campfires. Were Coppock and his men attempting to cover up a massacre? As historian Bain Attwood notes, they had been 'less than candid in the accounts they gave of this incident'.[8]

However, from the information Robinson gathered after the event it is clear that the warriors were ready for a battle, and whether or not Coppock's men attacked first, hoping to destroy them, they made a stand. Robinson was told that at the back of a hut where Munro and a stockworker were attacked and defended themselves, 'is the place where Bowman and Yaldwin and Ebden's men shot the blacks down. This is since called Waterloo Plains and Flat'. Robinson's account was obtained from a 'Scotch immigrant', who was a 'shepherd at the time, in charge of a flock of sheep'. According to Robinson,

> [He] said when the men came up with the blacks, the blacks called to them to come on and they would fight them. There were, I believe, 16 white men all armed and for the most part mounted. They fired from their horses; the blacks were down in the hollow. They were out of distance of their spears. One old man kept supplying them with spears and was soon shot. Great many were shot. Some other blacks held up pieces of bark to keep off the balls but it was no use. Some were shot dead with their bark in their hands.[9]

It would seem the stockmen used their firearms' longer range, as well as the hillside vantage point, to effect. The testimony of the musket and spear engagement is believable and consistent. It might have been the case that such a battle took place and the victorious stockmen either carried out a massacre afterwards, or simply wanted to remove the evidence of the numbers of dead.

The Counteroffensive

Whatever the case, any subsequent massacre should not completely overshadow what certainly appears to have begun as a defiant, defensive stand by warriors against Coppock's men. Coppock's reminiscences still leave us in doubt. Many years later he told a journalist:

> He reasoned the matter thus – I have always endeavoured to treat the natives with justice; they have been a great annoyance, and have killed a large number of my sheep, wounded three men, and have now murdered two. I have applied to the Government for protection, and received as answer that I would have to protect myself; these things being so, I must protect myself, and will give them a proper lesson whilst I am about it.[10]

'The words I used were Stand – (bael jerrand)'

Between mid-1838 and 1839, conflict continued right across the squatted lands in present-day Victoria. In late May 1839, Commandant of Mounted Police George Brunswick Smyth had had enough. He ordered Sergeant Dennis Leary and a party of troopers to the station of another ex-military squatter, 'Captain' Charles Hutton, on Djadja Wurrung and Taungurung lands on the Campaspe Plains 'for the purpose of apprehending the natives who had been committing these murders and robberies'.

'Captain' Charles Hutton had taken land at Campaspe Plains in 1838, which he named with an Aboriginal word, 'Moorabbee', despite, as we shall see, detesting Aboriginal people. 'Captain' Hutton was in fact a lieutenant in the East India Company's armed forces. It is unclear if he was still on the pay books while trying his hand at squatting, but he was certainly yet another squatter with military training. He might well have 'pulled rank' on Sergeant Leary, as he seems to have taken the lead in what happened next.

Leary said in his deposition to Edward Stone Parker some six months later that 'on the fourth day after leaving Captain Hutton's, we fell in with the natives on some plains on the Campaspe Creek. The day before we came in sight of the natives. I told my men that if on our coming in with the natives, [if] they threw any spears, or showed any thing like fight, we were to fire on them'.[11]

The troopers saw smoke rising in the distance and quietly set up camp nearby. As Leary reported, 'the following morning we charged the camp where we saw the smoke of the natives' fires ... to apprehend them if possible'. Leary said the orders he gave the men 'before seeing the blacks were the standing orders of the mounted police'. Obviously, these orders had been worked into some form of translation for the Djadja Wurrung to understand. Leary said he 'called out to the blacks when we charged them to stand, telling them not to be frightened. The words I used were Stand – (bael jerrand)'.

Leary seemed to see no inconsistency in performing a cavalry charge toward a group of people while at the same time calling on them to stand. Let alone if they even understood his version of the Aboriginal words he called out. Trooper Edward Beach testified that he 'did not hear Sergeant Leary say to them Stand (bael jerrand)' as Leary 'was some distance from me'.

Beach believed the warriors attacked first, even though 'nothing was said to the blacks before they threw their spears'. Hutton's overseer James Cosby testified that 'I thought I saw a spear thrown, and called out "there is a spear". Shortly after I heard some shots fired. I cannot say how many were fired. I cannot say how long the firing continued whether five minutes or half an hour'. Whether in the heat of the cavalry charge the Djadja Wurrung even noticed or understood these attempts to ask the warriors to stand is one thing. Whether the attempt was paying lip service to an attack on a camp that was consistent with mounted police 'standing orders' is another.

Hutton and Cosgrove rode to the place where they saw the group of warriors and it seems at least one woman and a child – all accounts suggest there were between ten and twenty people in the camp. The two men then rode on, away from Leary and his troopers. When Leary's men, Leary said, 'got close to them, they shipped their spears, and threw several of them at the party'. Precisely who started the skirmish is difficult to say. It seems that Hutton made the first move, charging in at the warriors. Hutton recalled that:

On seeing them I galloped forward with the intention of preventing their escape down the creek. I passed them quickly and from the hasty glance I had at their fires I suppose the number of aborigines was under twenty. After I got ahead of them I heard some firing behind me. I still kept on for about three quarters of a mile. I stayed there a short time, and then returned to the party. The firing had ceased. I saw the dead body of one of the natives on the bank of the creek. One of the policemen told me that six of the aborigines had been killed.[12]

A cavalry charge upon the Djadja Wurrung camp could only offer limited options – fight, flee or attempt to cover a retreat in the face of an overwhelming force. It seems the Djadja Wurrung chose the latter option. Leary said he personally saw two spears thrown but then 'they made off into the creek, and while they were running the party fired on them'. Leary believed 'five or six of them were killed'. Leary suggested the five mounted police under his command merely fired one round and the 'firing did not occupy more than a minute or two'. Trooper Edward Beach, however, said he 'fired three or four times' with his carbine and thought the firing continued 'for about five minutes'. The remaining warriors escaped and Leary's party 'saw no more of them' despite continuing 'in pursuit for two or three days longer'.[13]

Leary was not aware where Hutton, or 'Cosgrove, one of Captain Hutton's people' were at the time, but met Cosgrove when 'we came to the spot where the bodies lay'. Cosgrove said he 'joined Mr. Hutton who was on the other side of the creek. We shortly afterwards joined the party of police. I think I saw one dead body of a black'. Leary said he 'did not see more than fifteen blacks on the spot' and 'they were men' and he 'could distinguish no women or children'. Whereas Hutton said he saw 'one woman and child swimming from the creek'. Leary 'saw no sheep or remains of sheep at the spot where we saw the blacks' and failed to 'examine the bodies, but left them in and about the creek' in order to continue the pursuit.[14]

There was a deal of inconsistency in these accounts. Trooper Edward Beach didn't recall seeing any warriors shot, though he did note that as soon as spears were thrown, 'the party extended itself', or spread out into an extended line. Beach said, 'The blacks ran off at the time we fired. I saw no blacks fall. I cannot say whether any were killed. I saw no dead bodies'.[15]

When Protector of Aborigines Robinson was informed of the deaths, he pointed out that there was no proof these people were the 'guilty party' who had killed the stockmen and sheep. Hutton said he 'believe[d] the party of aboriginals on which the policemen fired to be the same party that attacked my station and murdered my men; as I found them on the same creek and near the spot where I had recovered the sheep. I had no other means of identifying them'.[16]

The statements by Hutton, Cosgrove, Leary and Beach were made six months after the event. These men were also now well aware that white men could indeed be hanged for killing black men. But still, it seemed quite reasonable to these men to kill Aboriginal people who might (or might not) have killed sheep, and who failed to hold up their hands in surrender when being charged by cavalry. The Protector of Aborigines George Augustus Robinson wrote in January 1840:

> Hutton avowed his [tactic] to be terror; to keep the natives in subjection by fear, and to punish them wholesale, that is, by tribes or communities. If a member of a tribe offend, destroy the whole. He believed they must be exterminated. This in his opinion was the best ... Mr Hutton said the [Murray] blacks will never be any good until they are scared as the Murrumbidgee blacks were; three parts killed.[17]

'White man no good'

Across Djadja Wurrung and Taungurung Country in 1839, Aboriginal people were taking dozens of sheep from their flocks and roasting them on fires. In July, when a flock of 600 sheep went missing, the now ubiquitous 'armed party' of stockmen found a group of people roasting several sheep, but they escaped into the bush. Assistant Protector Thomas investigated and reported to Protector Robinson that 'the men at the various stations seem bent on revenge' and that they had said to him that 'the first black that appears near any of the stations where outrages have been committed will have no mercy'.[18]

Despite this bravado, Lands Commissioner Henry Bingham believed the stockmen's 'evidence of <u>fear</u> and <u>alarm</u> displayed itself to the Blacks' and it was this fear that was encouraging the attacks (not any other reason such as food or defence of Country). There certainly was fear among the outstations. Protector Robinson saw it first hand. When he was at Munro's station interrogating the 'Scotch immigrant and shepherd' about what happened at 'Waterloo Plains', he noted how the man was 'frightened, he said, of the blacks'.

At other stations in early 1840, warriors took sheep and scattered them. Groups of Taungurung were reported turning up at various stations asking to be given sheep. When they were refused, according to several stockworkers, they said 'white man no good'. No wonder then at places such as 'Five Mile Station' they rushed the sheep, taking some and scattering the rest.[19]

'They had from 20 to 30 guns and muskets'

Since 1835, traders in Port Phillip, according to Protector Robinson, had been giving Kulin people firearms to shoot possums for their skins and lyrebirds for their tail feathers, which fetched a high price in London. By 1839, Protector Robinson was railing against how many firearms were in Aboriginal hands and being used against both blacks and whites. Indeed, Robinson was outraged when he heard that some squatters had given people guns to clear out an annoying local tribe, no doubt a traditional enemy.

In August 1839, a government notice was issued 'forbidding the use of firearms by natives'. It had little effect. In January 1840 at Yering, opposite Yarra Glen, the Port Phillip Commissioner of Crown Lands Henry Fyshe Gisborne, with a detachment of border police, fought a gun battle with a group of warriors armed with firearms. It seems no one was killed but Gisborne could not follow them up as they fired back at his men and the warriors retired in good order.

In May, the squatter Armyne Bolden wrote to Commandant La Trobe that he had 200–300 people from the 'Port Phillip and Goulburn tribes' encamped on his run. 'The blacks threatened to burn the huts and drive them [stockmen] away.' They also had 'from twenty to thirty guns and muskets'.

Bolden only saw twelve of the firearms. He counted 'eight single-barrel guns, percussion locks and quite new' as well as 'three old flint and steel guns and one musket'. By the 1830s, the percussion cap firearm was rapidly overtaking the older flintlock as a more reliable and quicker to reload weapon. In the small-scale skirmishes and guerilla warfare of the period, this was a well-armed force.[20]

In May 1840, a group of Aboriginal people turned up at Dr Mackay's Whorouly station and 'proffered their services to cut bark', which Commissioner Bingham noted was 'a sign of peace'. However, Mackay told them 'that none was wanted, and to be off'. According to Bingham's report on the subsequent attack, when they still 'came unarmed to the Huts Mr. Mackay and a second person prematurely rushed after them with arms in their hands in order to frighten them away'. They 'tried to gain their Camp before the natives, but failed in doing so, but when they did come up, broke their spears and took some of them away'. It seems they also killed some of the warriors' dogs. According to Bingham, 'this roused all the proud feeling of the savage ... for no greater insult can be offered them, than that [breaking spears] and killing their hunting Dogs'. Bingham continued that then 'commenced the scene of retaliation'.[21]

On 27 May, around twenty warriors launched an assault on Mackay's station. The renowned warrior Merriman apparently led the warband. These warriors also had firearms. One of the workers at Whorouly was Benjamin Read. Ever since the Battle at Broken River, trouble seemed to follow Read. Robinson noted that Read 'had several collisions with the natives and it [was] feared many have been of a fatal character to the Aborigines ... and there [was] reason to suppose that he was a cause, if not the principal one, why they attacked'. Whether the attack was solely aimed at Read or not, Merriman was also intent on destroying the entire station. As Mackay reported, 'they murdered one of my servants, burned my huts and stores and all my wheat ... Four horses each worth £100 were killed, and only seven head of cattle out of nearly three thousand were left alive on the run'.[22]

These were the sorts of victories that could end a squatter's occupation of Aboriginal land. Mackay was a broken man. Despite recovering the majority of his cattle, as he later wrote, 'one hundred and eighty head exclusive of those found dead were totally lost. The rest were recovered, at such expense of money and personal energy, as have left me an invalid for life, and to this day comparatively a poor man'.[23]

The destruction of Whorouly was a threat to squatters right across the region. And the warriors had firearms. Megan Carter believes the attack at 'Whorouly' was 'the catalyst to band together and destroy Aboriginal people'. It certainly sparked a massive response that was reminiscent of a pogrom more than a police action.[24]

'White Man take away Black Fellows country, now gun'

As we have seen, the squatter David Henry Wilsone complained vehemently in letters to his brother in Scotland about the Aboriginal Protectorate system. He believed the squatters had to take matters into their own hands. In September 1839, he wrote home that 'we will have a regular fight with the natives as they are becoming very troublesome & bold'. After warriors stole 'five fine ewe lambs', Wilsone gave all his workers firearms and 'advised to shoot any one they see attempt it again'. He believed that 'soon a regular affair will settle the business and clear our part of the country of these regular cannibals'.[25]

Wilsone could not be much clearer – the squatters 'have all united to defend to the utmost our properties & woe betide the blasted race when they are caught injuring us'. In May 1840, he wrote: 'The Blacks have been very annoying to us, having attacked our stations 2 times within the last 6 weeks & succeeded in carrying away guns, pistols, clothing, bedding, & provisions. Our people gave them chase, but they succeeded in getting away'. Wilsone believed that squatters had been 'left totally unprotected' even though they 'paid so dearly' (a levy on their leases) to have mounted police. He railed against the 'most expensive, pernicious and useless system of protectorates'.[26]

Meanwhile, some Aboriginal people believed firearms were some recompense for the loss of Country and the increasing difficulty in hunting kangaroos. In April 1840, constables were sent to collect firearms from people under the 'protection' of Protector William Thomas in a camp just outside Melbourne. John Batman had given firearms to some of the Boonwurrung from Mornington Peninsula even before the settlement was established, and they still carried them five years later. Thomas noted that the women regularly obtained powder and shot from the settlers.

The distinction between the use of firearms in hunting and in raiding settlers was lost on Commandant Lonsdale. All firearms in Aboriginal hands were to be taken. Thomas recorded the group of Boonwurrung with him had seven firearms. They objected strongly to handing in their guns:

> Their cry was what for White Man Guns? – Big one hungry – Black Fellows by and by – no kangaroo – White Man take away Black Fellows country, now gun. By and by all dead poor Black fellows.[27]

'Goaded with bayonets' and 'cut with the sabre'

In late 1839, Governor Gipps succumbed to the persistent lobbying. He ordered a number of squatters, including the distraught and now vengeful Mackay at 'Whorouly', be made magistrates. Now, a number of squatter-magistrates across the region had the power to appoint anyone they liked as a 'Special Constable'. They could also give orders to any mounted police in the area. Magistrate Mackay jumped at the opportunity. He quickly swore in other squatters as constables. These men now had official sanction to hunt down the so-called 'culprits' of the 'Whorouly' raid.[28]

Major Samuel Lettsom of the mounted police was sent to deal with attacks against squatters on the Ovens River. He was even ordered to take hostages if the actual attackers could not be found. When he couldn't find any Aboriginal people at all to apprehend at the Ovens, Lettsom returned south to Melbourne. He had been informed two of the 'troublemakers' – Merriman and a man known as 'Harlequin' – were headed there.[29]

For the Wurundjeri-willam, of the Wurundjeri balug – a large Woiwurrung clan – Merri Creek was an important meeting place and living site. Ceremonies and large gatherings were held there. The creek wanders through the present-day suburbs of Coburg, Brunswick East and Clifton Hill before it spreads into a river flat junction with the Yarra, now known as Yarra Bend Park. It had long been a gathering place for the Kulin.

Since the British appeared in their lands, Merri Creek had become a useful semi-permanent camp near the Melbourne township for many Kulin groups. But Superintendent of the Port Phillip District Charles La Trobe had plans for the Merri Creek flats. He thought it was a good site for a prison or a lunatic asylum. In the late 1830s he reserved the land and had been trying to move this unsightly camp from the outskirts of the growing township, but with no success. Even the Protectors of Aborigines could not budge them.[30]

Major Lettsom had heard that the 'Melbourne Blacks' and the 'Goulburn River tribe' were meeting at Merri Creek. He decided to raid the Merri Creek camp, where the 'ringleaders' must surely be. But there were now several hundred Kulin at the camp. Despite Protector Thomas warning him that if he took hostages, 'the colony might become a scene of carnage', Lettsom cobbled together all the police and military he could muster in Melbourne.[31]

According to a newspaper report, 'the whole of the Mounted and Border Police and the military stationed in Melbourne, amounting in all to twenty eight, were marched to the camp'. Along with them were 'Lieutenant Russell of the Mounted Police, and Captain Smith and Mr Vignolles of the 28th [Regiment], and Mr Powlett the Commissioner of Crown Lands'. Despite the entire military of Melbourne only consisting of around thirty soldiers and police, this was a powerful force at the time. According to the *Herald*, 'the display of a little of the "pomp and circumstances of glorious war"', would surely 'instil a little salutary dread, into the minds of the sable sons of the forest'.

In the first raid on the camp, the military drove a group of men, women and children across the river before they apparently scrambled up trees to safety. In the second raid on 10 October, La Trobe suggested to Lettsom that he 'overawe' the large group. Lettsom's force rode in at 6.30 am, carbines at the ready, galloping into the camp so that Protector Thomas said 'the earth shook under them'. Protector Robinson noted that '3 tribes, Boonerong, Waverong and Tar.doon.gerong' were there. All of them were arrested and marched to gaol at gun and bayonet point and held in custody overnight. Winberri (Tinbury), one of the senior men who attempted to intervene and raised a waddy threatening one of the officers, was shot down and killed.[32]

The event, so close to the township of Melbourne, was witnessed by many. A report in the *Sydney Herald* noted that:

> The captives were brought into town about 7 o clock in the morning, the more ferocious of the Goulburn blacks, hand-cuffed and chained together; they were all put into a yard adjoining the wooden building used as an hospital, and during the course of the morning, such as were suspected of being concerned in the murders were picked out and lodged in the jail; the Melbourne blacks were allowed to go at large about one o'clock, but the Goulburn tribe are still detained in custody awaiting the arrival of witnesses from the Goulburn [River].[33]

An eyewitness, 'Mr Wilkinson', recounted to Chief Protector George Robinson that slower-moving members of the group 'were goaded with bayonets by the soldiers and hit with the butt end of their muskets or cut with the sabre of the mounted police' and that he was 'shocked at the cruelty of the military and police'. At the police stockade, Robinson stated that, 'Thirty-five men and boys were chained, two by two, and separated from the rest. Their wives and children and mothers were there and witnessed a harsh and heart-rending scene'. Like Protector Sievwright, Robinson's pleas for proper justice were like words in the wind. He called the raid and capture an 'illegal proceeding'.[34]

While most people were subsequently freed, thirty Kulin were detained for more than a month. Apparently seventeen of the twenty-one on Lettsom's wanted list were among them. Lettsom had found his 'ringleaders' and La Trobe had seemingly finally cleared Melbourne of an annoying Kulin camp.

In the aftermath of the attack, Governor Gipps signalled a change to the operation of the Protectorate of Aborigines. In early 1841, Gipps noted that rather than have Protectors following Aboriginal people around, the Protectorate would establish permanent stations, which he hoped would become 'places of refuge to the natives'. Colonial policies of restricting Aboriginal people into reserves had begun.[35]

'Drive the white fellows from their country'

Despite, or perhaps because of Lettsom's raid, in 1840, threats to expel or kill all the white men continued. In September, Assistant Protector Edward Parker wrote in his journal 'I have been plainly told that the natives would, "bye and by", take to the mountains and try to drive the white fellows from their country'. So too, Robinson had heard this threat earlier that year.

And it was not only through warfare that they would conduct the fight. Assistant Protector Parker had met around thirty mostly Taungurung prisoners in the police stockade after the Lettsom raid. They asked him whether they were to be shot. After attempting to allay their fears, Parker was told that the Taungurung had threatened that a sorcerer or clever man was going to call up the Myndie or giant snake, to bring about a pestilence that would wreak destruction on all the whites in Port Phillip.[36]

Before people could take to the mountains or call up a pestilence, squatters and their stockmen went to work. One station owner, Robert

Pohlman, complained in April 1841 that because squatters lacked protection by police or military, they understood that they needed to conduct their own defence against resistance:

> in advancing beyond the bounds of location, we estranged ourselves voluntarily from the protection of government and took upon ourselves a state of responsibility as well as risk.

Pohlman was clear that it was up to the squatters to provide for their own 'defence'. What was less clear was whether this meant it was fine to shoot Aboriginal people who took sheep.[37]

These tactics of extermination continued across what is now Victoria through the 1840s. After heading north, the squatters branched out to the west and east. In the western districts of the present-day Port Fairy to Portland region, a strong fightback began around 1841. Often called the 'Eumeralla War', Gunditjmara people's resistance took the form of widespread attacks on stations and stock, to which squatters typically responded with a now well-learned response of retaliatory raids and massacres. The conflict continued until it was quashed around 1847.[38]

In the mid-1840s, to the east in Gippsland, lay the great region of the Gunaikurnai people that had not been occupied by squatters. But here, Angus McMillan and the infamous 'Highland Brigade' operated with impunity – and a secrecy so great that it took decades before the true extent of killings became known. Even by 1846 it had not ended. In that year squatter Henry Merrick wrote in a letter to relatives that in Gippsland 'men, women and children are shot wherever they can be met with'.[39]

It is difficult to get a clear picture of the murky operations of armed parties of squatters and stockmen in the 1840s. Some were obvious liars, trying to cover up what they knew were crimes. Others were full of such bravado and honesty in public about what they had done that it beggars belief that they were not held to account. Perhaps it is best left to one of the men who was at the start and finish of the rise and fall of the warriors of northeast Victoria – George Faithfull – to describe his own fall, and rise.

The Counteroffensive

By mid-1838 George Faithfull had sorted out his losses from the Battle at Broken River and returned to northeast Victoria, occupying land around Oxley. In 1853, as the warfare and any potential crimes were fading in memory, he could write candidly about how he took this land:

> The country was left to us [by other squatters] for some years in consequence of the hostility of the blacks, which became so unbearable that I could not keep shepherds, although well-armed, without employing a horseman, in addition to myself, to keep continually perambulating the woods lest the natives might cut them off. During my employment in this way my cattle were destroyed in numbers within the short distance of only six miles from my hut. I once found fourteen head of slaughtered cattle in one pond of water. They had been driven in by the natives ... Thus I and my men were kept for years in a perpetual state of alarm. We dared not move to supply our huts with food and water without a gun, and many of my men absconded from my service ...

Faithfull never denied that Aboriginal people put up a fight. Perhaps historians have been too quick of late to see the occupation of present-day Victoria (and elsewhere) as simply a string of bloody massacres. We might well be suspicious of later tales designed to cover up massacres by turning them into battles. But not all of them. Faithfull continued:

> At last, it so happened that I was the means of putting an end to this warfare. Riding with two of my stockmen one day quietly along the banks of the river ... we were at once met by some hundreds of painted warriors with the most dreadful yells I have ever heard ... The natives rushed on us like furies, with shouts and savage yells; it was no time for delay. I ordered my men to take deliberate aim, and to fire only with certainty of the destruction to the individual aimed at ... I fired my double barrel right and left, and two of the most forward fell ... I had time to reload and the war thus begun continued from ten o'clock in the morning until four in the afternoon. We were slow to fire which prolonged the

battle, and 60 rounds were fired, and I trust and believe that many of the bravest of the savage warriors bit the dust. It was remarkable that the children, and many of the women likewise, had so little fear that they boldly ran forward, even under our horses' legs, picked up the spears, and carried them back to the warrior men.

Faithfull is quite clear that it was only after such fierce resistance as this that the massacres began:

People formed themselves into bands of alliance and allegiance to each other, and it was then that the destruction of the natives really took place.[40]

CHAPTER ELEVEN
'It now became evident that they must be conquered'

'The unchristian system of colonisation'

When the Moreton Bay district around present-day Brisbane formally opened to free settlement in 1842, the duties of the military detachment rapidly expanded from policing a remote outpost into the frontline of a frontier war. In July 1842, 'A Squatter' from Moreton Bay wrote to the *Sydney Morning Herald* that 'the state of the district with respect to the aborigines appears now to have arrived at such a crisis that the necessity of some means being immediately adopted to suppress outrage on their part, and unwarranted retributions on the part of the settlers, is obvious'. The writer suggested that as the pastoralists 'injure the aborigines by occupying their country, we are in justice bound to make them an equivalent in some sort'. For this squatter, the answer was 'an extended system of missionary instruction' – this, along with 'a constabulary force', would remove 'the present evil'. While he could not understand why in 'many instances' attacks on the squatters and their stock were 'unprovoked', he certainly did not think that the occupation should cease, but rather that providing missionaries to instruct Aboriginal people would be a valid recompense for taking their lands.[1]

There were in fact some – albeit few and far between – calls to actually halt the occupation of more land. In August 1842, the editor of the *Australasian Chronicle*, William Augustine Duncan, wrote that 'some check must one day be put to the expansion of the system'. Duncan was an outspoken Catholic and critic of squatters' growing power and influence in the colony. He urged that discussion then occurring in the Legislative Council of New South Wales over an amendment to the Squatting Act should actually consider the 'rights of aborigines'.

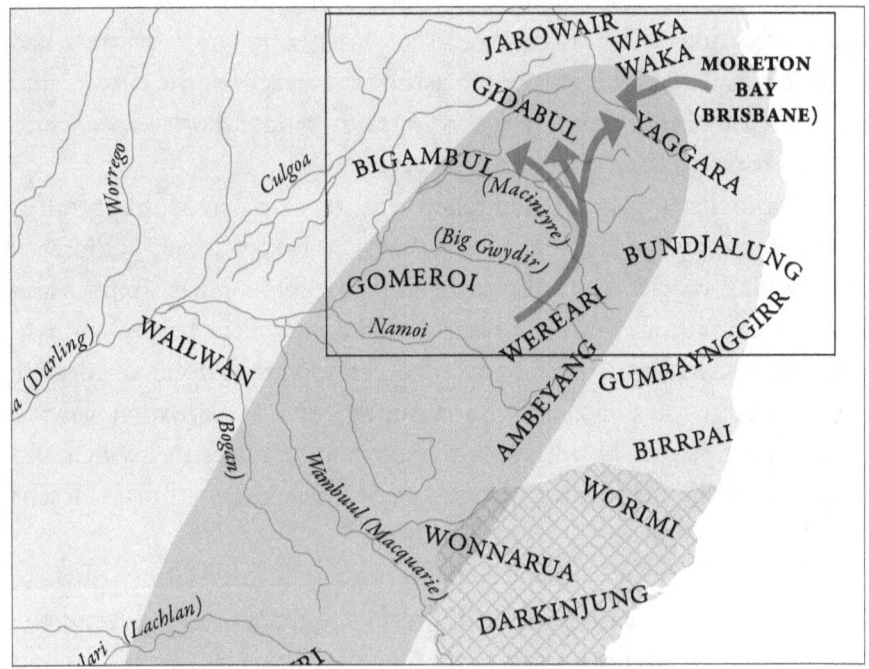

Southeast Queensland, late 1830s and early 1840s

Duncan might not have had much faith in the council's deliberations, as he also noted that one of the Legislative Council members had recently 'recommended the revival of the system which prevailed forty years ago, of marching a regiment of infantry against those unfortunate beings when they disturbed the settlers'. Perhaps Duncan was more concerned with the influence of squatters than Aboriginal rights (he even saw squatters as potentially establishing a rebellious independent state of their own), but he was very much a lone voice on what he called this 'horror at the unchristian system of colonisation which we have adopted'.[2]

Multuggerah's victory at the Battle of Meewah had struck such fear in the Moreton Bay and Darling Downs districts that a massive mobilisation of both militia and military forces began. In late September 1843, the 'Squatter's Friend' wrote to the *Sydney Morning Herald* that 'the [Lands] Commissioner and Lieutenant Johnston had proceeded with the military and the few mounted police of the district, to the scene of action'. He also reported that 'a large body of squatters had collected to defend their property against the attacks of the natives' and concluded by calling on Governor Gipps to 'render more assistance to the unprotected condition of the squatter'.[3]

Before they set out on their failed venture to destroy Multuggerah at Meewah, the vigilante party had sent a message for police help before they left the Half-way Inn in the Lockyer Valley. Commissioner Simpson and his police finally arrived – presumably the day after the battle – only to find the road had again been barricaded. Simpson then decided – despite having a large force of squatters and police – that the situation was too dangerous. Instead, he withdrew to gather more forces in Ipswich and Brisbane, while the squatters fanned out to various parts of the Downs and Lockyer to gather forces of their own.

After calls from 'the squatters and others in the vicinity of these out rages' and a meeting of their 'brother squatters' from beyond the Lockyer Valley, Simpson wrote to the Colonial Secretary that he believed it was his duty 'to afford protection to persons & property crossing the Range'. However, he thought he was 'unable to do anything effectively with [his] small Police Force'. In September, Simpson reported he and the three border police he could muster had been fifteen days constantly 'in the bush'. Simpson decided to return to Moreton Bay and gather a detachment of soldiers and 'returned with an Officer & twelve men to Helidon the nearest Station to the foot of the Range'. Here he left the soldiers 'with directions to afford every protection in their power'.[4]

'An Officer and twelve men' was a substantial detachment of the garrison at Moreton Bay. Simpson had also gathered three bush constables. Lieutenant Patrick Johnston marched his detachment to Helidon and by 19 September, Simpson now had a small army at his disposal – three border police, two land commissioners, three bush constables (including Bracewell, the escaped convict, who had lived with Aboriginal people and was now working with Simpson as an interpreter), a lieutenant and twelve soldiers – along with a 'strong body of settlers, and their servants, armed'. This was possibly over one hundred armed men in total. In open battle it would certainly need ten times that number of warriors to defeat them.[5]

But Multuggerah had no plans for open warfare. So the squatters set out after him. Under what authority is unclear, but Simpson, even if he wanted to rein them in, could have done little. It certainly seems Simpson allowed what he rather casually called 'inconvenient' bands of around thirty men to search for (and attempt to destroy) Multuggerah and his warriors, while he desperately called for military reinforcements. He wrote in early October to the Colonial Secretary:

> From the great number of the Mountain Tribes, extending nearly all round the District, & the uncertainty of their movement, I consider it highly advisable that a military Post should be permanently established at the foot of the Range, as their mere presence will, I have no doubt prevent further Aggressions on the high road & render the inconvenient assemblage of large bodies of Squatters in forays against the Aborigines unnecessary.[6]

It seems Simpson thought the 'forays' were indeed necessary. In effect, he was sanctioning an armed militia force, even if he did not give the order.

Colonial newspapers were generally the mouthpiece of one or other side of politics or they used conflict on the frontier for political purposes. In rare moments, they published letters from the frontier as news. In November, the editor of the *Maitland Mercury and Hunter River General Advertiser* newspaper was shown 'a private letter from Moreton Bay to a person in Maitland' dated 8 October. The letter writer said the 'aborigines are very troublesome in that neighbourhood; he had had two narrow escapes himself; he was once badly speared in the hip, and about two inches of the spear broke in the wound'. After 'robbing the drays and driving off flocks of sheep', Multuggerah's warriors were on the offensive and according to the letter writer, 'pillaging the shepherds has become an almost every day occurrence'.

The letter writer expressed the determination of the squatters or 'gentlemen' in pursuing the raiders: 'A short time back a party, consisting of about thirty gentlemen, went in pursuit of the blacks, taking with them a week's rations. They became so much fatigued before they could overtake them that they were obliged to stop for two days, and send for a further supply of rations'. They then started again, and the writer, with obvious first-hand knowledge of what happened, said, 'we were more successful in falling in with the blacks the second walk, but I do not wish to say too much on that subject'.

Rather than admonish the letter writer for his secrecy about the 'success' in 'falling in with the blacks' on the 'second walk', the newspaper editor thought this was sufficient news to 'shew the dreadful state in which this part of the country must be in'.[7]

In general, across the frontier, the horse was a key element in pursuing Aboriginal people. Here, in the thick Rosewood scrub, horses were dispensed with. As Campbell recalled:

> It now became evident that they must be conquered, or there really would be no more rations go to Darling Downs; so it was resolved to follow them up until they gave in. The horses were accordingly sent back, and some twenty men started on foot to follow the blacks, which they did persistently, giving them no time to procure their food and pouncing upon [them] by night or by day, in camp or in trees, when trying to procure food. The white men had this advantage that they could carry their own rations.[8]

As the *Sydney Morning Herald* reported on 12 October,

> the two Commissioners of Crown Lands, were ... immediately at the scene of outrage, and were speedily joined by Lieutenant Johnstone, with ten rank and file of Her Majesty's 99th regiment—these, with the Mounted Police force, and a strong body of settlers, and their servants armed, were immediately led out to scour the scrub, which in that part of the country is very dense.

The *Herald* correspondent was 'happy to say' that the 'hitherto inaccessible strong hold, the Rosewood Scrub, was penetrated, their camp stormed, and nearly the whole of the lost property recovered. An immense number of tomahawks, waddies, spears, and other offensive weapons were also taken, and as a matter of course brought away'.

The reporter was more circumspect about the extent of casualties. It was thought 'some of the ringleaders, amongst the rest the notorious Jackey Jackey, Peter, and other aborigines, who were concerned in the murder of Mr. Moore's child, at Lime-stone, have, I believe, fallen victims to the vengeance of the white man'.[9]

In another rare moment of Australian Wars history, a participant appears to have sketched one of the armed parties. Thomas John Domville Taylor, a young gentleman with some capital and in search of pastoral lands, arrived in Sydney in 1839 and after travelling south, headed for the newly opened Darling Downs. By 1842, Taylor had established himself with Dr John Rolland on a pastoral lease bordering the Condamine River known as the 'Broadwater', but which Rolland and Taylor renamed 'Tummaville' by 1843.

'Tummaville' was in the homelands of the Giabal, Gambuwal, Bigambul, and Jarowair people, many of whom joined the great alliance of tribes across south-east Queensland at this time. Taylor was known to have joined two armed conflicts – one in 1842 and another in 1844 – and it seems he also became part of the great army of squatters in 1843. Taylor's competent pencil drawings attempted to capture a range of vignettes of life as a squatter. Unsurprisingly, frontier conflict is prominent in Taylor's drawings. One image, *Party in search of Australian Aboriginal, Darling Downs*, either shows one of the bush 'commando units' of around thirty squatters and stockmen with one man in Border Police uniform in 1843, or at another point possibly in 1844. Long arms, pistols and swords abound.[10]

By late October, Simpson believed the situation was under better control. He wrote to the Colonial Secretary requesting approval of 'two Aborigines, Toby & Jemmy Fains being taken into the service', undoubtedly valuable trackers and informants. Simpson also requested that his 'establishment' be permanently increased to 'six mounted Troopers'. He was able to relate the increase to the expansion of the colony quite simply – the 'income derived from the Crown Lands in the Moreton Bay District being quite equal to meet the increased expenditure'. More squatters taking up leases on Crown Land meant more colonial revenue, which could fund more mounted police.[11]

Writing long after the Battle of Meewah, James 'Tinker' Campbell – not regarded by all as a reliable storyteller – was certainly proud that, as he said, 'now, in my old age, [I] have reason to thank God that I have never pulled a trigger upon a blackfellow'. As Campbell recalled, 'at the end of three weeks the blacks sent in a message to say that they would fight no more, but make peace now—they had had "plenty fight"'. It seems the work of the police, military, mounted parties of 'gentlemen' operating in the open and the 'infantry' of armed stockmen, well provisioned with rations, roaming through the dense bush where the warriors undoubtedly thought they could retreat in safety, had taken its toll. While Multuggerah's campaign had been thwarted and a kind of temporary peace established, the longer fight was far from over.[12]

'Establish a military fort'

The victory at the Battle of Meewah posed such a threat of cutting off the Darling Downs from Moreton Bay that drays or bullock trains crossing the Main Range were for a time provided with an armed escort. As the *Herald* reported, 'to prevent a recurrence of such robberies in future, it has been deemed advisable to station half a dozen soldiers at the Rocky Waterhole, at the foot of the Main Range, to escort such drays as may arrive at that part of the road over the mountains every Monday'. From late 1843 to 1846, a detachment of at first six, then twelve, soldiers of the 99th Regiment were posted to the Lockyer Valley. The detachment built a stockade named Fort Helidon at 'the Rocky Waterhole'. It seems the soldiers were active in their defence of the road across the range, conducting sorties from their fort against warriors.

Certainly, in August 1844, Simpson wrote to the Colonial Secretary that it was important not to remove the garrison of soldiers. He reported that:

'It now became evident that they must be conquered'

> The Aborigines have been very troublesome to the North of this District – commencing with Messrs. Graham & Ivory's Station, the most distant at the head of the western branch of the Brisbane, where they killed a Shepherd, they successively rushed every Station on that branch of the River, spearing & carrying off a considerable number of Sheep & Cattle – since the last fortnight they have taken up a position in the Rosewood Scrub & robbed several drays on the high road about 15 miles from Limestone – by means of patrols the Road has however been again cleared of them – they are I believe the same tribes who were recently so troublesome under the Dividing Range.

The attacks continued into 1844, Simpson noting that in the Lockyer Valley and 'the vicinity of the great Rosewood Scrub, they have been extremely troublesome, repeatedly attacking & dispersing the cattle of Mr. Wingate during the Winter'.[13]

The importance of holding the thin line of communication and transporting dray loads of wool between the Darling Downs hinterland and the port at Moreton Bay was underscored by the fact that soldiers sent to Moreton Bay from 1843 were diverted from the Māori Wars in New Zealand. Across most of the colony, military postings were either reduced or withdrawn and sent to New Zealand. However, the military presence in southern Queensland doubled in size.[14]

The concerns of the authorities at Moreton Bay were not just over Aboriginal victories such as at Meewah. The constant harassment of squatters meant many simply up and left their runs. In the early 1840s, squatter Jacob Lowe arrived in the Macintyre River area and as he later (1861) told a Queensland Legislative Assembly inquiry, in the early 1840s, many squatters had been 'all driven away by force from their stations'. When Lowe arrived in the district, he said he was 'only taking up runs from the settlers [who] had been driven by the natives, and which had been abandoned'. He also believed that when his cattle were speared in great numbers, it was done in order 'to drive us away out of the district'. Lowe was quite clear that the killing of cattle was a defence of Country.[15]

The Counteroffensive

In 1844, settlers were complaining 'that 26 white people had been killed in the Moreton Bay district without any enquiry by the Govt'. Thirteen had been killed in the Darling Downs from 1842 to 1844. Such raids and attacks on men and cattle that led to the abandonment of stations was common right throughout the push into Aboriginal lands in Queensland over the next few decades. In the late 1840s to 1853, the Badtjala and Gabbi Gabbi fiercely resisted the Europeans. But more and more squatters kept coming, sometimes taking up runs that had been abandoned two or three times before.[16]

It was a difficult task to attack the squatters and stockmen as they were a highly militarised set of men. In the 1840s, nearly every single man outside the townships in southern Queensland was part of some kind of military system, or came from one. The role of the military stationed at Moreton Bay transformed from largely guarding convicts and capturing escapees to being seconded to the mounted police or being posted to guard against Aboriginal attacks and make sorties against them, almost always in combination with armed stockmen who would be their guides. The stockmen not only added extra auxiliary firepower, but they gained first-hand knowledge of how the military conducted operations. The military presence itself was wider than just a detachment stationed in a fort or garrison. Officers became local magistrates and some became squatters.[17]

The squatters and their stockmen had developed an informal militia system. One recollection of the 1840s around northern New South Wales and southern Queensland outlined how this operated:

> Whenever the blacks committed any murder or killed any cattle, there was word passed around along from station to station, and the stockmen would collect at some appointed place, and follow up the tracks of the miscreants until they came up with them, and then the blacks were killed without mercy ... they came upon them in their camp ... and at daylight the next morning they opened fire, and killed every one they could get a shot at, whether man, woman or child. They let none escape.[18]

'It now became evident that they must be conquered'

A well-known phrase 'word had passed around' was a call to stockmen to muster – not that a horse had escaped as in the famous bush ballad 'The Man from Snowy River', but that cattle or sheep had been killed or stolen and stockmen were to gather and track Aboriginal people down and kill them.

The military stationed at Moreton Bay between 1843 and 1848, the 99th and 58th regiments, seem to have followed the squatters' lead in making reprisals against Aboriginal people as if it was in a time of complete war. While there is little information about their campaigns, the detachments went out in support of the armed squatters and stockmen. John James Knight, himself an early colonist at Moreton Bay, wrote one of the first histories of the colony in 1892. He talked to many people who had lived through the events of the 1840s. Knight noted that 'this period of military supervision was one of terrible slaughter, scores upon scores of the aborigines falling victims to the white man's gun'.

Like the many, many instances of armed reprisal and massacre across Australia, the documentation of these events was minimal or non-existent. While it is possible to reconstruct the number of white casualties (thirty-seven dead and at least forty-seven wounded) between 1840 and 1843, it is impossible to tally Aboriginal casualties. As Knight wrote in the *Brisbane Courier*, 'one of the men who assisted in putting many of the unfortunate blacks out of existence told the writer several incidents which if repeated here would scarcely be regarded as pleasant reading, nor yet redound to the credit of persons even now living'.[19]

Knight had spoken to an 'old resident' who said that

> the theft of a few stores or the killing of a few sheep by the blacks was avenged by wholesale shooting down by the whites – in fact as many blacks as could be found, whether offenders or not were swept away. This got so bad at last that for shame's sake a number of whites were arrested ... in the vicinity of Tent Hill, but on being brought before a magistrate – a squatter whose name he gave and who is now alive – their denial was regarded as sufficient to disprove the charges preferred against them.[20]

When Multuggerah sent a message suing for peace after the campaign in the Rosewood scrub, Campbell recalled that 'the white men heartily agreed, and so, in that direction, the war between the races ended'. Campbell saw it as a war, his contemporaries saw it as a war, and there can be little doubt Multuggerah and his warriors also believed they had been at war.

While Multuggerah led further raids, there was nothing on the scale of the planned campaign on the ranges with a prepared base in the Rosewood Scrub. The correspondent to the *Sydney Morning Herald* in October 1843 believed in the Lockyer Valley at least, the resistance could not continue:

> I am inclined to think the lesson now taught them, will banish them from that particular part of the country for some time to come at the same time it behoves all squatters and others throughout the entire district to be on their guard, as, although beaten in this particular instance, they are too numerous to be for ever intimidated.

In the broader region of southeast Queensland, Aboriginal people were indeed 'too numerous to be for ever intimidated'. Multuggerah's campaign was part of what has been called a 'Black War', which a major alliance of Aboriginal groups across southern Queensland conducted, and which was highly effective, impeding the conquest of the region. Warfare was to rage across the area for years to come. As historian Maurice French notes, 'the conflict was not over; it had merely shifted arenas'.[21]

EPILOGUE
'The blacks interfere with the profits of grazing'

'The advance posts of an army were not better kept'

The great uprising of 1838 to 1844 was a highpoint of resistance to the colonisers. It reached a peak around 1840. Yet conflict did not end there. Battles and skirmishes continued as squatters pushed further and further along riverways. In fact, during the 1840s, resistance warfare intensified in what is now southern Queensland. This called for drastic action. The policy that had worked so well across the British empire of recruiting Indigenous men to fight their own people was tried and tested in the Port Phillip region. The Native Mounted Police were deployed in Queensland from the 1860s with terrible consequences.[1]

Other alliances were formed. Far to the southwest, on the edge of present-day South Australia, the Maraura (Marrawarra) War broke out in 1839 as overlanders brought thousands of sheep across to Adelaide. After a series of Maraura victories that threatened the overland route, a strong armed party from Adelaide hunted down the Maraura at Rufus River in 1841, and killed many. The Maraura were known to have gathered around 500 warriors – the *Southern Australian* reported that 'all young men from everywhere' received messages 'to congregate on Rufus River' and fight the colonists.[2]

In far western New South Wales conflict continued during the mid-1840s. Indeed by 1845, the Baaka-Darling River was a landscape of ruined fortunes, a war zone. Major Thomas Mitchell wrote that when he travelled the area in December that year, he saw 'humiliating proof that the white man had given way'. This was 'visible in the remains of dairies burnt down, stockyards in ruins, untrodden roads'. At the lowest station on the Bogan River, Mitchell wrote:

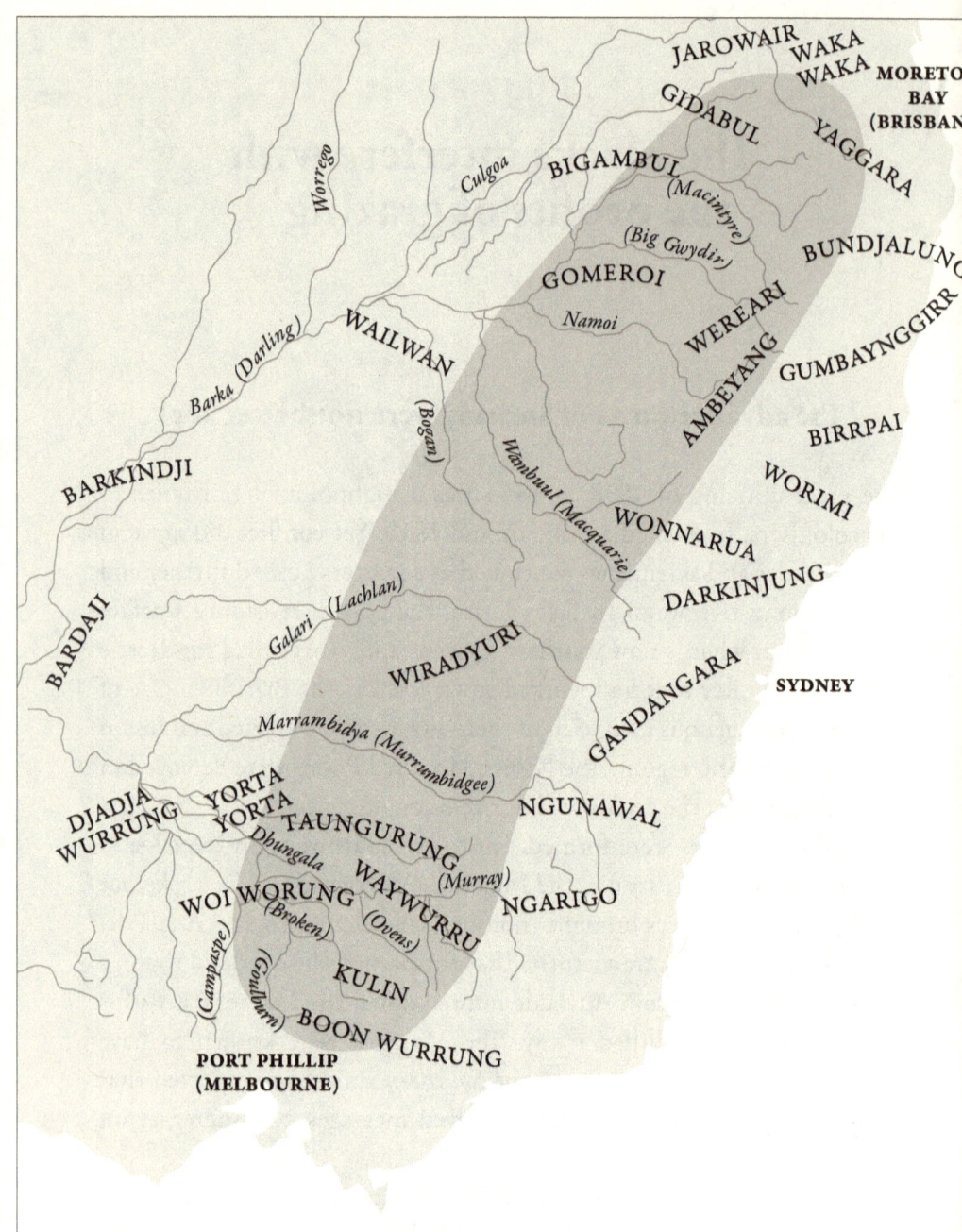

The Uprising, 1838 to 1844

The approximate main areas of conflict between colonists and Aboriginal people between 1838 and 1844. Not all First Nations and groups in southeast Australia are highlighted, only the main groups mentioned in the book. The maps are representational and intended to provide an overview of locations and Country.

Epilogue

The line of demarcation between the squatter and the savage had once been much lower down, at Muda and even at Nyingan, but the incursions of the blacks had rendered these lower stations untenable.

Mitchell was clear that this was more than just a drought-scape. He noted how the 'incursions of the savage, who is learning to "bide his time" on the Darling, are greatly encouraged by the hardships of the colonists when water is scarce'. Indeed, 'several stations have already been abandoned in consequence of the outrages of the aborigines of the Darling and Lachlan'. Mitchell thought that 'stone ovens' normally used for cooking kangaroo were now cooking 'about twenty head of cattle a day'.

Mitchell believed that 'half a million of acres, covered with the finest grass, have been abandoned'. He was very clear it was due to the 'Bogan Blacks'; 'the savages smile at the want of generalship by which they have been allowed to burn the white man's dairy station and stockyards on the banks of the Bogan'. Mitchell believed a police station or a township formed at the remains of his stockade 'Fort Bourke' would settle the issue.

Warriors along the lower Bogan River had taken back an immense tract of Country. They now did not have to build log barricades to stop cattle muddying the waterholes and making them undrinkable, as Mitchell had observed further upstream. When Mitchell's party arrived in what he called 'the neutral ground between savage and squatter' he was looking for clean water, 'unsoiled by cattle'. He thought the 'advance posts of an army' were 'not better kept'. While the Peninsular War veteran might have wanted to gild the lily somewhat about the dangers he faced, he was clear this was still some sort of war zone, and the devastation of this frontline was proof, with burnt-out buildings littering the landscape.[3]

This kind of 'no man's land' that Mitchell passed through in December 1845 was the result of unabated defiance and staunch resistance. In August that year, newspapers reported that 'the blacks' had 'assembled in considerable numbers, on the lower part of the Macquarie

River, plundering stations and destroying property', robbing 'six stations, and speared one man, a hutkeeper'. According to the newspaper report, 'the Commissioner of Crown Lands, accompanied by Sergeant Anderson, Corporal Lamborn, and four troopers of the mounted police, immediately started in quest of these marauders'. The police came upon them at a place called 'Bibbergibbery, beyond Mount Harris'. Sergeant Anderson apparently had an 'interpreter' with him and he ordered the warriors to lay down their weapons. They paid no attention to the order 'but immediately commenced an attack on the police, wounding Corporal Lamborn in the head'. The order to fire was given, and 'ten of the blacks were shot, and the rest dispersed'.

The mounted police were on a roll. They soon received information that 'the blacks were again mustering in great numbers at Narramine [Narromine], headed by the Bogan chief "Hughy" or "Joey", a very powerful and resolute fellow'. The police came upon them, and, as before, ordered them to lay down their weapons. Yet again, these warriors refused, upon which 'the order to fire was given, and the Bogan Chief was shot, as was another black named Davy. This chief received no less than seven balls in various parts of his body before he fell'.[4]

Money and fear

This 'immense tract of Country' from what is now Melbourne to Brisbane was one of the greatest frontiers of a colony in modern history. Between 1838 and the early 1840s, the following groups of Aboriginal people went to war with the colonists in New South Wales: the Gomeroi and Wiradyuri in the southern and northwestern inland, the Bigambul, Werearai and Ambēyang in northern New South Wales; the Barkindji, Bardaji, Murrawari, Nyemba and Nyirrpa in the west; the Kulin confederacy, Taungurung and Ngurai Illum Wurrung, Waywurru, Woiwurrung, Boonerong, Djadja Wurrung, Yorta Yorta and Gunaikurnai among others in present-day Victoria; the Ningy Ningy, Yaggara, Yuggarapul, Yugambeh, Geynyon, Gnarabal, Gidhabal (Giabal), Turrbal, Nunukul, Barrungam, Jarowair, Jinaburra, Wooganbarah,

Epilogue

Dallambarah, Coccombraral, Giggabarah, Quandamooka, Kabi Kabi, Jarowair and Western Wakka Wakka in southern and central Queensland; the Birrpai, Worimi, Darkinyung and Wonnarua in the central and lower to mid-north coast; the Bundjalung on the north coast, and many others.[5]

From 1838 to the early 1840s these people made a defiant stand against the push into their lands in the huge arc from Port Phillip to Moreton Bay. It was a moment where warriors could target the squatters and their men and stock at their weakest – as overlanding parties, as bullock trains on isolated roads, as often poorly armed stockmen constructing their bark shelters after having just staked out a new run, or deep in the bush out with sheep and cattle grazing on unfenced lands. It was an opportunity to counterattack before more and more men and sheep poured through the breaches made along the riverways and mountain passes of inland New South Wales. And it was a chance to communicate and co-ordinate these attacks.

There were two important tactics that underpinned the uprisings of 1838 to 1844. The first was to attack the squatters' money: bleeding them dry through the loss of hundreds, sometimes thousands of pounds' worth of stock that halted many in their tracks. Some up and left, ruined. As we have seen, Europeans could understand Aboriginal people killing sheep and cattle to eat. But the 'wanton destruction' of stock and property was less comprehensible.[6]

It was certainly aimed at pushing the whites out. As we have seen, many squatters were forced to move elsewhere, hoping to find less aggressive locals. Historians have recycled the reasons of drought and over-investment in the squatting boom for its period of bust in the early 1840s. A detailed study of the economic impact of frontier warfare awaits.[7]

The other major common tactic in The Uprising was fear. This age-old method of spreading terror forced convict shepherds to cower in their huts, swim rivers and flee for their lives, refuse to work for their overseers, destroy their firearms, or simply go insane in the bush. As Uncle Wayne Fossey notes, the 'fire people' of the Condamine Valley were renowned for generating 'fear through fire'.[8]

Both tactics worked perhaps too well. They also panicked squatters into buying more guns, building defences and shooting on sight. Squatter Edward Curr once met a wounded Aboriginal man who had approached a hut and been shot. When he confronted the man who shot him, 'Jack the soldier', as he was known, Jack replied that 'as many of them as comes here when I am alone I will shoot'.[9]

'A comparatively weak and contemptible force'

By 1838, from the Broken to the Bogan to the Big River, warriors had significant successes in halting the massive push of sheep and cattle into their lands. They worked with bushrangers, had experience clashing with mounted police, conducted numerous raids on isolated stations, killed, culled and collected sheep and cattle, and gathered and used firearms. The time was then ripe for a massive counteroffensive – attacks designed to drive the stockmen out and to exact revenge for their crimes.

1838 was a decisive year in the struggle between pastoralists, squatters and stockworkers and Aboriginal people right across the eastern Murray-Darling Basin. And it was not because of an internal colonial debate about justice over the Myall Creek Massacre in June of that year. It was because retaliation by warriors intensified at this time. It was an explosion of resistance aimed at the heart of the pastoral enterprise: stockworkers and their sheep and cattle.

Importantly, the counteroffensive was unified by where it occurred – River Country, from Broken River, the Murrumbidgee, the Bogan, Namoi and Macintyre as well as in Big River Country. It occurred across the vast edge of what is now called the Murray-Darling Basin, the edge of where pastoralism was having the greatest impact. The Uprising must be seen as a defence of this River Country.

In 1975, historian Malcolm Prentis declared that Aboriginal resistance in Australia 'was not in any way organised, except on a very local basis'. Twenty years later, military historians in the *Oxford Companion to Australian Military History* agreed. They stressed the 'egalitarian, non-cohesive nature of Indigenous society prevented inter-tribal alliances and associated military strategies'. Until recently, this narrative dominated the story of the Australian Wars.[10]

The idea of Aboriginal military weakness has a long history. Take for example this observation from the editor of the *Perth Gazette* in 1837, quite bizarrely written just after a serious period of conflict around York in Western Australia:

> The accounts we receive from Graham's Town of the disturbed state of the country in South Africa, from the incursions of the Caffres, afford us the means of congratulation, that we are surrounded [in Western Australia] by a comparatively weak and contemptible force. Our natives have never been found a barrier to the occupation of the country, neither have they united in a body for the purpose of plunder. Their aggressions have been a succession of petty and treacherous outrages.[11]

And if we jump forward to 1966, the *Australian Dictionary of Biography* entry for Governor Gipps noted that during 'an atmosphere of force and fear' on the frontier under Gipps's reign, 'the Aborigines did not combine, and most of the incidents were small in size'. As we have seen, the warfare that the beleaguered governor had to contend with both 'in the north and the south' in 1838 was far from insignificant – he was in fact being harassed to declare war, arm stockmen and squatters as a militia, build a border police force and establish a string of military outposts.[12]

Another long-standing idea about the Australian Wars has been that Aboriginal warriors could not adapt traditional warfare (which was inherently less violent than colonial war) to war against the colonisers. This is far from the truth. As we have seen, warriors built barricades, herded cattle for mobile food supplies, stockpiled weapons and used firearms. As historian Ray Kerkhove has outlined in his remarkable work *How They Fought – Indigenous tactics and weaponry of Australia's Frontier Wars*, warriors were in fact highly adaptive to new technologies and circumstances, when these were useful.[13]

In 1838, a colonial surveyor, bushman, pastoralist and speculator,

John Holder Wedge, wrote to the Colonial Office in London. Wedge believed in the late 1830s there was a 'general and simultaneous movement of hostility' across the frontier. But back in London in 1839 after many arduous years of surveying, travelling, fighting bushrangers and assisting John Batman's land grab in Victoria, he had changed his tune. Wedge now thought that it was a scenario of 'occasional attacks either upon, or by the distant Stock keepers' that was 'acted upon by the impulse of passion, the hope of plunder, or from motives of revenge'.

In the same batch of letters to Lord John Russell, Wedge was pressing his claims for compensation for his services to the colony. It appears his initial thoughts did not quite fit a picture of the successful relations with Aboriginal people he claimed he was largely responsible for at Port Phillip. The erasure of the true history of the Australian Wars had well and truly begun.

Many others over the years repeated that passion, plunder and revenge were the motivations for warfare. These wars from north to south were, in hindsight especially, a case of 'a succession of petty and treacherous outrages' rather than sustained resistance. All this worked to portray a quiet colonisation – one where there was little serious resistance to white people's land claims.[14]

But ask Uncle James Ingram, or Uncle Bill Allen Jnr or Uncle Wayne Fossey or Uncle Paul Spearim if warriors could communicate and combine over vast distances, and the answer is a very different one. Not only did they combine but they gathered for hundreds of kilometres, following songline routes and kinship obligations, calling gatherings to decide how to fight back, where to fight back and who and what to target. Uncle Bill notes how stories and knowledge travelled a long way along the rivers, but also across mountains from the inland plains to the coast.[15]

Scratch below the surface of the dominant narrative of Aboriginal military weakness and read some of the keener white observers of The Uprising such as squatters Edmund Curr, James Demarr or John Henderson, and they describe combination, coordination, planning and supply.

It has been difficult for Australians to grasp The Australian Wars as military history. The wars were unique in the British military conquest of

Indigenous lands across the globe. They were rarely the stand-up battles that Britons read about in their broadsheets of Napoleonic victories, or the short, sharp bloody confrontations of South Africa or New Zealand. Those sorts of conflicts were easier for the British to understand – and to deal with. They were more like the warfare they were used to – standing in line and firing at each other or holding fortifications to the last man.[16]

The Australian Wars were arguably *more* of a threat to the colonial enterprise *precisely because* they were small-scale guerrilla war campaigns. It was far more challenging for the British Army to fight such warfare – indeed it was forced to adapt to this warfare during the 19th century by introducing 'light infantry' and skirmish formations.

The end result of this challenge by Australia's warriors to Britain was that British settlers not only jumped to their own defence, but were encouraged to do so because the colony of New South Wales was so overstretched. Squatters with guns and horses and stockmen who feared for their lives put down The Uprising of 1838 to 1844. The British Army had very little to do with it.

'Warfare there will be wherever a new country is found, and new stations formed'

In 1851 John Henderson reflected on his experiences as a squatter in the 1840s. He observed that 'warfare there will be wherever a new country is found, and new stations formed. This is to be expected, and cannot be prevented'. Henderson had experience on the ground. When his workers were attacked, he decided to place himself 'in a better posture of defence ... in case of another attack'. He gave his assigned convict workers some of his stock of firearms and 'cut loop holes in all sides of [his] hut, as well as one on each side of the door, so as to command it, and give a cross fire in front of it'. Henderson was, like many of the educated overseers and squatters at the time, well schooled in the military history of the British empire. They knew how to apply this knowledge to the small-scale warfare they had become swept up in.[17]

The gradual decline in The Uprising during the 1840s was due to the absolute militarisation of the squatters and their men. They had become expert bushmen and knew they needed horses, dogs and guns when working in the bush. Rather than compete for runs, they made alliances to concentrate their firepower. They also made their stations and runs into defensive locations. By the early 1840s, squatters and stockworkers knew the score. They had well and truly become the foot soldiers of the wars for the occupation of Aboriginal lands.

It was also a particularly Australian war in that it unfolded according to Australian terrain. It was fought along the riverways, in the reedy swamps and billabongs, and across the rocky high tops. Rarely was it fought on the plains. The plains were a death trap for Aboriginal people once the horse had become almost symbiotic with any white person in the bush. Despite all the warriors' advantages of terrain knowledge, if a mounted force caught them in the open, they stood little chance.

The colonists knew that Aboriginal people would fight back and not give up their lands easily. As Wedge put it to Lord Glenelg in April 1839:

> The act of taking possession of their Country, unless ample provision be made for them, cannot be looked upon with indifference by the Aborigines when they begin to feel the consequence of being dispossessed of the haunts, which have hitherto afforded them the means of subsistence. Their only alternative will be either to try to maintain their own possessions by committing depredations on the flocks, and not unfrequently I fear by the murder of the shepherds, or to fall back and encroach up on the hunting grounds of the adjoining Tribes.

Wedge believed it was 'Our duty and our interest to compensate them'. Despite such laudable sentiments, Wedge was still a coloniser. He was certain that 'food and raiment to minister to their wants, to teach them domestic and useful habits, and to instil into their minds Religious precepts' was the right approach.[18]

But to what extent was The Uprising co-ordinated and communicated? Was it more a case of Aboriginal people resisting the squatting invasion as it affected them simultaneously? Historian Jacqui Durrant agrees that 'chains of neighbouring groups could communicate effectively over quite a distance'. In Victoria, 'Kulin people in Melbourne and beyond knew well what was going on in Northeast Victoria and the Snowy Mountains; and perhaps as far as coastal Yuin lands [far south coast New South Wales]'. However, Durrant reminds us that it would be difficult to suggest that 'a warrior in Melbourne ever knew about what was going on in Queensland'.[19]

It might be difficult, but not impossible. Of course there would never be a pan-Aboriginal alliance across the country. But news certainly travelled far and wide. There are many accounts of performed stories of battles that were relayed extensively. The story of the 1884 stand by around 1000 Kalkadoon warriors against a force of 200 Native Mounted Police and armed civilians at Battle Mountain formed part of ceremonies for years later across northern Queensland.[20]

There were other examples of alliances. In southeast Queensland, warriors followed their long-held tradition of travelling hundreds of kilometres for bunya feasts and ceremonies. They used the same alliances when they gathered to attack the whites. Across inland New South Wales and northeastern Victoria, it was the same story.

Aboriginal groups communicated information among themselves in ways that colonists generally failed to comprehend. In 1844, the explorer Ludwig Leichhardt described what he called a 'pantomime' or a performance. Leichhardt was at Baroon during a bunya gathering. Even though it was by then a year after the Kilcoy massacre where, as we have seen, people were poisoned by arsenic, he saw 'several powerful main figures ... among the warriors', each painted red, who 'found fault' with 'those who join the whites' – those who worked on squatting stations. According to Leichhardt, the 'pantomime' played out with a warrior reproaching the men who no longer hunt kangaroos or catch possums, and who 'don't take part in [traditional] battles'. In the performance, a man stepped up and said: 'I do not live in the dwelling of the whites; the whites are angry with me. I have no pipe, no tobacco, no hatchet. I live in the bush'. This call to reject white society was played out in a performance that could travel across language boundaries.[21]

Along the Bogan River far to the south, in 1845 Major Thomas Mitchell noted a similar divide: 'These latter savages naturally regard those who are half civilised ... as we should look on [as] deserters to the enemy'.[22]

What Leichhardt called 'pantomimes' were in fact intricate performances of stories, knowledge, news and politics. It seems that some could be 'calls to action'. In April 1835, a 'Grand Corrobory' (Corroboree) was reported in detail in the *Colonist* newspaper. It was held on the banks of the Nepean River, probably at Emu Plains, as the newspaper report noted the Blue Mountains 'rose in primeval grandeur immediately behind the encampment'. The gathering was an important one. The *Colonist* reported that it was 'on a scale of extent and magnificence never before witnessed in the colony' with people 'in attendance from all parts of the territory'.

The entire performance was undoubtedly addressing its white audience. Various characters and scenes critiqued the invasion and colonisation of Aboriginal lands. According to the *Colonist*, 'Yellamundy ... from the Hawkesbury ... was in the character of a native mourner, his body being pipe-clayed all over'. He appeared to be 'mourning for the loss of his hunting grounds, and the independence of his nation – the unfortunate but unavoidable consequence of European colonization'. Yellamundy pointedly said that 'White fellow sit down all about; black fellow murry [very] miserable!'

'Jibbinwy' was also from 'the Hawkesbury' and 'was in the character of a native warrior; his face, limbs, arms, and breast being ornamented with streaks of red paint' and his 'military evolutions' reminded the reporter of 'a European [military] review'. This performance obviously referred to the warriors' resistance to the colonists that had occurred across Sydney, Bathurst and the Hunter Valley by 1835.

The next performance was from 'Terribalong, from Broken Bay', who was 'in the character of a colonial Barrister'. In an ironic scene that showed incredible insight into the centre of colonial authority now ruling Aboriginal lives, the reporter noted:

His gown was a cloak of bandicoot skins, and his bushy hair was tied up tastefully with native grass, in imitation of a wig. In the whole corrobory there was no character better sustained than this; for Terribalong's powers of imitation were admirable, and he successively and most successfully personated the whole Australian Bar [judges].

People had come to this gathering from the Hawkesbury, the Hunter Valley, the Murrumbidgee River and the Bathurst Plains. Perhaps this incredible theatre was an adaptation of a traditional gathering that had been transformed into political critique of colonial society:

Yakabil, from the Morumbidgee [Murrumbidgee], and Black Boy, from Hunter's River, were both in the character of Colonial Attorneys, and, being somewhat forward, were going to address the Meeting, when Terribalong, personating the Attorney General, and insisting that they had no right to speak since the late division of the Bar, they were silenced, and turned out of the corrobory.

When the next performance began there could be no mistaking the irony. Windradyne, the Wiradyuri leader who had fought a bloody struggle during the Bathurst War of 1822–1824, took the 'stage' dressed 'in the character of a free settler'.

Finally, the son of the famous Sydney Aboriginal man Bungaree, 'Young Bungary', donned 'his late father's old military surtout [surcoat] cocked hat and sash' and performed 'in the character of Governor Darling'.

The performance on the banks of the Nepean River was a remarkable parody of colonial society, arguably an early part of the history of Aboriginal political struggle. It also shows just how Aboriginal people from different language groups and Country across vast distances could meet and convey precise and accurate stories. It seems entirely feasible that the performance of a great victory at Broken River could travel as far as One Tree Hill.[23]

'The blacks interfere with the profits of grazing'

Many years later in 1849, the Legislative Council of New South Wales was debating a bill to admit the evidence of Aboriginal people in court. The editor of the *Herald* newspaper gave credit to the council for 'having argued this knotty question with consummate ability, and of having disposed of it with sound discretion'. But he called 'several of its members' to task:

> Their cool suggestions for the coercion of the blacks by brute force, and their scarcely concealed wish that the law and the Government should connive at the extermination of the race, would have been more seemly in a barbarian camp than in the hall of civilized legislation. The motive of such cold-blooded atrocity is too transparent to be misunderstood.

Incredibly, he ended by summarising the position of several of the ten members of the nascent New South Wales parliament who voted against the bill:

> The blacks interfere with the profits of grazing: a sufficient reason why they should be shot down like kangaroos, or be dosed, with arsenic like native dogs.

In the Legislative Council of New South Wales in 1849, most of the council members believed genocide was simply a way to maximise the profits of squatters.

In 1849 it was the likes of William Wentworth who railed that the conflict between squatters and Aboriginal people was simply due to the meddling of liberals and humanitarians who 'had worked so much evil for the colonies'. Wentworth said it was 'unadvisable to interfere in the battles between the aboriginals and the borders of the colonies'. He believed 'a few good defeats of the blacks by the whites would always permanently quiet a district'.

The author of the 1819 *A statistical, historical, and political description of the colony of New South Wales and its dependent settlements etc...* knew his history: 'under former Governors the policy had been to help the whites to effect this, and such a policy had been invariably successful, with the most trivial slaughter'. The idea that 'slaughter' could be 'trivial' in the face of progress toward a profitable colony was certainly taking hold in the early writing of Australian history.[24]

'A ceaseless war'

As historian Ray Kerkhove notes about incredible moments of resistance such as The Uprising, 'for many First Nations people, it may not have been a lasting victory, but it was certainly a chapter of great courage and genius for which their ancestors deserve to be honoured'.[25]

Such recognition by the wider Australian community has been thin on the ground. Before the contemporary accounts and settler reminiscences were swamped by war stories from France and Gallipoli, historian and author Arthur Lincoln Haydon noted that Australia was still, when he was writing in 1911, 'a country where nearly every native is hostile'. Haydon wrote a history of what he called the 'Trooper Police'. He believed they had been involved in a 'ceaseless war' since 1825.

Haydon was quite remarkable for his time. He said Aboriginal people were 'not without grounds for adopting this [hostile] attitude'. He believed the settlers 'to a great degree are responsible for the ceaseless war'. Haydon admitted this was 'a dark page in Australian history, a page one would willingly blot out if it were possible'.

It certainly was possible to 'blot out' this 'dark page'. In 1912, just a year later, other historians got to work. Edward Jenks in his *A History of the Australasian Colonies* completely brushed aside Aboriginal resistance. Jenks ignorantly wrote: 'they could offer no resistance to the invaders, and they have, in fact, been entirely ignored (except as objects of charity or aversion) in the settlement of the country'. Jenks preferred to cast the resistance by Māori warriors in Aotearoa/New Zealand as 'unknown to the colonists of Australia'. On closer examination, The Australian Wars lasted longer, occurred over vast distances, saw incredible pound-for-pound battles and skirmishes, were bloodier and cost far more First Nations lives. Jenks's idea of Aboriginal weakness compared to other First Nations is still deeply ingrained in Australians' understanding of colonisation. One day, they may be compared very differently.[26]

The Uprising

As we have seen, Roderick Flanagan, Alexander Harris and others noted the 'simultaneous aggressive movement of the Aborigines throughout the entire colony, and along its boundaries' around 1840. In recent times, Ray Kerkhove and Jack Clear are two of the few historians to have noted this emerging line of conflict. As Clear notes:

> With the abolition of free land grants within the limits of location, and the legalisation of squatting beyond it, settler colonisation swept across the river systems of New South Wales at a pace with few comparisons in the British Empire. The ultimate result was the emergence of an extensive frontier of Indigenous-settler conflict from Moreton Bay to Port Phillip.[27]

It will be up to future historians working with Communities and knowledge-holders to conduct further detailed research into all the vast areas covered by The Uprising of 1838 to 1844, all the numerous Aboriginal peoples and groups, and all the numbers of squatters' and stockmen's descendants. It will be up to local historians to revisit their archives. And as is happening in Victoria today, new historical societies such as the Benalla History Group need to arise. This book could never cover all these stories in the fine-grained detail required to get even closer to the truth, closer perhaps to a clearer knowledge of all the massacres that occurred, all the battles that were fought, and all the Aboriginal victories that could one day truly be part of Australian military history.

Acknowledgments

First and foremost I thank the 'Bathurst Elders' Dinawan Uncle Bill Allen Junior, Wirribi Aunty Leanna Carr, and Yahnadarrambal Uncle Jade Flynn for their ongoing guidance and support. Many thanks too to Lisa Paton for her enthusiasm and support. I also acknowledge the knowledge and wisdom of the late Mallyan Uncle Brian Grant. I hope this book honours all the work toward Dhuluny (truth, Wiradyuri) and truth-telling the Bathurst Elders have led in recent years.

This is my third book with NewSouth Publishing and their faith in my work is so much appreciated. Thanks go to Elspeth Menzies, Paul O'Beirne and copyeditor Jocelyn Hungerford.

Many historians have assisted in this book. In particular, I thank Queensland historian Ray Kerkhove. Ray's work over many years in understanding the tactics and strategies of Australian warriors, his efforts in scouring settler records for hints about communication and alliances between different First Nations groups, as well as his ongoing support and encouragement, have been central to this book.

A huge thank you to Victorian historian Jacqui Durrant for her enthusiasm and help with Victoria, a colonial history I once knew very little about beyond bushrangers, gold, and a battle at a stockade.

To Jack Clear for his research assistance and work on the Wiradyuri resistance wars, a huge thank you.

Wiradyuri historian Mina Murray has been an inspiration. I can't begin to describe how important her work in this field is, and will be in future.

Thanks go to Hamish McPherson for his important work on Benalla and northeast Victoria. The fine-grained local histories of The Australian Wars that still need to be done are in good hands.

To many other colleagues including the late Lyndall Ryan, Bill Gammage, Kate Auty, Mark Dunn, Samantha Leah, Naomi Parry Duncan, Bruce Pennay, Iain Stuart, Kiera Lindsay, Catharine Coleborn, Trevor Leahman, Raymond Evans and in particular Henry Reynolds and Rachel Perkins, I give thanks for their encouragement, inspirational discussions and their important work in broadening understanding of The Australian Wars.

Thanks go to many local historians, in particular Geoff Burch of Wagga Wagga for his support and assistance.

A huge mandaang guwu (thank you, Wiradyuri) to Anita Heiss whose historical fiction work continues to amplify the often tedious work of historians and inspire people to engage with these histories.

To Jye Murray '@theKooriePhysio' – this is the third part of the trilogy for your bookshelf. I hope it in some small way acknowledges your strength and resilience.

To another wonderful proud Cowra Wiradyuri Trilby Ryan, thank you for your enthusiasm for truth-telling and Community resilience.

Thanks so much for the support during the last few years to Sandra Wallace, Michael Lever, Jackson Pellow and all my colleagues at Artefact Heritage and Environment, especially the inspirational Aboriginal Cultural Heritage Officers Kelly Barton and Cole Perry.

Thanks go to Nick Bryant for the Yass rest stops, Francis Daley and Beattie Lanser at 'Boobook Hill' farm for the organic veg and camping, and to Jim Casey for the use of 'Jim's Gym' to keep me from cracking up at my computer, as well as his always insightful comments on the economics of colonialism. To Miranda Nagy, Beatrix and Seamus – thanks heaps from 'Stevie G' for the music, chats and football.

Thank you Larissa Trompf and Finn for minding 'Shadie the Wonder Staffy' on all those Thursday visits to the State Library.

Thanks to my family, Barbara, Les and Sue for their ongoing support for my obsessive projects. And to my partner Alex, I can't thank you enough for all the support and advice you have given and all the amazing road trips we have done together.

Finally, thanks go to Shadie the Wonder Staffy for travelling with me over thousands of kilometres, barking at those dangerous cows and for being so friendly to everyone we talked to.

Bibliography

Abbreviations
ADB	*Australian Dictionary of Biography*
AIATSIS	Australian Institute of Aboriginal and Torres Strait Islander Studies
CCL	Copies of Letters to Commissioners of Crown Lands
CSC	Colonial Secretary Correspondence
CSLR	Main Series of Letters Received (Colonial Secretary)
CSSB	Colonial Secretary Special Bundles
SLV	State Library of Victoria
SRNSW	State Records New South Wales
HRA	*Historical Records of Australia*
HRV	*Historical Records of Victoria*
LRCS	Letters received from the Colonial Secretary
ML	Mitchell Library
NLA	National Library of Australia
RHSV	Royal Historical Society of Victoria
RAHS	Royal Australian Historical Society
VPRS	Victorian Public Record Office
NSWVP	*New South Wales Votes and Proceedings*

Research trips and site visits
Central West, Blayney, Cowra, August 2023
Benalla, Wangaratta, Northeast Victoria, October 2023
Yass, Albury, Wagga, Narrandera, September 2023
Liverpool Plains, Hunter Valley, Central West, February 2024
Cowra and Bathurst, May and June 2024
Bingara, Myall Creek, Toowoomba, Southeast Queensland, Moree, June 2024

Interviews
Hamish McPherson, 29 September 2023, Benalla, Victoria
Aunty Cheryl Cooper and Aunty Carol Alliman, 29 September 2023, Benalla, Victoria
Megan Carter, fourth great granddaughter of 'King Brangy of the Ovens River', 7 October 2023, Sydney
Uncle James Ingram, 20 October 2023, Wagga Wagga
Uncle Robert Carroll, 22 October 2023, Narrandera
Uncle Robert Carroll and Uncle Clem Christian, 22 October 2023, Narrandera
Uncle Bill Allen Jnr, Aunty Leanna Carr, Lisa Paton, 1 December 2023, Bathurst
Uncle Bill Allen Jnr, 6 June 2024, Bathurst
Ray Kerkhove and Birrpai and Dhungutti man on Jaggara Country, Terry Royan, 11 June 2024, Toowoomba
Ray Kerkhove, Terry Royan, Gomeroi and Kooma man Boe Spearim, and Elder in Residence, University of Southern Queensland, Uncle Wayne Fossey, 11 June 2024, Toowoomba
Moree Elders Group, 13 June 2024, Dhilyaan Aboriginal Centre, Moree
Uncle Paul and Boe Spearim, 24 October 2024, online

Personal communications
Hamish McPherson, emails, 20 September, 2022; 28 September 2023
Ray Kerkhove, email, 27 August 2023
Geoffrey Burch, Wagga Wagga and District Historical Society, email, 2 November 2023
Jacqui Durrant, emails, 2, 17 April 2024
Aunty Glenda Chalker, email, 16 April 2024
Mina Murray, various pers. comms., 25 May, 17 August 2024
Dinawan Uncle Bill Allen Junior, Bathurst, 15 August 2024

Newspapers
Argus
Australasian
Australasian Sketcher with Pen and Pencil
Australian
Bathurst Free Press and Mining Journal
Benalla Standard
Bent's News and Tasmanian Register
Colonial Observer
Colonial Times
Colonist
Commercial Journal and Advertiser
Courier
Daily Advertiser
Empire
Hunter River Gazette
Leader
Ovens and Murray Advertiser
Sydney Gazette
Sydney Herald
Sydney Monitor
Sydney Morning Herald
Sydney Times
The Courier-Mail
The Holy Name Monthly
The Moreton Bay Courier
Town and Country Journal
Wingham Chronicle and Manning River Observer

Archives, records, maps, images and manuscripts
Baker, W, 'Map of a portion of Australia showing the area of the twenty located counties of New South Wales with the adjoining eight grazing districts', W Baker, Sydney, 1841, National Library of Australia, MAP F 479
Barnett, E, 'Survey of the Intermediate Country between the Ovens and Broken Rivers, 1850', *VPRS* 8168, Historic Plan Collection; <mapwarper.prov.vic.gov.au/maps/6742>
Benalla Historical Society Archives, Benalla, Victoria
Bonney, C, 'Autobiographical Notes', 1897, NLA, JAF P10 55
Bourke, JC, Letters to Edmund Finn ['Garryowen'] (1888), Correspondence and papers (1821–1908), *RHSV*, MS 004116.02

Bibliography

Cannon, M & Macfarlane, I (eds), *The Aborigines of Port Phillip, 1835–1839, HRV, Foundation Series*, vol. 2A, Public Record Office, Victorian Government Printing Office, Melbourne, 1982

Cannon, M & Macfarlane, I (eds), *Aborigines and Protectors 1838–1839, HRV, Foundation Series*, vol. 2B, Public Record Office, Victorian Government Printing Office, Melbourne, 1983

Colonial Secretary's Papers, Main Series of Letters Received, SRNSW

Colonial Secretary's Papers, Special Bundles, SRNSW

Crawford, JC, Papers, NLA, M600 M687-M688

Cunningham, A, 'Report of a tour between Liverpool Plains and Moreton Bay', April – 7 July 1827, Allan Cunningham papers, 1827–1832, ML, SLNSW, *D79

Dowse, T, 'Recollections and reminiscences, 1828–1878', Thomas Dowse Papers, John Oxley Library, State Library of Queensland, OM79-68

Dredge, J, Assistant Protector of Aborigines at the Goulburn River, Diary, 7 December 1839, SLV, MS 11625

Eyre, JE, ML, SLNSW, CY Reel 118, A1806

Fraser, C, 'Journal of a residence on the banks of the Rivers Brisbane and Logan from 30 June to 6 September 1828', 2 and 3 July 1828, SRNSW, CSSB, 9/2738

'Faithfull papers', NLA, MS 1146, Boxes 1–10

Finn, E, Letter received re attack on Bourke by blacks in 1839, RHSV, MS 004114

Fowles, J (att.), 'Colonel James Nunn, Australian Mounted Infantry', circa 1840, ML, SLNSW, ML 1321

Gardner, W, 'Northern and Western Districts of New South Wales', ML SLNSW, A 176/vol. 2

HRA, Series 1, Governor's Despatches to and from England, vols 18–23, July 1835 to 1844, The Library Committee of the Commonwealth of Parliament, Alfred James Kent, Government Printer, Sydney, 1923–1924

Lang, JD, 'The journal of the Brethren Nique and Rode at Umpieboang', 16 March 1842, vol. 20, John Dunmore Lang papers. German mission, Moreton Bay, 1837–1867, ML, SLNSW, A 2240

Langevad, G (ed.), *The Simpson Letterbook*, Cultural and Historical Records of Queensland, Number 1, 1979, Anthropology Museum, University of Queensland, Brisbane, 1979

Melbourne Survey Office, 'Survey of the intermediate country between the Ovens and Broken Rivers, 1850', Victorian Public Record Series 8168, Historic Plan Collection

New South Wales Government Gazette, Government Printer, Sydney, (various numbers)

New South Wales Votes and Proceedings, 1839, vol. 2

Parliamentary Select Committee on Aboriginal Tribes (British Settlements), *Report from the Select Committee on Aborigines (British Settlements); with the Minutes of Evidence, Appendix and Index*, The House of Commons, London, 1837

Royal Historical Society of Victoria, MS 004116.02; MS 004114

Select Committee on the Condition of the Aborigines, Legislative Council New South Wales, *Report from the Select Committee on the Condition of the Aborigines, with Appendix, Minutes of Evidence and Replies to a Circular Letter*, W.W. Davies, Government Printing Office, Sydney, 1845

Select Committee on the Condition of the Aborigines, *Report of the Select Committee of the Legislative Council on the Aborigines; Together with etc.*, John Ferres, Government Printer, Melbourne, 1859

Taylor, TJD, 'Drawings, sketchbook and journal by Thomas Domville Taylor, 1840–1848', NLA, PIC MSR 14/1/6, Volume 1190

Thomas Papers, ML, SLNSW, uncatalogued MSS, set 214 CY732

Thomas, W, 'Journals and papers', 1838–1843, ML, SLNSW, MS 214.1-2

Threlkeld, L, 'Report of the mission to the Aborigines at Lake Macquarie, New South Wales, 1837', NLA, <trove.nla.gov.au/newspaper/article/31719534>
Uren, S, 'The massacre of the Faithfull party', c. 1913, State Library of Victoria, MS 14903
Wagga Wagga and District Historical Society Archives, Wagga Wagga, NSW

Published works

Andrews, A, *The First Settlement of the Upper Murray, 1835 to 1845, with a short account of over two hundred runs 1835 to 1880*, Ford Printer, Sydney, 1920. Facsimile reprint, Library of Australian History, North Sydney, 1979

Arkley, L, *The Hated Protector: The story of Charles Wightman Sievwright, Protector of Aborigines 1839–42*, Orbit Press, Melbourne, 2000

Attwood, B, *The Good Country: The Djadja Wurring, the settlers and the Protectors*, Monash University Publishing, Melbourne, 2017

Attwood, B, *Possession: Batman's treaty and the matter of history*, Meigunyah Press, Melbourne, 2009

Backhouse, J, *A Narrative of a Visit to the Australian Colonies*, Hamilton, Adams and Co., London, 1843

Balfour, JO, *A Sketch of New South Wales*, Smith, Elder and Company, London, 1845

Bartley, N, *Australian Pioneers and Reminisces, together with portraits of some of the founders of Australia*, Gordon and Gotch, Brisbane, 1896

Barwick, D, *Rebellion at Coranderrk*, Aboriginal History Inc., Canberra, 1998

Belich, J, *Replenishing the Earth: The settler revolution and the rise of the Anglo world 1783–1939*, Oxford University Press, Oxford, 2009

Bennett, G, *Wanderings in New South Wales, Batavia, Pedir Coast, Singapore, and China: Being the journal of a naturalist in those countries, during 1832, 1833, and 1834*, Richard Bentley, London, 1834

Bennett, G, *The Earliest Inhabitants: Aboriginal tribes of the district: The blacks of Dungog, Port Stephens, and Gresford*, Chronicle Print, Dungog, 1964 (c. 1930)

Beresford, Q, *Wounded Country: The Murray-Darling Basin – A contested history*, NewSouth Publishing, Sydney, 2021

Boldrewood, R, *The Squatter's Dream*, Macmillan, London, 1890

Bottoms, T, *Conspiracy of Silence: Queensland's frontier killing times*, Allen & Unwin, Sydney, 2013

Boyce, D, *Clarke of the Kindur: Convict, bushranger, explorer*, Melbourne University Press, Melbourne, 1970

Boyce, J, *1835: The founding of Melbourne and the conquest of Australia*, Black Inc., Melbourne, 2011

Boswell, A, *Recollections of some Australian blacks: Bathurst district, 1835–40, Port Macquarie, 1844, Hunter's River, 1850*, np, nd, c.1890

Bride, TF, (ed.) *Letters from Victorian Pioneers: Being a series of papers on the early occupation of the colony, the Aborigines, etc.*, Government Printer, Trustees of the Public Library, Melbourne, 1898

Brodribb, WA, *Recollections of an Australian Squatter or, Leaves from my journal since 1835*, John Woods & Co., Sydney, 1883

Broome, R, *Aboriginal Australians: A history since 1788*, Allen & Unwin, Sydney, 2010 (1982)

Broome, R, *Aboriginal Victorians: A History Since 1800*, Allen & Unwin, Sydney, 2005

Byrne, JC, *Twelve Years' Wanderings in the British Colonies from 1835 to 1847*, 2 vols, Richard Bentley, London, 1848

Bibliography

Cahir, F, *'My Country all gone the white men have stolen it': The invasion of Wadawurrung Country 1800–1870*, Revolution Print, Ballarat, Victoria, 2019

Campbell, J, *Invisible Invaders: Smallpox and other diseases in Aboriginal Australia, 1780–1880*, Melbourne University Press, Melbourne, 2002

Campbell, J, *The Early Settlement of Queensland*, Bibliographical Society of Queensland, Brisbane, 1936

Cannon, M, *Who killed the Koories?*, William Heinemann Australia, Melbourne, 1990

Carlson, B & Farrelly, T, *Monumental Disruptions: Aboriginal people and colonial commemorations in so-called Australia*, Aboriginal Studies Press, Canberra, 2023

Cash, M, (Burke, JL, (ed.)), *The Adventures of Martin Cash, comprising a faithful account of his exploits etc.*, Mercury Steam Press Office, Hobart, 1879

Clark, C, *The Encyclopedia of Australia's Battles*, Allen & Unwin, Sydney, 2010

Clark, ID, *Aboriginal Languages and Clans: An historical atlas of western and central Victoria, 1800–1900*, Monash University, Melbourne, 1990

Clark, ID, *Scars in the Landscape: A register of massacre sites in western Victoria, 1803–1859*, AIATSIS, Canberra, 1995

Clark, ID (ed.), *The Journals of George Augustus Robinson, Chief Protector, Port Phillip Aboriginal Protectorate, Volumes One and Two: 1 January 1839 – 30 September 1840, 1 October 1840 – 31 August 1841*, Heritage Matters, Ballarat, 2000

Clark, ID & Heydon, T, *A Bend in the Yarra: A history of the Merri Creek Protectorate Station and Merri Creek Aboriginal School 1841–1851*, Aboriginal Studies Press, AIATSIS, Canberra, 2004

Clayton, I & Barnes, A, *Wiradjuri of the Rivers and Plains*, Heinemann, Melbourne, 1997

Clayton-Dixon, C, *Surviving New England: A history of Aboriginal resistance and resilience through the first forty years of the colonial apocalypse*, Anaiwan Language Revival Program, Armidale, 2019

Cliento, R & Lack, C, *Triumph in the Tropics: An historical sketch of Queensland*, Smith and Patterson, Brisbane, 1959

Collins, P, *Goodbye Bussamarai: The Mandandanji land war, Southern Queensland 1842–1852*, University of Queensland Press, Brisbane, 2002

Connor, J, *The Australian Frontier Wars 1788–1838*, UNSW Press, Sydney, 2002

Connors, L, *Warrior: A legendary leader's dramatic life and violent death on the colonial frontier*, Allen & Unwin, Sydney, 2015

Cooper, F, *Wild Adventures in Australia and New South Wales: Beyond the boundaries: with sketches of life at the mining districts*, James Blackwood, London, 1857

Coutts Crawford, J, *Recollections of travel in New Zealand and Australia*, Trübner & Co., London, 1880

Cox, R, *Broken Spear: The untold story of Black Tom Birch, the man who sparked Australia's bloodiest war*, Wakefield Press, Adelaide, 2021

Critchett, J, *A Distant Field of Murder: Western District frontiers 1834–1848*, Melbourne University Press, Melbourne, 1990

Curr, EM, *The Australian Race: Its origins, languages, customs, place of landing in Australia and the routes by which it spread itself out over that continent*, 4 vols, John Ferres Government Printer, Melbourne, 1886–1887

Curr, EM, *Recollections of Squatting in Victoria, then called the Port Phillip District (1841–1851)*, George Robertson, Melbourne, 1883

Darragh, TA & Fensham, RJ (eds), *The Leichhardt Diaries: Early travels in Australia during 1842–1844*, Memoirs of the Queensland Museum, Cultural Heritage Series, Queensland Museum, Brisbane, 2013

Darmangeat, C, *Justice and Warfare in Aboriginal Australia*, Lexington Books, New York, 2020

De Marr, J, *Adventures in Australia fifty years ago: Being a record of an emigrant's wanderings through the colonies of New South Wales, Victoria and Queensland during the years 1839–1844*, Swan Sonnenschein, London, 1893

Dennis, P, Grey, J, Morris, E & Prior, R (eds), *The Oxford Companion to Australian Military History*, Oxford University Press, Melbourne, 1995

Drake, J, *Queensland's Frontier Wars*, Boolarong Press, Tingalpa, Brisbane, 2021

Dunn, M, *The Convict Valley: The bloody struggle on Australia's early frontier*, Allen & Unwin, Sydney, 2020

Ellender, I & Christiansen, P, *People of the Merri Merri: The Wurundjeri in colonial days*, Merri Creek Management Committee, Melbourne, 2001

Evans, R, *A History of Queensland*, Cambridge University Press, Melbourne, 2007

Evans, R, *Fighting Words: Writing about Race*, University of Queensland Press, Brisbane, 1999

Fels, MH, *Good Men and True: The Aboriginal police of the Port Phillip District 1837–1853*, Melbourne University Press, 1988

Fels, MH, *'I Succeeded Once': The Aboriginal Protectorate on the Mornington Peninsula, 1839–1840*, Aboriginal History Monograph 22, ANU Press, Canberra, 2011

Finalson, WF, *A Treatise on Martial Law, as allowed by the Law of England in time of Rebellion, with Practical Illustrations Drawn from the Official Documents in the Jamaica Case and the Evidence Taken by the Royal Commission of Inquiry with Comments, Constitution*, Stevens and Sons, London, 1866

Fison, L & Howitt, AW, *Kamilaroi and Kurnai: Group-marriage and relationship, and marriage by elopement, drawn chiefly from the usage of the Australian aborigines: Also the Kurnai tribe, their customs in peace and war*, George Robertson, Melbourne, 1880

Flanagan, R, 'The Aborigines of Australia – No. XIV: The "Rising of 1842–4"', *Empire*, 15 April 1854

Flood, J, *Archaeology of the Dreamtime*, University of Hawaii Press, Honolulu, 1983

Ford, L, *Settler Sovereignty: Jurisdiction and Indigenous people in America and Australia 1788–1836*, Harvard University Press, Cambridge, 2011

Foster, R, Hosking, R & Nettelbeck, A, *Fatal Collisions: The South Australian frontier and the violence of memory*, Wakefield Press, Adelaide, 2001

French, M, *Conflict on the Condamine: Aborigines and the European invasion*, Darling Downs Institute Press, Toowoomba, 1989

Furphy, S, *Edward M. Curr and the Tide of History*, ANU Press, Canberra, 2013

Gammage, B, *Narrandera Shire*, Narrandera Shire Council, Narrandera, 1986

Gapps, S, *Gudyarra: The first Wiradyuri war of resistance: The Bathurst War 1822–1824*, NewSouth Publishing, Sydney, 2021

Gapps, S, *The Sydney Wars: Conflict in the early colony 1788–1817*, NewSouth Publishing, Sydney, 2018

Gardiner, E, *Terrible Vale: No time like the past: History of a New England grazing run between 1830 and 1940*, DSAMC Education, Tamworth, c.1998

Garran, JC & White, L, *Merinos, Myths and Macarthurs: Australian graziers and their sheep, 1788–1900*, ANU Press, Canberra, 1985

Gerstaecker, F, *Narrative of a Journey Round the World, etc.*, vol. 3, Hurst and Blackett, London, 1853

Gilmore, M, *Old Days, Old Ways: A book of recollections*, Angus & Robertson, Sydney, 1934

Gilmore, M, *More Recollections*, Angus & Robertson, Sydney, 1935

Gormly, J, *Exploration and Settlement in Australia*, Ford, Sydney, 1921

Grant (Senior), S & Rudder, J, *A New Wiradjuri Dictionary: English to Wiradjuri, Wiradjuri to English, categories of things and reference tables*, Restoration House, Canberra, 2010

Bibliography

Grey, J, *A Military History of Australia*, Cambridge University Press, Melbourne, 1990

Gunson, N (ed.), *Australian Reminiscences and Papers of L. E. Threlkeld: Missionary to the Aborigines 1824–59*, 2 vols, AIATSIS, Canberra, 1974

Hall, T, *The Early History of the Warwick District and the Pioneers of Darling Downs*, Robertson & Provan, Toowoomba, c. 1920–29

Halls, C, *Guns in Australia*, Hamlyn, Sydney, 1974

Hardy, B, *Lament for the Barkindji: The vanished tribes of the Darling River Region*, Rigby, Adelaide, 1976

Harris, A, *Settlers and Convicts, or, Recollections of sixteen years' labour in the Australian backwoods by an emigrant mechanic*, Melbourne University Press, Melbourne, 1969 (1847)

Haydon, AL, *The Trooper Police of Australia: A record of mounted police work in the Commonwealth from the earliest days of settlement to the present time*, A. Melrose, London, 1911

Henderson, J, *Excursions and Adventures in New South Wales: With pictures of squatting and of life in the bush: An account of the climate, productions, and natural history of the colony, and of the manners and customs of the natives, with advice to emigrants, &c.*, W Shoberl, London, 1851

Hinkins, JT, *Life Amongst the Native Race, with Extracts from a Diary of the Late John T. Hinkins*, Hasse, McQueen and Co., Melbourne, 1884

Hodgson, CP, *Reminiscences of Australia with Hints on the Squatters' Life*, W. N. Wright, London, 1846

Hood, J, *Australian and the East; Being a journal of a narrative of a voyage to New South Wales in an emigrant ship with a residence of some months in Sydney and the bush etc. in the years 1841 and 1842*, John Murray, London, 1843

Johnston, A & Rolls, M (eds), *Reading Robinson: Companion essays to Friendly Mission*, Quintus Publishing, University of Tasmania, Hobart, 2008

Kabaila, P, *Wiradjuri Places: The Murrumbidgee River Basin*, Black Mountain Projects, Canberra, 1995

Kabaila, P, *Wiradjuri Places: The Lachlan River Basin*, Black Mountain Projects, Canberra, 1996

Kerkhove, R, *How They Fought: Indigenous tactics and weaponry of Australia's Frontier Wars*, Boolarong Press, Brisbane, 2023

Kerkhove, R & Uhr, F, *The Battle of One Tree Hill: The Aboriginal resistance that stunned Queensland*, Boolarong Press, Brisbane, 2019

Kerwin, D, *Aboriginal Dreaming Paths and Trading Routes: The colonisation of the Australian economic landscape*, Sussex Academic Press, Brighton, 2010

Kidd, R, *The Way We Civilise: Aboriginal Affairs – the untold story*, University of Queensland Press, Brisbane, 1997

Lang, G, *The Australian Aborigines in their Original Condition*, Wilson & Mackinnon, Melbourne, 1865

Lang, JD, *An Historical and Statistical Account of New South Wales, both as a Penal Settlement and a British Colony*, vol. 1, Cambridge University Press, Cambridge, 2011 (1834)

Lang, JD, *An Historical & Statistical Account of New South Wales From the Founding of the Colony in 1788 to the Present Day: In two volumes: The history of the last twenty-five years entirely new*, vol. 1, Sampson Low, Marston, Low, & Searle, London, 1875

MacAllister, C, *Old Pioneering Days in the Sunny South*, C MacAlister, Goulburn, 1907

Macklin, R, *Hamilton Hume: Our greatest explorer*, Hachette, Sydney, 2016

Mackenzie-Smith, J (ed.), *Brisbane River Valley, 1841–50: Pioneer observations and reminiscences*, Sources No. 5, Brisbane History Group, Brisbane, 1991

Marr, D, *Killing for Country: A family story*, Black Inc., Melbourne, 2023

Milliss, R, *Waterloo Creek: The Australia Day massacre of 1838, George Gipps and the British conquest of New South Wales*, McPhee Gribble Penguin Books, Ringwood Victoria, 1992

Mitchell, TL, *Journal of an Expedition into the Interior of Tropical Australia in Search of a Route from Sydney to the Gulf of Carpentaria*, Longman, Brown, Green and Longmans, London, 1848

Mitchell, TL, *Three Expeditions into the Interior of Eastern Australia: With descriptions of the recently explored region of Australia Felix, and of the present colony of New South Wales*, 2 vols, T & W Boone, London, 1838

Mollison, AF (Randall, JO (ed.)), *An Overlanding Diary: April–December 1837, from Uriara Station, on the Murrumbidgee, to Port Phillip, Victoria*, Mast Gully Press, Melbourne, 1980

Muir, P (ed.), *N.S.W. Journals of Robert Muir Pioneer Cattleman & Grazier 1839–1851*, Peter Muir, Leonora, 1986

Mulvaney, J & Kamminga, J, *Prehistory of Australia*, Allen & Unwin, Sydney, 1999

Musgrave, S, *The Wayback*, Cumberland Argus, Parramatta, 1925

Nettelbeck, A, *Indigenous Rights and Colonial Subjecthood: Protection and reform in the nineteenth-century British Empire*, Cambridge University Press, Cambridge, 2019

O'Gorman, E, *Wetlands in a Dry Land: More-than-human histories of Australia's Murray-Darling Basin*, University of Washington Press, Seattle, 2021

O'Sullivan, *Mounted Police in N.S.W*, Rigby, Adelaide, 1979

O'Rourke, MJ, *Raw Possum and Salted Pork: Major Mitchell and the Kamilaroi Aborigines*, Plowpress, Canberra, 1995

Oxley, J, *Journals of Two Expeditions into the Interior of New South Wales*, John Murray, London, 1820

Parker, ES, *The Aborigines of Australia: A lecture, delivered in the Mechanics' Hall, Melbourne, before the John Knox Young Men's Association, on Wednesday, May 10th, 1854*, Hugh McColl, Melbourne, 1854

Parsons, D, *Wadingh Wadingh: A history of Aboriginal People in the Warwick Area and their Land*, David Parsons, Maryvale, 2003

Petrie, C (ed.), *Tom Petrie's Reminiscences of Early Queensland*, Angus & Robertson, Sydney, 1983 (1904)

Phillips, J, *Reminiscences of Australian Early Life by a Pioneer*, AP Marsden, London, 1893 (2014)

Prentis, M, *A Study in Black and White: The Aborigines in Australian history*, Methuen, Sydney, 1975

Presland, G, *First People: The Eastern Kulin of Melbourne, Port Phillip and Central Victoria*, Museum Victoria Publishing, Melbourne, 2010

Queensland Legislative Assembly, *Native Police Force: Report from the select committee on the Native Police Force and the condition of the Aborigines generally, etc.*, Fairfax and Belbridge, Brisbane, 1861

Ranken, WB, *The Rankens of Bathurst*, Townsend, Sydney, 1916

Reynolds, H, *This Whispering in Our Hearts, Revisited*, NewSouth Publishing, Sydney, 2018 (1998)

Reynolds, H, *The Other Side of the Frontier: Aboriginal resistance to the European invasion of Australia*, UNSW Press, Sydney, 2006 (1981)

Reynolds, H, *The Law of the Land*, Penguin, Melbourne, 1992

Reynolds, H, *Forgotten War*, NewSouth Publishing, Sydney, 2022 (2013)

Reynolds, H & Clements, N, *Tongerlongeter: First Nations leader and Tasmanian war hero*, NewSouth Publishing, Sydney, 2022

Richards, J, *The Secret War: A true history of Queensland's Native Police*, University of Queensland Press, Brisbane, 2008

Ridley, W, *Kámilarói and other Australian languages*, Thomas Richards, Government Printer, Sydney, 1875

Bibliography

Roberts, SH, *The Squatting Age in Australia 1835–46*, Melbourne University Press, Melbourne, 1964

Robinson, F & York, B, *The Black Resistance: An introduction to the history of the Aborigines' struggle against British Colonialism*, Widescope, Camberwell, Victoria, 1977

Rodwell, ME (ed.), *The Ollera Papers 1838–1857: The family letters of George, John and Edwin Everett*, Journal of Australian Colonial History, Occasional Publication No. 1, University of New England, Armidale, 2017

Rusden, GW, *History of Australia*, Volume 2, Chapman and Hall, London, 1883

Russell, HS, *The genesis of Queensland: An account of the first exploring journeys to and over Darling Downs: The earliest days of their occupation; social life; station seeking; the course of discovery, northward and westward; and a resumé of the causes which led to separation from New South Wales, &c.*, Turner & Henderson, Sydney, 1888

Russell, P (ed.), *This Errant Lady: Jane Franklin's Overland Journey to Port Phillip and Sydney, 1839*, NLA, 2002

Ryan, L & Lydon, J (eds), *Remembering the Myall Creek Massacre*, NewSouth Publishing, Sydney, 2018

Sidney, J, *Sidney's Australian hand-book: How to settle and succeed in Australia: Comprising every information for intending emigrants / by a bushman*, Pelham Richardson, London, 1848

Stanley, P, *The Remote Garrison: The British Army in Australia 1788–1870*, Kangaroo Press, Sydney, 1986

Steele, JG, *Aboriginal Pathways in Southeast Queensland and the Richmond River*, University of Queensland Press, Brisbane, 1983

Stephens, M (ed.), *The Journal of William Thomas, Assistant Protector of the Aborigines of Port Phillip and Guardian of the Aborigines of Victoria, 1839–1867, Volume 1: 1839 to 1843*, Victorian Aboriginal Corporation for Languages, Melbourne, 2014

Stone, B, *The Squatters: The story of Australia's pastoral pioneers*, Allen & Unwin, Sydney, 2019

Sturt, C, *Two Expeditions into the Interior of Southern Australia*, Public Library of South Australia, Adelaide, 1963

Suttor, WH, *Australian Stories Retold and Sketches of Country Life*, Glyndwr Whalan, Bathurst, 1887

Sveiby, K, and Skuthorpe, T, *Treading Lightly: The hidden wisdom of the world's oldest people*, Allen & Unwin, Sydney, 2006

Telfer, W, and Milliss, R, *The Wallabadah manuscript: The early history of the northern districts of New South Wales. Recollections of the early days*, UNSW Press, Sydney, 1980

Vale, M, *Warby: My excellent guide*, Sydney, M. Vale, 1994

Walker, W, *The Squatters' Grab: Where it all went wrong*, WW Walker, 2023

Walsh, K & Hooton, J, *Australian Autobiographical Narratives: An annotated bibliography, Volume 1 to 1850*, Australian Scholarly Editions Centre, Canberra, 1993

Waugh, DL, *Three Years' Practical Experience of a Settler in New South Wales: Being extracts from letters to his friends in Edinburgh, from 1834 to 1837*, John Johnstone, Edinburgh, 1838

Wentworth, WC, *A Statistical, Historical, and Political Description of the Colony of New South Wales and its Dependent Settlements in Van Diemen's Land etc.*, G and WB Whittaker, London, 1819

Wheeler, GC, *The Tribe and Intertribal Relations*, John Murray, London, 1910

Wolfe, P, *Settler Colonialism and the Transformation of Anthropology*, Cassell, New York, 1999

Woolmington, J, *Aborigines in Colonial Society 1788–1850: From 'noble savage' to 'rural pest'*, Cassell, Melbourne, 1973

Book chapters and journal articles

Allen, MW, 'Hunter-gatherer violence and warfare in Australia', in Allen, MW & Jones, TL (eds), *Violence and Warfare Among Hunter-Gatherers*, ProQuest Ebook Centra, Taylor & Francis, 2014, pp. 97–98

Backhouse, J, 'Account of a journey from Parramatta across the Blue Mountains to Wellington, 1835', in Mackaness, G (ed.), *Fourteen Journeys Over the Blue Mountains of New South Wales 1813–1841*, Review Publications, Dubbo, 1978

Barwick, DE, 'Mapping the past: An atlas of Victorian clans 1835–1904 Part 1', *Aboriginal History*, vol. 8, no. 2, ANU Press, Canberra, 1984, pp. 100–131

Bassett, J, 'The Faithfull massacre at the Broken River, 1838, *Journal of Australian Studies*, vol. 13, no. 24, 1989, pp. 18–34

Bassett, J, 'The Faithfull Massacre of 1838', *Quadrant*, 20 February 2019, <quadrant.org.au/magazine/2019/01-02/the-faithfull-massacre-of-1838/>

Baylie, WH, 'On the Aborigines of the Goulburn district', *Port Phillip Magazine*, vol. 1, no. 2, 1843, pp. 86–92

Baylis, JJ, 'The Murrumbidgee & Wagga Wagga', *JRAHS*, vol. 13, nos. 4 & 5, 1927, pp. 253–256, 294–304

Brodie, N, 'The Vandemonian War as genocidal moment: Historiographical refrains and archival secrets', *Journal of Genocide Research*, vol. 20, no. 3, 2018, pp. 472–481

Burke, H, Roberts, A, Morrison, M, Sullivan, V & The River Murray and Mallee Aboriginal Corporation (RMMAC), 'The space of conflict: Aboriginal/European interactions and frontier violence on the western Central Murray, South Australia, 1830–41', *Aboriginal History*, vol. 40, 2016, pp. 145–179

Cambage, RH, 'Exploration between Wingecarribee, Shoalhaven, Macquarie and Murrumbidgee rivers', *JRAHS*, vol. 7, pt. 5, 1921, pp. 204–217

Cowlishaw, G, 'Roger Milliss: Waterloo Creek: The Australia Day Massacre of 1838: George Gipps and the British Conquest of New South Wales', *The Australian Journal of Anthropology*, vol. 4, no. 1, pp. 62–67

Davidson, I, Burke, H, Wallis, LA, Barker, B, Hatte, E & Cole, N, 'Connecting Myall Creek and the Wonomo', in Lydon, J & Ryan, L (eds), *Remembering the Myall Creek Massacre*, NewSouth Publishing, Sydney, 2018, pp. 100–110

Dredge, R, '"An awful silence reigns": James Dredge at the Goulburn River', *The La Trobe Journal*, no. 61, Autumn 1998, pp. 17–26

Evans, R, 'Against the grain: Colonialism and the demise of the Bunya Gatherings, 1839–1939', in Haebich, A (ed.), *On the Bunya Trail: Queensland Review Special Edition*, vol. 9, no. 2, 2002, pp. 47–64

Evans, R, 'On the utmost verge: Race and ethnic relations at Moreton Bay 1799–1842', *Queensland Review*, vol. 15, no. 1, 2008, pp. 1–31

Evans, R, 'The mogwi take mi-an-jin: Race relations and the Moreton Bay penal settlement 1824–42', in Shaw, B (ed.), *Brisbane: The Aboriginal presence 1824–1860*, Brisbane History Group, Kelvin Grove and Boolarong Press, Brisbane, 2020 (1992), pp. 1–36

Fisher, R, 'From depredation to degradation: The Aboriginal experience at Moreton Bay 1842–60', in Fisher, R (ed.), *Brisbane: The Aboriginal presence 1824–1860*, Brisbane History Group Paper no. 11, 1992, pp. 31–47

Floud, R & Harris, B, 'Health, height, and welfare: Britain, 1700–1980', in Steckel, R & Floud, R (eds), *Health and Welfare during Industrialization*, University of Chicago Press, Chicago, 1997, pp. 91–126

Fuller, R, Trudgett, M, Norris, R & Anderson, M, 'Star maps and travelling to ceremonies: The Euahlayi people and their use of the night sky', *Journal of Astronomical History and Heritage*, vol. 17, no. 2, 2014, pp. 149–160

Bibliography

Gammage, B, 'The Wiradjuri War 1838–40', *The Push from the Bush*, vol. 16, no. 1, 1838 Volume Collective of the Australian Bicentennial History, 1978–1988, Canberra, 1983, pp. 3–17

Grguric, N, 'The fortified homestead of the Australian frontier', in Clark, G & Litster, M (eds), *Archaeological Perspectives on Conflict and Warfare in Australia and the Pacific*, 2022, ANU Press, Canberra, 2022, pp. 191–209

Gunson, N, 'A missionary expedition from Zion Hill (Nunah) to Toorbul, Moreton Bay District in 1842–43: The journal of the Reverend K. W. W Schmidt', *Aboriginal History*, vol. 2, no. 2, 1978, pp. 114–121

Hamilton, HG, 'The Country between Liverpool Plains and Moreton Bay in New South Wales: Extracts from two letters from Commander H G Hamilton R. N. to W. R. Hamilton Esq.', 4, 24 March 1843, *Journal of the Royal Geographical Society of London*, vol. 13, 1844, pp. 245–253

Jarrott, JK, 'Gorman's Gap', *Queensland Heritage*, vol. 3, no. 4, 1976, pp. 24–38

Kenny, A, 'The "Society" at Bora ceremonies: A manifestation of a body of traditional law and custom in Aboriginal Australia relevant to Native Title Case Law', *Oceania*, vol. 82, no. 2, 2012, pp. 129–151

Kent, D, 'Frontier conflict and Aboriginal deaths: How do we weigh the evidence?', *Journal of Australian Colonial History*, vol. 8, 2006, pp. 23–42

Kerkhove, R, 'Frontier War defences of early Queensland', *Queensland History Journal*, vol. 24, no. 7, 2020, pp. 673–690

Kerkhove, R, 'Reconstructing the Battle of Narawi', *Queensland Review*, vol. 26, no. 1, pp. 1–24

Kerkhove, R, 'Tribal alliances with broader agendas? Aboriginal resistance in southern Queensland's "Black War"', *Cosmopolitan Civil Societies Journal*, vol. 6, no. 3, 2014, pp. 38–62

Langevad, G (ed.), 'Narrative of David Bracewell regarding his sojourn at Wide Bay, 30 May 1842', *The Simpson Letterbook*, Cultural and Historical Records of Queensland No.1, Brisbane, 1979

Lester, A, 'British settler discourse and the circuits of empire', *History Workshop Journal*, vol. 54, no. 1, 2002, pp. 24–28

Mackenzie-Smith, J, 'The Kilcoy poisonings: The official factor 1841–43', in Fisher, R (ed.), *Brisbane: The Aboriginal presence 1824–1860*, Brisbane History Group Paper no. 11, 1992, pp. 76–91

Martens, J, '"In a state of war": Governor James Stirling, extrajudicial violence and the conquest of Western Australia's Avon Valley, 1830–1840', *History Australia*, vol. 19, no. 4, 2022, pp. 668–686

McBryde, I, 'Travellers in storied landscapes: A case study in exchanges and heritage', *Aboriginal History*, vol. 24, 2000, pp. 152–174

Pardoe, C, 'Conflict and territoriality in Aboriginal Australia: Evidence from biology and ethnography' in Allen, MW & Jones, TL (eds), *Re-examining a Pacified Past: Violence and warfare among hunter-gatherers*, Left Coast Press, Walnut Creek, 2014, pp. 112–132.

Parris, HS, 'Early Mitchellstown and Nagambie', *The Victorian Historical Magazine*, vol. 22, 1947–50, pp. 126–133

Pennay, B, 'Interpreting an image: Picturing sound and song at the Murray River crossing place', *Victorian Historical Journal*, vol. 93, no. 1, June 2022, pp. 229–234

Pratt, R, 'The military at Moreton Bay, 1825–1842', *Queensland History Journal*, vol. 21, no. 12, 2013, pp. 819–825

Pratt, R & Hopkins-Weise, J, 'Redcoats in the 1840s Moreton Bay and New Zealand frontier wars', *Queensland Review*, vol. 26, no. 1, 2019, pp. 34–51

Presland, G, 'The Kulin People and the failure of the Aboriginal Protectorate during the superintendency of C J La Trobe', *La Trobeana Journal of the C J La Trobe Society Inc*, vol. 16, no. 1, Special Edition: La Trobe and the Aboriginal People 1, March 2017, pp. 5–13

Rogers, TJ & Bain, S, 'Genocide and frontier violence in Australia', *Journal of Genocide Research*, vol. 18, no. 1, 2016, pp. 83–100

Ryan, L, 'Settler massacres on the Port Phillip Frontier, 1836–1851', *Journal of Australian Studies*, vol. 34, no. 3, 2010, pp. 257–273

Ryan, L, 'The Myall Creek Massacre: Was it typical of the time?' in Ryan, L & Lydon, J (eds), *Remembering the Myall Creek Massacre*, NewSouth Publishing, Sydney, 2018, pp. 89–109

Semelin, J, 'In consideration of massacres', *Journal of Genocide Research*, vol. 3, no. 3, 2001, pp. 377–389

Serle, G, 'Manuscripts: Excerpts from the letters of Dr. David Henry Wilsone, squatter, 1839–1841', *La Trobe Library Journal*, vol. 5, no. 19, pp. 53–62

Standfield, R, '"The vacillating manners and sentiments of these people": Mobility, civilisation and dispossession in the work of William Thomas with the Port Phillip Aboriginal Protectorate', *Law Text Culture*, no. 15, 2011, pp. 162–184

Strong, M, '"One ring to rule them all?" Towards understanding the plethora of bora grounds in southeastern Queensland', *Queensland History Journal*, vol. 22, no. 12, 2016, pp. 859–877

Swain, T, 'Australia', in Swain, T & Trompf, G, *The Religions of Oceania*, Routledge London, 1995, pp. 19–118

Taçon, P & Chippindale, C, 'Australia's ancient warriors: Changing depictions of fighting in the rock art of Arnhem Land, N.T.' *Cambridge Archaeological Journal*, vol. 4, no. 2, 1994, pp. 211–248

Williams, M, 'Charles Bonney and the fertile Kilmore Plains', Historical Notes, *Victorian Historical Journal*, vol. 90, no. 1, June 2019, Royal Historical Society of Victoria, pp. 105–120

Windschuttle, K, 'Guerrilla warrior and resistance fighter? The career of Musquito', *Labour History*, no. 87, November 2004, pp. 221–235

Young, S, 'Reminiscences of Mrs Susan Bundarra Young (formerly Mrs James Buchanan) of Bundara', *JRAHS*, vol. 8, 1923, Supplement, pp. 394–407

Essays, unpublished works and websites

Albury Historical Society, 'Extract from the Diary of Lady Jane Franklin', <alburyhistory.org.au/wp-content/uploads/2023/02/Lady-Franklin-diary-1839.pdf>

'Bunya Pine (Araucaria bidwillii) – Traditional Aboriginal food & beverage', Koori History, 2017, <koorihistory.com/bunya/>

Carter, M, 'Djimbi Ngai – "Here I am" A history of First Nations people in North East Victoria', <dhudhuroaandwaywurruancestors.wordpress.com/>

Century Humanities, University of Newcastle, 'Colonial Frontier Massacres 1788–1930', nd, <c21ch.newcastle.edu.au/colonialmassacres/detail.php?r=506>

Cumpston, Z, 'Indigenous plant use: A booklet on the medicinal, nutritional and technological use of indigenous plants', Clean Air and Urban Landscapes Hub, University of Melbourne website, 2020, <nespurban.edu.au/wp-content/uploads/2020/08/Indigenous-plant-use.pdf>

Darmangeat, C, 'The Aboriginal Collective Conflicts Database' website, University of Paris, nd, <cdarmangeat.ghes.univ-paris-diderot.fr/australia/index.php>

Dawn, R, 23 March 2024, Facebook post in 'Gomeroi of the Namoi' Facebook Group

Durrant, J, 'Circa 1840 – in the north east valleys', Jacqui Durrant website, 2019–2024, <jacquidurrant.com/2019/03/>

Durrant, J, 'First Nations "Kings" of Benalla', *Life on Spring Creek – A blog by Jacqui Durrant*, 2020, <lifeonspringcreek.com/2020/09/15/aboriginal-benalla/>

Bibliography

Carter, M, Finding Merriman website until 2023 (no longer operational)
Finding Merriman, <https://findingmerriman.com.au/merriman/>
Gardner, PD, 'Gippsland massacres: The destruction of the Kurnai Tribes 1800–1860', 3rd edition, self-published, Ensay, Victoria, 2001
Geographical Names Board, 'Murrumbidgee River', <proposals.gnb.nsw.gov.au/public/geonames/abcdc84c-3a23-4077-a645-26c6ddccf2a3>
James, D, 'Benwhalla – The fallen and forgotten', personal website nd, <www.danieljames.com.au/words/2018/10/21/benwhalla-the-fallen-and-forgotten>
Kerkhove, R, 'Notes from audio recordings: Indigenous knowledge of Bunya Mtns Region/Bunya Festival; Routes and Traditions from Groups of the West Flank of Bunyas (Darling Downs etc.)', 28 April 2010, unpublished
Kerkhove, R, 'The Great Bunya Gathering: Early accounts', Academia.edu website, nd, <www.academia.edu/8244371/The_Great_Bunya_Gathering_Early_Accounts>
Kitson, B, 'From Runs to Closer Settlement', QLD Historical Atlas website; <www.qhatlas.com.au/content/runs-closer-settlement>
Roberts, T, 'Thomas John Domville Taylor (ca. 1817–1889)', Harry Gentle Resource Centre, Griffith University, 2020, <harrygentle.griffith.edu.au/life-stories/thomas-john-domville-taylor/>
Sullivan, B, 'Wagga and the Murrumbidgee: The Wagga Community's relationship with the Murrumbidgee River and wetlands over time', Charles Sturt University Archives, 2012, <cdn.csu.edu.au/__data/assets/pdf_file/0008/679796/Bernard-Sullivan-Wagga-and-the-Murrumbidgee.pdf>
Taungurung Land and Waters Council website, nd, <taungurung.com.au/>

Unpublished other

Auty, K, 'Land theft and Victoria', Submission to Yoorrook Truth Telling Commission, 2024
Burch, G, 'Exploration & settlement on the Murrumbidgee', personal paper, 2023
Kerkhove, R, 'A different mode of war? Aboriginal "guerilla tactics" in defining the "Black War" of Southern Queensland 1843–1855', Paper for Australian Historical Association Conference, University of Queensland, Brisbane, 2014
Kerkhove, R, 'Analysis of the Corn Fields Raids', unpublished paper, nd
Kerkhove, R, 'White casualties and events in the Lockyer-Downs War 1840–1850', unpublished paper, 2022
McPherson, H, 'Frontier war on the "Port Phillip road": Colonisation and resistance in Benalla and north-east Victoria', Benalla Aboriginal History Group, Benalla, Victoria, 2023
McPherson, H, '"Original Rights": Colonial invasion and Aboriginal resistance in Benalla and northern Victoria 1838–1858', Benalla Aboriginal History Group, Benalla, Victoria, 2024

Theses

Allen, L, 'A history of the Aboriginal people of the Central Coast of New South Wales to 1874', PhD thesis, The University of Newcastle, 2022
Bassett, J, 'The Faithfull Massacre – A case study', thesis, School of Humanities, Deakin University, 1986
Clear, J, 'The Wiradjuri Wars: Analysing the evolution of settler colonial violence in New South Wales, 1822–1841', PhD thesis, Department of Modern History, Macquarie University, 2021.
Stuart, I, 'Squatting landscapes in South-Eastern Australia (1820–1895)', PhD thesis, Prehistoric and Historic Archaeology, University of Sydney, 1999.
Withycombe, P, 'The Twelfth Man: John Fleming and the Myall Creek Massacre', BA Hons thesis, University of Newcastle, 2015

Reports
Bennett, M, 'Aboriginal Heritage Study for the Cabonne and Blayney Council Local Government area', 2016
Gall, L & Australian Heritage Specialists, 'Jinibara Traditional Inputs for the Sunshine Coast Heritage Study for Sunshine Coast Regional Council', 2017, <hdp-au-prod-app-suncst-haveyoursay-files.s3.ap-southeast-2.amazonaws.com/4016/2321/1315/2021-06-09_14-01_978.pdf>
Kass, T, 'A thematic history of Bogan Shire', 2012, <www.bogan.nsw.gov.au/images/PlanningAndDevelopment/Heritage/BSC_Thematic_History_-_Draft_March_2012.pdf>
Kerkhove, R, 'Indigenous historical context of the Sunshine Coast. A report for Converge, Kabi Kabi Corp and Sunshine Coast Council', June 2018
Kerkhove, R, 'Mapping Frontier War on the Sunshine Coast/Noosa Region', Report for the Sunshine Coast Reconciliation Group, 2020
Kerkhove, R, 'Report for Jagera Daran: Indigenous historical context of Toowomba Bypass: Lockyer Valley and Helidon, with special attention to events surrounding the "Battle of One Tree Hill", 2015
OzArk Environmental Heritage Management, 'Bourke Shire Aboriginal Heritage study', 2019, <bourke.nsw.gov.au/wp-content/uploads/2019/02/Bourke-Shire-Aboriginal-Heritage-Study-Draft-2019.pdf>
State of New South Wales and Office of Environment and Heritage, 'Draft plan of management, Terry Hie Hie Aboriginal Area', Office of Environment and Heritage, Sydney, p. 12, 2017, <www.environment.nsw.gov.au/resources/planmanagement/draft/terry-hie-hie-aboriginal-area-draft-plan-management-170540.pdf>

Australian Dictionary of Biography and Obituaries Australia
Australian Dictionary of Biography (ADB) and Obituaries Australia references are published by the National Centre of Biography, Australian National University, Canberra.

Anderson, H, 'Macdonald, Donald Alaster (1859–1932)', *ADB*, <adb.anu.edu.au/biography/macdonald-donald-alaster-7335/text12731>, published first in hardcopy 1986
Arkley, L, 'Sievwright, Charles Wightman (1800–1855)', *ADB*, <adb.anu.edu.au/biography/sievwright-charles-wightman-13194/text23887>, published first in hardcopy 2005
Austin CG & Lack, C, 'Russell, Henry Stuart (1818–1889)', *ADB*, <adb.anu.edu.au/biography/russell-henry-stuart-2618/text3613>, published first in hardcopy 1967
Baker, DWA, 'Lang, John Dunmore (1799–1878)', *ADB*, <adb.anu.edu.au/biography/lang-john-dunmore-2326/text2953>, published first in hardcopy 1967
Bartram Trott, M, 'Backhouse, James (1794–1869)', *ADB*, <adb.anu.edu.au/biography/backhouse-james-1728/text1899>, published first in hardcopy 1966
Bassett, M, 'Gisborne, Henry Fyshe (Fysche) (1813–1841)', *ADB*, <adb.anu.edu.au/biography/gisborne-henry-fyshe-fysche-2099/text2647>, published first in hardcopy 1966
Bodi, L, 'Gerstaecker, Friedrich (1816–1872)', *ADB*, <adb.anu.edu.au/biography/gerstaecker-friedrich-3604/text5593>, published first in hardcopy 1972
Currey, CH, 'Therry, Sir Roger (1800–1874)', *ADB*, <adb.anu.edu.au/biography/therry-sir-roger-2723/text3837>, published first in hardcopy 1967
Cranfield, LR, 'Logan, Patrick (1791–1830)', *ADB*, <adb.anu.edu.au/biography/logan-patrick-2367/text3107> published first in hardcopy 1967
Dunlop, EW, 'Oxley, John Joseph (1784–1828)', *ADB*, <adb.anu.edu.au/biography/oxley-john-joseph-2530/text3431>, published first in hardcopy 1967

Bibliography

Dutton, G, 'Eyre, Edward John (1815–1901)', *ADB*, <adb.anu.edu.au/biography/eyre-edward-john-2032/text2507> published first in hardcopy 1966

Eastwood, J, 'La Trobe, Charles Joseph (1801–1875)', *ADB*, <adb.anu.edu.au/biography/la-trobe-charles-joseph-2334/text3039>, published first in hardcopy 1967

Farrow, F, 'McCombie, Thomas (1819–1869)', *ADB*, <adb.anu.edu.au/biography/mccombie-thomas-4068/text6489>, published first in hardcopy 1974

Gibbney, HJ, 'Sturt, Charles (1795–1869)', *ADB*, <adb.anu.edu.au/biography/sturt-charles-2712/text3811>, published first in hardcopy 1967

Godfrey, M, 'Robertson, Gilbert (1794–1851)', *ADB*, <adb.anu.edu.au/biography/robertson-gilbert-2595/text3563>, published first in hardcopy 1967

Gray, N, 'Dangar, Henry (1796–1861)', *ADB*, <adb.anu.edu.au/biography/dangar-henry-1954/text2349>, published first in hardcopy 1966

Gray, N, 'Scott, Robert (1799–1844)', *ADB*, <adb.anu.edu.au/biography/scott-robert-2642/text3673>, published first in hardcopy 1967

Gross, A, 'Snodgrass, Peter (1817–1867)', *ADB*, <adb.anu.edu.au/biography/snodgrass-peter-2676/text3739>, published first in hardcopy 1967

Gross, A, 'Sturt, Evelyn Pitfield Shirley (1816–1885)', *ADB*, <adb.anu.edu.au/biography/sturt-evelyn-pitfield-shirley-4663/text7709>, published first in hardcopy 1976

Gunthorpe, SG, 'Dowse, Thomas (1809–1885)', *ADB*, <adb.anu.edu.au/biography/dowse-thomas-3440/text5243>, published first in hardcopy 1972

Hume, SH, 'Hume, Hamilton (1797–1873)', *ADB*, <adb.anu.edu.au/biography/hume-hamilton-2211/text2869>, published first in hardcopy 1966

Kenny, MJB, 'Hall, Edward Smith (1786–1860)', *ADB*, <adb.anu.edu.au/biography/hall-edward-smith-2143/text2729>, published first in hardcopy 1966

Kerkhove, R, 'Old Moppy (c. 1787 – c. 1842)', *ADB*, <ia.anu.edu.au/biography/old-moppy-29802/text36892>

Kerkhove, R, 'Multuggerah (c. 1820 – c. 1846)', *ADB*, <ia.anu.edu.au/biography/multuggerah-29904/text37020>

Kerr, RS, 'Lack, Clem Llewellyn (1900–1972)', *ADB*, <adb.anu.edu.au/biography/lack-clem-llewellyn-10769/text19095>, published first in hardcopy 2000

Lea-Scarlett, EJ, 'Snodgrass, Kenneth (1784–1853)', *ADB*, <adb.anu.edu.au/biography/snodgrass-kenneth-2675/text3737>, published first in hardcopy 1967

McCulloch, SC, 'Gipps, Sir George (1791–1847)', *ADB*, <adb.anu.edu.au/biography/gipps-sir-george-2098/text2645>, published first in hardcopy 1966

Na, 'Hewitt, Thomas (1805–1876)', Obituaries Australia, <oa.anu.edu.au/obituary/hewitt-thomas-14210/text25223>

Na, 'McLeay, Alexander (1767–1848)', *ADB*, <adb.anu.edu.au/biography/mcleay-alexander-2413/text3197>, published first in hardcopy 1967

Na, 'Warby, John (1774–1851)', *ADB*, <adb.anu.edu.au/biography/warby-john-2772/text3939>, published first in hardcopy 1967

Osborne, ME, 'Thomson, Sir Edward Deas (1800–1879)', *ADB*, <adb.anu.edu.au/biography/thomson-sir-edward-deas-2732/text3855>, published first in hardcopy 1967

Parsons, V, 'Faithful, William (1774–1847)', *ADB*, <adb.anu.edu.au/biography/faithful-william-2035/text2513>, published first in hardcopy 1966

Perry, TM, 'Hovell, William Hilton (1786–1875)', *ADB*, <adb.anu.edu.au/biography/hovell-william-hilton-2202/text2847>, published first in hardcopy 1966

Perry, TM, 'Cunningham, Allan (1791–1839)', *ADB*, <adb.anu.edu.au/biography/cunningham-allan-1941/text2323>, published first in hardcopy 1966

Persse, M, 'Wentworth, William Charles (1790–1872)', *ADB*, <adb.anu.edu.au/biography/wentworth-william-charles-2782/text3961>, published first in hardcopy 1967

Stancombe, GH, 'Wedge, John Helder (1793–1872)', *ADB*, <adb.anu.edu.au/biography/wedge-john-helder-2778/text3951>, published first in hardcopy 1967
Thomsen, G, 'Mollison, Alexander Fullerton (1805–1885)', *ADB*, <adb.anu.edu.au/biography/mollison-alexander-fullerton-2466/text3303>, published first in hardcopy 1967
Waller, KGT, 'Leslie, Patrick (1815–1881)', *ADB*, <adb.anu.edu.au/biography/leslie-patrick-2351/text3073>, published first in hardcopy 1967
Walsh, GP, 'Jamison, Sir John (1776–1844)', *ADB*, <adb.anu.edu.au/biography/jamison-sir-john-2268/text2907>, published first in hardcopy 1967
Ward, JM, 'Flanagan, Roderick (1828–1862)', *ADB*, <adb.anu.edu.au/biography/flanagan-roderick-3535/text5449>, published first in hardcopy 1972
Wilde, WH, 'Gilmore, Dame Mary Jean (1865–1962)', *ADB*, <adb.anu.edu.au/biography/gilmore-dame-mary-jean-6391/text10923>, published first in hardcopy 1983

Notes

Introduction

1. Macdonald, D, 'The fight on Broken River. An incident of the thirties', *Argus*, 3 November 1906, p. 7.
2. In the late 1830s, some squatters were expecting to receive 20 pounds per bale. In 1830, the total value of wool exports was 2 million pounds. The annual colonial wool clip in 1838 was over two million kilograms and wool had by far become the colony's primary export. A key to high prices was the quality, washing and lack of burrs. In 1837, it was noted that dirty and burred wool from New South Wales reduced the price at sales in London. The wool barons needed to reduce any interruption to their grazing, shearing and washing processes as much as possible to achieve maximum profits. 'Price current of colonial wool', *Australian*, 30 January 1838, p. 2; Garran, JC & White, L, *Merinos, myths and Macarthurs: Australian graziers and their sheep, 1788–1900*, ANU Press, Canberra, 1985, p. 183.
3. Parsons, V, 'Faithful, William (1774–1847)', *ADB*. Daniel James suggests they were ambushed by 'between 100 to 300 Aboriginal men': James, D, 'Benwhalla – The Fallen and Forgotten', blog, <www.danieljames.com.au/words/2018/10/21/benwhalla-the-fallen-and-forgotten>; Interview, Aunty Cheryl Cooper and Aunty Carol Alliman, 29 September 2023, Benalla, Victoria.
4. Uren, S, 'The Massacre of the Faithfull Party', c. 1913, SLV, MS 14903, p. 2.
5. 'Benalla', *Leader*, 19 May 1894, p. 32.
6. When the *Benalla Standard* published Uren's story in 1907, locals replied to the newspaper that such an event had never happened. As Uren recalled it, 'The opposition by a few to the writer's account of the massacre as taking place in Benalla would need to be experienced to be believed. A couple of columns of letters appeared in the local paper and inferred that the story was a myth. Proofs were demanded. In the next issue appeared a second batch of letters written from the opposite angle. The Municipal Council took up the matter and the writer was invited by the Shire Secretary, Mr. J. Knox, to supervise a party of men to dig round the Faithfull Tree to get evidence of burials there. Arrangements were made and the skeletons of two men were quickly exhumed, a third later'. Uren, 'The Faithfull Massacre', p. 10; Uren's 1906 oral history taken from John Brown's son, Jim, and his 1945 revision may not match the 1838 depositions by Walker and others precisely, but they certainly can't be dismissed. Uren's 'History of Benalla' was written after the Victorian Department of Education invited him to write text for an exhibition on local history, inspired by Uren's investigation into the events. Uren, S, 'The Faithfull Massacre', *Australasian*, 6 July 1907, p. 44; 'The fight of the Broken River', *Benalla Standard*, 6 November 1906, p. 4.
7. Clark, C, *The Encyclopedia of Australian Battles*, Allen & Unwin, Sydney, 2010, p. 14.
8. Barton, GB, 'Old time memories. The Overlanders in '38. By G. B. Barton.', *Australasian*, 12 December 1896, p. 25.
9. Andrews, A, *The First Settlement of the Upper Murray, 1835 to 1845, with a short account of over two hundred runs 1835 to 1880*, Ford Printer, Sydney, 1920, p. 31; 'Faithfull Massacre, Benalla', Colonial Frontier Massacres 1788–1930, Centre for 21st-century Humanities website, <c21ch.newcastle.edu.au/colonialmassacres/detail.php?r=506>, University of Newcastle, 2022.

10 Parris, HS, 'Early Mitchellstown and Ngambie', *The Victorian Historical Magazine*, vol. 22, The Historical Society of Victoria, Melbourne, 1947–50, p. 126.
11 'Colonial Frontier Massacres, Australia, 1788 to 1930'; McPherson, H, 'Frontier War on the "Port Phillip Road": Colonisation and resistance in Benalla and north-east Victoria', Benalla Aboriginal History Group, Benalla, Victoria, 2023, p. 3; Auty, K, 'Land theft and Victoria', Submission to Yoorrook Truth Telling Commission, 2024, p. 3; Aunty Cheryl Cooper and Aunty Carol Alliman, interview, 29 September 2023, Benalla, Victoria. In *Monumental Disruptions*, Bronwyn Carlson and Terri Farrelly address events like this, including the 'Wills Massacre' (p. 115 ff) and how they are memorialised in plaques and monuments, compared to the massacres of Aboriginal peoples who have barely warranted a mention in Australia's commemorative landscape.
12 Harris, A, *Settlers and Convicts or, Recollections of sixteen years' labour in the Australian backwoods by an emigrant mechanic*, Melbourne University Press, Melbourne, 1969 (1847), p. 212.
13 Flanagan, R, 'The Aborigines of Australia – No. XIV: The "Rising of 1842–4"', *Empire*, 15 April 1854, p. 3.
14 'More aggressions by the blacks,' *Sydney Morning Herald*, 19 September 1843, p. 4; 'The blacks – Moreton Bay', *Sydney Morning Herald*, 27 September 1843, p. 4.
15 Flanagan, 1854, p. 3. Flanagan stands out at this period as both an early historian and a voice in support of Aboriginal people. Flanagan's serialised histories were posthumously published in 1888 as *The Aborigines of Australia* as part of a growing interest in establishing an 'Australian history' at the centenary of the first colony in 1788. This was a time when a growing sense of Australian national identity was awkwardly attempting to incorporate Indigenous history while erasing it and its people. Ward, JM, 'Flanagan, Roderick (1828–1862)', *ADB*.
16 Cooper, F, *Wild Adventures in Australia and New South Wales: Beyond the boundaries: With sketches of life at the mining districts*, James Blackwood, London, 1857, p. 77f; 'Domestic intelligence – Ipswich', *The Moreton Bay Courier*, 17 April 1852, p. 2; Halloran, A, to Colonial Secretary, 7 February 1854 and 23 June 1854 in Halloran, A, 1st Report on Aborigines Wide Bay, December 1853, quoted in Kerkhove, R, *How They Fought: Indigenous tactics and weaponry of Australia's frontier wars*, Boolarong Press, Brisbane, 2023, p. 49.
17 Historian Jack Clear notes that 'the ongoing war in and around the Narrandera area [1839–1840], and the setbacks suffered by the British in their effort to quell Aboriginal resistance, were emblematic of a broader theatre of conflict that stretched from the Moreton Bay settlement in what is now south-east Queensland to Port Phillip Bay in present-day Victoria': Clear, J, 'The Wiradjuri Wars: Analysing the evolution of settler colonial violence in New South Wales, 1822–1841', PhD thesis, Department of Modern History, Macquarie University, 2021, p. 251; Bartley, N, *Australian Pioneers and Reminisces, together with portraits of some of the founders*, Gordon and Gotch, Brisbane, 1896, p. 167. There have only been brief outlines of this conflict by Bill Gammage, Peter Rimas Kabaila and Iris Clayton. Jack Clear's 2021 doctoral thesis, 'The Wiradjuri Wars', is an important recent study that includes the second Wiradyuri war, however while Clear focuses on the two Wiradyuri wars 'within a broader theatre of violence' identified by Flanagan and others, he sees this as a more 'indirect' connection (p. 9). I suggest the connections along the 'whole boundary' of the colony of New South Wales were much greater. See Gammage, B, 'The Wiradjuri War 1838–40', *The Push from the Bush*, vol. 16, no. 1, 1983, esp. p. 3; Kabaila, P, *Wiradjuri Places: The Murrumbidgee River Basin*, Black Mountain Projects, Canberra, 1995; Clayton, I & Barnes, A, *Wiradjuri of the Rivers and Plains*, Heinemann, Melbourne, 1997. Another contemporary to note 'united tribes' and, according to Kerkhove and Uhr,

that they were in a 'state of open warfare', to quote Leichhardt, was the 'explorer' himself: Kerkhove R & Uhr, F, *The Battle of One Tree Hill: The Aboriginal resistance that stunned Queensland*, Boolarong Press, Brisbane, 2019. (See also Darragh, TA & Fensham, RJ (eds), *The Leichhardt Diaries: Early travels in Australia during 1842–1844*, 1 January 1844, pp. 379–380. Also, that they were 'reproaching' people who 'join with the whites'.) Gormly, J, *Exploration and Settlement in Australia*, Ford, Sydney, 1921, pp. 127–128.

18 It is unclear how Clem Lack obtained the story of John 'Tinker' Campbell's encounters with Multugerrah and his account of the Battle of One Tree Hill, but Lack reported it in a sensationalised manner, typical of the 1930s, writing that 'the blacks were troublesome'. According to Lack, 'Campbell's first salting season was nearly over at Kangaroo Point, when one day a messenger sent by his "brother", Multuggerah, the aboriginal chief, warned him to keep away from the Darling Downs. Campbell refused to take the warning seriously, but it was quite true. News constantly filtered into Brisbane of shepherds being killed, and out-stations more or less in a state of siege, with the sheep closely guarded in pens': Lack, C, 'A pitched battle of the early days, and something about "Tinker" Campbell's adventures', *Courier-Mail*, 16 April 1938, p. 7. See also Kerkhove & Uhr, 2019; Kerr, RS, 'Lack, Clem Llewellyn (1900–1972)', *ADB*.

19 Broome, R, *Aboriginal Australians: A history since 1788*, Allen & Unwin, Sydney, 2010 (1982), p. 47. In the past, warriors were certainly not incapable of uniting in warfare against neighbouring tribes, and like non-'hunter-gatherer' societies, seem to have developed warfare techniques in response to environmental changes. See Taçon, P & Chippindale, C, 'Australia's Ancient Warriors: Changing depictions of fighting in the rock art of Arnhem Land, N.T.', *Cambridge Archaeological Journal*, vol. 4, no. 2, 1994, pp. 211–248. Some have seen conflict in the period 1838 to the early 1840s as generated not just by the great squatting boom but by drought and financial crash. This erases any agency of Aboriginal people to have taken co-ordinated decisions to resist the wave of settlers and stock pushing into Aboriginal lands. See Clark, ID, *Scars in the Landscape: A register of massacre sites in western Victoria, 1803–1859*, AIATSIS, Canberra, 1995, p. 9, and Ryan, L, 'Settler massacres on the Port Phillip Frontier, 1836–1851', *Journal of Australian Studies*, vol. 34, no. 3, 2010, p. 268; O'Rourke, MJ, *Raw Possum and Salted Pork: Major Mitchell and the Kamilaroi Aborigines*, Plowpress, Canberra, 1995, p. 48.

20 Milliss, R, *Waterloo Creek: The Australia Day massacre of 1838, George Gipps and the British conquest of New South Wales*, McPhee Gribble, Melbourne, 1992, p. 43; Flanagan, 1854, p. 3. Flanagan may have been writing for a burgeoning Goldrush burst in newspaper coverage, and keen to introduce local stories of note, but his later publications show more than a passing interest and his role as an early Australian historian should be further explored. He begins his piece with a sentence noting that 'the simultaneous aggressive movement of the Aborigines throughout the entire colony, and along its boundaries ... belongs to the history of the country'. Some historians have noted that 'frontier warfare intensified' from around 1838 but have not considered how connected these wars were. John Connor, for example, saw this as part of a perfection of 'tactics for attacking cattle and sheep': Connor, J, *The Australian Frontier Wars, 1788–1838*, UNSW Press, Sydney, 2002, p. 103.

21 In his study of frontier defences, Nicolas Grguric notes that 'settler societies' developed 'narratives of reversal' that focused on the settlers who were on the defensive against attacks by warriors, rather than the other way around. While it is certainly the case these narratives make little or no mention of Aboriginal motives for these attacks, often the colonists were indeed on the defensive, and we need to ask why. Grguric, NK, 'Fortified Homesteads: The architecture of fear in frontier South Australia and the Northern Territory, ca. 1847–1885', *Journal of Conflict Archaeology* 4, no. 1–2 (2008), p. 82.

Note to page 11

22 For descriptions of 'tribes' uniting for hunting, ceremonies and war, see the early ethnographers: Curr, EM, *The Australian Race*, vol. 1, John Ferres, Melbourne, 1886, p. 67; Wheeler, GC, *The Tribe and Intertribal Relations,* John Murray, London, 1910, pp. 57–59; Roth, WE, *North Queensland Ethnography Bulletin*, no. 8, Australian Museum, Sydney, 1910, p. 5, and Taplin, FW, 'Some Aboriginal customs', *Australasian Sketcher with Pen and Pencil*, 16 May 1889, p. 71. When Ludwig Leichhardt passed through the Wide Bay region in 1843 he noted that 'united tribes' were 'now (in)... open warfare' with the colonisers: Leichhardt, L, 30 July 1843, in Darragh & Fensham, 2013, p. 266. Ray Kerkhove has noted that after the Kilcoy Massacre of 1842, several language groups made alliances, including Kabi, Yuggera, Wakka and Batjala. Kerkhove notes this 'Post-Kilcoy' alliance to have been a 'super-alliance' that combined five traditional confederacies and included around fifteen sub-groups: Kerkhove, 2023, p. 48. See also Strong, M, '"One ring to rule them all?" Towards understanding the plethora of bora grounds in southeastern Queensland', *Queensland History Journal*, vol. 22, no. 12, 2016, pp. 859–877. There is no doubt about Aboriginal people's capacity for alliances, often across great distances. In 1889, a Queensland journalist remarked how it was 'well known' that Aboriginal groups frequently held what he called inter-tribal 'assemblies' or 'councils' where they negotiated 'peace, war, and alliances with other tribes'. According to another Queensland man who witnessed the bunya festival, Tom Petrie, these gatherings worked as an 'inter-tribal parliament', wherein 'each tribe would tell the others what happened in his part of the country', 'somewhat after the style of a Salvation Army gathering' (each person standing up in turn to state their news or issues). Today, Uncle Wayne Fossey notes how Elders made decisions in consensus, with 'head warriors' who worked 'in line with their decisions'. In an 1861 inquest into the Native Police in Queensland, two witnesses were asked whether at the bunya and other gatherings, Aboriginal people 'hatch mischief against the whites' and both agreed this was the case, where they 'planned their mode of attack': 'Australian Aborigines customs', *Brisbane Courier*, 18 May 1889, p. 7; Petrie, C (ed.), *Tom Petrie's Reminiscences*, Angus & Robertson, Sydney, 1983 (1904), pp. 22–23. Ray Kerkhove has listed these and further examples including James Davis (an escaped convict), who described a meeting after the bunya gathering being arranged to organise resistance after the Kilcoy Massacre, where 'a great meeting of the native tribes, 13 or 14 in number called a *toor* (ring) by the blacks – a great circular ditch being dug out by the women ... These meetings may be called by any tribe, the messengers being despatched in every direction': Stephen Simpson, 30 May 1842 to Colonial Secretary. In *The Simpson Letterbook*, Kerkhove notes another recollection of meetings of fifty delegates from fifty tribes as well as the evidence to the inquest: Kerkhove, 2023, pp. 86–87; Langevad, G (ed.), *The Simpson Letterbook*, Cultural and Historical Records of Queensland, no. 1, 1979, Anthropology Museum, University of Queensland, Brisbane, 1979. See McBryde, I, 'Travellers in storied landscapes: A case study in exchanges and heritage', *Aboriginal History*, vol. 24, 2000, pp. 157–164; Mulvaney, J & Kamminga, J, *Prehistory of Australia*, Allen & Unwin, Sydney 1999, p. 95; and Flood, J, *Archaeology of the Dreamtime*, Manoa, University of Hawaii Press, 1983, pp. 235–236, have all shown that well-established trade routes connected the inland with coastal Queensland and down the Great Dividing Range to the Snowy Mountains. Dale Kerwin's *Aboriginal Dreaming Paths and Trading Routes: The colonisation of the Australian economic landscape*, Sussex Academic Press, Brighton, 2010, outlined how 'dreaming paths' formed travel routes along which goods and knowledge flowed. Commodities traded over vast distances included bunya nuts, pituri, stone axes, ochre, skins and a myriad of wooden implements. It is clear that stories and ceremonies were also traded along the same routes. As Henry Reynolds put it, 'large ceremonial gatherings provided the venue for gossip, trade and cultural inter-change':

Reynolds, H, *The Other Side of the Frontier, Aboriginal resistance to the European invasion of Australia*, UNSW Press, Sydney, 2006 (1981), pp. 11–12.

23   Uncle Paul Spearim, interview, 24 October 2024.

24   After this unification, attacks on colonists substantially increased from thirty-three in 1827 to 124 in 1830. Reynolds, H & Clements, N, *Tongerlongeter: First Nations leader and Tasmanian war hero*, NewSouth Publishing, Sydney, 2022, pp. 101, 148; Godfrey, M, 'Robertson, Gilbert (1794–1851)', *ADB*. So too at Bathurst in central west New South Wales in 1824, after threats to 'tumble down' all the 'white men', attacks occurred within days of each other across a wide region, indicating a sophisticated communications network and broad alliances. See Gapps, S, *Gudyarra: The first Wiradyuri war of resistance: The Bathurst War 1822–1824*, NewSouth Publishing, Sydney, 2021, esp. pp. 136–177.

25   Selheim, P, 'Treatment of Aborigines', *Courier*, 5 March 1862, p. 2. Historians looking at the Australian Wars have generally seen Aboriginal groups as either too small to mobilise in large numbers, or that resistance was generally a local response. See for example: Prentis, M, *A Study in Black and White: The Aborigines in Australian history*, Metheun Australia, Sydney, 1975, p. 27; Pearson, M, 'Bathurst Plains and beyond: European colonisation and Aboriginal resistance', *Aboriginal History*, vol. 8, no. 1, 1984, p. 76; Owen, C, 2016, *'Every Mother's Son Is Guilty' – Policing the Kimberley Frontier of Western Australia, 1882–1905*, UWA Publishing, Perth, p. 65; Dennis, P, 1995, 'Aboriginal armed resistance to white invasion', in Dennis, P, Grey, J, Morris, E & Prior, R (eds), *The Oxford Companion to Australian Military History*, Oxford University Press, Melbourne, p. 3. However as Ray Kerkhove notes, small numbers of warriors in localised groups is no impediment to forming alliances. Kerkhove compares other First Nations warrior resistance in North America and elsewhere, also noting that such combinations from different areas in fact have their own tactical advantages in being able to threaten from different directions. He identifies three forms of warrior military organisation: 'Totemic warrior lodges'; 'Confederacies (intertribal alliances)' and 'Region-wide resistance movements': Kerkhove, 2023, pp. 33, 39–40. Some historians have argued that warriors might be defending 'spiritually significant areas'. For example, Grace Karskens suggests that 'the geography of the [Dyarubbin-Hawkesbury] river from Cattai to Sackville Reach suggests that they were defending a spiritually significant area': Karskens, G, *People of the River: Lost worlds of early Australia*, Allen & Unwin, Sydney, 2020, p. 499. While this may be important, the role of economic (resource-rich areas) and military (defensible terrain) factors must also be considered. Most engagements have some element of terrain for a surprise attack or for a covered retreat or withdrawal. Attacks on colonists most commonly occurred at places that offered a tactical advantage rather than anything else. For a classic example see the 1816 Battle at Razorback in Gapps, S, *The Sydney Wars: Conflict in the early colony 1788–1817*, NewSouth Publishing, Sydney, 2018, pp. 217–221. Attacks were designed to cut off supplies to the colonists, gain supplies for themselves, and push colonists out from their farms and stock runs. The idea of a 'spiritual defence' tends to limit Indigenous agency as an emotional response, rather than responses calculated in strategic and military terms by a warrior culture steeped in such abilities and practices.

26   Uncle Paul Spearim, interview, 24 October 2024; Bonney, C, 'Autobiographical notes', NLA, JAF P10 55, 1897, p. 7.

27   Cahir, F, *'My Country all gone the white men have stolen it': The invasion of Wadawurrung Country 1800–1870*, Revolution Print, Ballarat, 2019, p. 53.

28   Uncle Bill Allen Junior, interview, Bathurst, 6 June 2024. In northern New South Wales in the 1890s, early anthropologist and ethnographer RH Mathews observed people travelling from the Namoi River in the south to Maronoa in the north to the MacIntyre

River – a circumference of area around 300 kilometres. See Kenny, A, 'Custom in Aboriginal Australia relevant to Native Title Case Law', *Oceania*, vol. 82, no. 2, 2012, pp. 138–142 for an overview of a series of bora ceremonies Mathews witnessed in the 1890s. As Kenny notes, 'the data on the three boras attended by Kogai from the St George area, Pickum Welltown, Callandoon, Winton, Umbercollie and Goondiwindi and Kamilar Gundabïoui, Meroe and other places, show how the frequent holding of ceremonies together of diverse peoples from a wide area renewing, invigorating and reconfiguring regional polity'. Kenny continues: 'The reaches of such societies went beyond an immediate group of people who lived together, shared a common language or owned a particular stretch of land and were open to or influenced by changing political, social and environmental circumstances'. While traditional Aboriginal nations, groups or shared boundaries are not always linked to features such as waterways or catchments or mountain ranges or rivers, they often are. The Murray-Darling Basin covers many diverse nations, but these groups share some broadly common cultural traits. Some conception of the identity of people as Koori, Goori, Murri, Palawa, Noongar and other terms that are not pan-Aboriginal but extend beyond language groups, appears to link region-wide gatherings and other forms of shared culture and knowledge. Kerkhove suggests there were 'distinctive features of economy and lifestyle' across the Murray-Darling Basin, including similar social and kinship systems, intermarriage and kin ties, shared linguistic, artistic and social features and long-distance ceremonial attendance. These people shared similar hunting (large plains game such as emu, kangaroo and goanna), riverine resources (fish, turtles, freshwater mussels, reeds and waterfowl) and many other practices including harvesting, tools, weapons, villages, ancestral stories and knowledge (see 'The Rising and regional borders', Ray Kerkhove, pers. comm., 27 August 2023). The extent of shared cosmologies and ancestral stories between different language groups certainly breaks apart the misconception that resistance could not be 'pan-Aboriginal' or that different groups (despite some having traditional enmities) could not unite against a common foe. See Pardoe, C, 'Conflict and territoriality in Australia', in Allen, MW & Jones, TL (eds), *Re-examining a Pacified Past: Violence and warfare among hunter-gatherers*, Left Coast Press, Walnut Creek, 2014, pp. 112–114 and Kenny, 2012, pp. 129–151.

29   At the tri-annual Bunya Gathering in southern Queensland people travelled from central New South Wales and south-west Queensland to feast on the nuts from the bunya pine tree that once stood in numerous groves across southern Queensland. Kerkhove, 2023, p. 54. Kerkhove compares a later 'spiritual resistance' known as the 'Kooroongoora' in the manner it was communicated across huge distances in Central Australia. See also Kerkhove, 'The Great Bunya Gathering. Early Accounts', <www.academia.edu/8244371/The_Great_Bunya_Gathering_Early_Accounts>, 2012, p. 4; Flanagan, 'The Aborigines of Australia. No. XIV. The "Rising" of 1842–4', *Empire*, 15 April 1854, p. 3. Fred Cahir notes the Kulin nation's 'extensive communication networks' were 'frequently mentioned by colonial writers': Cahir, 2019, p. 53. For reports on the use of fires and smoke in communication see Kerkhove, 2023, pp. 88–90. For songlines using the night sky see Fuller et al, 'Star maps and travelling to ceremonies', *Journal of Astronomical History and Heritage*, vol. 17, no. 2, 2014, pp. 149–160. As Fuller notes, 'a way to use the stars for travelling which was not a form of navigation by the stars … was the use of patterns of stars (star maps) to teach people how to travel in and outside of their country … technique could be considered a memory aid to assist in teaching and as a reminder for future travel'. Fuller summarises: '… the Euahlayi people [northern New South Wales and southern Queensland] used a known pattern of stars in the night sky to teach and remember a number of waypoints on a route to a

destination, often a ceremonial gathering place. This star map was used in winter during the planning for the summer travel, and we have identified at least three routes from Euahlayi country to ceremonial or resource destinations'.

30 Aunty Glenda Chalker, pers. comm., 16 April 2024; Lt. Adamson George Parker, SRNSW, 4/1735, 6045, pp. 60–62.
31 18 April 1839, in Serle, G, 'Manuscripts: Excerpts from the letters of Dr. David Henry Wilsone, squatter, 1839–1841', *La Trobe Library Journal*, vol. 5, no. 19, 1977, p. 57.
32 30 August 1840, in Serle, 1977, p. 61.
33 Flanagan, 1854, p. 3.
34 Uncle James Ingram, interview, 20 October 2023. See also Gammage, B, *Narrandera Shire*, Narrandera Shire Council, Narrandera, 1986, p. 17; Aunty Flo Grant quoted in Sullivan, B, 'Wagga and the Murrumbidgee: The Wagga Community's relationship with the Murrumbidgee River and wetlands over time', Charles Sturt University Archives, 2012, <cdn.csu.edu.au/__data/assets/pdf_file/0008/679796/Bernard-Sullivan-Wagga-and-the-Murrumbidgee.pdf>, p. 45. Barry Stone's 2019 history of squatting notes 'outbreaks of violence increased across the entire frontier, from the Port Phillip District in the south through New South Wales to Southern Queensland'. Stone echoes Flanagan, suggesting this was 'a culmination of mistreatment and mutual distrust dating back 50 years' but fails to consider the resistance in finer grained detail. See Stone, B, *The Squatters: The story of Australia's pastoral pioneers*, Allen & Unwin, Sydney, 2019, esp. p. 58. Quentin Beresford's 2021 *Wounded Country* certainly focuses on the riverways and resistance warfare as a defence of Country, but does not focus on connections between the terrain of the Murray-Darling as being of tactical and strategic importance. See Beresford, Q, *Wounded Country: The Murray-Darling Basin – A contested history*, NewSouth Publishing, Sydney, 2021, especially p. 81. Perhaps if we are to extend Emily O'Gorman's recent push for an understanding of 'socioecological landscapes', the history of defending rivers and waterways needs closer examination. They were certainly 'the places first sought out' by Europeans, and often places of refuge for Aboriginal people in marshes or wetlands that were not 'productive' for stocking sheep and cattle. That they were also the places first defended has had little attention: O'Gorman, E, *Wetlands in a Dry Land: More-than-human histories of Australia's Murray-Darling Basin*, University of Washington Press, Seattle, 2021, especially pp. 7 and 42.
35 As Ray Kerkhove notes, 'First Nations resistance had to contend with a trickle of tiny but rapidly expanding cells. Its "frontline" was largely empty – vast, unfenced leases or "runs", later called "stations" – with "outstations" many miles apart. There was no actual "boundary". The frontier was indistinct, porous and mosaiced': Kerkhove, 2023, p. 16. Ray Kerkhove is one of the few historians to have identified numerous points of alliances, but also broader 'resistance movements' including 'The Rising' in south-eastern Australia and the 'Kooroongoroo' across central and northern Australia. As Kerkhove points out, increasing focus on understanding the detail of Australia's First Nations resistance has occurred over the last ten years or so. In 2014, Mark Allen demonstrated how archaeological and ethnographic evidence indicated quite complex and large-scale military engagements within so-called 'hunter-gatherer societies': Allen, M, 'Hunter-gatherer violence and warfare in Australia', in Allen, MW & Jones, TL (eds), *Violence and Warfare among Hunter-Gatherers*, ProQuest Ebook Centra, Taylor and Francis, 2014, pp. 97–98. More recently, Christophe Darmangeat analysed hundreds of early accounts of intra-Indigenous collective conflicts in Aboriginal Australia, developing an extensive database and then publishing a comprehensive examination of Aboriginal warfare in *Justice and Warfare in Aboriginal Australia*, Lexington Books, New York, 2020. In this,

he identified four modes of regulated fighting, often involving very large numbers. The database, containing all the bibliographic references, is available online at: <cdarmangeat.ghes.univ-paris-diderot.fr/australia/index.php>. See also Darmangeat, C, 'Vanished wars of Australia: The archaeological invisibility of Aboriginal collective conflicts', *Journal of Archaeological Method and Theory*, vol. 26, 2019, p. 1559. Kerkhove argues that through such changes, it gradually became apparent that First Nations resistance was indeed highly organised: Kerkhove, 2023, p. 12. While Kerkhove maps the area of the circa 1840 'Rising' as a swathe of southeastern Australia from the Darling Downs in Queensland to all of present-day Victoria and the eastern half of New South Wales, I believe we can consider this as a front line rather than such a huge zone, which encompasses areas that had no or little conflict at this time. Beresford's chapter on resistance warfare in the Murray-Darling basin notes how Aboriginal victories were 'short lived' and have been difficult for historians to explain in 'military terms' and due to the scattered information in historical sources they have to 'imagine' how Aboriginal people heard news of encroaching squatters and colonisers. Beresford does note that 'cooperation among clans and nations' occurred, following Kerkhove's descriptions of typical 'tactical measures' deployed by warriors in frontier warfare: Beresford, 2021, pp. 86–87.

Chapter 1

1. *Australian*, 2 January 1835, p. 2; Walsh, 'Jamison, Sir John (1776–1844)', *ADB*.
2. Historians have usually seen the conflict in the Hunter region as petering out by the early 1830s. The 1835 warfare and bushranging spree may be connected, and there was a period of conflict, possibly related, at this time at 'Brisbane Water' that historians have not seen as part of Hunter Valley histories and have rarely studied. See Dunn, M, *The Convict Valley: The bloody struggle on Australia's early frontier*, Allen & Unwin, Sydney, 2020 and Allen, L, 'A history of the Aboriginal people of the Central Coast of New South Wales to 1874', PhD thesis, The University of Newcastle, 2022; *New South Wales Government Gazette*, no. 177, 22 July 1835, p. 501; *Sydney Gazette*, 4, p. 2 and 13 June 1835, p. 2.
3. In 1827 at a station on the Liverpool Plains, what seems to have begun as a scuffle between stockmen with whips and warriors with clubs turned into a mass shooting. It appears to have been hushed up by squatters keen not to get into trouble after the Mounted Police Officer Nathaniel Lowe had been put on trial earlier that year for killing Aboriginal people. Roger Milliss appears to have untangled what occurred from the embellished and scant records: Milliss, R, *Waterloo Creek: The Australia Day Massacre of 1838: George Gipps and the British conquest of New South Wales*, McPhee Gribble, Melbourne, 1992, pp. 78–81; O'Rourke, MJ, *Raw Possum and Salted Pork: Major Mitchell and the Kamilaroi Aborigines*, Plowpress, Canberra, 1995, p. 12.
4. O'Rourke notes the farthest stations in 1831 to have been around the Mooki River and included Druitt's 'Phillips Creek', Blaxland's 'Kilcoobil', Lawson's 'Premer' and 'Bone Creek', Cox's 'Nombi', Eales's 'Duri', Brown's 'Wallamoul' and Dangar's 'Waldoo' (near Tamworth): O'Rourke, 1995, p. 13.
5. See Gapps, S, *The Sydney Wars: Conflict in the early colony 1788–1817*, NewSouth Publishing, Sydney, 2018, pp. 121–122.
6. *Sydney Herald*, 1 June 1835, p. 3 and 11 June 1835, p. 2; *Australian*, 4 August 1835, p. 2; *Colonist*, 13 August 1835, p. 3.
7. 'Williams' River Blacks', *Sydney Herald*, 3 August 1835, p. 3.
8. *Australian*, 4 August 1835, p. 2.
9. In late 1835, Bourke received assent from Glenelg to reward convicts who protected their masters' property. This was in response to a memorial [or petition] from 'a large number of the most respectable Inhabitants of New South Wales' in support of a land grant to a

convict who had defended his 'employer's property against an armed party of runaway Convicts': Glenelg to Bourke, 13 December 1835, *HRA*, XVIII, p. 227.

10 For a detailed account of Clarke's life and four or five years with the Gomeroi see Boyce, D, *Clarke of the Kindur: Convict, bushranger, explorer*, Melbourne University Press, Melbourne, 1970, pp. 26–37.

11 Mitchell, TL, *Three Expeditions: With descriptions of the recently explored region of Australia Felix, and of the present colony of New South Wales*, T & W Boone, London, 1838, vol. 1, p. 36; O'Rourke, 1995, pp. 13, 23.

12 Mitchell, 1838, vol. 1, pp. 62, 140–141; O'Rourke, 1995, p. 29.

13 Mitchell noted that 'the population of the Darling seemed to have been much reduced by smallpox': Mitchell, 1838, vol. 1, p. 218. So too, Charles Sturt came across people who had 'violent cutaneous eruptions' on their bodies. He noted the number of houses he saw didn't seem to equate to the small number of people he met: Sturt, C, *Two expeditions into the interior of Southern Australia*, Public Library of South Australia, Adelaide, 1963, pp. 124–125; O'Rourke, 1995, p. 13; White, GB, *Journal*, 1832, quoted in O'Rourke, 1995, p. 15.

14 As Peter Kabaila notes: 'with no immunity to the virus, tribes were decimated. As the disease moved inland through the Wiradjuri region river system into South Australia it was interpreted as the result of the powerful magic of distant tribes who had unleashed the terrifying power of the Rainbow Serpent ... in the Wiradjuri region these times remained vivid for generations as a time of death. Fifty years later, the old people recalled how the sickness "Followed down the rivers" ... Burying bodies was no longer attempted and the atmosphere became tainted with decomposing bodies'; Kabaila, P, *Wiradjuri Places: The Lachlan River Basin*, Black Mountain Projects, Canberra, 1996, p. 10. The devastating path of smallpox was confirmed later by, as Beresford writes, the 'squatters, magistrates and the ministers of religion' who all gave evidence to a Select Committee on the Condition of the Aborigines in 1845. A magistrate at Dungog north of the Hunter Valley explained that 'about ten years ago an epidemic of a variolous nature carried off about half their number'. These were Wonnurua families. Others who gave evidence reported 'a great number' and another, 'a third' of the population had been killed around 1830 by the disease. So it seems that around 30 to 50 per cent of the Aboriginal population across what was to become New South Wales was killed by smallpox: Beresford, *Wounded Country: The Murray-Darling Basin – A contested history*, NewSouth Publishing, Sydney, 2021, p. 77; Campbell, J, *Invisible Invaders: Smallpox and other diseases in Aboriginal Australia, 1780–1880*, Melbourne University Press, Melbourne, 2002, p. 126. At the same time, other diseases were spreading. In mid-1836, the *Colonist* newspaper disinterestedly reported that 'great havoc is being made, we understand, among the blacks in the neighbourhood of Port Macquarie, by a disease of the nature of a diarrhoea, which threatens speedily to extirpate the race', *Colonist*, 23 June 1836, p. 5.

15 White, GB, *Journal*, 1832, quoted in O'Rourke, 1995, p. 15; Beresford, 2021, p. 79.

16 'Private interior discovery', *Sydney Monitor*, 18 April 1835, p. 2.

17 The report suggested that the 'Bogan tribe' would assist any action against the 'Mials', indicating a traditional enmity: 'The king of the Bogan tribe, and Sandy, the historian of the bloody transaction, are desirous, with assistance, of conducting the police to Warrandurry's retreat, for the purpose of apprehending him and his accomplices': 'Bathurst', *Gazette*, 23 July 1835, p. 3. According to Governor Bourke, Richard Cunningham, 'Colonial Botanist', 'wandered from the Exploring Party near the River Bogan on 17 April last' (1834). Bourke wrote to Lord Glenelg to inform him 'with regret' that 'a Party sent out to seek him' had informed him that 'he was murdered by the Black natives soon after his separation from his Companions'. Bourke waited for more information on the circumstances: Bourke to Glenelg, 30 November 1835, *HRA*, XVIII, p. 214. In December

he received a report from Lieutenant Zouch of the Mounted Police to Captain Williams that described how Zouch left Bathurst on 24 October with 'Sandy', a 'black native', toward 'Borea' and on 2 November 'met with two Blacks who knew the particulars of a Whiteman having been murdered on the Bogan'. Zouch took them as guides and then a few days later approached the smoke 'from the fires of the Myall Blacks' on the 'borders of a Lake called Budda'. Zouch then rounded up forty people with no resistance and they named the three responsible. Zouch took the men 'Wongangegery, Boree-boomalee and Bureemall' prisoner and the only reason Zouch could obtain for Cunningham's death was that when they took him in and gave him food he was 'repeatedly getting up in the night' and this 'excited suspicion'. We can only surmise as to what Cunningham was doing – perhaps he was delirious. Whatever the case, Zouch followed orders, marched to the site of the killing and buried Cunningham's remains. He returned to find two men had escaped and that only Burremall was to be sent to Sydney for trial: Zouch to Williams, 7 December 1835, *HRA*, 1, XVIII, pp. 236–237.

18   Mitchell, 1838, vol. 1, p. 114.
19   On what the military-schooled man called his 'first retreat' from the Barka-Darling River, he 'found the party who were awaiting me, with a supply of provisions, under very great alarm, in consequence of the proceedings of the Mount Harris tribe. The men had been obliged to put the camp in a state of defence. The blacks had attempted to surprise them, and would, had I not returned, have combined in some general attack': 'Obstacles that attend travelling into the interior of Australia', *Colonist*, 29 October 1835, p. 2; Gibney, 'Sturt, Charles (1795–1869)', *ADB*.
20   As Beresford notes, both Sturt and Mitchell did not like putting themselves in 'the position where Aboriginal people had the tactical advantage'. According to Beresford, Mitchell 'tended to view Aboriginal people as a natural enemy as if he were engaged in an undeclared war ... often contemplating military tactics in his dealings with them'. He reflected that 'war and victory, with all their glory ... [spreads] the light of civilization': Beresford, 2021, pp. 34, 42, 47; Mitchell, 1838, vol. 1, pp. 26, 86–87; 'Exploration', *Commercial Journal and Advertiser*, 13 August 1836, p. 2; McCombie in *Report from the Select Committee on the Condition of the Aborigines*, p. 70; Farrow, 'McCombie, Thomas (1819–1869)', *ADB*.
21   *Australian*, 3 July 1835, p. 2.
22   'Police report', *Sydney Monitor*, 16 September 1835, p. 2. It was obvious to Mitchell he was not welcomed by the various groups he met along the Baaka-Darling: 'Some of their ceremonies were different from those of any other Aboriginal tribes nearer the colony, such as waving the green bough, first setting it on fire, with furious gestures at us; throwing dust at us with their toes, and spitting at our men ... We remained masters ever after of the left bank of the Darling, although a very savage tribe, 120 miles higher, crossed one day in a scrub, and immediately set about burning the bushes and grass close to our tents, until we drove them across the river': 'Exploring expedition to the interior to the Honorable the Colonial Secretary, Camp West of Harvey's Range, Sept. 4, 1835', *Colonist*, 24 September 1835, p. 2. Mitchell's report of killings generated some harsh criticism in the press. Governor Bourke was forced to write to Lord Glenelg for his opinion on whether Mitchell had gone beyond the limits of his duty. A legal opinion on 'the attack made on the Black Natives by the exploring party under Major Mitchell on the 27th May 1836' by the 'Law Officers of the Colony' was sent in April 1838 to Lord Glenelg by Governor Gipps: Gipps to Glenelg, 18 April 1838, *HRA*, XVIII, p. 390. For Mitchell's defence and the Executive Council's assessment see Appendices A–M, Extract from Minutes No. 29–31 of the proceedings of the Executive Council, 16th, 19th, 24th December, 1836, *New South Wales Government Gazette*, 21 January 1837, no. 259, Supplement, p. 59.

23 OzArk Environmental Heritage Management, 'Bourke Shire Aboriginal Heritage Study', p. 19; 'Bathurst', *Gazette*, 23 July 1835, p. 3. As Iain Stuart notes, 'when William Lee, a squatter from Bathurst, took up a station on the Bogan in September 1841 Aborigines attacked his men and three of them were killed. This required an expedition by the Mounted Police in which a number of Aborigines were killed and captured. Governor Gipps cancelled Lee's licence no doubt because he saw Lee's disregard of instructions as the cause of the trouble. Lee's case however was taken up as a cause celebre in the squatter's struggle with Governor Gipps. The ban on settlement remained until 1858 no doubt helped by the lack of water in the region': Stuart, I, 'Squatting landscapes in South-Eastern Australia (1820–1895)', PhD thesis, Prehistoric and Historic Archaeology, University of Sydney, 1999, p. 55.

24 In March, Sir James Stirling addressed the Legislative Council and was happy to report that although there was apparently little progress in 'their civilization' he noted the 'satisfactory state [of] communications with the Natives' and in recent months only 'one single interruption of an accidental character'. He would soon be disappointed: 'Tuesday 23rd of March 1836', *Sydney Herald*, 28 July 1836, p. 4; *Commercial Journal and Advertiser*, 17 August 1836, p. 3.

25 The editor asked in reply whether it would be preferable to 'live among savages than with civilized whites who would perpetrate wholesale murder?': 'Native Blacks', *Sydney Gazette*, 2 February 1836, p. 2. In August, a 'Correspondent' to the *Sydney Herald* believed that when Aboriginal peoples' 'favourite spots have become the sites of towns and villages, or the possessions of unfeeling tyrants' and their 'daughters have been dragged from the camp from before the eyes of the mother', in their 'attempts to resist', 'their brothers have been murdered'. Yet such observations and calls for restraint were drowned out by others who could only see that white lives mattered: 'The Aboriginal natives', *Sydney Herald*, 22 August 1836, p. 2; 'Port Phillip', *Sydney Gazette*, 30 August 1836, p. 2.

26 The writer to the *Monitor* called them 'Mullinbudgee Blacks', possibly meaning Murrumbidgee. The 'Warwick Blacks' they were in search of seem to have been from near present-day Cowra. The people they found were 'Taylor, Billy, Budger, John Watterman and two gins'. 'They fired two shots, one of which wounded Taylor through the back' and 'committed great depredations' including killing a calf and four pigs: *Sydney Monitor*, 30 January 1836, p. 2.

27 'Port Phillip', *Sydney Herald*, 21 July 1836, p. 4.

28 The *Colonist* described the run as 'at a station belonging to the Messrs. Hall of Pitt Town, situated on Liverpool Plains, on the banks of the River Anglo, one of the sources of the Gaddo' though it is unclear where this is today: 'Liverpool Plains', *Colonist*, 30 June 1836, p. 4. See also 'List of Europeans killed by the Aborigines on the Liverpool Plains 1832–8', *Colonist*, 22 September 1838. The other newspapers drew on the *Colonist*'s report of events. Millis suggests it could have occurred near present-day Bingara. He also considers Threlkeld's reference to what may have been this attack as actually provoked by the Europeans. Later references to pre–Myall Creek conflict in that area must be considered in the light of the opposing 'sides' of the 1838 trials, as evidence of European aggression was both being sought and covered up. Threlkeld wrote that a party of Mounted Police under Sergeant John Temple was sent to the area and 'combined with stockmen' to exact 'a terrible retribution ... upwards of eighty were shot in retaliation for this affair'. Millis believes this was in retaliation for the Hall brothers' attack. However there are no known historical records of Temple, who was stationed in the Mounted Police in the Hunter Valley, taking such action beyond Threlkeld's brief note: Milliss, 1992, pp. 101, 789.

29 *Sydney Times*, 8 October 1836, p. 2. In November, the *Sydney Herald* noted: 'The blacks at New England are very troublesome, they have lately speared both men and cattle' and the

Australian that 'We hear that the blacks at New England have lately been very troublesome, they having speared several men, and destroyed a great number of cattle': *Sydney Herald*, 28 November 1836, p, 2; *Australian*, 28 November 1836, p. 2.

30 Young, S, 'Reminiscences of Mrs Susan Bundarra Young (formerly Mrs James Buchanan) of Bundarra', *JRAHS*, pp. 401–402; Gardiner, E, *Terrible Vale: No time like the past: A history of a New England grazing run between 1830–1940*, DSAMC Education, South Tamworth, c. 1998, pp. 17–18. Harry Macdonald was the overseer for 'Mr. Wiseman' and he 'took up' a station on behalf of the businessman of Wiseman's Ferry fame. The family connections in pushing sheep and cattle north from the Hawkesbury to the Hunter, through the Liverpool Plains and on into Gomeroi Country, were common.

31 See Callum Clayton-Dixon, C, *Surviving New England: A history of Aboriginal resistance and resilience through the first forty years of the colonial apocalypse*, Anaiwan Language Revival Program, Armidale, 2019, for an overview of the resistance in the region, largely conducted post-1838.

32 'Conflict with the natives', *Wingham Chronicle and Manning River Observer*, 25 April 1922, p. 2.

33 After the attack at Kiripit: 'after this outrage the natives divided – one body seeking shelter south west towards the source of the Gloucester River, and the other going north west towards the Upper Arundel'. Apparently, 'Ganghat became anathema to the tribe – a valley of death. The adjoining parish Belbora (correctly Baal Bora) owes its name to this tragedy. It means a place to be shunned': 'Conflict with the Natives', *Wingham Chronicle and Manning River Observer*, 25 April 1922, p. 2. The author of 'Conflicts with the natives' seems to be 'J.E.W.' who went by this name in the preceding article 'Peeps into the past. Berrico Public School. ABORIGINES. PART II'. The author was certainly knowledgeable about the people of the region and seemed concerned to remind readers of the origins of the place names across the Wingham and Gloucester areas in particular: 'The Kabook Tribe of aborigines which inhabited this district, were linguistically allied to and apparently a branch of that strong tribe that ranged over the Manning and Wallamba water sheds. The boundaries of their "Town" – tribal territory – seems to have been well defined geographically, by adopting the watersheds of these two rivers. To their west and throughout the Hunter Valley roamed the powerful Kamileroi Tribe and its branches, and on the north was a distinct New England tribe. The Williams River blacks were apparently a branch of the Kamileroi, but the Port Stephens Tribe seems to have been distinct from either by their place names': 'Peeps into the past. Berrico Public School. ABORIGINES. PART II. Written for the "Wingham Chronicle" (By J.E.W.)', *Wingham Chronicle and Manning River Observer*, 25 April 1922, p. 2. Contemporary reports confirm this and possibly other uses of poison. The *Australian* newspaper in early 1838 noted that 'a number of the "poor blacks", as one of our contemporaries sneeringly calls the aborigines, have been lately shot at Port Macquarie under circumstances which loudly call for enquiry. A correspondent informs us that another mode of destroying these unhappy creatures – and one which is daily practised by the stockmen and others in the neighbourhood – is to mix corrosive sublimate!! with food, which is given to them by those white murderers under pretence of regaling them': *Australian*, 9 February 1838, p. 3. The *Gazette* demanded that the police magistrate at Port Macquarie 'explain his conduct in reference to certain blacks who were shot it has been publicly asserted by his orders at Port Macquarie, and whose ears were cut off and brought to Mr. Gray, in proof of their having been so shot': 'Port Macquarie', *Sydney Gazette and New South Wales Advertiser*, 17 February 1838, p. 2.

34 *Launceston Advertiser*, 23 March 1837, p. 3; 'The Poor Blacks', *Sydney Herald*, 7 December 1837, p. 2.

35 *Sydney Monitor*, 27 October 1837, p. 2; *Bent's News and Tasmanian Register*, 25 November 1837, p. 2.

36 'Maneroo Plains', *Australian*, 18 November 1836, p. 2. In 1837 the Port Phillip district seemed no safer. The editor of the *Sydney Monitor* believed it was no wonder that warriors were attacking settlers in the region: 'When the native blacks can be tied to trees, and deliberately shot to death by the convicts, and when those convicts on being tried, get acquitted, we cannot wonder, though we deeply regret retaliation by the natives': 'Port Phillip', *Sydney Monitor*, 27 March 1837, p. 2.

37 'The Bogan blacks', *Colonial Observer*, 25 November 1841, p. 59; Kass, T, 'A thematic history of Bogan Shire', 2012, <www.bogan.nsw.gov.au/images/PlanningAndDevelopment/Heritage/BSC_Thematic_History_-_Draft_March_2012.pdf>, p. 9.

38 Balfour, JO, *A Sketch of New South Wales*, Smith, Elder and Company, London, 1845, pp. 20–21.

39 Balfour, JO, 1845, p. 21.

40 See Connor, J, *The Australian Frontier Wars 1788–1838*, UNSW Press, Sydney, 2002, p. 112 for an overview of the pressures from 'reformist zeal'.

41 Equivalent to 9.2 million hectares. See Roberts, SH, *The Squatting Age in Australia 1835–47*, Melbourne University Press, Melbourne, 1964, pp. 69–84. Besides all this, 'adventurers' were making treaties with Aboriginal people and claiming their own chunks of what the authorities believed was Crown Land. Governor Bourke saw the treaty made by John Batman and the Port Phillip Association with Kulin people to be a threat to British claims of possession. The colonial office in London agreed to Bourke asserting formal legal jurisdiction over the entire colony of New South Wales. Batman's land grab for Port Phillip became illegal under British law. This also seemed to deny any sovereignty of Aboriginal people to their land. Yet the colonial office did actually hold that Aboriginal people had rights to land, but that the laws of England would now determine them: Attwood, B, *Possession: Batman's treaty and the matter of history*, Meigunyah Press, Melbourne, 2009, pp. 84–86; Reynolds, H, *The Law of the Land*, Penguin, Melbourne, 1992, pp. 126–132. However it took until 1850 for the Colonial office to recognise that a squatters pastoral lease did not extinguish all Aboriginal rights to land. In the meantime, squatters believed they had the right to shoot 'trespassers' and people who stole or killed their stock. See Reynolds, H, *This whispering in our hearts, revisited*, NewSouth Publishing, Sydney, 2018 (1998), pp. 46–50.

42 Bourke to Glenelg, 8 September, 1837, *HRA*, XVIII, pp. 80–84.

43 Glenelg to Bourke, 13 April 1836, *HRA*, XVIII, p. 380.

44 As soon as he received Glenelg's signal, Bourke lost no time in acting to 'open the Country about Port Phillip to Settlers'. The sale of town allotments for what would become Melbourne soon added to the colonial coffers. But he also wanted to establish 'Civil Authority in the District for the protection of the Aborigines and the due administration of the Laws'. The fees from land sales could cover the cost of constables and magistrates to keep order. Bourke to Glenelg, 15 September 1836, *HRA*, XVIII, p. 540. *Government Gazette*, 5 November 1836, no. 247, p. 858.

45 As James Boyce notes, 'By the end of the 1840s squatters had seized nearly twenty million hectares of Aboriginal land'. Boyce sees the turning point in this occupation as 1835 when a Whig government under Lord Melbourne led to 'evangelical activism' permeating government. At the same time, 'colonisation turned into a frenzied land grab'. Boyce argues this occurred through a consensus struck in 1835–1836 that saw policies of containment align with colonists' 'right' to take land wherever they saw fit: Boyce, 1835, pp. xi–xiii. Bourke to Glenelg, 10 October 1835, *HRA*, XVIII, p. 156–158; Milliss, 1992, p. 793.

Chapter 2

1. Curr, EM, *Recollections of squatting in Victoria, then called the Port Phillip District (1841–1851)*, George Robertson, Melbourne, 1883, pp. 122, 177.
2. Curr, 1883, pp. 120–121.
3. Fowles, J (att.), 'Colonel James Nunn, Australian Mounted Infantry', circa 1840, ML, SLNSW, ML 1321. See Milliss, R, *Waterloo Creek: The Australia Day massacre of 1838, George Gipps and the British conquest of New South Wales*, McPhee Gribble, Melbourne, 1992, pp. 9–11, for an overview of Nunn's family and career. In fact, there was not much else Fowles could find important in Nunn's career in the colonies than his link to security for the far-off squatters and stockmen; not that was without criticism at least. By 1840, after the Waterloo Creek affair had finally been investigated, Nunn was desperately trying to resurrect his career as a British soldier.
4. Cobban, GGM, deposition, 17 May 1839, Extracts from the Minutes of the Executive Council, Enclosure A 8 to Minute No. 20 of 1839, *HRA*, XX, p. 254; Breton evidence in House of Commons Select Committee 1837 in Connor, J, *The Australian Frontier Wars 1788–1838*, UNSW Press, Sydney, 2002, p. 105. Gipps was also soon to be disappointed that military officers were reluctant to settle in the colony, having lost the advantages of land grants. As Gipps wrote to the Marquess of Normanby in November 1839, he was 'always happy to see officers of the Army or Navy settle in the Colony'. They were valued. In 1838 the governor and the Executive Council were concerned that these 'best behaved men' could simply up and leave their policing roles and go back to their regiments. The Secretary for the Colonies soon put the governor's mind to rest; any soldier in the mounted police was henceforth to be a 'supernumerary' and not 'belong to [or be paid by] their respective regiments', and would not be 'ordered to rejoin their Regiments even when those Regiments leave the Colony'. While it might have seemed a way of retaining police, secondment from the Army had suddenly become far less attractive. The colonial government would soon have to turn elsewhere for recruits. The ex-convicts of the border police were nowhere near as efficient. The Native Mounted Police, however, were incredibly so: Gipps to Glenelg, 27 April 1838, *HRA*, XIX, p. 399; Glenelg to Gipps, 15 September 1838, *HRA*, XIX, p. 584; Gipps to Normanby, 1 November 1839, *HRA*, XX, p. 385.
5. Roger Milliss outlines the push north, noting the constantly shifting nature of early runs searching for the perfect pasture as well as way runs were being treated and traded as actual property. Milliss, R, *Waterloo Creek: The Australia Day Massacre of 1838: George Gipps and the British conquest of New South Wales*, McPhee Gribble, Melbourne, 1992, pp. 90–96.
6. Major Fitton, deposition, 4 April 1839, *HRA*, XX, p. 252.
7. Boe Spearim, interview, 24 October 2024; Cobban to Nunn, 24 October 1837, Enclosure A6, Executive Council Minute, 27 March 1838, in Letters on Aborigines 1839, SRNSW, CSLR, 4/2433.1. Milliss provides an account of Cobban's journey in *Waterloo Creek*, pp. 150–151. Milliss suggests the white man was possibly James Feeny of John Macdonald's bushranging gang, who surrendered himself at the Gwydir in 1840.
8. Paterson's first tour in May only went as far as present-day Tamworth before he returned, saddle-sore and exhausted, to Jerry's Plains. He set off again in October. Thomson to Paterson, 27 April 1837, SRNSW, CCL, 4/3659, pp. 9–10.
9. Bingham to Thomson, 23 August 1837, SRNSW, CCL, 37/8239; *Government Gazette*, 20 September 1837, p. 652.
10. State of New South Wales and Office of Environment and Heritage, 'Draft Plan of Management, Terry Hie Hie Aboriginal Area', Office of Environment and Heritage website, Sydney, 2017; <www.environment.nsw.gov.au/resources/planmanagement/draft/terry-hie-hie-aboriginal-area-draft-plan-management-170540.pdf>, p. 12.

11 Aboriginal people had been managing their own cattle and sheep for years. In the 1820s around Bathurst, Wiradyuri people took large herds of cattle from the colonists and drove them away for their own source of regular beef. People watching how the squatters and their stockworkers moved, herded, and then butchered cattle as needed saw how the colonists used their cattle, and did the same. Sometimes it was just the spearing and butchering of one or two cattle, at other sites dozens of head of cattle were recorded being herded away: Stone, B, *The Squatters: The story of Australia's pastoral pioneers*, Allen & Unwin, Sydney, 2019, p. 44; Gapps, S, *Gudyarra: The first Wiradyuri war of resistance: The Bathurst war 1822–1824*, NewSouth Publishing, Sydney, 2021, pp. 5–7; Mitchell, TL, *Three Expeditions: With descriptions of the recently explored region of Australia Felix, and of the present colony of New South Wales*, T & W Boone, London, 1838, vol. 1, p. 351.

12 Paterson, Evidence to Supreme Court, 8 May 1838, encl. Dowling 'Report on the case of John Waggoner', Gipps to Glenelg, 7 May 1838, *HRA*, XIX, p. 410.

13 Threlkeld '8th Annual Report', 18 December 1838, in Gunson, N (ed.), *Australian Reminiscences and Papers of LE Threlkeld: Missionary to the Aborigines 1824–59*, 2 vols, AIATSIS, Canberra, 1974, p. 145.

14 Roger Milliss is confident that the Gravesend Massacre occurred based on these two reports and was the event that sparked retaliation. Milliss, 1992, p. 159. Mayne, 'Evidence to Legislative Council Committee on police and gaols, 19 June 1839', in *Votes and Proceedings* 1839, p. 25.

15 Paterson to Thomson, 6 December 1837, SRNSW 37/11, 557; Uncle Paul Spearim, interview 24 October 2024.

16 When a mounted police detachment did arrive in the area in January, some warriors were found 'perched upon ledges and rocks quite inaccessible'. According to Lieutenant Cobban, 'they shouted out defiance at us', as he understood it. So too, later at Waterloo Creek, the 'appearance of the Blacks' camp' indicated to Cobban 'a much larger number of men than [he] had ever seen together before'. He counted 'a great number of spears and other weapons ... three or four hundred in all': Cobban, GGM, deposition, 17 May 1839, Extracts from the Minutes of the Executive Council, Enclosure A 8 to Minute No. 20 of 1839, *HRA*, XX, pp. 254–256.

17 Despite all the assistance the boy had given Paterson, the Lands Commissioner recommended 'securing' him to assist in any police operation: Alexander Paterson, Bell's Station, Manilla River, 6 December 1837, Extracts from the Minutes of the Executive Council, Enclosure A 6 to Minute No. 20 of 1839, *HRA*, XX, pp. 252–253.

18 Glennie to Scott, 21 November 1837 and Scott to Thomson, 28 November 1837, Miscellaneous Correspondence relating to Aborigines 1797–1840, SRNSW, 55A, 5/1161, pp. 306, 308–311.

19 'Proclamation of the Queen', *Sydney Herald*, 30 October 1837, p. 2; 'The Proclaiming Queen Victoria', *Australian*, 31 October 1837, p. 2. The *Herald* claimed to have received letters about the destruction of cattle 'by the hundreds': 'The Poor Blacks', 'Accidents, Offences, etc.', *Sydney Herald*, 7 December 1837, pp. 2, 4; Extracts from the Minutes of the Executive Council No. 20 and No. 22, 1839, Encl. No. 1, Gipps to Glenelg, 22 July 1839, *HRA*, XX, p. 247. Milliss notes that Paterson's perhaps over-excited reports helped to wreak havoc at Big River, yet the situation was undoubtedly spiralling out of control and would have prompted intervention sooner rather than later: Milliss, 1992, p. 159.

20 Nunn reported Snodgrass as saying 'words to that effect' in his later deposition on Waterloo Creek. It was not disputed: JW Nunn, deposition, Encl. A 6 to Minute No. 20 of 1839, *HRA*, XX, p. 250. The mounted police had rarely been used beyond the limits of location prior to this. See Connor, 2002, p. 107. For a dramatic interpretation of the meeting and

issue of orders to Nunn see Milliss, 1992, pp. 1–3, 163–165. Milliss suggests the meeting must have given Nunn a sense of 'absolute carte blanche' for his campaign. However, this ignores Mounted Police standing orders and there is nothing in Nunn's orders or records of the meeting directly allowing Nunn to do as he pleased, but to 'suppress these outrages' with 'utmost exertion' and to 'act according to your own judgement'.

21 Interview, Aunty Leanna, 1 December 2023, Bathurst. The battle was between 'coast and mountains tribes' near the Taylors Range in present-day southeast Queensland: 'J.W.', 'Romance of real life in Australia', *Colonial Times*, 24 May 1850, p. 4.

22 See O'Rourke, MJ, *Raw Possum and Salted Pork: Major Mitchell and the Kamilaroi Aborigines*, Plowpress, Canberra, 1995 and Milliss, 1992, pp. 21–43 for an outline of the Kamilaroi (Gomeroi) and squatters at this time. Milliss suggests a 'pre-contact' figure of '12–15,000 for the Kamilaroi, or even more': Millis, 1992, p. 26. More recently Karl-Erik Sveiby and Nhunggabarra man, Tex Skuthorpe, from Nhunggal country in northwestern New South Wales suggested 15 000 but with possible fluctuations in size as large as 60 000: Sveiby, K & Skuthorpe, T, *Treading Lightly: The hidden wisdom of the world's oldest people*, Allen & Unwin, Sydney, 2006, pp. 25–26.

23 See Fison, L & Howitt, AW, *Kamilaroi and Kurnai: Group-marriage and relationship, and marriage by elopement, drawn chiefly from the usage of the Australian Aborigines: Also the Kurnai tribe, their customs in peace and war*, George Robertson, Melbourne, 1880 and Ridley, W, *Kamilaroi and other Australian Languages*, Thomas Richards, Government Printer, Sydney, 1875.

24 Aunty Resa Dawn describes how 'the Gwydir River rises at the junction of the Rocky River and Boorolong Creek, at Yarrowyck (Bulagaranda) northwest of Uralla and flows generally northwest and west, joined by over thirty-four tributaries, including the Horton and Mehi rivers, before reaching the Barwon River, north east of Collarenebri over a 488-kilometre course. Before the construction of Copeton Dam and much diversionary work, the Gwydir River flowed into the Gingham and Lower Gwydir Wetlands': Resa Dawn, Facebook post in 'Gomeroi of the Namoi', 23 March 2024. Yarrowyck Crossing is a popular camping ground today, one of many incredible riverside camp spots the author visited during research for this book.

25 Mitchell, 1838, vol. 1, pp. 90, 94. For an overview of Kamilaroi agriculture, aquaculture and stories of great floods see Milliss, 1994, pp. 26–29.

26 Mitchell, 1838, vol. 1, pp. 74–76, 114–115; Cunningham, A, 'A report of a tour', April – 7 July 1827, Allan Cunningham papers, 1827–1832, ML, SLNSW, *D79, p. 72.

27 Paul Spearim, interview, 24 October 2024. Roger Milliss's analysis of the lead-up to Waterloo Creek is extraordinarily detailed. Milliss notes in his inimitable way how 'most of the inland Aborigines had already heard about the whites and their ways on the inter-tribal telegraph even if they had never seen them at first-hand'. He adds: 'one can only speculate on the animated debates that must have ensued in the elders' councils on the best tactics to adopt': Milliss, 1992, p. 100.

28 For an overview of Nunn's route both known and conjectural, see Connor, 2002, pp. 108–109. For a far more detailed account see Milliss, 1992, pp. 166–203.

29 Nunn to Thomson, 5 March 1838, SRNSW, Misc. Correspondence relating to Aborigines, 38/2279; Nunn, deposition, Merton, 4 April 1839, *HRA*, XX, p. 251; Cobban, deposition, Merton, 17 May 1839, *HRA*, XX, p. 254; Lee, deposition, Merton, 4 April 1839, *HRA*, XX, p. 251; Connor, 2002, p. 108, Millis, 1994, p. 170.

30 See, for example, Richard Broome, R, *Aboriginal Australians: A history since 1788*, Allen & Unwin, Sydney, 2010 (1982), p. 47. Even military historian John Connor makes a similar assessment. See Connor, 2002, pp. 49, 62, 66–67, 107–118.

31 Nunn and Cobban's reports and later depositions are vague at times with periods of activity unmentioned. Milliss's efforts in piecing together the route are remarkable, though they remain speculative and perhaps paint too much of a picture of Nunn simply trying to find and destroy any Aboriginal people at all at this point – suggesting it had purely become a punitive expedition rather than attempting to find the raiders and killers: Milliss, 1992, pp. 173–174. See Connor, 2002, p. 110 for an assessment of Milliss on Nunn. Nunn may have gathered several stockmen at Cobb's, but as Connor notes, it is unlikely the 'ten or twenty' suggested by Milliss. Overseers and station owners could not deplete their own defences too much.

32 'The Fiftieth Anniversary of the Colony', *Australian*, 26 January 1838, p. 3; 'The Jubilee', *Australian*, 30 January 1838, p. 2. While Milliss is confident the attack and killings occurred on 26 January, Connor is not as certain. We can't be certain of the date because Nunn seems not to have kept a diary and other Mounted Police who later gave evidence were not exact with dates. Whatever the case, it was a day or two either side of the Jubilee Celebrations: Milliss, 1992, p. 180; Connor, 2002, p. 110.

33 Cobban, deposition, Merton 17 May 1839, *HRA*, XX, p. 254. Milliss locates the scene as Waterloo Creek through two later accounts from a stockman and a travelling journalist. The *Town and Country* journalist interviewed 'Peter', the only 'now living but one blackfellow [he didn't name the other] who escaped that dreadful slaughter'. Peter said 'the greater part of the tribe' had been slaughtered, suggesting around sixty people if there were a hundred camped there. Peter also seems to have called it a 'fight', or the journalist at least called it that: 'the scene of a fight, and the slaughter of a large number of blacks': 'A Tour to the North: Liverpool Plains – Gurley and Edgeroi', *Town and Country Journal*, 28 February 1874, p. 337; Milliss, 1992, pp. 176–177. Milliss worked out from talking to locals during the 1980s that what is now known as Millie Creek and Lower Water were once Waterloo Creek and Snodgrass Lagoon: Milliss, 1992, p. 179.

Chapter 3

1 The Taungurung Land and Waters Council describe Taungurung Country as going 'to the Campaspe River in the east (where we meet up with Dja Dja Wurrung), nearly up to Echuca in the north just south of where the Campaspe River meets the Murray River (Yorta Yorta/Bangerang country), down to Murchison, over to Mooroopna and then the Ovens and Broken Rivers in the east near Wangaratta and Bright (Dhudhuroa and Yaitmathang are our alpine neighbours in the north east, and Gunai/Kurnai in the south east)': 'Tuangurung Country Plan', Taungurung Land and Waters Council website, <taungurung.com.au/wp-content/uploads/2021/01/Taungurung_Country-Plan.pdf>.

2 Bonney, C, 'Autobiographical notes', NLA, JAF P10 55, 1897, pp. 3–4. Bonney then took a run at Kilmore, but moved to Mount Macedon as he had great 'trouble in getting men' to work for him. Several convict workers took his guns and left his run to become bushrangers: *Colonist*, 1 June 1837, p. 3.

3 Snodgrass to Glenelg, 23 February 1838, *HRA*, XIX, pp. 290–291.

4 Perry, TM, 'Hovell, William Hilton (1786–1875)', *ADB*; Hume, SH, 'Hume, Hamilton (1797–1873)', *ADB*; Mollison, *An Overlanding Diary: April–December 1837*, pp. 10–29; Thomsen, 'Mollison, Alexander Fullerton (1805–1885)', *ADB*. See Presland, G, *First People: The Eastern Kulin of Melbourne, Port Phillip and Central Victoria*, Museum Victoria Publishing, Melbourne, 2010, pp. 12–15 for an overview of the Kulin confederacy, language groups and traditional lands.

5 Parsons, V, 'Faithful, William (1774–1847)', *ADB*.

6 Lang, JD, *An Historical & Statistical Account of New South Wales From the Founding of the*

Colony in 1788 to the Present Day: In two volumes: The history of the last twenty-five years entirely new, vol. 1, Sampson Low, Marston, Low, & Searle, London, 1875, pp. 194–195; Baker, DWA, 'Lang, John Dunmore (1799–1878)', *ADB*.

7 According to Samuel Uren's account, as reported to him by the son of one of the survivors, the first party went to Colonel White's station, Three Mile Creek, and was there increased to nineteen men before heading to Broken River: Uren, S, 'The Faithfull Massacre', *Australasian*, 6 July 1907, p. 3. Accounts are conflicting. Patrick Drain's deposition suggests Faithfull followed a day later with eight men and Drain recalled the advance party being attacked well beforehand, three weeks before the battle at Broken River, it seems. See: Statement by Patrick Drain, 1 June 1838, enclosed with JR Hardy to Thomson, 1 June 1838, SRNSW, CSLR, 38/5770.

8 Sturt, C, 'Obstacles that attend travelling into the interior of Australia', *Colonist*, 29 October 1835, p. 2; Gibney, 'Sturt, Charles (1795–1869)', *ADB*.

9 In mid-1840, Lands Commissioner Henry Bingham spent some time with Aboriginal people at the Ovens River when he was looking for 'ringleaders' of an 'affray' between 'the Aboriginal natives and young Mr. Mackay and his men at Warouley [Whorouly]', Doctor Mackay's station, on the Ovens River. Bingham spent a surprising amount of time with the people around the Hume [Murray] and Ovens rivers over a two-month period, asking them questions about the reasons for a spate of attacks in mid-1840. He even asked them to draw a series of a kind of 'identikit' pictures of the people he was seeking over the Whorouly affray. Simon might be referring to Mundy's attacks. Bingham noted another man from the rear section of the Faithfull party who was connected with 'the recent murder at Mr. Chisolm's station', William Brown, who was living at Chisholm's station in mid-1840: Bingham to Colonial Secretary, 'Affray between Dr. Mackay's Men and Black Natives, Head Quarters, Tumut River, October 13th 1840', SRNSW, CSLR, 4/2486.1, 1841, p. 45. In February 1841, Robinson took three men, who had been arrested following the raid on Mackay's station, when they were released from Melbourne prison and accompanied them back to Wangaratta. They included Simon or 'Tare.rang.er' of the 'Wayayjeree tribe or nation': Clark, ID (ed.), *Journals of George A. Robinson, Chief Protector, Port Phillip Aboriginal Protectorate, Volume 2: October 1840 – August 1841*, Heritage Matters, Ballarat, 2000, p. 66. Jacqui Durrant believes the 'Wayayjeree tribe or nation' (Bingham wrote 'traggerah') that Simon was noted as coming from was 'Waggerah', or Wagra, present-day Wymah: Durrant, pers. comm., 2 April 2024.

10 Bingham to Colonial Secretary, 'Affray between Dr. Mackay's Men and Black Natives, Head Quarters, Tumut River, October 13th 1840', SRNSW, CSLR, 4/2486.1, 1841, p. 45.

11 Megan Carter, interview, 7 October 2023. Megan is a descendant of 'King', often known as Brandy, Brandie or 'Frank'. Brangy was a brother-in-law to 'King' Michie's son Tommy Banfield: Durrant, 2 April 2024.

12 Historians have noted the years 1838 to 1842 as the most intensive period of resistance warfare in Australian history. As Ian Clark notes, in Victoria, this was 'when Aboriginal resistance to European invasion was at its greatest'. Hamish McPherson suggests the Battle at Broken River was 'a key incident in a wider colonial frontier war across north-east Victoria'. Clark suggested the 'pace of dispossession, the drought of 1838–39, and the subsequent financial crash of 1842 threatened the economic existence of both Aborigines and Europeans'. It seems strange then that even in 2022 historians can write about Broken River as 'the Faithfull Massacre ... in which overlanders were murdered'. Old stories die hard: McPherson, H, 'Original rights: Colonial invasion and Aboriginal resistance in Benalla and northern Victoria 1838–1858', Benalla Aboriginal History Group, Benalla, Victoria, 2024, p. 3; Pennay, B, 'Interpreting an image: Picturing sound and song at the

Murray River crossing place', *Victorian Historical Journal*, vol. 93, no. 1, June 2022, p. 232. See also the Colonial Frontier Massacres 1788–1930, Centre for 21st-century Humanities, <c21ch.newcastle.edu.au/colonialmassacres/detail.php?r=506>, University of Newcastle, 2022, which continues to represent this as a massacre, despite being notified otherwise by the author. See also Clark, ID, *Scars in the Landscape. A register of massacre sites in western Victoria, 1803–1859*, AIATSIS, Canberra, 1995, p. 9; Parker to Robinson, 1 April 1840, *HRV*, vol. 2B, p. 692.

13   Clark, ID (ed.), *The Journals of George Augustus Robinson, Chief Protector, Port Phillip Aboriginal Protectorate, Volume One: 1 January 1839 – 30 September 1840*, Heritage Matters, Ballarat, 2000, p. 129.

14   Baylie, WH, 'On the Aborigines of the Goulburn district', *Port Phillip Magazine*, vol. 1, no. 2, 1843, p. 90; Thomas, 22 April 1843 (Stephens, M, ed.), *The Journal of William Thomas, Assistant Protector of the Aborigines of Port Phillip and Guardian of the Aborigines of Victoria, 1839–1867, vol. 1: 1839 to 1843*, Victorian Aboriginal Corporation for Languages, Melbourne, 2014, p. 518.

15   As Gary Presland notes, 'the similarities of languages with those of a number of groups in central and western Victoria, connected the Woiwurrung and Boon Wurrung speaking clans to a confederacy or nation called "Kulin". The Taungurung and Nguraiillam Wurrung (whose estates were in the Goulburn and Ovens River valleys on the northern side of the Great Dividing Range) made up what is now referred to as the Eastern Kulin. The Woiwurrung and Boon Wurrung language groups of the Kulin to the south "was a nation of more than forty-five clans"'. Importantly, 'Kulin people practiced exogamy; i.e. they married out of their clan, into clans of the opposite moiety, and preferably in a distant language group. Connections of this kind were used, in part, to cement political alliances' and for economic benefits: Presland, G, 'The Kulin People and the failure of the Aboriginal Protectorate during the superintendency of C J La Trobe', *La Trobeana Journal of the C J La Trobe Society Inc*, vol. 16, no. 1, Special Edition: La Trobe and the Aboriginal People 1, March 2017, pp. 6–7. See also Barwick, DE, *Rebellion at Coranderrk*, Aboriginal History Inc., Canberra, 1998, pp. 13–15 for the divisions into moieties for prescribing marriage connections. Alliances between nations and groups in the Kulin confederacies were long standing: Presland, 2010, pp. 14–21.

16   Faithfull, WP, 3 May 1838 in Gibson to Thomson, 11 May 1838, SRNSW, CSLR, 38/4853; statement by surviving member of overland party William McKay, 1853, in Bassett, J, 'The Faithfull Massacre – A case study', thesis, School of Humanities, Deakin University, 1986, p. 26. William Lonsdale to Colonial Secretary, 2 July 1838, *HRV*, vol. 2a, p. 340. Attempting to gather evidence later, Police Magistrate Stewart reported he did not 'learn that any of these, or of the nieghbouring [sic] Tribes, have ever in any way been molested by Europeans' but the information he was 'able to get upon this point' was 'not altogether to be depended upon'. Stewart to Thomson, 20 June 1838, SRNSW, CSLR, 4/2423.3. Judith Bassett is a lone voice arguing that 'the Faithfull Massacre nor any of the other raids mentioned in [Richard Broome's] The Colonial Experience were intended to resist the encroaching settlement by Europeans...' While it seems some of Bassett's other contentions with Broome's account of Broken River are worth noting, it is difficult to say these attacks had nothing to do with resisting the 'encroaching Europeans'. Indeed Bassett admits that the overlanders were attacked prior to this on the Ovens River and they responded by firing at their attackers and suggests the attack was in revenge for the warriors being fired upon, but ignores the fact the warriors attacked first. Bassett's arguments show a lack of understanding of frontier warfare and her assertions that 'tribal' societies merely attack for revenge or plunder only, are now widely disproven. Bassett, J, 'The Faithfull

Massacre of 1838', *Quadrant*, 20 February 2019, <quadrant.org.au/magazine/2019/01-02/the-faithfull-massacre-of-1838/>.

17 Robinson, journal entry 23 February 1841, in Clark, vol. 2, 2000, p. 87; Barwick, DE, 'Mapping the past: An atlas of Victorian clans 1835–1904, Part 1', *Aboriginal History*, vol. 8, no. 2, ANU Press, Canberra, 1984, pp. 105–107. According to Barwick, the clan of the Benalla local area were the Yeerun-illam-balluk of the Taungurung language group, and their moiety was Bunjil the eagle.

18 Protector of Aborigines George Augustus Robinson noted in 1841 that the name of the river at Benalla was '*By.en.good.der.re*' and the crossing place by the large waterhole '*Mer.ry.gan.der*'; according to Jacqui Durrant the shorter form was Marangan and the local people often known by Europeans as the 'Maragan tribe': Robinson, journal entry 23 February 1841, in Clark, vol. 2, 2000, p. 87; Durrant, 'First Nations "Kings" of Benalla', Life on Spring Creek – A blog by Jacqui Durrant, website, 2020, <lifeonspringcreek.com/2020/09/15/aboriginal-benalla/>. Uren had witnessed the flood times, noting that, 'The writer saw these conditions exemplified in 1906, when, even the Show Grounds were inundated and the Show, which was to be held on the day of the flood, was reluctantly postponed'. Uren was a school teacher in Benalla. Uren, S, 'The Massacre of the Faithfull Party' c. 1913, State Library of Victoria, MS 14903, p. 1.

19 As Yorta Yorta man Daniel James (who grew up in Euroa, near Benalla) notes, 'the men, in their ignorance had chosen a kangaroo ground to camp alongside the main watering hole [Marangan], which doubled as a sacred site and where clans from the three tribes, Bangerang, Taunarong and Way wurru would often meet': James, D, 'Benwhalla – The fallen and forgotten' personal website, nd, <www.danieljames.com.au/words/2018/10/21/benwhalla-the-fallen-and-forgotten>; Megan Carter, interview, 7 October 2023; Uren, S, 'History of Benalla', *Benalla Standard*, 9 October 1906, p. 3; Uren, 1907, p. 5; Presland, 2010, p. 26.

20 Megan Carter, interview, 7 October 2023; Uren, 1906, p. 3.

21 'Now and then', *Ovens and Murray Advertiser*, 25 May 1869, p. 2; 'Benalla', *Leader*, 19 May 1894, p. 32; *Benalla Standard*, 9 October 1906, p. 3. The commemoration of foundational moments in Benalla began in the 1860s with the declaration by a 'Petrus Lambertus Alkemade' that 'I am the man who fixed the forty-feet pole five feet deep, in the soil of the eminence from which Mr Piper reviewed the fighting men of the famed Broken River tribe of aboriginals, which the Ensign poetically describes. I am the man who audaciously ventured to attach to that assuming pole the Union Jack, within view of the tree into which Mr Piper fired the historical bullet': Letter to the editor by Petrus Lambertus Alkemade, *Ovens and Murray Advertiser*, 25 May 1869, p. 3; see: Robert Dorning to Truus Gribben, 6 March 2019, Benalla Historical Society Archives for an overview of these claims.

22 For early arrivals in the area see: Williams, M, 'Charles Bonney and the fertile Kilmore Plains', Historical Notes, *Victorian Historical Journal*, vol. 90, no. 1, June 2019, Royal Historical Society of Victoria, pp. 105–120. Smyth and Mundy arrived in Melbourne at the end of February 1838, as the *Melbourne Advertiser* reported, 'Lieutenants Smith and Munday arrived last week overland from Sydney. Lieut. Smith relieves Lieut. Hawkins': *Melbourne Advertiser*, vol. 1, no. 10, 5 March 1838, p. 3; *Sydney Morning Herald*, 10 March 1847, p. 3.

23 Glenelg to Gipps, 31 January 1838, *HRA*, XIX, pp. 252–255.

24 Assistant Protector of Aborigines at the Goulburn River, James Dredge, Diary, 7 December 1839, SLV, MS 11625, p. 31. Lady Jane Franklin met Mundy in April 1839 and rather politely, considering she was talking to a self-avowed mass murderer, said she had heard stories of him that 'were not in his favour': Russell, P, *This Errant Lady: Jane Franklin's*

Overland Journey to Port Phillip and Sydney, 1839, National Library of Australia, Canberra, 2002, p. 41. Dredge took up his Protectorate 'station' with his family by a bend in the Goulburn River at what is now Michelton in May 1839. The Dredges 'planted a garden, built their bark hut and distributed blankets and food to the local people' and were regularly visited by several hundred Aboriginal people. But already 'nearby [was] an inn, a police barracks and a bark homestead'. Dredge's station itself attracted what he called 'lawless villains' seeking 'intercourse with the [Aboriginal] women': Dredge, R, '"An awful silence reigns": James Dredge at the Goulburn River', *The La Trobe Journal*, no. 61, Autumn 1998, pp. 17–26. See also 'Correspondence between the Black Protectorate and the Government', *Australian*, 26 December 1840, p. 3, outlining Dredge's reasons for resigning from his post and Robinson's reply. Jacqui Durrant, pers. comm., 17 April 2024.

25   Lonsdale to Colonial Secretary, 2 July 1838, *HRV*, vol. 2a, p. 340. Historian Jacqui Durrant is not convinced, however, that the warriors in these raids were involved in the attack on Crossley's party as these were not traditional alliances and stretched into Djadja Wurrung Country. At the least, the raids formed part of a pattern of attacks at the time and any successes may well have been communicated across the wider region: Jacqui Durrant, pers. comm., 2 April 2024; Flanagan, R, 'The Aborigines of Australia – No. XIV: The "Rising of 1842–4"', *Empire*, 15 April, 1854, p. 3. See Williams, 2019, for the location and period of Mundy's station at Pyalong, esp. p. 112.

26   While it is possible, as Barwick suggests, Faithfull's men had stumbled across the advance group for a larger gathering that was about to occur at Marangan, there is no certainty of this. In April–May 1838, according to Barwick, senior men from Kulin and Waveroo clans, accompanied by their wives and children, were travelling throughout central and northeast Victoria to attend a series of male initiation rites and inter-clan gatherings. However, there is no known link to Marangan: Barwick, 1984, p. 120. Uren recounts Brown's understanding of his father's story about meeting Aboriginal people in the area in 'The Faithfull Massacre', 1907, p. 4.

27   Uren notes from Brown that 'The travellers crossed and pitched camp at the river bend, known to travellers as The Winding Swamp, where a flour mill later stood, and near which spot the Black Swan Hotel was subsequently erected. The railway bridge is now also adjacent': Uren, 1907, p. 5.

28   William Read, sworn statement, Melbourne Court Register, 22 April 1838, *HRV*, p. 316; James Crossley, sworn statement, Melbourne Court Register, 14 April 1838, *HRV*, p. 314. Uren notes that 'Bentley found bundles of spears at advantageous spots around the camp. He entreated the overseer to take all precautions in case of attack. Again his warning was ignored'. The discrepancies between the various contemporary depositions and Uren's account (based largely on Brown) cannot be ignored. But overall, they still contain a similar outline of events: Uren, 1907, p. 5.

29   Uren relies on Brown's account of Crossley's statement, but Crossley's inaction at the time of attack suggests an overconfidence at the least: Uren, 1907, p. 5.

30   William Read, sworn statement, Melbourne Court Register, 22 April 1838, *HRV*, p. 316.

31   Uren notes: 'In spite of a close watch, sheep were speared and carried off by the blacks, who sent out smoke signals which soon brought hundred of natives into the locality' but this is unclear if it comes from Brown or might have been assumed by Uren. If so, it is a reasonable assumption knowing the use of smoke signals right across the region: Uren, 1907, p. 5. Mitchell was clear that such communication was as fast and effective as a telegraph; 'When we reached the head of the highest slope, near the place whence I first saw these ponds, a dense column of smoke ascended from Mount Frazer, and subsequently other smokes arose, extending in telegraphic line far to the south, along the base of the mountains; and

thus communicating to the natives who might be upon our route homewards the tidings of our return': Mitchell, TL, *Three expeditions into the interior of Eastern Australia: With descriptions of the recently explored region of Australia, and of the present colony of New South Wales*, 2 Volumes, T & W Boone, London, 1838, vol. 1, p. 129.

32 Stewart thought there were four muskets with the party. Stewart to Thomson, 20 June 1838, SRNSW, CSLR, Port Phillip, 38/6427, 4/2423.3.

33 William Bateman, sworn statement, Melbourne Court Register, 22 April 1838, *HRV*, p. 316.

34 'Port Phillip', *Sydney Gazette*, 22 May 1838, p. 2.

35 William Read, sworn statement, Melbourne Court Register, 22 April 1838, *HRV*, p. 316; William Walker, sworn statement, Melbourne Court Register, 22 April, *HRV*, p. 317.

36 Gibson to Thomson, 11 May 1838, CSLR, 38/4853. Gibson wrote to Thomson of the 'melancholy intelligence' he received on 23 April that the Faithfull party had been 'attacked on the 13th instant between the Ovens and Goulburn Rivers by a party of Native Blacks, eight of Mr. Faithfull's men were killed, and his Drays plundered'. George Faithfull had told Gibson he was 'was in hourly expectation of a fresh attack from the Blacks': Gibson to Thomson, 23 April 1838, SRNSW 4/2404.3, 38/4004, 2212; *Sydney Monitor*, 18 May 1838, p. 2. The report wrongly suggested that the men broke 'through the circle of blacks, fairly out-ran them, and got off'. The white men 'beat the native in running' and 'from where the first man was killed, to the last slain, was a space of seven miles'.

37 The numbers of attackers have been disputed. Daniel James suggests a likely number of attackers as 'between 100 to 300 Aboriginal men': James, 'Benwhalla – The fallen and forgotten'. Bassett suggests there were only twenty, however that number of warriors is totally implausible. The number of men seen following the party at one point does not mean that was the number of attackers. Bassett disputes they were 'warriors' and among various other errors of fact, incorrectly asserts that women were never involved in combat: Bassett, 'The Faithfull Massacre of 1828', 2019. Crossley said he saw 'from 150 to 200 natives in all directions round' and then 'about 40 of the natives made for the drays and commenced ransacking them' while Read said twenty. Daniel Bateman (Balmain) said the shepherds had been 'followed by about 200 blacks who were throwing spears at them'. William Walker stated that he 'saw between 200 and 300 natives'. The variations between the survivors' depositions might well reflect both the 'fog of war' and Crossley's embarrassment at fleeing the situation while Read stayed and fought. There were known to be large ceremonial gatherings of hundreds of people at this very spot, and it would seem that large numbers of warriors were involved at least, definitely well more than twenty. The threat that superiority of numbers posed was well known. As 'Colo' George Suttor, who had experience with Wiradyuri attacks during the Bathurst War of 1824, noted in 1826, 'they seldom attack but when they are sure of overpowering': 'Colo', Brucedale near Bathurst, *Australian*, 14 October 1826, p. 3. If the 1906 *Benalla Standard* newspaper report about the 'Fight of the Broken River' is correct, it described how the warriors had daubed themselves with 'war paint' – a clear sign that all overlanders would have known meant preparing for combat, however it seems from the survivors' testimony it was a surprise attack: 'The Fight of the Broken River', *Benalla Standard*, 6 November 1906, p. 4. See also: Uren, 1907, p. 44. For the most considered overviews of the battle see: Milliss, 1992, pp. 247–249 and McPherson, H, 'Frontier War on the Port Phillip Road: Colonisation and resistance in Benalla and north-east Victoria', Benalla Aboriginal History Group, Benalla, Victoria, 2023, p. 7.

38 'Port Phillip', *Sydney Gazette*, 22 May 1838, p. 2.

39 Durrant has 'no doubt that the Faithfull incident was coordinated between Waywurru and Taungurung, and that knowledge of those events would have shortly reached most spheres of Kulin influence. But Taungurung were not on good terms with Wiradjuri (unlike western

Waywurru, who were on good terms with southern Wiradjuri), so on this count I do not think Kulin and Wiradjuri were coordinating. I think there was an awareness of events. I think the Benalla Taungurung knew what was coming down the pike when they made that attack, because Waywurru told them of their recent experience, and of recent southern Wiradjuri experience, with whom Waywurru were equally allied'. Durrant notes that 'some southern Wiradjuri groups (from the Holbrook/Culcairn and Corowa/Howlong areas) were allied with Western Waywurru (Wangaratta/ Tarrawingee/Oxley/Beechworth). Eastern Waywurru were allied with Dhudhuroa, and Yaitmathang (a Ngarigu-speaking group at Omeo). But Eastern Waywurru and Dhudhuroa neighbours were violent enemies with Wiradjuri. Taungurung at Benalla and Mansfield were allied with Dhudhuroa and Waywurru, but definitely were violent enemies with Wiradjuri. As for Bangerang, there is no solid evidence they were allied to Waywurru or Taungurung. But it is almost certain the two geographically closest Bangerang groups (Kailtheban near Benalla and Angootheran nearer Wangaratta), were on cordial terms with their neighbours for practical reasons, and it's likely some individual families had alliances'. However, Durrant is clear that Bangerang's Wongatpan clan and other Bangerang clans nearer Echuca were traditional enemies of Taungurung and Waywurru, as well as Wiradyuri: Jacqui Durrant, pers. comm., 2 April 2024.

40 The report seems at variance with Crossley and others' depositions about running a long distance and being picked off by pursuers, but perhaps it was a mix of both: Gibson to Thomson, 11 May 1838, CSLR, 38/4853.

41 Sturt, C, *Two Expeditions into the Interior of Southern Australia: Volume II*, Public Library of South Australia, Adelaide, 1963, pp. 104–107. See: Kerkhove, R, *How They Fought: Indigenous tactics and weaponry of Australia's Frontier Wars*, Boolarong Press, Brisbane, 2023, pp. 105–200, for a detailed outline of various strategies and tactics of warriors against armed stockmen, military and police.

42 Statement by Patrick Drain, 1 June 1838, enclosed with JR Hardy to Thomson, 1 June 1838, SRNSW, CSLR 38/5770.

43 As Barton recounted, 'McKenzie, with the consent of the others, selected the King Parrot; Dixon, for McFarlane, selected the Cheviot Hills; Campbell selected a piece of country on the north side of the Goulburn, since called Gin Gin; Snodgrass selected the Muddy Creek for himself, and a place now called Doogalook for McFarlane; Hughes preferring to remain where he was': Barton, GB, 'Old time memories. The Overlanders in '38. By G. B. Barton.', *Australasian*, 12 December 1896, p. 25.

44 John Conway Bourke, Letters to Edmund Finn ['Garryowen'] (1888), correspondence and papers (1821–1908), Royal Historical Society of Victoria, MS 004116.02; Letter (1886) to Edmund Finn re attack on Bourke by blacks in 1839, Royal Historical Society of Victoria, MS 004114.

45 Drain obviously did not want to be seen as an escaped convict and gave himself up to the watchman. Drain also recalled that before they had arrived at the Ovens River, around 160 miles before the Murray (possibly near Gundagai) they met around twenty 'Murray Blacks'. The Europeans often referred to southern Wiradyuri people as 'Murray Blacks' and the Taungurung were their traditional enemies. He said they followed them all the way to the Ovens River from Gundagai. Drain also noted that 'two of these Murray blacks' who had stayed with Drain's party 'left us the same day that the shepherds were murdered ... an hour or two after sunrise'. Had they gone to a planned rendezvous at Marangan after keeping tabs on the other shepherds? Drain certainly implies they had time to make it across to Broken River that morning before the attack began. He also noted that the two men later returned and were 'friendly' with the other Aboriginal people there. Durrant

suggests 'Murray Blacks' (if Drain was correct they were indeed Wiradyuri) would not have been accepted in Taungurung Country at Ovens River. Yet these were strange times and we should not assume traditional enmities continued to prevail: Durrant, pers. comm., 2 April 2024; Statement by Patrick Drain, 1 June 1838, enclosed with JR Hardy to Thomson, 1 June 1838, SRNSW, CSLR 38/5770. See also the Finding Merriman website: Carter, M, <findingmerriman.com.au/merriman/merrimans-places/>.

46 The attack might well have begun as revenge or payback for crimes committed at the Ovens River or might have been an opportunistic attack by warriors who had spent time with the stockmen and discovered their limited firepower. The first group of warriors with Charlie might have felt humiliated lying on the ground under the eye of William Walker and his musket all night long. It could have been conducted at a moment when a large force of warriors arrived at Marangan for other ceremonial reasons, or simply that they were on a raiding spree, having just attacked several other stations. Yet there was no great need for these warriors to plunder a dray. In her 1984 article, Diane Barwick suggested that 'In April–May 1838 the senior men of every Kulin and Waveroo clan, accompanied by their wives and children, were travelling throughout central and northeastern Victoria to attend a scheduled series of male initiation rites, each requiring the attendance of members of distant clans ... This journeying, dictated by religious and family obligations was not deterred by long-continued drought or the depredations of overlanding pastoralists ...'. Barwick might well be correct that Kulin and Waveroo clans had scheduled male initiation rites every April–May and they were travelling at this time, but to suggest these were disrupted by Faithfull's party firing on them doesn't take into account the depositions and other records relating to the events, including the fact that the 'Murray Blacks' in Drain's deposition were travelling south back towards the Murray. Barwick notes that 'Overlanders' journals, depositions and reminiscences reveal that planning for a series of initiations involving Taungurung, neighbouring Waveroo clans, and adjacent Wiradjuri about Albury was underway' but does not provide any sources. Barwick suggests 'fearful squatters and ignorant officials misinterpreted the necessary travels of messengers and the resulting inter-tribal assemblies as planning for "concerted warfare"'. The latter in fact seems to be more correct, or at the very least, the ceremonies were also going on – though the fact Faithfull noted there were no 'youth' among the attackers does not mean they were held back from fighting or that there was a ceremony to be held. Such an attack against an armed force would only be conducted by initiated men, traditionally, and it must be assumed, in conflict with Europeans: Barwick, 1984, p. 120. Historian Jacqui Durrant, who specialises in northeast Victoria history, is also suspicious of Barwick's lack of sources on this. Durrant believes 'it is far more reasonable to assume that Waywurru Wangaratta were intermarried with Benalla Taungurung, and that those two groups' called in some allies and mustered the large number of warriors: Durrant, pers. comm., 2 April 2024. See: Statement by Patrick Drain, enclosed with JR Hardy to Thomson, 1 June 1838, SRNSW, CSLR 38/5770. Milliss suggests that the edict by Governor Bourke 'forbidding interference' with Aboriginal women was at the back of the minds of all those who gave depositions or wrote about the affair, and they did not admit that this was a cause. He cites Rusden, writing in 1883, who had talked to one of the survivors and Rusden believed 'the convict men had trafficked with the women'. However, this was admitted to have occurred at the Ovens River station prior to Benalla. While this still might have been part of the reason, a hatred of 'white bastards' has a more general ring to it: Milliss, 1992, pp. 252–253; Rusden, GW, *History of Australia*, vol. 2, Chapman and Hall, London, 1883, p. 228.

47 Uren's later version of events seems to have embellished the story of Brown and Glenn (Walker). In his 1945 account they beat a heroic retreat with one musket and a few cartridges. He also notes they went toward Goomalibee and then turned northeast to White's Three Mile Creek station. Uren, 1907, pp. 7–8.

48   Uren, 1907, pp. 7–8; Uren, c. 1913; Uren, 1906, p. 3; Melbourne Survey Office, 'Survey of the Intermediate Country between the Ovens and Broken Rivers, 1850', Victorian Public Record Series, 8168, Historic Plan Collection; Faithfull in Gibson to Thomson, 23 April 1838, SRNSW, CSLR 38/4004. William Faithfull's camps at this point were at Oxley and Bontharambo. There were still men occupying country on the Ovens (some of Bowman's men), at Bontharambo (Faithfull's sheep station being held for Joseph Docker), Oxley (some of Faithfull's men with his cattle), down the King River at what is now Docker (Mackay), and at the Three Mile (Col. White). Durrant, pers. comm., 2 April 2024.
49   Uren, 1906, p. 3.
50   Barton, 1896, p. 25.
51   John Conway Bourke, Letters to Edmund Finn ['Garryowen'] (1888), Correspondence and papers (1821–1908), Royal Historical Society of Victoria, MS 004116.02; Letter (1886) to Edmund Finn re attack on Bourke by blacks in 1839, Royal Historical Society of Victoria, MS 004114. Jacqui Durrant notes Mackay reported all the stations were abandoned but she believes Bowman's and Faithfull's were not. Still, White had moved south to safety and Mackay had fled. The *Sydney Monitor* noted others: 'Several Europeans have been driven from their stations, amongst whom are the Messrs. White, Hume, Mackey, Smith, and Dr. Harris's overseer': 'Atrocities of the Natives', *Sydney Monitor*, 25 June 1838, p. 3; Durrant, pers. comm., 2 April 2024. By May, the desire to find which 'tribe' was responsible grew and the *Monitor* reported that 'the blacks, which, it is now known, belonged to the River Ovens tribe': *Sydney Monitor*, 18 May 1838, p. 2. Stewart had 'been informed that Mr. Faithful's party had gone on to Port Phillip' so they carried on 'direct to the Broken River or Winding Swamp (where the outrage had been committed)'. Here they 'remained two days in search of the Tribe who frequent that place, but not having succeeded in falling in with it we returned to the Murray River': Stewart to Thomson, 20 June 1838, SRNSW, CSLR, Port Phillip, 38/6427, 4/2423.3; Mackay to Broughton, 15 May 1838, encl., JR Hardy to Thomson, 1 June 1838, SRNSW, CSLR, 38/5770, 4/2423.3. Jacqui Durrant notes 'the psychological impact was absolutely huge on the Europeans. The whites in Benalla were killed and scared off … and for a period of time that meant the entire Broken River was emptied of Europeans again. They frightened off Mackay, who was at Myrrhee (present-day Docker), and this meant that the left bank of the King [River] as far as Docker and upstream was cleared out. Colonel White left, so pretty much the left bank of the Ovens at Wangaratta was cleared out. However, it does not seem like Faithfull and Bowman's men left, and if they did, it wasn't for long. Certainly, by June they were all back, and fighting'. Durrant suggests that 'in terms of actually regaining land it was brief, maybe a week or two in some places, maybe a month or more' in others. The significance of retaking Country however should not be dismissed. It was the weight of firearms, horses and men that followed in the counterattacks that meant the reoccupation of Country was only so brief: Durrant, pers. comm., 2 April 2024.

Chapter 4

1   Phillips, J, *Reminiscences of Early Australian Life by a Pioneer*, A. P. Marsden, London, 1893, p. 31; Uncle Wayne Fossey, interview, 11 June 2024, Toowoomba.
2   Roger Milliss suggests it could have been 'Tati Tati' people who were visiting Menindee in 1835 who returned, however Mitchell was relying on his guide Piper, who it seems understood what this war party was doing: Milliss, R, *Waterloo Creek: The Australia Day massacre of 1838, George Gipps and the British conquest of New South Wales*, McPhee Gribble, Melbourne, 1992, pp. 128–129, 797. See Hardy, B, *Lament for the Barkindji: The vanished tribes of the Darling River Region*, Rigby, Adelaide, 1976, pp. 44, 225; Mitchell, TL, *Three Expeditions: With descriptions of the recently explored region of Australia*

Felix, and of the present colony of New South Wales, T & W Boone, London, 1838, vol. 2, p. 92.

3 While it appears there might have been traditional combat between people at Wagga and Narrandera reported in 1844, this might well have been dispute resolution and does not mean alliances against common enemies could not have occurred: Gammage, B, *Narrandera Shire*, Narrandera Shire Council, Narrandera, 1986, p. 17; Aunty Flo Grant quoted in Sullivan, B, 'Wagga and the Murrumbidgee: The Wagga Community's relationship with the Murrumbidgee River and wetlands over time', Charles Sturt University Archives, 2012, <cdn.csu.edu.au/__data/assets/pdf_file/0008/679796/Bernard-Sullivan-Wagga-and-the-Murrumbidgee.pdf>, p. 45; Uncle James Ingram, interview, 20 October 2023.

4 There are various reports of the meaning of the name for the river including 'track goes down here', 'a very good place' or 'big water' and 'often turned aside' (flooded). See Geographical Names Board, 'Murrumbidgee River', nd, <proposals.gnb.nsw.gov.au/public/geonames/abcdc84c-3a23-4077-a645-26c6ddccf2a>; Sullivan, 2012, p. 2.

5 Cambage, RH, 'Exploration between Wingecarribee, Shoalhaven, Macquarie and Murrumbidgee Rivers', *JRAHS*, vol. 8, part V, 1921 p. 217.

6 Baylis, J, 'The Murrumbidgee & Wagga Wagga', *JRAHS*, vol. 13, no. 4, 1927, p. 254.

7 Uncle James Ingram, interview, 20 October 2023.

8 Uncle James Ingram, interview, 20 October 2023.

9 Gammage, 1986, pp. 29–30; Gammage, B, 'The Wiradjuri War 1838–40', *The Push from the Bush*, vol. 16, no. 1, 1983, p. 4.

10 Gammage, 1986, p. 29.

11 According to James Belich, 'settler Australasia was founded in 1788, but it exploded in 1828, and the second date was arguably more significant than the first': Belich, J, *Replenishing the Earth: The settler revolution and the rise of the Anglo world 1783–1939*, Oxford University Press, Oxford, 2009, pp. 261–262.

12 According to Geoff Burch, 'the first settlement around Wagga took place in the year 1832, when the Tompsons took up Oura and Eunonyhareenyah; R. H. Best took up the Wagga Wagga station, and the Jenkins family took up Tooyal and Buckingong. Tooyal was first known as "Toyeo", which means the jag of a spear': Burch, G, 'Exploration & settlement on the Murrumbidgee', personal paper, 2023, p. 3.

13 'War by the Blacks', *Sydney Herald*, 21 March 1833, p. 3. See also Neville Lyons suggesting that when the Wiradyuri 'couldn't get any food they speared the cattle' in Kabaila, *Wiradjuri Places: The Murrumbidgee River Basin*, Black Mountain Projects, Canberra, 1995, p. 90. Wagga Wagga local historian Geoff Burch believes 'Mr M' is probably Anthony Marshall, who was the head stockman on Best's 'Wogga Wogga' run, though it could also have referred to Macleay's run – Borambola: Burch, pers. comm., Wagga Wagga and District Historical Society, 2 November 2023. See also George Bennet's *Wanderings in New South Wales, Batavia, Pedir Coast, Singapore, and China: being the journal of a naturalist in those countries, during 1832, 1833, and 1834*, Richard Bentley, London, 1834, esp. pp. 148–179.

14 Baylis, 1927, p. 255.

15 Baylis, 1927, p. 255. Gormly appears to have spoken with Jenkins in the early 1900s: Gormly, J, *Exploration and Settlement in Australia*, Ford, Sydney, 1921, p. 118.

16 Burch, 2023, p. 2; 'Warby, John (1774–1851)', *ADB*. See: Vale, M, *Warby: My Excellent Guide*, St Ives, NSW, 1994, esp. pp. 1–12.

17 *Sydney Herald*, 21 March 1833, p. 3.

18 See Gapps, S, *The Sydney Wars: Conflict in the early colony 1788–1817*, NewSouth Publishing, Sydney, 2018 and *Gudyarra: The first Wiradyuri war of resistance: The Bathurst War 1822–1824*, NewSouth Publishing, Sydney, 2021.

19 *Sydney Herald*, 21 March 1833, p. 3. Whether this was a new tactic developed by some warriors specifically for warfare against the colonists or had been part of traditional warfare is unclear, but it certainly had a powerful effect. It undoubtedly added to stressful, sleepless nights in bark huts at the isolated edges of the colony. The threat might have been even more effective than the reality – a classic moment of psychological warfare.
20 Gammage, 1986, p. 32.
21 The experiences of Aboriginal people dealing with squatters and stock on their lands was mixed. Not all the stockmen and overseers regarded them as savages and many outstations became 'places of refuge' for those seeking shelter from vengeful armed whites. As the missionary Lancelot Threlkeld noted in 1837: 'Generally speaking, however, there is a kindly feeling, a friendly disposition, manifested towards the Blacks by the Colonists, and many of the out-stations prove places of refuge in cases of danger, whilst other stations are dreaded on account of the alleged barbarity and violence inflicted on the Aborigines': Threlkeld, L, 'Report of the Mission to the Aborigines at Lake Macquarie, New South Wales, 1837', NLA, <trove.nla.gov.au/newspaper/article/31719534>.
22 See Gapps, 2021. Governor Brisbane had urged the colonial authorities in England for the formation of a 'colonial cavalry', writing to Earl Bathurst in June 1824, at the height of the Bathurst War, that this was necessary 'not only with the view of keeping the Aborigines in check, against whom Infantry have no chance of success, but also for the general Police of the Country': Despatch, Governor Brisbane to Earl Bathurst, 18 June 1824, in *HRA*, vol. XI, p. 283. Also see Morisset's requests for horses for infantry around Bathurst: Letter, Morisset to Goulburn, 26 July 1824, SRNSW CSC 6065, 4/1800: pp. 126–127.
23 There were other elements of conflict after the Bathurst War, but no serious warfare. In June of 1825, Bathurst Superintendent of Government Stock John Maxwell was compelled to send two soldiers to the Molong Plains stock stations 'to prevent a recurrence of trouble from the black natives' (see Gapps, 2021, p. 203) and James Backhouse noted the killing of cattle in the Wellington Valley as late as 1835. In 1828, the public execution by hanging of a man only named as 'Tommy' for murder, was apparently to be a great deterrence to other Aboriginal people 'from future acts of barbarity upon the peaceful and unoffending settler': *Sydney Gazette*, 2 January 1828, p. 3; James Backhouse, 'Account of A Journey from Parramatta Across the Blue Mountains to Wellington, 1835', in *Fourteen Journeys Over the Blue Mountains of New South Wales 1813–1841*, p. 213; Ranken, WB, *The Rankens of Bathurst*, Townsend, Sydney, 1916, pp. 22, 65–66; Despatch, Earl Bathurst to Governor Darling, 1 October 1826, in *HRA*, XII, pp. 593–596. The granting of 'inducements' to the military was notable in areas where conflict was greatest such as in Van Diemen's Land (Tasmania). See: Brodie, N, 'The Vandemonian war as genocidal moment: Historiographical refrains and archival secrets', *Journal of Genocide Research*, vol. 20, no. 3, 2018, p. 478. While this was not, as John Connor and Jack Clear have suggested, the 'start of a new phase of frontier warfare in which private settlers and paramilitary police forces assumed near-total responsibility for the dispossession and suppression of the Aboriginal population' (this had happened before in Bathurst), it certainly raised the stakes in the colonial state, sanctioning frontier colonists as a military force: Clear, 2021, p. 192; Connor, 2002, p. 120.
24 Eyre, EJ, Autobiography, December 1838, SLNSW, ML, CY Reel 118, A1806, p. 150; Dutton, 'Eyre, Edward John (1815–1901)', *ADB*.
25 Gammage, 1986, p. 32. While some accounts have suggested the killing of a woman who pulled a gun on a Wiradyuri party seeking rations ignited conflict, it seems raids on cattle and sheep had in fact continued through the 1830s around Narrandera. Peter Kabaila retells a Wiradyuri man's account of an incident in which 'a group of Aborigines went up to the homestead because in those days they used to give the Aborigines flour rations' but the overseer's wife was the only one present and the Wiradyuri party 'gave her a bit of a scare:

so she pulled a gun on them and they killed her'. According to his informant, this incident was 'when the trouble started': Kabaila, 1995, p. 90.
26   Williams to Hardy, 'Bangus', 11 January 1839, SRNSW, CSLR, 4/2470.4, p. 17.
27   *Sydney Monitor and Commercial Advertiser*, 13 February 1839; Matthew Donovan to Commissioner Cosby, deposition, 6 May 1839, SRNSW CSLR 4/2438.
28   It remains unclear, but the evidence of a large footprint suggests either that colonists had an intimate knowledge of 'Brian Boru' at this stage, or had information from Aboriginal people working as guides or 'trackers'. Letter, Hardy to Thomson, 18 January 1839; SRNSW, CSLR 4/2470.4; pp. 20–22.
29   Hardy to Colonial Secretary, Yass, 18 January 1839, SRNSW, CSLR 4/2470.4, pp. 20–21.
30   Gammage, 1983, p. 5; Gammage, 1986, pp. 32, 38; Williams to Jenkins, 11 January 1839; SRNSW, CSLR 4/2470.4, pp. 17–18; Matthew Donovan to Commissioner Cosby, deposition, 6 May 1839, SRNSW CSLR 4/2438; Burch, 2023, p. 3.
31   When Crawford arrived in Adelaide he established a station and Charles Sturt named Mount Crawford in his honour: Papers of James Coutts Crawford, Diary entry 13–14 February 1839; NLA M600. Interestingly in Coutts Crawford's *Recollections of travel in New Zealand and Australia, Truebner and Co., London, 1880*, p. 9, by 1880 he had changed his tone to 'The blacks were numerous and rather troublesome'.
32   Gammage, 1986, p. 32. According to Gilmore they were young boys tasked with learning several languages to assist in communication between language groups: Gilmore, M, *Old Days, Old Ways: A book of recollections*, Angus & Robertson, Sydney, 1934, pp. 114–116; Wilde, WH, 'Gilmore, Dame Mary Jean (1865–1962)', *ADB*.
33   'Aboriginal epic. Youth's fight with eagle. Story of early Wagga', *Daily Advertiser*, 16 August 1932, p. 3. See Kerkhove, R, *How They Fought. Indigenous tactics and weaponry of Australia's Frontier Wars*, Boolarong Press, Brisbane, 2023, pp. 79–81 for a discussion on insignia and markings. Duncan McFarlane describes a typical 'march' to battle in the Clarence River area in: 'Tribal fights', *Daily Examiner*, 25 January 1935, p. 11.
34   Uncle James Ingram, interview, 20 October 2023. A cyclical drought arrived in the summer of 1837 and at first little could distract from the land rush. But soon, crop harvests failed and large imports of grain were needed – between 1839 and 1842 around one-third of the wheat and flour consumed in the colony was imported from India and other places: Introduction, *HRA*, vol. 20, p. x.
35   Letter, Hardy to Thomson, 17 January 1839, SRNSW CSLR, 4/2470.4; pp. 14–16.
36   Michael Byrne to Commissioner Cosby, deposition, 8 March 1839; Thomas Supple to Commissioner Cosby, deposition, 5 May 1839; John Newton to Commissioner Cosby, deposition, 5 May 1839; John Tomkinson to Commissioner Cosby, deposition, 30 April 1839; *SRNSW* CSC 4/2438. For mutilation as a military tactic see Gapps, 2021, pp. 115–116.
37   John Tomkinson to Commissioner Cosby, deposition, 30 April 1839, SRNSW, CSC 4/2438. Clear speculates 'the two muskets in Tomkinson and Ferguson's possession were the main objects of their attention': Clear, 2021, p. 239.
38   Diary, John Coutts Crawford, 13–14 February 1839, NLA M600; Papers of John Coutts Crawford, M687-M688; Michael Byrne to Commissioner Cosby, deposition, 8 May 1839, SRNSW, CSLR 4/2438; Evidence of Henry Cosby, 9 July 1839, *New South Wales Legislative Council Votes and Proceedings* (*NSWVP*) II, pp. 68–69; Gammage, 1983, p. 9.
39   *Sydney Herald*, 24 May 1839, p. 3.
40   Commissioner Cosby to Colonial Secretary Thomson, deposition, 12 May 1839, SRNSW, CSLR 4/2438; Evidence of Henry Cosby, 9 July 1839, *NSWVP* II, pp. 68–69.
41   Commissioner Cosby to Colonial Secretary Thomson, deposition, 12 May 1839; SRNSW, CSLR 4/2438; Evidence of Henry Cosby, 9 July 1839, *NSWVP* II, pp. 68–69.

42	*Sydney Herald*, 24 May 1839; John Tomkinson to Commissioner Cosby, deposition, 30 April 1839; Commissioner Cosby, deposition, 12 May 1839; SRNSW, CSLR 4/2438.
43	Based on a survey of cattle auction prices over 1839 across various colonial newspapers.
44	As Gammage notes, this shift from offensive to defensive conduct was a testament to the effective and unexpectedly aggressive Wiradyuri offensives of early 1839: Gammage, 1983, p. 5. Military historian Jeffrey Grey noted the Narrungdera warriors had 'not only halted the spread of settlement in their district, but may have even forced a temporary retreat on the part of the settlers'. It is clear from a close analysis of this period that a retreat was indeed the case: Grey, J, *A Military History of Australia*, Cambridge University Press, Melbourne, 1990, pp. 32–33.

Chapter 5

1	For an excellent overview of the early settlement and interactions see: Evans, R, 'On the utmost verge: race and ethnic relations at Moreton Bay 1799–1842', *Queensland Review*, vol. 15, no. 1, 2008, esp. pp. 1–12.
2	Even though Cunningham observed, on the banks of the Condamine River, several Barunggan people 'firing the dried herbage' as Raymond Evans notes, he 'did not directly associate this activity ... with the "extraordinary luxuriance of growth" across vast reaches of the Downs': Evans, R 'The mogwi take mi-an-jin: Race relations and the Moreton Bay penal settlement 1824–42', in Shaw, B., (ed.), *Brisbane: The Aboriginal presence 1824–1860*, Brisbane History Group, Brisbane and Boolarong Press, Brisbane, 2020 (1992), p. 7. Gorman to Colonial Secretary, 16 November 1839, SRNSW, INX-45-1895, Moreton Bay, CSLR, 1840, 752, 4/2499.2. See: Evans, 2008, pp. 1–3 for an overview of the mostly Irish but surprisingly diverse convict population, including George Brown.
3	Macdonald to Colonial Secretary, 24 September 1839, SRNSW, INX-45-1895, Moreton Bay, CSLR, 1840, 752, 4/2499.2. Kerkhove, R & Uhr, F, *The Battle of One Tree Hill: the Aboriginal resistance that stunned Queensland*, Boolarong Press, Brisbane, 2019, p. 23; Perry, TM, 'Cunningham, Allan (1791–1839)', *ADB*; Evans, 2008, p. 20.
4	'Interior discovery', *Sydney Gazette*, 30 November 1839, p. 2; Macdonald to Colonial Secretary, 24 September 1839, SRNSW, INX-45-1895, Moreton Bay, CSLR, 1840, 752, 4/2499.2.
5	It was a matter that perplexed the Lands Commissioner at New England, George Macdonald. Bush Constable Brown deserted his party on the return journey, taking the provisions he had been given at McIntyre's station. Macdonald was 'unable to ascertain any probable motive' for Brown's actions. Two of the Aboriginal men went back to McIntyre's station and Brown proceeded on with only one other man, who was reported as 'their Uncle'. All of them had firearms, and Gorman noted that Thompson and Giles 'had two Firelocks and thirty Rounds of ammunition belonging to the Police Force of this Settlement in their possession'. It is unclear who provided the information on the journey, but Bush Constable Thomson was regarded as 'the more intelligent' of the trio by Macdonald: 'Thompson also states, that after getting [over] the Gap (the <u>northern</u> descent from which he says presented the only difficulty to a Road being made) they came down upon a fine ... country – with vast Park-like plains, running from East to West as far as the Eye could reach and intersected by innumerable streams, all running to the westward – that they neither crossed nor saw any large river – nor any Eastern water; – that the only broken country they passed through was during the <u>last four days</u> of their journey – and that he considers Moreton-Bay to be not more than 150 miles from the most northern Stations of this District': Macdonald to Colonial Secretary, 24 September 1839, SRNSW, INX-45-1895, Moreton Bay, CSLR, 1840, 752, 4/2499.2.

6   French, M, *Conflict on the Condamine: Aborigines and the European invasion*, Darling Downs Institute Press, Toowoomba, Queensland, 1989, pp. 32–33; Stuart, I, 'Squatting landscapes in South-Eastern Australia (1820–1895)', PhD thesis, Prehistoric and Historic Archaeology, University of Sydney, 1999, p. 56.
7   Kitson, B, 'From runs to closer settlement', QLD Historical Atlas website, 2010, <www.qhatlas.com.au/content/runs-closer-settlement>; Waller, KGT, 'Leslie, Patrick (1815–1881)', *ADB*; Love, B, 'The Blucher Tribe', *The Holy Name Monthly*, 2 July 1962, p. 3.
8   Thomas Archer quoted in Kerkhove, R, 'Frontier War defences of early Queensland', *Queensland History Journal*, vol. 24, no. 7, Royal Historical Society of Queensland, 2020, p. 673.
9   Parsons, D, *Wadingh Wadingh: A history of Aboriginal people in the Warwick area and their land*, David Parsons, Maryvale, 2003, p. 145; Cooper, F, *Wild Adventures in Australia and New Zealand: Beyond the boundaries: With sketches of life in the mining districts*, James Blackwood, London, 1857, p. 86; Gary, D, *Warwick Argus*, 27 June 1903, p. 1; Leslie, P, in Hall, H, *The Early History of the Warwick District and the Pioneers of Darling Downs*, Robertson & Provan, Toowoomba, c. 1920–29, p. 10.
10 *Australian*, 25 July 1827, p. 3.
11 Petrie, C, *Tom Petrie's Reminiscences of Early Queensland*, Angus & Robertson, Sydney, 1983 (1904), p. 231. For an overview of the impact of the cornfield raids see: Kerkhove, R, 'Analysis of the corn fields raids', unpublished paper, nd.
12 Watkins (1892) quoted in Bottoms, T, *Conspiracy of Silence, Queensland's frontier killing times*, Allen & Unwin, Sydney, 2013, p. 11; Evans, R, *Fighting Words: Writing about race*, University of Queensland Press, Brisbane, 1999, pp. 65–66. As military historians Rodd Pratt and Jeff Hopkins-Wiese note, while there had been a few minor clashes between local Aboriginal clans and the military during this convict period, they had been rare and could barely be described as skirmishes in scale. In 1827, Captain Logan reported that a lone Aboriginal man had been shot by a sentry while raiding the settlement's maize crop and a few years later, during Commandant James Clunie's tenure, there had been a series of skirmishes in and around the Dunwich pilot station on North Stradbroke Island during 1830–31, which have been collectively described as the Battle of Narawai (Moongalba). See Kerkhove, R, 'Reconstructing the Battle of Narawi', *Queensland Review*, vol. 26, no. 1, pp. 3–31. Likewise, the posting at Limestone (near present-day Ipswich) had seen at least one clash involving a lone corporal of the 4th Regiment and some local Yuggera men. There had been little need to expand the military presence at Moreton Bay before 1842. As Pratt and Hopkins-Wiese note, while a detachment of the 99th Regiment had been despatched from Brisbane on two occasions to deal with gangs of bushrangers in the interior, the most common cause of military deployments from Moreton Bay were either in response to a reported Aboriginal depredation or in anticipation of one: Pratt, R & Hopkins-Wiese, J, 'Redcoats in the 1840s Moreton Bay and New Zealand frontier wars', vol. 26, no. 1, 2019, p. 36. Evans outlines the sporadic conflict around Moreton Bay from 1824 to 1839 and suggests Aboriginal people would have seen the shrinking penal establishment as evidence that it was either well under control or even about to cease: Evans, 2008, pp. 14–19. Kerkhove outlines the details of the constant raids on crops around the settlement that required 'crow minders' to keep watch and at times shoot at Aboriginal people in 'Analysis of the Corn Fields Raids'. See also Evans, 2020, esp. pp. 20–23.
13 Hodgson, CP, *Reminiscences of Australia with hints on the squatters' life*, W. N. Wright, London, 1846, p. 77; Parsons, 2003, p. 145. For an excellent overview of the squatters' push into the Darling Downs from 1840 to 1842 see French, 1989, pp. 63–80, 94–95.
14 Parsons, 2003, p. 146.

15 Parsons, 2003, p. 145; Gorman Journal entry, 1 November 1840, quoted in Jarrott, JK, 'Gorman's Gap', *Queensland Heritage*, vol. 3 no. 4, 1976, p. 24.
16 Kerkhove and Uhr cite 'The naming of Mt Rascal', Anthropological Society of Queensland, 25 June 1971. They also note a 2019 interview with Shannon Bauwens, a Western Wakka/Jarowir man at Gowrie who 'recalls being told that Mt Rascal was so fiercely protected on account of it being an important site for men's business' with 'stone tomahawks of great warriors' placed there, but provide no context for this or further information about Bauwens: Kerkhove & Uhr, 2019, p. 66.
17 'Return of the number of White men killed and wounded by the Aborigines in the District of Moreton Bay from the year 1841 to 1844 inclusive', SRNSW, CSLR, 4/2656.2.
18 Kerkhove & Uhr, 2019, pp. 76–80; Evans, 2008, pp. 20–21; Evans, 2020, pp. 24–25.
19 Other names for the group occupying what is now the Toowoomba escarpment down to Helidon were 'Lockyer Creek blacks', 'Tent Hill blacks', 'Limestone blacks', 'Mountain tribes', 'Darling Downs blacks', and 'Rosewood blacks'. Kerkhove notes that 'whether these broad names are any indication of sub-groups (clans or bands) of a single tribal group, or a broader political or linguistic affiliation is difficult to surmise from the limited interest and fragmentary knowledge of colonial reports': Kerkhove, R, 'Report for Jagera Daran: Indigenous historical context of Toowomba Bypass: Lockyer Valley and Helidon, with special attention to events surrounding the "Battle of One Tree Hill"', 2015, pp. 2–5, 8. A squatter ('J. W.') in the Moreton Bay area in the 1830s apparently met Moppy at a battle between the 'the Coast Tribes and the Beppo Jockeroos (Mountain Wild Black-fellows)': 'J.W.', 'Romance of real life in Australia', *Colonial Times*, 24 May 1850, p. 4.
20 Lieutenant Gorman reported to the Colonial Secretary on 'the Death of Mr. Assistant Surveyor Granville C. Stapylton and one of the men belonging to his Party named William Tuck'. Stapylton had been sent out 'for the purpose of surveying part of the Logan and Teviot Rivers and marking an inland trace to the Richmond and if possible to get down that River towards the Sea coast'. Stapylton's journey ended near Mount Lindsay on the present-day Queensland – New South Wales border. Gorman believed 'the natives in that part of this District are very treacherous'. As 'Prisoner of the Crown Abel Sutton' described it, when he returned to the survey party's camp that day, 'Mr. Stapylton was dead, his clothes torn off him, he was wounded in the breast and in the side of the head, his right Eye was much swelled, and his left Eye was open he was lying on his back [and] the boxes were all broken open. The arms, blankets, clothes, sugar and flour was all gone'. After the deaths of Stapylton and his assistant, Gorman believed 'the Surveying parties are too small to proceed thro' those wild parts at such a Distance from Brisbane Town' and 'that altho Mr. Stapylton had some arms with him he would not allow them to be Kept Loaded or in a state of preparation'. Gorman recommend that 'each of those parties going into the wild parts of this district should consist of Twelve men with Six stand of Arms so as that three of those men might mount Guard at the Tents daily always Keeping one man on sentry'. Gorman believed that if these precautions were taken he was 'quite certain that no Blacks will attempt to attack any Party so constituted'. Abel Sutton Gorman to Colonial Secretary, deposition, 27th August 1840, re Murder of Asst. Surveyor Moreton Bay 22nd June 1840, SRNSW, INX-45-1895, Moreton Bay, CSLR, 752, 4/2499.2. Gorman continued that, 'The Blacks are very much afraid of arms when loaded and they are quite as well aware as white men when the arms are loaded. In this case two Blacks had been for several days with the party a couple of days before the murder [and] one of those Blacks had a piece belonging to Mr. Stapylton in his hand and said to the men that it was no use as it was not loaded': Gorman to Colonial Secretary, 27th August 1840, re Murder of Asst. Surveyor Moreton Bay 22nd June 1840, SRNSW, INX-45-1895, Moreton Bay, CSLR, 752, 4/2499.2.

21 Kerkhove suggests the attack on Staplyton's party led to interest in finding other routes than via Cunningham's Gap. The Ugurapul people who destroyed Staplyton's expedition were traditional allies of the Yaggara but it was Old Moppy who reported them to Gorman, perhaps reflecting Moppy's faith in Gorman at this time, or traditional Law being followed: Kerkhove, R, pers. comm., 31 December 2023. Kerkhove and Uhr note that Moppy was undoubtedly a warrior leader, but he should not be considered, as the colonists did, 'chief' of his 'tribe': Kerkhove & Uhr, 2019, pp. 31–32. Kerkhove notes that 'Old Moppy invited Gorman to his base camp at Grantham to meet with him and to meet Jarowair/Western Wakka people (who the Yaggara got their wives regularly from). Moppy then sent his son (possibly Multuggerah) with Gorman to show him the best route up to the Downs. The Jarowair came to the camp at Old Moppy's invite specifically to meet Gorman and petition him about how the squatters were invading their lands and killing them. Gorman promised to investigate. However, when he got to Eton Vale and met the squatters, they complained that "the blacks" were trying to burn them out (they certainly were!) so Gorman decided to ignore the Jarowair protests'. Kerkhove believes 'this incident sparked Moppy's change of heart towards Gorman and all settlers and set him on his path of vengeance. It must have been a severe loss of face for him, when he had such faith in Gorman, only to have his sincere efforts to help his neighbours (the Jarowair) ignored'. Kerkhove suggests 'Old Moppy' was highly regarded all over the region and that was why the initial alliance was so far-reaching. He would have taken a prominent role in airing grievances and formulating plans at the Bunya Gatherings that generated the larger alliance. However, 'Cocky' Rogers killed Moppy before his leadership could be fully effective: Kerkhove, pers. comm., 31 December 2023. For an outline of the deaths of Mullan and Ningavil see: Evans, 2020, pp. 34–35.

22 Balfour to Lt. Owen Gorman, 6 October 1841, in Mackenzie-Smith, J. (ed.), *Brisbane River Valley, 1841–50: Pioneer Observations*, Sources No. 5, Brisbane History Group, Brisbane, 1991, p. 35.

23 Kerkhove & Uhr, 2019, p. 80.

24 David McConnell letters, September to November 1840, in Kerkhove & Uhr, 2019, pp. 80–81.

25 Bottoms, 2013, p. 16. Kerkhove and Uhr point out the difficulties understanding traditional domains today and use colonists' terms for the Aboriginal groups in the region such as 'Moppy's Tribe'. See: Kerkhove & Uhr, 2019, pp. 27–29, 76–78; Parsons, 2003, p. 145.

26 Rogers had taken hundreds of sheets of ironbark from the Yaggara village, which Kerkhove and Uhr suggest was one possible cause for the earlier raids in the area: Kerkhove & Uhr, 2019, pp. 79–81.

27 As Raymond Evans has noted, 'what eventuated was more of a massacre than a battle': Evans, 2008, p. 24. In 2005, Richard Broome cautioned historians to carefully interrogate massacres: 'the word is overused and portrays Aboriginal people as passive victims. Some incidents were not "massacres" but battles in which one side suffered severe losses. The details of the action are too vague in many incidents to confidently label them "massacres" rather than "defeats"': Broome, R, *Aboriginal Victorians: A history since 1800*, Allen & Unwin, Sydney, 2005, p. 81.

28 In August 1840, Gorman had 'found it necessary to forward by the Schooner Harliquin Bush Constable George Brown who has of late behaved in so insolent and disrespectful a manner as to convince me that he is of no further use as a Constable here [and begged] ... to suggest that he may not be permitted to enter this district again which he is most likely to do if not prevented': Gorman to Colonial Secretary, 13 August 1840, SRNSW, INX-45-

1895, Moreton Bay, CSLR, 1840, 752, 4/2499.2. It is unclear if Brown went to Sydney or not but he was certainly back at Moreton Bay in mid-1841. Timothy Bottoms agrees with Raymond Evans that George 'Black' Brown was an 'ally' of the Yuggerah: Bottoms, 2013, pp. 16–17; Evans, R, *A History of Queensland*, Cambridge University Press, Melbourne, 2007, p. 53. See Kerkhove & Uhr, 2019, pp. 23–25 and pp. 87–90. Kerkhove and Uhr suggest there were 'potentially 20 Aboriginal casualties' and are suspicious of the shepherds' testimony that they committed no crimes and some denied even firing their muskets. While it seems Brown was not captured at the time according to Evans (2008, p. 24), Campbell, who met Brown as a prisoner afterwards, did not mention casualties, but said that 'white men, well mounted dashed into the camp and upon his calling out that he was a Christian like themselves, spared and made him a prisoner': Campbell, J, *The Early Settlement of Queensland*, Bibliographical Society of Queensland, Brisbane, 1936, pp. 9–12.

29 Therry to Gorman 23 December 1841, Letters to Police Magistrates, SRNSW, 4/6658; Currey, CH, 'Therry, Sir Roger (1800–1874)', *ADB*.
30 Therry to Gorman 23 December 1841, Letters to Police Magistrates, SRNSW, 4/6658; Evans, 2008, p. 26.
31 Evans, 2008, p. 26; Kerkhove & Uhr, 2019, p. 97. As John Mackenzie-Smith has noted, Governor Gipps had reason to think the 'gentlemen squatters' would behave better beyond the eyes of the authorities in the squatting districts than convict and ex-convict frontiersmen, or would control their stockworkers: 'Gipps was content merely to give each of these aspiring pastoral capitalists a stern warning before they set forth to the interior. The squatting parties were informed in no uncertain terms that they would be encroaching upon dangerous territory; they could expect no protection from the government and would be accountable for any Aboriginal loss of life. This was reiterated by Commissioner G.J. McDonald as the droving parties traversed the New England district': Mackenzie-Smith, J, 'The Kilcoy Poisonings: The official factor 1841–43', in Fisher, R. (ed.), *Brisbane: The Aboriginal presence 1824–1860*, Brisbane History Group Paper no. 11, 1992, p. 78.

Chapter 6

1 John Mackenzie-Smith suggests the poisoning might have been ordered by another squatter: Mackenzie-Smith, J, 'The Kilcoy poisonings: The official factor 1841–43', in Fisher, R (ed.), *Brisbane: The Aboriginal presence 1824–1860*, Brisbane History Group Paper no. 11, 1992, pp. 81–88.
2 Gunson, N, 'A missionary expedition from Zion Hill (Nunah) to Toorbul etc: The journal of the Reverend KWW Schmidt', *Aboriginal History*, vol. 2, no. 2, 1978, pp. 114–121. Two other missionaries, Nique and Rode, noted in March that 'the Natives from Toorbul told us also that at one of the Squatters station's, many Natives had died from having received for eating something "ban" (nasty, poison)': 'The Journal of the Brethren Nique and Rode at Umpieboang', 16 March 1842, vol. 20, John Dunmore Lang papers, German mission, Moreton Bay, 1837–1867, ML, SLNSW, A 2240; Langevad, G (ed.), *The Simpson Letterbook*, May 30 1842, Cultural and Historical Records of Queensland, no. 1, 1979, Anthropology Museum, University of Queensland, Brisbane, 1979, p. 1.
3 Handt, JCS, Report of Transactions relative to the Aborigines in the District of Moreton Bay for the year 1842, SANSW, CSLR, INX-106-46108, 43/218, 4/2618.1.
4 Simpson migrated to Australia in 1839 with well-connected recommendations. His wife and child died soon after, and Simpson then threw himself with gusto into the task of running Moreton Bay. Langevad, 1979, p. xxi.
5 Simpson was at first circumspect about whether the poisoning was 'by design or accident'. He wrote: 'It is well known that Arsenic has been extensively used at some of the Stations

in the North for the cure of the Scab & it is a question how far the carcasses of Sheep dying under the treatment, if eaten by the Blacks, may be capable of inducing the symptoms named, which are certainly those of Arsenic': Simpson to Colonial Secretary, 30 May, 3 October 1842, in Langevad, 1979, p. 27.

6   Historian Libby Connors notes that 'from August 1841 the Aboriginal men west of the D'Aguilar Rannge had decided on campaigns to evict them [Europeans] from their lands'. She notes that 'opinions differed among the various tribal groups over how to deal with the European settlers' but by late 1841, the Brisbane Valley was under attack: Connors, L, *Warrior: A legendary leader's dramatic life and violent death on the colonial frontier*, Allen & Unwin, Sydney, 2015, pp. 57, 66–67. Connors may be referring to Charles White, the editor of the *Bathurst Free Press* in the late 19th century, who under the name 'The Chatterer' wrote a series on 'The Aborigines in Australia' in 1890. Chapter 13 was called 'Massacres' and in this he noted 'German missionaries' first reported the Kilcoy poisoning, 'stating that between 50 and 60 natives, of the Gigabarah tribe, had been poisoned on one of the squatter's stations, and that the neighbouring tribes had determined to kill the whites whenever they might meet with any of them': 'The Aborigines in Australia', *Bathurst Free Press and Mining Journal*, 1 April 1890, p. 4. See also 'J.W.', 'Romance of Real Life in Australia', *Colonial Times* 24 May 1850, p. 4. Timothy Bottoms brings together reports from various sources that point to the shepherds of Evan Mackenzie's station: Bottoms, T, *Conspiracy of Silence: Queensland's frontier killing times*, Allen & Unwin, Sydney, 2013, pp. 83–84. Kerkhove and Uhr note that these were 'Giggabarah' (Jinibara) people. According to traditional owners today, 'the Jinibara People are considered by other tribal groups in Southeast Queensland as "mountain people"' with traditional country including the D'Aguilar Ranges, much of Brisbane Forest Park, the Blackall Ranges, many of the Glasshouse Mountains, and the southern side of the Jimna Ranges. The word Jinibara means 'people of the lawyer vine' (jinni = lawyer vine; bara = people), thus referring to the mountainous nature of our country where the lawyer vine grows in riparian areas and rain forests': Gall, L & Australian Heritage Specialists, 'Jinibara Traditional Inputs for the Sunshine Coast Heritage Study For Sunshine Coast Regional Council', 2017, <hdp-au-prod-app-suncst-haveyoursay-files.s3.ap-southeast-2.amazonaws.com/4016/2321/1315/2021-06-09_14-01_978.pdf>, p. 8. Frontier wars historian Ray Kerkhove has detailed how there was a vast network of traditional alliances of 'tribes' across the south-east Queensland region stretching from the Gold Coast inland to Warwick and north to Bundaberg. In the early 1840s, these traditional alliances expanded dramatically. It seems Multuggerah's Yaggara people from the Lockyer Valley and Ipswich area had joined with the 'Blucher Tribe' from the Warwick area (Gidhabal), the Yugambeh from Cunningham's Gap, the Geynyon from the Severn River (probably Stanthorpe and Tenterfield), and the Barrungam, Jarowair, Wakka Wakka and Jinaburra from the (Toowoomba) 'ranges' and 'Mount Brisbane' or the D'Aguilar Range. While it is difficult to be precise about the groups that united at this point, it seems there was an alliance across 400 kilometres of what is today south-east Queensland. That is certainly what Commissioner Simpson believed – 'from Wide Bay to beyond Cunningham's Gap'. Kerkhove and Uhr note that in the 1940s Kilcoy Elder Gaiarbau (Willie Mackenzie) described the Birin and Jinabara alliances for combined activities such as hunting, ceremony and marriage exchange: Kerkhove, R & Uhr, F, *The Battle of One Tree Hill: The Aboriginal resistance that stunned Queensland*, Boolarong Press, Brisbane, 2019, pp. 38. A 'JW' (possibly John Watts) reminiscing in the Hobart *Colonial Times* in 1850 about his experiences at Moreton Bay in the 1830s described Multuggerah's father 'Old Moppy' as having influence over 'approved *tribes*' from amongst the 'Beppo Jockeroos (Mountain

Wild Blackfellows)'. Kerkhove mistakes 'approved men' (not tribes) and excludes 'kippers' or young boys that were not included in J. W.'s assessment of Moppe's force: 'J.W.', 'Romance of real life in Australia', *Colonial Times*, 24 May 1850, p. 4; Kerkhove, R, *How They Fought: Indigenous tactics and weaponry of Australia's Frontier Wars*, Boolarong Press, Brisbane, 2023, p. 50.

7   Koori History, 'Bunya Pine (Araucaria bidwillii) – Traditional Aboriginal food & beverage', Koori History website, 2017, <koorihistory.com/bunya/>.
8   Simpson to Colonial Secretary, May 30 1842, in Langevad (ed.) 1979, p. 2.
9   Ray Kerkhove, Terry Royan, Boe Spearim and Uncle Wayne Fossey, interview, 11 June 2024, Toowoomba; interview, Ray Kerkhove and Terry Royan, 11 June 2024, Toowoomba.
10 Bell in Kerkhove, R, 'Notes from audio recordings: Indigenous knowledge of Bunya Mtns region/Bunya Festival', 28 April 2010, unpublished, pp. 3–4; Uncle Wayne Fossey recalls his grandfather who lived 'at the back of Toowoomba in a tent' speaking of a stone arrangement on nearby Gunnaburra Mountain as part of a travel route. Wayne thinks they might have been part of 'star maps': Ray Kerkhove, Terry Royan, Boe Spearim and Uncle Wayne Fossey, interview, 11 June 2024, Toowoomba.
11 'Domestic intelligence', *Sydney Herald*, 20 April 1842, p. 2. As Kerkhove notes, 'this was extraordinary for the time, but there was little attempt to define the boundaries of the Bunya Reserve or restrict European access to the area': Kerkhove, R, 'Indigenous historical context of the Sunshine Coast: A report for Converge, Kabi Kabi Corp and Sunshine Coast Council', June 2018, p. 4.
12 Bottoms, 2013, p. 21. See: Petrie, C (ed.), *Tom Petrie's Reminiscences of Early Queensland*, Angus & Robertson, Sydney, 1983 (1904), pp. 11–17 for an early account of the festival and Cliento, R & Lack, C, *Triumph in the Tropics: An historical sketch of Queensland*, Smith & Patterson, Brisbane, 1959, esp. pp. 177–186 for a 1950s assessment of conflict on the frontier which calls this period 'The Guerilla War' and 'The Black War' that in southern Queensland lasted twenty years. Kenny notes that at bora and other gatherings 'linguistic and other cultural differences between the people who participated in these initiations, these gatherings reflected a broader, open regional system that had common laws relating to land, and that both reflected and created a regional polity': Kenny, 'The "Society" at Bora Ceremonies: A manifestation of a body of traditional law and custom in Aboriginal Australia relevant to Native Title case law', *Oceania*, vol. 82, no. 2, 2012, p. 131; Ray Kerkhove, Terry Royan, Boe Spearim and Uncle Wayne Fossey, interview, 11 June 2024, Toowoomba. For an overview of the bunya forests and gatherings see Evans, R, 'Against the grain: Colonialism and the demise of the Bunya Gatherings, 1839–1939', in Haebich, A (ed.), *On the Bunya Trail: Queensland Review special edition*, vol. 9, no. 2, University of Queensland Press, Brisbane, 2002, pp. 47–64.
13 Davis told Petrie this had led to 'a cry for vengeance'. See Russell, HS, *Genesis of Queensland Etc*, Turner & Henderson, Sydney, 1888, esp. pp. 279–282 for Russell's first-hand account of meeting Davis and Bracewell, and reports of the Petrie expedition retreating due to concerns over warriors mobilising after the poisoning: Austin & Lack, 'Russell, Henry Stuart (1818–1889)', *ADB*; Ray Kerkhove, Terry Royan, Boe Spearim and Uncle Wayne Fossey, interview, 11 June 2024, Toowoomba.
14 The Toor was according to Simpson 'held for the purpose of settling any differences which may arise amongst them'. Simpson noted that the meetings 'may be called by any Tribe' and that messengers were 'despatched in every direction': Simpson to Colonial Secretary, May 30 1842, in Langevad (ed.), 1979, p. 2. Davis's report could not be ignored – he had lost 'three of his adopted brothers' who 'died as a consequence of the food they eat there'. Simpson noted that 'the statement of Davis fully confirms that of Bracewell with regards

to this poisoning'. Davis was told that the poison had been laced in mutton, not at all an accidental circumstance as Simpson first thought possible. It was a desperate and callous ploy by the isolated and possibly unarmed stockmen who were confronted by 'the Blacks having assembled near the Station in numbers'. The people who gathered there were, according to Davis, 'told by the white men to remain at their camp & that they would bring them some food'. Simpson reported that 'Nine or Ten Tribes suffered more or less – one the Woogambarah very severely, so that they were unable to come to the [Bunya] meeting'. Libby Connors is among several historians to suggest the Bunya Gathering was a point where a collective decision to fight was made, as after this, conflict escalated: Connors, 2015, pp. 81–84.

15 It was found the men who resorted to poison came from Mackenzie's station as one of the warriors had a pocket watch that belonged to one of Mackenzie's shepherds, who had been killed 'out of revenge, as Davis says, for the loss of their poisoned friends'. Davis attempted to pacify the warriors to prevent them taking out revenge on Petrie's party, whom they were asking 'whether they belonged to the White men who had poisoned their friends' and Davis warned them to 'lose no time in getting off': Simpson to Colonial Secretary, 30 May 1842, in Langevad (ed.), 1979, pp. 2–3; Evans, R, 'On the utmost verge: Race and ethnic relations at Moreton Bay 1799–1842', *Queensland Review*, vol. 15, no. 1, Griffith University, 2008, p. 27.

16 McConnell also believed he had 'already killed two' when he met him and around one hundred warriors who had stolen his sheep. McConnell, in a precarious situation, negotiated the return of all but seventy sheep that he agreed the warriors could keep, in an exchange that probably saved the squatter and his stockworkers' lives: McConnell in Kerkhove & Uhr, 2019, p. 98.

17 He reported that 'A Hutkeeper of Mr. Bigge was murdered a few weeks since & within these few days another of Mr. Balfour's; besides several other individuals have been attacked on their way from one station to another': Simpson to Colonial Secretary, 13 July 1842, in Langevad, 1979, p. 3.

18 Simpson reported that 'in an attempt to take three of the most desperate characters, supposed to be the murderers of Mr. Bigge's man, at Mr. McConnels Station, a black named Commandant was killed & two others escaped wounded': Simpson to Colonial Secretary, 13 July 1842, in Langevad, 1979, p. 3; McConnell and Balfour quoted in Kerkhove & Uhr, 2019, p. 114.

19 Dowse, T, 'Recollections and Reminiscences, 1828–1878', Thomas Dowse Papers, John Oxley Library, State Library of Queensland, OM79-68, p. 27; McConnell quoted in Kerkhove & Uhr, 2019, p. 115.

20 Commissioner Simpson was also alarmed. He forwarded a letter to the Colonial Secretary from Balfour that contained 'an account of a series of aggressions committed by the Aborigines at his Station'. Simpson was worried about 'this state of insecurity to the Squatters' and that they could not get any workers 'to engage for the duty of Shepherd, & Stockman' as they would 'sooner earn a scanty existence near the Settlement than expose themselves to the dangers of the bush': Simpson to Colonial Secretary, 8 August 1842 in Langevad, 1979, p. 3. Simpson might have felt significant pressure from the squatters to act. He later noted that the German missionary Schmidt seemed to have been reluctant to follow up on reports of the Kilcoy Massacre 'from fear of offending the squatters': Simpson to Colonial Secretary, 20 January 1843, in Langevad, 1979, p. 5.

21 The margin note on Rolleston's return also says: 'The report of the Murder of these four men did not reach the Commissioner for some months after the occurrence': 'Return of the number of White men killed and wounded by the Aborigines in the District of Moreton

Bay from the year 1841 to 1844 inclusive', CSLR, INX-45-4685, 4/2656.2. Simpson even went so far as to 'be allowed right of preemption', putting up the whole of the building at his own expense: Simpson to Colonial Secretary, 19 September 1842 in Langevad, 1979, p. 3. The standing orders were published in May 1839 and clearly establish the 'Crown Commissioner' as the head of a force that in every respect was in line with military structure and procedures. See 'Standing Orders for the Border Police', *HRA*, XX, p. 257.

22 'News from the interior', *Sydney Morning Herald*, 25 November 1842, p. 2. An incident in March, described in the press as 'a most diabolical murder', was committed 'at Limestone by two black fellows, upon the person of a poor little infant only two years and nine months old, the daughter of a Mr. W. Moore, wheelwright and blacksmith'. Yet unreported around the same time was the fact, much later established by Assistant Land Commissioner Rolleston, that a man had 'forcibly abused a Black woman'. It is difficult from the news report to uncover a motivation beyond rage. Dowse, T, 'News from the interior', *Sydney Morning Herald*, 19 April 1843, p. 3. Four shepherds were killed in retaliation. The shepherds Hassel, Noonan, Cummins and McKin (and J Essex wounded) were all of Eales station at Wide Bay. According to the 'Return of the number of White men killed and wounded', 'Sussex [Essex] forcibly abused a Black woman, and hence the attack': 'Return of the number of White men killed and wounded by the Aborigines in the District of Moreton Bay from the year 1841 to 1844 inclusive', CSLR, INX-45-4685, 4/2656.2.

23 Dowse, 1843, p. 3. According to Kerkhove the warriors were led by Jackey Jackey, a Yaggara leader. After unsuccessfully attacking a property, 'in humiliation at their defeat, they killed a child as a way of reaping some vengeance against the family': Kerkhove, pers. comm., 31 December 2023. In April, Commissioner Simpson felt the threat of attack first-hand. He was undertaking a tour of Wide Bay and one evening near 'the crossing place of the Numabulla' was alarmed 'by a cry that the Natives were rushing a party of Mr. Eales' men, who were following us for protection – & had encamped a short distance from us.' Simpson allowed them to join his party and 'divided the men into 3 watches for the night'. When the next day 'a party of the Cuccombaruh Tribe' joined Simpson's camp, he ordered the sentries to 'watch them closely': Langevad, 1979, p. 9.

24 Dowse, 1843, p. 3.

25 'Moreton Bay – August 14', *Colonial Observer*, 26 August 1843, p. 2.

26 'Return of the number of White men killed and wounded by the Aborigines in the District of Moreton Bay from the year 1841 to 1844 inclusive', CSLR, INX-45-4685, 4/2656.2; Kerkhove, pers. comm., 31 December 2023.

27 The low number of wounds (which usually outnumber deaths around ten to one in conflict) might reflect a lack of reporting, but also could be due to the fact that small groups of one or two stockmen could be picked off and killed, rather than left wounded: 'Return of the number of White men killed and wounded by the Aborigines in the District of Moreton Bay from the year 1841 to 1844 inclusive', CSLR, INX-45-4685, 4/2656.2.

28 Campbell, J, *The Early Settlement of Queensland*, Bibliographical Society of Queensland, Brisbane, 1936, p. 13.

29 The 'Squatter's Friend' reported that on the Darling Downs recently, 'two squatters, Messrs. Hicks and Campbell, narrowly escaped being murdered by these savages, the former having his horse killed under him, and several spears passed through the clothes of both, but luckily their persons escaped uninjured'. 'The Squatter's Friend' was incensed that 'these marauders' had the temerity to 'show themselves at the head stations and carry off the sheep before the owner's face'. He called for 'protection from the Government': 'The Blacks – Moreton Bay', *Sydney Morning Herald*, 27 September 1843, p. 4.

30 Dowse, 1843, p. 3.
31 Dowse urged that 'the settlers must have an eye upon their movements, as it plainly appears there is no dependence to be placed upon their good faith, for they will one week visit a station on the most friendly terms, and the next drive off a flock of sheep, and if possible murder their shepherds': Dowse, 1843, p. 3.
32 Simpson to Colonial Secretary, 3 October 1843 in Langevad, 1979, p. 12.
33 For the importance of bullock trains in the Downs during the 1840s see: Kerkhove & Uhr, 2019, pp. 135–136.
34 The battle is now signposted with interpretation at the lookout thanks to the efforts of, among others, historian Ray Kerkhove: Ray Kerkhove, Terry Royan, Boe Spearim and Uncle Wayne Fossey, interview, 11 June 2024, Toowoomba.
35 Campbell, 1910, p. 6; Simpson to Colonial Secretary, 3 October 1843 in Langevad, 1979, p. 12; Strong, M, '"One ring to rule them all?' Towards understanding the plethora of bora grounds in southeastern Queensland', *Queensland History Journal*, vol. 22, no. 12, 2016, p. 870. In 1828 Fraser noted that 'at Moreton Bay the blacks were in thousands … [and] dwelt in regular built huts, forming a sort of village': Fraser, C, 'Journal of a Residence on the Banks of the Rivers Brisbane and Logan from 30 June to 6 September 1828', 2 and 3 July 1828, SRNSW, CSSB, 9/2738; Strange, Flinders and Oxley quoted in Evans, 2008, pp. 4–5.
36 Campbell, 1936, p. 20; Dowse, 1843, p. 3; Simpson to Colonial Secretary, 3 October 1843 in Langevad, 1979, p. 12.
37 Campbell, 1910, p. 6.
38 Campbell, 1910, p. 6. While the squatters and their stockmen gathered at the Half Way House and called Lands Commissioner Simpson to a meeting, Simpson later reported he tried to discourage 'all large assemblies of squatters for [the] purpose of retaliation'. He recommended instead 'the union of two or three neighbouring stations for their mutual defence': Simpson to Colonial Secretary, 3 October 1843 in Langevad, 1979, p. 12; Campbell, 1936, p. 20. Intriguingly, Dowse did not initially report the squatters' repulse at Meewah: Dowse, 1843, p. 3.
39 Campbell, 1910, p. 6.
40 Simpson to Colonial Secretary, 3 October 1843 in Langevad, 1979, p. 12.
41 Kerkhove, 'Report for Jagera Daran: Indigenous historical context of Toowomba Bypass: Lockyer Valley and Helidon: With special attention to events surrounding the "Battle of One Tree Hill"', 2015, p. 8; Kerkhove, 2023, pp. 280–281; Gapps, S, *The Sydney Wars: Conflict in the early colony 1788–1817*, NewSouth Publishing, Sydney, 2018, pp. 218–221.
42 Kerkhove and Uhr suggest the pursuers apparently became confident and with 'wild cheers', 'charged up the steep incline'. Kerkhove and Uhr are confident the mountain was One Tree Hill, though note that the single contemporary observation by Simpson only remarked 'a hill in the vicinity' and Mount Davidson, closer to the ambush site, could have been the location: Kerkhove & Uhr, 2019, p. 156. The 'large body of squatters' that had been gathered could have been around a hundred armed and mounted men. Kerkhove and Uhr have shown there were around 200 men across the eighteen or so stations of the Lockyer, Upper Brisbane and The Downs at this time, and if they left half their workers at the head stations on guard, the mobile force available would have been around one hundred. Kerkhove and Uhr also estimate that the allied forces of warriors that Multuggerah could bring to bear were around 1500 to 2000 men, though it appears this number were not gathered in the Rosewood scrub: Kerkhove & Uhr, 2019, pp. 126–127.

Part 2

1. Ryan, L, 'Settler massacres on the Port Phillip Frontier, 1836–1851', *Journal of Australian Studies*, vol. 34, no. 3, 2010, p. 262. See also: Semelin, J, 'In consideration of massacres', *Journal of Genocide Research*, vol. 3, no. 3, 2001, pp. 377–389.

Chapter 7

1. There is certainly some discrepancy between his first report and the deposition made later in 1839 at a time, after the Myall Creek trials, when he might not have wanted to be connected to ordering his men to open fire: Nunn, deposition, Merton, 4 April 1839, *HRA*, XX, p. 251; Cobban, deposition, Merton, 17 May 1839, *HRA*, XX, p. 254; Lee, deposition, Merton, 4 April 1839, *HRA*, XX p. 251; Nunn to Thomson, 5 March 1838, SRNSW, CSL, 38/2279.
2. Warriors often stockpiled their weapons, sometimes as back-up for an attack or a defence, sometimes when heading to a ceremony, at other times to have them ready to hand in camp. Often the stockpiles were extra weapons, or a cache of arms. See Kerkhove, R, *How They Fought: Indigenous tactics and weaponry of Australia's Frontier Wars*, Boolarong Press, Brisbane, 2023, p. 269; Flanagan, R, 'The Aborigines of Australia – No. IX', *Empire*, 5 November 1853, p. 4.
3. Deposition at Merton, 4 April 1839, *HRA*, XX, p. 251; Cobban, deposition, Merton, 17 May 1839, *HRA*, XX, p. 254; Lee, deposition, Merton, 4 April 1839, *HRA*, XX p. 251; Nunn to Thomson, 5 March 1838, SRNSW, CSL, 38/2279. Connor suggests the large number of 200–300 deaths to be unlikely 'dinner party boastings'. The sheer number of rounds expended to achieve such casualties from around thirty firearms is quite impossible. He does not agree with Nunn and Cobban's four or five bodies, but suggests Sergeant Lee's 'forty or fifty seems the best calculation'. Connor also suggests that even though the people at Waterloo Creek were armed, 'Nunn's attack on them was unprovoked'. This goes against Cobban, Nunn, Hannan and Lee's depositions that Hannan was speared before any shooting commenced, which seems to be one of the few details that matched across all reports. Even Threlkeld called it a battle, or at least 'the blacks stood battle' before anything else transpired: Threlkeld in Gunson, 1974, p. 138. We might not believe these men making depositions well after the events and in the light of the Myall Creek Massacre perpetrators' deaths, but in the climate of fear, terror and defiance on the Big River it is not difficult to understand warriors launching an attack on mounted police who were approaching their camp. There was not a lot else they could do other than surrender or flee. Connor admits 'there is no evidence for Nunn's motives' but suggests he attacked the first group of people he could find as a means of spreading fear amongst them and stopping their attacks on settlers and their sheep. Rather, it seems the fact that one of their own was speared surprised the police and that was the catalyst for a spree of vengeful shooting in the scrub: Connor, 2002, p. 111. Milliss argues Cobban's account in particular was suspect, sanitised and an attempt to 'obscure the true dimensions of the slaughter at Waterloo Creek'. Milliss considered the depositions at Merton to have been co-ordinated, but that Lee's estimate of 'forty to fifty' was a more honest assessment only because he had a falling out with Nunn. Unfortunately, Milliss's speculation seems to want to find evidence of a major massacre as part of a post-Myall Creek cover-up and lacks an appreciation of both Aboriginal and European military tactics and operations. He suggests that the firing from the first encounter would have meant 'any Aborigines within earshot would have cleared off at the crack of Cobban's pistol': Milliss, R, *Waterloo Creek: The Australia Day massacre of 1838, George Gipps and the British conquest of New South Wales*, McPhee Gribble, Melbourne, 1992, pp. 188, 628–649. This patronising view of Aboriginal people who would run at

the first sound of gunfire is unfortunate and not supported at all by other attacks and encounters with armed and mounted white men. The warriors were in strong numbers and had stockpiled weapons. Governor Gipps reported the death toll was 'not less than ten or twelve, besides a number wounded', based on Nunn's initial report. Nunn's unusual assessment, 'not less than', suggests he was carefully leaving it open as to how many deaths there were above 'ten or twelve', but to suggest as Milliss does that even Lee's assessment of forty to fifty deaths was below the mark is difficult to sustain: Gipps to Glenelg, 27 April 1838, *HRA*, XIX, p. 399.

4   In 1849, Colonial Secretary Edward Deas Thomson, forced to jog his memory by the forthright lawyer and member of the Legislative Council, George Robert Nichols, came to Nunn's defence. Thomson recalled 'a complaint had been made by Mr. Park, formerly a candidate for the representation of Durham, of depredations committed by the blacks, and a party of mounted police was despatched for their protection, with instructions to disperse the aborigines, but not to fire upon them unless they were attacked. It was clear from the report that there was no attack upon the natives until a trooper had been speared, and it became necessary to order the attack in self-defence. The Government had never attempted to deny that persons actually attacked by blacks had a perfect right to defend themselves, and no more was done in this case'. The Colonial Secretary was clear that 'all who recollected the kind-hearted Major Nunn must know that he was utterly incapable of the cruelty laid to his charge, and that he could only have acted as he had done in self-defence': 'Legislative Council. The Aborigines.' *Sydney Morning Herald*, 2 July 1849, p. 2.

5   Historian John Connor argues 'Nunn's expedition enabled settlers to consolidate their hold on the Gwydir and advance north to the Barwon and Macintyre rivers': Connor, J, *The Australian Frontier Wars 1788–1838*, UNSW Press, Sydney, 2002, p. 111. When word reached Sydney of Nunn's 'recontre' or 'collision' as the governor called it, with 'a Tribe of the Natives', Gipps was duty-bound to inform Lord Glenelg. Glenelg's 'Despatch of the 26th July 1837, No. 353 on the subject of the treatment of the Aboriginal Inhabitants of this Country' explicitly required the governor to report on any 'measures which are to be adopted when any of them come to a violent death by the hands of the Queen's officers or by persons acting under their orders'. In his letter, Gipps had to 'very much regret' to state that 'a case has already occurred' where he had 'found it necessary to act upon your Lordship's Instructions': Gipps to Glenelg, 25 April 1838, *HRA*, XIX, pp. 396–397. Governor Gipps understood the attacks right across the edge of the colony in 1838 to be in retaliation for the actions of squatters and stockmen. He interviewed Major Nunn, who informed him that 'the party of Natives he fell in with must have consisted of not far short of 1,000 persons, including women and children' and that 'they consisted of tribes but little accustomed to intercourse with white men'. They were also skilled fighters; Gipps noted that 'they are particularly dextrous with their spears as well as with a peculiar instrument called a Boomering which they hurl with great effect'. Nunn was almost certainly outlining a case for the threat posed by such warriors as justification for his actions at Waterloo Creek: Gipps to Glenelg, 27 April 1838, *HRA*, XIX, p. 399.

6   But the governor was not hopeful these measures would be entirely successful. He added that 'outrages' are 'now of frequent occurrence beyond the boundaries of Location': Gipps to Glenelg, 27 April 1838, *HRA*, XIX, pp. 397–399.

7   It took until July 1839 for the Executive Council to make a decision on Major Nunn's actions at Waterloo Creek. In the council's verdict, 'the Savage Tribes' were 'unquestionably the Aggressors'. While the council deplored the 'numbers of the Native Tribe who … fell under the fire of the Police', they argued that Nunn's party were 'under a persuasion that it was necessary in self-defence'. Governor Gipps duly reported to London that 'no further

proceedings' in Nunn's case were necessary, especially due to the 'amount of excitement produced in the Colony' by the execution of 'seven men for a massacre of the Aborigines' at Myall Creek in June 1838: Extracts from the Minutes of the Executive Council No. 20 and No. 22, 1839, Encl. No. 1, Gipps to Glenelg, 22 July 1839, *HRA*, XX, p. 247; Gipps to Glenelg, 22 July 1839, *HRA*, XX, pp. 243–244.

8   Gipps noted, 'a man in charge of a Cattle Station, belonging to a person named Fitzgerald, has been found barbarously murdered, and also two other men belonging to a Surveying party under Mr. Finch'. So too 'some Cattle belonging to the same person [were] slaughtered … ': Gipps to Glenelg, 27 April, 2 May 1838, *HRA*, XIX, p. 398–400; Gipps to Glenelg, 21 July 1838, *HRA*, XIX, pp. 508–509.

9   Russell to Gipps, 21 December 1839, *HRA*, XX, p. 440.

10 Gray, 'Dangar, Henry (1796–1861)', *ADB*; 'Supreme Court', *Gazette*, 20 November 1838, p. 2. With intense public interest in the trial, reports of the first trial appeared in full in the *Australian*, the *Monitor* and the *Gazette* in November 1838.

11 Telfer, W, *The Wallabadah manuscript: The early history of the northern districts of New South Wales: Recollections of the early days*, UNSW Press, Sydney, 1980, p. 37; Day to Thomson, 31 July, 1838, SRNSW CSL 38/9458.

12 Roger Milliss outlines what he calls the 'Bingara tradition' in *Waterloo Creek*, pp. 200–203. Local oral tradition suggests up to 300 people were massacred at Slaughterhouse Creek; however elements of the story appear mixed, as a group of the perpetrators were then supposed to have headed to Myall Creek and conducted that massacre as well.

13 For an overview of the lead-up to Myall Creek see: Milliss, 1992, pp. 274–292. While Milliss speculates a great deal about events and motivations, his account stands as an important version of the massacre. For Fleming's role as leader see: Withycombe, P, 'The Twelfth Man: John Fleming and the Myall Creek Massacre', BA (Hons) thesis, University of Newcastle, 2015, esp. pp. 41–58.

14 'Supreme Court', *Sydney Gazette*, 20 November 1838, p. 2.

15 'Supreme Court', *Sydney Gazette*, 20 November 1838, p. 2.

16 Foot to Thomson, 4 July 1838, SRNSW, CSLR, 38/6929. Gipps believed 'the number of persons murdered … was not less than 28'. Gipps noted there had been what he called some 'old quarrels' between the stockmen and the 'not less than fifty Blacks' who had 'been living at these different stations (along with Dangar's) in perfect tranquillity'. He also understood that 'occurrences in other quarters' had led to 'a determination … formed by the white men to put the whole of the Blacks to death': Gipps to Glenelg, 19 December 1838, *HRA*, XIX, pp. 700–702; Gipps to Glenelg, 21 July 1838, *HRA*, XIX, pp. 510–511. See Withycombe, 2015, pp. 60–61 for an overview of Fleming's later life.

17 *Sydney Gazette*, 19 April 1836, p. 2; *New South Wales Government Gazette*, 18 May 1836, no. 222, p. 395.

18 Gipps to Glenelg, 1 October 1838, *HRA*, XIX, p. 601; Gipps to Glenelg, 10 November 1838, *HRA*, XIX, p. 669; Glenelg to Gipps, 16 November 1838, *HRA*, XIX, p. 678; Gipps to Glenelg, 19 December 1838, *HRA*, XIX, p. 704; Normanby to Gipps, 17 July 1839, *HRA*, XX, p. 243. According to Withycombe, 'Henry Keck, principal gaoler in Sydney, reported that all seven convicted murderers … confessed their guilt, and declared, "it was done … in defence of their masters' property … they were not aware … they were violating the law…"': Withycombe, 2015, p. 52.

19 Milliss, 1992, p. 304. Roger Milliss's chapter 'The Massacre at Myall Creek' in his incredible 1992 *Waterloo Creek* stands today as the most comprehensive analysis of the vast numbers of depositions, court transcripts, correspondence and news reports about the events. His research into the backgrounds of the perpetrators provides an insight into men drawn from

convictism conducting horrific, genocidal acts deep in the Australian bush. While Milliss is prone to speculation, there is so much material about Myall Creek due to the intense public scrutiny and murder trials that not much guesswork is needed to understand this particular massacre. He also makes the very important point that it was only part of a series of massacres, arguably a systematic approach by stockmen to cattle and sheep raids at this time. See Milliss, 1992, pp. 640–641.

20   Bennett, G, *The earliest inhabitants: Aboriginal tribes of the district: The blacks of Dungog, Port Stephens, and Gresford*, Chronicle Print, Dungog, 1964 (c. 1930), p. 23. As the *Australian* newspaper reported: 'THE BLACKS.—Great hostilities have long existed and still exist among the different tribes of the aborigines in this quarter, to the great annoyance of the authorities, and continual jeopardy on the part of the natives. Some few nights back a body of blacks from the Dungog and Gloucester tribes came to a camp of the Stroud and Booral tribes in the dead hour of the night, and having first fired a gun to awaken and alarm, immediately discharged a volley of musketry and spears into the camp, and killed one man and wounded five others, among whom was a woman and a boy. This is the eighth murder committed by these savages within the last five months, nor is it likely to end with this. Orders have been given by the magistrates to the police to disarm all the natives found with firearms, till such time as a reconciliation can be effected among them': 'Port Stephens', *Australian*, 16 April 1844, p. 3. For earlier conflict see: 'Forty pounds reward', *New South Wales Government Gazette*, 29 March 1837, no. 269, p. 281; 'To the editor', *Colonist*, 6 July 1837, p. 2. The editor of the *Australian* called it the 'Brisbane water outrages': *Australian*, 24 February 1837, p. 3; *Colonist*, 20 April 1837, p. 6; *Sydney Herald*, 13 November 1837, p. 2; *Bent's News and Tasmanian Register*, 9 December 1837, p. 2.

21   Bill Gray (an early settler of the Lockyer and Macintyre regions), from Gray, WB, 'The early days of the Big River and McIntyre and Severn', Private Collection, 1902, quoted in Kerkhove, 2020, p. 680.

22   'The Bogan Blacks', *Colonial Observer*, 25 November 1841, p. 59.

23   Stuart, I, 'Squatting landscapes in South-Eastern Australia (1820–1895)', PhD thesis, Prehistoric and Historic Archaeology, University of Sydney, 1999, p. 55.

24   'More black murders', *Australian*, 11 April 1839, p. 2; 'Another black massacre', *Sydney Gazette*, 11 April 1839, p. 2.

25   'Original poetry. A dream of life', *Sydney Gazette*, 22 January 1831, p. 4. Ambēyang historian Callum Clayton-Dixon is clear warriors had an organised and communicated response to the crisis that was unfolding across the New England region in the late 1830s. Clayton-Dixon notes Gardner's 1840 observation that people across the region 'would resort in great numbers at certain seasons, to convenient and central situations, to deliberate and decide on their affairs'. Gardner described how a 'great meeting took place on the Sovereign [Dumaresq] River among the various tribes', in 1840. Soon after, the Sydney newspapers were noting how the New England area was 'again being ravaged by the blacks': Clayton-Dixon, C, *Surviving New England: A history of Aboriginal resistance and resilience through the first forty years of the colonial apocalypse*, Anaiwan Language Revival Program, Armidale, 2019, p. 66; *Sydney Herald*, 4 May 1840 p. 3.

26   'A bushman. Peel's river, April 3rd, 1839', *Sydney Herald*, 12 April 1839, p. 3.

27   George Everett, 1 August 1840, John Everett, 21 June 1841, in Rodwell, ME (ed.), *The Ollera Papers 1838–1857: The family letters of George, John and Edwin Everett, Journal of Australian Colonial History*, Occasional Publication No. 1, University of New England, Armidale, NSW, 2017, pp. 59, 76. John may be referring to a shepherd killed on Henry Dangar's 'Gostwyck' station a few months prior. See Clayton-Dixon, 2019, p. 81.

28 'Murder by the blacks', *Sydney Herald*, 1 May 1840, p. 2. The commissioner had to deal with a spree of bushranging as well. One squatter noted, 'while the white men are plundering and annoying us on the one side, the blacks are committing their daily depredations on the other, by killing both shepherds and sheep. Three white men have been killed for certain, and many others are now missing': 'Original Correspondence, New England, April 29, 1839', *Sydney Herald*, 24 May 1839, p. 3.
29 'Clarence River Historical Society. The Bawden lectures. A massacre of the blacks', *Daily Examiner*, 16 November 1935, p. 7. See: Kent, D, 'Frontier conflict and Aboriginal deaths: How do we weigh the evidence?', *Journal of Australian Colonial History*, vol. 8, 2006, pp. 35–41 for an account describing how stockmen were sworn in as special constables, surrounded a Bundjalung camp at night and at daybreak charged and killed indiscriminately. According to Kent, a man named Lynch was later charged with the stock theft: Macdonald to Colonial Secretary, 13 January 1843, *HRA*, XXII, p. 654.
30 'Hewitt, Thomas (1805–1876), 'People Australia', online; *Clarence and Richmond Examiner*, 11 March 1876, p. 2; 'Hewitt, Thomas (1805–1876)', Obituaries Australia website, <oa.anu.edu.au/obituary/hewitt-thomas-14210>; Robert Muir diary, 23 May 1840, in Muir, R, *NSW journals of Robert Muir, pioneer cattleman & grazier 1839–1851, collected and compiled by his great, great grandson Peter Muir*, Peter Muir, Leonora, 1986.
31 'C. E. S. to the editor', *Sydney Gazette*, 9 February 1841, p. 2. The correspondent complained that the 'young Assistant Commissioner to Mr. Mayne' needed to oppose 'cunning to cunning' if he was to successfully ambush the raiders: 'Peel's River. Outrages by the Blacks and Bush-rangers', *Sydney Monitor and Commercial Advertiser*, 24 November 1841, p. 2.
32 'Depredations of the blacks at Liverpool Plains', *Colonial Observer*, 23 November 1842, p. 626.
33 'News from the interior. Liverpool Plains – The blacks', *Sydney Morning Herald*, 21 November 1842, p. 2.
34 'New England', *Hunter River Gazette*, 16 April 1842, p. 3.
35 Macdonald to Thomson, 13 January 1843, *HRA*, XXII, p. 654.
36 Hamilton, HG, 'The country between Liverpool Plains and Moreton Bay in New South Wales: Extracts from two letters from Commander H G Hamilton R. N. to W. R. Hamilton Esq.', 4, 24 March 1843, *Journal of the Royal Geographical Society of London*, vol. 13, 1844, p. 248; Clayton-Dixon, 2019, pp. 74, 95–105.

Chapter 8

1 *Sydney Monitor*, 14 January 1839; Hardy to Thomson, 17 January 1839, SRNSW, CSL, 1912, 4/2470.4, 14–16.
2 Gammage, B, 'The Wiradjuri War 1838–40', *The Push from the Bush*, vol. 16, no. 1, 1838, Volume Collective of the Australian Bicentennial History, 1978–1988, Canberra, 1983, p. 9; Commissioner Cosby, deposition, 12 May 1839, SRNSW, CSL 4/2438. An assigned servant named George Palmer did capture one of Denay's alleged murderers, a man they called 'Boney' (possibly after Napoleon Bonaparte). 'Boney' escaped, however, but Palmer joined Cosby on his sweeps of the river, and the commissioner 'found him useful and intelligent, and he displayed every wish to render himself of service', despite – or perhaps because of – being injured by Boney in his escape: Commissioner Cosby, deposition, 12 May 1839, SRNSW, CSL, 4/2438.
3 Evidence of Henry Cosby, 9 July 1839, *New South Wales Legislative Council Votes and Proceedings (NSWLCVP)* II, p. 68. On 14 January, the *Sydney Monitor* described the country around Yass as having 'again resumed its dreary appearance' after six weeks without rain. By May the *South Australian Gazette* reported that the cattle of New South Wales were 'dying

in great numbers around the exhausted water holes' and that the Murrumbidgee River had 'decreased so considerable as to become dry in many places, and fish may be seen lying in a putrid state on the bed of the river'. In July, Cosby had noted that hostilities on the Murrumbidgee had existed during the previous two years but only in the first six months of 1839 did they intensify. Gammage suggests 'the high summer of a drought year' as a probable reason for attacks on cattle – though this does not explain cattle killed 'wantonly': *Sydney Monitor*, 14 January 1839; *South Australian Gazette and Colonial Register*, 11 May 1839; Evidence of Henry Cosby, 9 July 1839, *NSWLCVP* II, p. 68; Gammage, B, *Narrandera Shire*, Narrandera Shire Council, Narrandera, 1986, p. 32.

4   *Sydney Gazette*, 20 September 1838; O'Sullivan, J, *Mounted Police in N.S.W.*, Rigby Limited, Hong Kong, 1979, pp. 35–36; *Colonist*, 20 February 1839; *Sydney Standard and Colonial Advocate*, 11 March 1839. The *Commercial Journal and Advertiser* noted the use of stockmen would 'not only be cruel, but unjust, to empower any man to call away the men of stock-owners or agriculturalists': *Commercial Journal and Advertiser*, 16 March 1839.

5   O'Sullivan, 1979, p. 36. For example, the 20th Light Dragoons were a 'penal regiment' of court-martialled cavalrymen and were stationed in the West Indies: Sargent, C, 'The Governor's Body Guard of Light Horse 1801–1834', *Sabertache*, vol. 34, no. 1, 1998, p. 10. Similarly, the New South Wales Corps, as Peter Stanley notes, 'was no more a repository for criminals than any other British line regiment recruited during the Revolutionary and Napoleonic wars': Stanley, P, *The Remote Garrison: The British Army in Australia 1788–1870*, Kangaroo Press, Kenthurst, 1986, p. 18.

6   By July 1839 there were six border police stationed in the District of Lachlan, a force that Commissioner Cosby was unhappy with and he called for 'one party at the most remote stations' as well as 'others for the general duties of the district': Evidence of Henry Cosby, 9 July 1839, *NSWLCVP* II, p. 69.

7   Byrne, JC, *Twelve Years' Wanderings in the British Colonies From 1835 to 1847*, Richard Bentley, London, 1848, p. 225. Byrne's party came under attack near Rufus River. See Byrne's account: pp. 226, 227, 228–229.

8   As Clear notes, 'it was a natural feature that enabled British expansion that was being used to shield the Wiradjuri from Byrne's party': Clear, J, 'The Wiradjuri Wars: Analysing the evolution of settler colonial violence in New South Wales, 1822–1841', PhD thesis, Department of Modern History, Macquarie University, 2021, p. 269.

9   Phillips, J, *Reminiscences of Early Australian Life by a Pioneer*, A. P. Marsden, London, 1893 (2014), pp. 19–20.

10 Phillips, 1893, pp. 22–23.

11 Gammage, 1986, p. 34; Gammage, 1983, p. 11; *Adelaide Chronicle and South Australian Advertiser*, 28 January 1840.

12 *Adelaide Chronicle and South Australian Advertiser*, 18 February 1840; Gammage, 1983, p. 12; Gammage, 1986, p. 32.

13 Harrington to Cosby, 31 December 1839, SRNSW, 2996, CSL 4/3659, p. 266. An itinerary produced by Cosby in January 1840 of the stock stations in his district noted the weapons in the possession of colonists as six muskets, three pistols, and a fowling piece: Itinerary – Henry Cosby, January 1840, SRNSW, 2784, X813, pp. 19–21. There might have been numbers of other unrecorded weapons, including cutlasses and swords. Harrington wrote to Cosby in January 1840 that an Aboriginal man had been 'stabbed by one of Mr. Thompson's men on the Morumbidgee': Letter – Harrington to Cosby, 23 January 1840, SRNSW, 2996, CSL 4/3659, p. 273.

14 Harrington to Cosby, 15 May 1840, SRNSW, 2996, CSL 4/3659, p. 326; Gammage, 1983, pp. 12–14.

15 As Clear notes, historical details on how the battle unfolded are lacking. Gammage asserts that the settlers succeeded in 'killing many' of the Wiradyuri and 'driving the rest away', but cites no evidence. Iris Clayton suggests the Wiradyuri 'fought openly against a band of well-armed and mounted settlers' and suggests the Wiradyuri were defeated because they chose open battle rather than the guerrilla tactics that had thus far served them well: Clear, 2021, p. 264; *Narrandera Argus and Riverina Advertiser*, 25 June 1935, p. 162; Gammage, *Narrandera Shire*, 1986, p. 35; Clayton, I, *Wiradjuri of the Rivers and Plains*, Heinemann Library Australia, Melbourne, 1997, p. 67.

16 Uncle Robert Carroll, interview, 22 October 2023, Narrandera. Hollow Rush (*Juncus amabilis*) is used in many ways including as string, body adornment and basket making, as a water filtering straw, and for hunting, both as spears and to act as a snorkel when underwater (e.g. for sneaking up on ducks): Cumpston, Z, 'Indigenous plant use: A booklet on the medicinal, nutritional and technological use of indigenous plants', Clean Air and Urban Landscapes Hub website, the University of Melbourne, Melbourne, 2020, <nespurban.edu.au/wp-content/uploads/2020/08/Indigenous-plant-use.pdf>.

17 'Toyeo' and 'Tooyal' are not in the Wiradyuri dictionary. The reed spear or dyiriil was used with a woomera. While it might not have been as deadly as other spears, used in numbers it would have an impact. Burch, G, 'Exploration and settlement on the Murrumbidgee', personal paper, 2023, p. 3; Uncle Robert Carroll, interview, Narrandera, 22 October 2023.

18 Peter Kabaila suggests 'Massacre' or Murdering Island might not have been the location of a massacre, based on its small size and unsuitability for defending a camp. However it retains important significance regarding the events. Kabaila did investigate the site in 1995, including using a metal detector, but found nothing of significance. Kabaila's oral accounts come from Ossie Ingram and Neville Lyons in March 1995. Bill Gammage suggested the origin of the name of poison waterholes might be that settlers laid wild dog baits in the creek bed during the 1890s: Gammage, 1986, app. 4. Kabaila agrees the events around these massacres are 'very sketchy' and no historical information for either massacre events appears until much later. Kabaila does suggest the local Narrandera oral tradition 'undoubtedly springs out of the memory of killing by white settlers in the Wiradjuri region during this [1830s] darkest period of Aboriginal history in NSW': Kabaila, P, *Wiradjuri Places: The Murrumbidgee River Basin*, Black Mountain Projects, Canberra, 1995, pp. 93–96.

19 *Wagga Wagga Express*, 4 July 1914; *Freeman's Journal*, 5 January 1895; *Narrandera Argus and Riverine Advertiser*, 12 April 1929; *Daily Advertiser*, 27 May 1935; *Murray Pioneer and Australian River Record*, 22 January 1926. Rolfe Boldrewood's fictionalised account of the massacre noted one colonist killed and several wounded, but these are not mentioned in any other sources: Boldrewood, R, *The Squatter's Dream*, Macmillan, London, 1890, p. 110. See: Gapps, S, *The Sydney Wars: Conflict in the early colony 1788–1817*, NewSouth Publishing, Sydney, 2018 and *Gudyarra: The First Wiradjuri War of Resistance, the Bathurst War 1822–1824*, NewSouth Publishing, Sydney, 2021 for several examples of similar circumstances. Mary Gilmore also suggested the 'Poisoned Waterholes' near Narrandera were named from the deliberate poisoning of Wiradyuri people, however in 1951 George Gow claimed the name was in fact derived from the accidental poisoning of a drover's dogs after they consumed bait laid out for dingoes: *Advertiser*, 10 November 1925; *Narrandera Argus and Riverina Advertiser*, 5 February 1951. Peter Kabaila noted 'the first report of Massacre Island appears to have been as late as 1890' and that there is 'no contemporary record' of this or the poisoned waterholes incident that has 'yet been uncovered as historical "proof"': Kabaila, 1995, p. 90. In 1925, an anonymous 'Victorian official' dismissed 'the Narrandera Massacre story' as romantic fiction and believed 'the one massacre on the

Murray or Murrumbidgee was the battle of Rufus Creek, where the South Australian armed Government forces killed 17 blacks': *Murray Pioneer and Australian River Record*, 24 December 1925. Other later reports suggested 'the blacks made their presence so troublesome that the whites determined to deal with them in a summary manner': *Narrandera Argus and Riverina Advertiser*, 25 December 1925 and 12 April 1929. The *Daily Advertiser* suggested that 'the aborigines gave the selectors a lot of trouble spearing cattle just for the sheer delight of it', completely failing to understand the Wiradyuri intent: *Daily Advertiser*, 5 January 1931. See: 'Dyiriil', in Grant (Senior), S & Rudder, J, 'Categories of things and reference tables', in *A New Wiradjuri Dictionary: English to Wiradjuri, Wiradjuri to English*, Restoration House, Canberra, 2010.

20 Gammage, 1986, p. 35; Harrington to Cosby, 22 June 1840, SRNSW, 2996, CSL 4/3659, p. 336; *Sydney Herald*, 19 August 1840. A petition by Murrumbidgee stockmen in 1841 for an additional police force was also denied by Gipps, who refused 'to add, more than is indispensably necessary, to the expenses of the colony': *Geelong Advertiser*, 8 May 1841; Clear, 2021, pp. 265–266.

21 Gammage, 1983, p. 4. The Wagga *Daily Express* claimed in 1924 that 'the squatters were left more or less in peace' by the Wiradyuri after the Murdering Island massacre: *Daily Express*, 18 December 1924. The *Narrandera Argus* suggested in 1941 that 'the poisoning of the water is supposed to have accounted for many unfortunate blacks and lessened the troubles of the settlers': *Narrandera Argus and Riverina Advertiser*, 9 December 1941.

22 'Introduction', *HRA*, XIX, p. vii.

23 Eyre quoted in Dutton, 'Eyre, Edward John (1815–1901)', *ADB*.

24 Uncle Robert Carroll, interview, Narrandera, 22 October 2023; Beresford, Q, *Wounded Country: The Murray-Darling Basin – A contested history*, NewSouth Publishing, Sydney, 2021, p. 68.

Chapter 9

1 Faithfull to Thomson, 8 May 1838, SRNSW, CSLR, Port Phillip, 4/2423.3.

2 *Sydney Gazette*, 22 May 1838, p. 2; Faithfull to Gibson in Gibson to Thomson, 11 May 1838, SRNSW, CSLR, 38/4853, 4/2423.3; 'Port Phillip', *Sydney Gazette*, 22 May 1838, p. 2. Milliss accounts for the movements of Crossley, Smyth and others over the few days after the attack, although it remains somewhat unclear as to their sequence. Milliss also suggests remains of the stockmen were never found, however they were discovered in 1907: Milliss, R, *Waterloo Creek: The Australia Day massacre of 1838, George Gipps and the British conquest of New South Wales*, McPhee Gribble, Melbourne, 1992, p. 250.

3 After the initial burst of sympathy and support, a few weeks later the newspaper urged restraint. It reported that the 'Government have sent a party of mounted police, under their officer, from Goulburn, accompanied by Mr. Stewart, the police magistrate, to enquire into the affair, and, if possible, to apprehend the blacks that were concerned; but they are not to SHOOT any of them, unless in their own defence'. Frenzied talk of revenge might have been filtering back to the offices of Edward Smith Hall's *Sydney Monitor*, always keen for an opportunity to criticise what Hall believed was an authoritarian colonial government: 'Yass', *Sydney Monitor*, 27 April, p. 2 and 18 May 1838, p. 2; Kenny, 'Hall, Edward Smith (1786–1860)', *ADB*.

4 Waddy confirmed the men were armed: 'Mr. Faithfull told me that his men were 20 in number & that 5 or 6 of them were armed' and that 'the Blacks attacking them suddenly', had 'killed 8 men and drove the others away and then plundered the Drays of all the articles in them': Waddy to Nunn, 25 April 1838, in Nunn to Thomson, 30 April 1838, SRNSW, CSLR, 38/4239, 4/2423.3.

5   Lieutenant Smyth thought the postman, the young convict John Bourke, was a man of 'intrepid conduct' to carry on with the Sydney to Melbourne mail run just days after the attack: Milliss, 1992, p. 821; Letters from miscellaneous persons, 1838 'G', SRNSW 4/2404.3. Uren is suspicious of White's account: 'The account given by Colonel White is scrappy, disjointed and uninformative. The part his own men played in taking a terrible revenge on the men, women and children of the tribe may have swayed him in this matter'; Uren, S, 'The Massacre of the Faithfull Party', c. 1913, State Library of Victoria (SLV) MS 14903, p. 2.

6   Williams, M, 'Charles Bonney and the fertile Kilmore Plains', Historical Notes, *Victorian Historical Journal*, vol. 90, no. 1, June 2019, RHSV, pp. 105–120. Smyth and Mundy arrived in Melbourne at the end of February 1838, as the *Melbourne Advertiser* reported: 'Lieutenants Smith and Mundy arrived last week overland from Sydney. Lieut. Smith relieves Lieut. Hawkins', *Melbourne Advertiser*, vol. 1, no. 10, 5 March 1838, p. 3; Assistant Protector of Aborigines at the Goulburn River, James Dredge, Diary, 7 December 1839, SLV, MS 11625, p. 31.

7   Smyth to Lonsdale, 22 April 1838, *HRV*, 2a, pp. 321–322.

8   John Conway Bourke, Letters to Edmund Finn ['Garryowen'] (1888), Correspondence and papers (1821–1908), RHSV, MS 004116.02; Letter (1886) to Edmund Finn re attack on Bourke by blacks in 1839, RHSV, MS 004114; Lea-Scarlett, 'Snodgrass, Kenneth (1784–1853)', *ADB*. Alan Gross's 1967 *ADB* entry for Peter Snodgrass notes his career as a pastoralist and Victorian politician but mentions nothing of his actions at Broken and King Rivers in 1838: Gross, A, 'Snodgrass, Peter (1817–1867)', *ADB*.

9   It is unclear how Bourke got his information on what happened at King River (or indeed how well he recalled events from 1838 in the 1880s). The returning massacre party might have told him what happened: John Conway Bourke, Letters to Edmund Finn ['Garryowen'] (1888), Correspondence and papers (1821–1908), RHSV, MS 004116.02; Letter (1886) to Edmund Finn re attack on Bourke by blacks in 1839, RHSV, MS 004114.

10 Gross, A, 'Sturt, Evelyn Pitfield Shirley (1816–1885)', *ADB*; 'Attacks on the Overland Routes to Port Phillip', *HRV*, vol. 2a, The Aborigines of Port Phillip 1835–1839, pp. 312–331.

11 'Yass', *Sydney Monitor*, 27 April 1838, p. 3.

12 *Sydney Monitor*, 18 May 1838, p. 2.

13 Hobson, 12 April 1839, Jane Franklin to John Franklin, 20 April 1839, Albury Historical Society, online; Hobson and Franklin in Russell, P (ed.), *This Errant Lady: Jane Franklin's overland journey to Port Phillip and Sydney, 1839*, NLA, Canberra, 2002, pp. 49–50.

14 Robinson, entry for 8 February 1841, in Clark, ID (ed.), *Journals of George Augustus Robinson, Chief Protector, Port Phillip Aboriginal Protectorate, Volume Two: 1 October 1840 – 31 August 1841*, Heritage Matters, Ballarat, 2000.

15 McPherson, H, 'Frontier war on the Port Phillip Road: Colonisation and resistance in Benalla and north-east Victoria', Benalla Aboriginal History Group, Benalla, Victoria, 2023, p. 7. Jacqui Durrant notes that Robinson stated two names for Merriman, 'but the one frequently used was Minnup, similar to the Kulin word Munip, meaning ash or dust'. Durrant also notes that 'King Michie had been a formidable leader in the local resistance to European invasion'. By late 1852, Marangan was overrun with gold rush traffic en route to the Ovens diggings. As Durrant notes, despite these incursions into his country, Wulkidjaduwil (King Michie) had continued to live next to Marangan, 'in what could be considered, in retrospect, to be one of the greatest acts of civil defiance of European rule imaginable', Durrant, J, 'First Nations "Kings" of Benalla': Life on Spring Creek – A blog by Jacqui Durrant', 2020; 'The Blacks,' *Port Phillip Patriot and Melbourne Advertiser*, Thursday

Notes to pages 175–177

29 September 1842, p. 2. By the 1850s Wulkidjaduwil had become known as 'King Michie' and in 1853 he was buried in Benalla on the banks of Marangan.

16   McPherson notes several possible named individuals including Merriman, Charlie, Wellington or Walledigun, Merriman or Min-nup, Jackendebby and Wul-kidja-duwil or Michie, all noted in various contemporary reports: McPherson, 2023, p. 8; Bassett, J, 'The Faithfull massacre – A case study', thesis, School of Humanities, Deakin University, 1986, p. 24; Megan Carter, interview, 7 October 2023. See: Robinson, entry for 23 February 1841, in Clark, vol. 2, 2000, p. 52 and <findingmerriman.com.au> for Merriman's Country.

17   Megan Carter, interview, 7 October 2023. Durrant notes that 'between Waywurru and Taungurung and Ngurai-ilum (who spoke Taungurong and who got along with Waywurru, also having kin relations), they could easily amass a few hundred men': Durrant, pers. comm., 2 April 2024. The Taungurung, Waveroo and Ngurai-ilum had strong kinship, cultural and social connections. There were bonds between the Woi-Wurrung of the Yarra River, the Taungurung and Ngurai-illam Wurrung of the Goulburn River and Central Victoria, and the Waveroo (Waywurru) of the Ovens and King Rivers. Barwick asserted that historical accounts in journals and reminiscenses suggest that 'planning for a series of initiations involving Taungurung, neighbouring Waveroo clans, and adjacent Wiradjuri about Albury was underway by January 1838', but it is difficult to find evidence of this, rather than assumption: Barwick, DE, 'Mapping the past: An atlas of Victorian clans 1835–1904 Part 1', *Aboriginal History*, vol. 8, no. 2, ANU Press, Canberra, 1984, p. 120. In February 1841, Robinson took three men, arrested following the raid on Mackay's Whorouly station, when they were released from Melbourne prison and accompanied them back to Wangaratta. They included Simon or 'Tare.rang.er' of the 'Wayayjeree [Wiradyuri] tribe or nation'. On 9 February 1841, Robinson was at Docker's station at Wangaratta and met many of the '150 or 200' Aboriginal people who were there: Robinson in Clark, vol. 2, 2000, pp. 66, 73–74. For the most detailed, recent and accurate overview of northeast Victoria see Durrant, J, 'Understanding Aboriginal group names in North East Victoria', <jacquidurrant.com/2024/07/31/understanding-aboriginal-group-names-in-north-east-victoria/>.

18   These bonds were united by shared language features, moiety totem systems and marriage laws. Each of the Eastern Kulin clans was either associated with the Bunjil (Eagle) or Waa (Black Crow) ancestral spirit or totem: Barwick, 1984, pp. 105–106; Presland, 2010, pp. 15, 33–37.

19   *Sydney Monitor*, 7 May 1838, p. 3.

20   Curr, 1883, pp. 132–33. Barwick suggests 'Curr's ignorance of Aborigines was publicly criticised in a series of official investigations of Board policy, culminating in an 1881 Parliamentary inquiry [and] Better-informed contemporaries (notably Howitt, who demolished Curr's false statements about kinship and leadership in 1889) attacked his self-serving propaganda'. Barwick noted in 1984 that 'Recent reprints have made Curr's books widely accessible and his views are often uncritically quoted by modern writers unaware of their falsity'. Now they are available in full, online and without critical annotation they do provide some valuable information, and it must be noted here that the role of 'messengers' and message sticks is well known in other areas of Australia: Barwick, 1984, p. 103. More recently, historians have been critical of Barwick's work, as it has failed to provide sources and offered much speculation.

21   Thomas noted that 'to comfort me they left lots of spears ... saying "they must go but would soon return"': Standfield, R, '"The vacillating manners and sentiments of these people": Mobility, Civilisation and Dispossession in the Work of William Thomas with the Port Phillip Aboriginal Protectorate', *Law Text Culture*, no. 15, 2011, pp. 177–181; Thomas

Papers, ML, SLNSW, uncatalogued mss, set 214 CY732, p. 115. The Djadja Wurrung and other nations to the north and south were certainly very much in contact with each other. When Robinson was in the Loddon District at Munro's station in late January 1840, a neighbouring station was raided by 'wild black fellows' who were 'going to fight the Melbourne blacks'. Robinson noted that 'I believe the Murray blacks are in communication with the tribes of this country': Robinson in Clark, ID (ed.), *The Journals of George Augustus Robinson, Chief Protector, Port Phillip Aboriginal Protectorate, Volume One: 1 January 1839 – 30 September 1840*, Heritage Matters, Ballarat, 2000, p. 132.

22 Mackie to Broughton in Hardy to Thomson, 1 June 1838, SRNSW, CSLR 38/5770.

23 Franklin suggested that Faithfull was targeted – adding that 'Mr. Faithfull's neighbours do not suffer in the same way' and while this may be the case, there were certainly many other raids and attacks. In fact Franklin noted that a few weeks previously, 'a servant of Mr Ebden's was set upon by Blacks, stripped completely naked and robbed of rations and clothes. The police shortly afterwards found the tracks of the offending Blacks but all search for them was useless'. Later, writing from the Murray River at the Mounted Police outpost, Franklin noted that 'the blacks in general in this neighbourhood are said to be quite quiet, but at Mr Brown's sheep station 18 miles off, they had been spearing someone's cattle and between this and the Murrumbidgee, had attacked several men in a similar manner': Franklin, 12 April 1839, in Russell, 2002, p. 17. McPherson has listed other subsequent attacks in the northeast Victoria region: George Faithfull's station in August 1838 (shepherd George Graham killed); David Reid's Currargarmonge station near Wangaratta in 1839; Rutledge and Forster's station on the Goulburn River in November 1838 (convict George Mould killed); Docker's Bontharambo station in April 1839 (shepherd James Doyle killed); Mackellar's Lima station in late 1839; Stuckey's Barjarg station, Bodribb's Junction station and Chisholm's Myrrhee station in early 1840; Robert and George Benson's Junction station in 1841 (sheep stolen by 'Goulburn blacks'); Mackay's Whorouly station in May 1840; Gray's Pelican Lagoon station in 1842 (an 'American Black' station hand killed); the Jameson brothers' Tallarook station in the Goulburn River area in 1845; Mr Curlewis's Tatong and Emu stations in 1846; McPherson, H, '"Original Rights": Colonial invasion and Aboriginal resistance in Benalla and northern Victoria 1838–1858', Benalla Aboriginal History Group, Benalla, 2024, p. 18.

24 Faithfull, G, Wangaratta, 8 September, 1853, in Bride, TF (ed.), *Letters from Victorian Pioneers: Being a series of papers on the early occupation of the colony, the Aborigines, etc.*, Government Printer, Trustees of the Public Library, Melbourne, 1898, pp. 218–222.

25 Sievwright, C, in *Journal of William Thomas*, 1 April 1839, in Cannon, M, *Who killed the Koories?*, William Heinemann Australia, Port Melbourne, 1990, p. 520; Arkley, L, 'Sievwright, Charles Wightman (1800–1855)', *ADB*. Protector Sievwright, despite his limited ability to address their needs, won great respect from the people who lived with him at several camps – as many as 270 at a time. With sporadic supplies, he attempted, as his biographer writes, 'unprecedented food-for-work schemes, hoping to replace some of the lost traditional food with crops grown by the Aborigines themselves'. But raids, attacks and stock thefts continued. The squatters and the press actually blamed Sievwright for failing to stop them. See: Arkley, L, *The Hated Protector: The story of Charles Wightman Sievwright, Protector of Aborigines 1839–42*, Orbit Press, Mentone, Victoria, 2000, and Attwood, B, *The Good Country: The Djadja Wurring, the settlers and the Protectors*, Monash University Publishing, Melbourne, 2017, esp. pp. 53–77 for an outline of the complex relationships that developed between the Djadja Wurrung and the squatters – often co-operative, sometimes in conflict, with the conflict largely about getting food.

26 'The Blacks', *Australian*, 8 June 1838, p. 2; 'Port Phillip', *Sydney Gazette*, 22 May 1838, p. 2.

27 'Port Phillip', *Sydney Gazette*, 22 May 1838, p. 2; 'News of the Day', *Sydney Monitor*, 18 May 1838, p. 2.
28 'Legislative Council', *Sydney Herald*, 13 August 1838, p. 2; King et al. to Gipps, 8 June 1838, *HRV*, vol. 2A, pp. 349–351; Gipps to Glenelg, 21 June 1838, *HRV*, vol. 2A, pp. 354–356. The memorialists were desperate and also appealed to the Executive Council – a fact Gipps described as 'contrary to the usual practice': Gipps to Glenelg, 21 July 1838, *HRA*, XIX, pp. 508–510.
29 Gipps to Glenelg, 21 July 1838, *HRA*, XIX, p. 510.
30 'Outrages Committed by Aborigines', (Memorial) To His Excellency Sir George Gipps ... and the Honorable Executive Council of New South Wales', 8 June 1838, SRNSW, CSL, 38/6250. The governor also made sure to note the expense to government – the mounted police needed supplies if they were to continue to search for the 'hostile tribes'. Gipps's later proclamation on Aboriginal equality before British law noted that 'to permit the stronger to regard the weaker party as aliens, with whom a war can exist and against whom they may exercise belligerent right, is not less inconsistent with the spirit of the Law than it is at variance with the dictates of justice and humanity'. It was both against the law and inhumane to declare war on Aboriginal people: Notice in Note 47, *HRA*, XX, p. 856. For an overview of the seriousness of the situation as recalled by Barton in the 1890s, see Barton, GB, 'Old time memories. The Overlanders in '38. By G. B. Barton', *Australasian*, 12 December 1896, p. 25.
31 Gipps to Glenelg, 1 May 1838, *HRA*, XIX, p. 403.
32 Glenelg to Gipps, 15 May 1838, *HRA*, XVIII, p. 417; Barrow to Baring, 23 May 1838, *HRA*, XIX, p. 455; Deniston and others to Lord Glenelg, 23 October 1838, *HRA*, XIX, p. 658; Gipps to Glenelg, 21 July 1838, *HRA*, XIX, p. 510. As McPherson notes, the geography of the unprotected Port Phillip Road heightened colonial anxiety about the attack and would shape the response of colonial authorities: McPherson, 2023, p. 3. See also: Colonial Secretary to Phillip G King et al, 23 June 1838, *HRV*, vol. 2A, p. 352.
33 A short note in the margin of the letter to the governor set out the train of orders: 'Let measures now be taken for carrying the arrangement into effect. Inform the Police Magistrate at Melbourne – the Commandant of the Mounted Police, & the Surveyor General that it is determined to establish Posts at these places': M. Hunter (Asst. Military Secretary's Office) to Colonial Secretary, 10 July 1838, SRNSW, CSLR, 38/7067, 4/2423.3. As historian Marie Fels notes, 'the presence of law and order [was] considerably greater than the show of power and authority elsewhere' across the colony: Fels, MH, *Good Men and True: The Aboriginal police of the Port Phillip District 1837–1853*, Melbourne University Press, Melbourne, 1988, p. 42.
34 Gipps to Glenelg, 6 April 1839, *HRA*, XX, p. 90. A temporary solution to staffing the outposts on the Port Phillip Road was to attract mounted police with a system that had propped up the expanding British empire for decades – bounties. Mounted police at these isolated outposts were, according to Lady Jane Franklin, who interviewed several at Broken River in 1839, offered '20 shillings for every runaway they take and 30 shillings for a man escaped from irons 30 hours after his missing': Franklin in Russell, 2002, p. 52.
35 Gipps to Glenelg, 6 April 1839, *HRA*, XX, p. 90.
36 Gipps to Glenelg, 21 July 1838, *HRA*, XIX, pp. 508–509; Wedge to Glenelg, 22 April 1839, *HRA*, XX, p. 450.
37 Gipps to Glenelg, 21 July 1838, *HRA*, XIX, p. 510; Glenelg to Gipps, 10 November 1838, *HRA*, XIX, p. 660.
38 Gipps to Glenelg, 6 April 1839, *HRA*, XX, p. 90.
39 *Sydney Gazette*, 1 May 1838, p. 2; Gipps to Glenelg, 27 April 1838, *HRA*, XIX, pp. 397–398. See: Milliss, 1992, pp. 238–243 for an overview of the politicking between Gipps,

40 Gipps to Glenelg, 27 April 1838, *HRA*, XIX, pp. 397–400. Gipps was very concerned to halt any settler retaliation and worked hard to set up an inquiry, sending a magistrate to the area with a series of specific questions to investigate, including whether there had been 'previous hostility' and whether the party had 'any black women with them at the time of the attack'. He reinforced that 'Black Natives of NS Wales are in every respect to be considered Subjects of the Queen and not as aliens against whom the Queen's troops may exercise belligerent rights'. Gipps wanted the murderers caught, but if they could not be found, 'other individuals' could be taken as, in effect, hostages to bargain with. For this he was later reprimanded by Lord Glenelg. Magistrate George Stewart was sent with a party of ten mounted police from Goulburn: Glenelg to Gipps, 21 December 1838, *HRA*, XIX, p. 706; encl. instructions, Nunn to Thomson 30 April 1838, SRNSW, CSLR, 38/4329; Gipps to Glenelg, 1 May 1838, *HRA*, XIX, p. 403. As Governor Gipps put it to Lord Glenelg in February 1839, 'in consequence of the numerous depredations which have of late been committed by the Aboriginal Inhabitants of this Country on the Flocks and Herds of the Colonists, depastured beyond the Settled Limits of the Colony, and of the atrocities which in return have been committed on the Aborigines by the Shepherds and Stockmen in charge of those flocks and herds, I have deemed it proper to call an extraordinary Meeting of the Legislative Council for the purpose of submitting to it a Bill for the establishment of a Police force in those distant Districts': Gipps to Glenelg, 20 February 1839, *HRA*, XX, p. 6. In March 1839, 'An Act further to restrain the unauthorised occupation of Crown Lands and to provide the means of defraying the expense of a Border Police' was passed. Gipps to Glenelg, 6 April 1839, *HRA*, XX, p. 90. By July 1839, Downing Street stressed to Gipps it was important to 'check that feeling of recklessness in sacrificing the lives of the Natives': Normanby to Gipps, 17 July 1839, *HRA*, XX, pp. 242–243; Gipps to Glenelg, 22 July 1839, *HRA*, XX, p. 244.

Chapter 10

1 George Faithfull, 8 September, 1853, in Bride, T, *Letters from Victorian Pioneers: A series of papers on the early occupation of the colony, the Aborigines etc*, Government Printer, Melbourne, 1898, p. 221. Daniel James has noted how the '*Melbourne Herald* on the 2nd of April 1958 published a two-page spread on the massacre, entitled, "The worst of our early massacres", "Our" meaning European of course. The article goes into great detail about the circumstances in which the men were "murdered" and the story of the pioneering spirit of the Faithfulls who overcame the odds to become "rich and substantial" landowners'. The *Melbourne Herald* continued: 'The Faithfull massacre touched off a fierce warfare of raids and reprisals that made the settlement of north-eastern Victoria the most dramatic episodes in colonising history … [and] 'not until years later, after a day-long battle along the Ovens River, could George Faithfull declare the aboriginal [sic] tribes were finally crushed and his name "made a terror to them forever"': James, D, website, nd, 'Benwhalla – The Fallen and Forgotten', <www.danieljames.com.au/words/2018/10/21/benwhalla-the-fallen-and-forgotten>. Judith Bassett's 1989 article on the Battle at Broken River, which she calls the 'Faithfull brothers massacre' in the *JAS* (and republished online by *Quadrant* in 2009) makes several statements that are at odds with the historical sources and in one area, for example, shows a lack of understanding of how firearms actually work: Bassett, J, 'The Faithfull massacre of 1838', *Quadrant*, 20 February 2019, <quadrant.org.au/magazine/2019/01-02/the-faithfull-massacre-of-1838/>, pp. 18–34. See Niel Black, Journal entry, 9 December 1839, quoted in Stone, B, *The Squatters, The story of Australia's pastoral pioneers*, Allen & Unwin, Sydney, 2019, pp. 133–134.

2   As Diane Barwick noted in 1984, 'these two -(w)urrung [Taungurung and Ngurai Illum Wurrung] have been loosely labelled the "Goulburn tribe" since the 1840s; their dispossession and near extermination by pastoralists who occupied the Campaspe, Goulburn and Broken rivers 1837–41 is documented in archival records only recently publicised by historians': Barwick, DE, 'Mapping the past: An atlas of Victorian clans 1835–1904 Part 1', *Aboriginal History*, vol. 8, no. 2, ANU Press, Canberra, 1984, p. 124.
3   Samuel Faloon, deposition, 28 May 1838, SRNSW, CSLR, 4/2423.3, p. 45.
4   Megan Carter, interview, 7 October 2023.
5   Lonsdale did not believe it was local Aboriginal people: 'From the enquiry I have made into the circumstance there is no doubt but the murder was committed by Blacks, but not of those about this part of the country': Lonsdale to Colonial Secrerary, 3 June 1838, SRNSW, CSLR, 4/2423.3, p. 45.
6   Attwood, B, *The Good Country: The Djadja Wurring, the settlers and the Protectors*, Monash University Publishing, Melbourne, 2017, pp. 15–17; Samuel Faloon, deposition, 28 May 1838, SRNSW, CSLR, 4/2423.3, p. 45.
7   Robinson noted when he passed through the area in early 1840 that it was a 'military station' on the Campaspe River and consisted of a single mud hut: Robinson in Clark, ID (ed.), *The Journals of George Augustus Robinson, Chief Protector, Port Phillip Aboriginal Protectorate, Volume One: 1 January 1839 – 30 September 1840*, Heritage Matters, Ballarat, 2000 pp. 119–120.
8   Coppock in *HRV*, vol. 2a, pp. 337–338; Attwood, 2017, pp. 15–17.
9   When Robinson was touring the Loddon district in January 1840 he passed by an abandoned hut to where Munro and a stockworker had retreated after being attacked and his horse had been speared. According to Robinson, 'it seems the blacks had been robbing another of Mr Munro's huts, and were then endeavouring to get to the sheep when Mr Munro, who had been out in quest of them, happened to be on his return and came upon their manoeuvres'. Munro and his worker then retreated to the hut with 'the blacks run after them, shouting and hallowing, but the men in the hut fired four shots. The report stopped them': Robinson in Clark, vol. 1, 2000, p. 122–123.
10 Attwood, 2017, pp. 15–17; 'Barfold Station, Coliban River, Campaspe Plains', Colonial Frontier Massacres in Australia 1788–1930, website, <c21ch.newcastle.edu.au/colonialmassacres/detail.php?r=520>. Coppock told a journalist, 'C. J. W.', that his men were 'were anxious to avenge their comrades, and at the same time satiate their bloodthirsty natures' and that '23 blacks were left dead on the field' and that 'they made but a feeble resistance'. Was it bravado in his old age or the opportunity to be more honest? 'Old time memories. Trials and experiences of a pioneer', *Australasian*, 31 October 1885, p. 1.
11 Attwood suggests Leary was ordered to 'disperse' the Aboriginal people there; however there is no mention of this in Leary's testimony, rather it was 'for the purpose of apprehending the natives who had been committing these murders and robberies': Attwood, 2017, p. 29; Dennis Leary, deposition to Edward Parker Stone, 6 January 1840, SRNSW, CSLR, 4/2511.
12 Charles Hutton, deposition to Edward Parker Stone, 8 January 1840, SRNSW, CSLR, 4/2511.
13 Leary noted that 'After falling in with the blacks we travelled down the creek about 7 or 8 miles, but did not see the junction of the creek with any river; we then turned to the Eastward, and at the close of the second or third day I cannot say which we came on the tracks of the drays proceeding from the Goulburn to South Australia, and made the river near the junction. We were out about eight days from the time of leaving Captain Hutton's, till the party arrived at the Police Station on the river Goulburn. Captain Hutton

accompanied us the whole distance': Dennis Leary, deposition to Edward Parker Stone, 6 January 1840, SRNSW, CSLR, 4/2511.
14 Dennis Leary, deposition to Edward Parker Stone, 6 January 1840, SRNSW, CSLR, 4/2511.
15 Attwood suggests six is the correct number of deaths, as Parker later said Djadja Wurrung had told him six: Attwood, 2017, p. 30. Beach deposed that 'To the best of my recollection I saw about ten blacks. They were men. They threw several spears, I cannot say how many. The sergeant then ordered us to load and fire. Our carbines were not loaded, but our pistols were. I fired three or four times with my carbine. I did not fire my pistols at all. The firing continued for about five minutes. The party extended itself when the spears were thrown, and I cannot say how many times the rest of the party fired. The blacks ran off at the time we fired. I saw no blacks fall. I cannot say whether any were killed. I saw no dead bodies. It was in the evening that this happened. We saw no more of the blacks after they ran away. We encamped about four or five hundred yards from the spot where we fired for the night': Edward Beach, deposition to Edward Parker Stone, 6 January 1840, SRNSW, CSLR, 4/2511.
16 Hutton ruled out two other 'tribes' they met with, one of which had recently come from Melbourne: Charles Hutton, deposition to Edward Parker Stone, 8 January 1840, SRNSW, CSLR, 4/2511. See George Brunswick Smyth, deposition, 6 January 1840, SRNSW, CSLR, 4/2511 (includes Smyth to Leary, 21 June 1839); Dennis Leary, Edward Beach, depositions, 6 January 1840; Hutton, deposition, 8 January 1840; James Cosgrove, deposition, 24 January 1840, SRNSW, CSLR, 4/2511.
17 Robinson in Clark, 2000, vol. 1, p. 132. Attwood tabled twenty-seven incidences of conflict on Djadja Wurrung Country between 1838 and 1842, largely in the Campaspe area and Campaspe Plains. Attwood, 2017, pp. 31, 45–46, 69.
18 Attwood, 2017, p. 31. See *Port Phillip Patriot*, 22 July 1839; Thomas to Robinson, 23 July 1839 and 12 August 1839 in *HRV*, vol. 7, pp. 332–333, 341. McPherson lists the following examples of conflict in the north-east Victoria region 1838–1845: 'George Faithfull's station (August 1838: shepherd killed), David Reid's Currargarmonge Station, Rutledge and Forster's Station on the Goulburn River (November 1838), Richard Clarke publican at Broken River (early 1839), Docker's "Bontharambo" station (April 1839: shepherd killed), Mackellar and Black's Lima Station (late 1839), Mackay's Whorouly Station (April 1840), Cumberland Creek station (1841), Gray's "Pelican Lagoon" station (1842: "American Black" station hand killed) and the Jameson brothers' Tallarook station and in the Goulburn River area (1845)': McPherson, H, 'Frontier war on the "Port Phillip road": Colonisation and resistance in Benalla and north-east Victoria', Benalla Aboriginal History Group, Benalla, 2023, p. 13.
19 Bingham to Colonial Secretary, 'Affray between Dr. Mackay's Men and Black Natives, Head Quarters, Tumut River, October 13th 1840', SRNSW, CSLR, 4/2486.1, p. 45. Sometimes, the climate of fear was exploited by convict workers who had lost their sheep. In January 1840 at Munro's station, Protector Robinson met 'Mr Christie, Mr Munro's overseer and Mr Liston, a distant relation of Mr Munro and a sub-overseer' as well as another man who 'were all armed [and] going in pursuit of the blacks at Mount Alexander'. They said 'the blacks had taken away 1500 sheep, 825 ewes, 700 lambs'. The two shepherds who reported the raid said that '36 blacks, all men' and who had 'no spears, only throwing sticks and clubs', had taken flour and meat and 'drove away the flocks in two drives'. They said one of the men told them his name was 'Jaggy Jaggy' (probably Jagga Jagga, who was well known in Port Phillip). Robinson said the 'report of the robbery by the blacks has created an excitement, incredible'. In fact, when Robinson later met Christie

he was told 'the blacks had not taken the sheep. The shepherds had left their flocks, had slept and the wild dogs had rushed them'. The false alarm did show Robinson just how a raid created 'excitement' and fear, and how squatters and stockmen went automatically on the offensive: Robinson in Clark, vol. 1, 2000, p. 124.

20   This fight has been regarded by some historians as the beginning of an ongoing guerrilla war, however the Battle at Broken River in 1838 is a more appropriate point for the beginning of this period of warfare. See Robinson to Assistant Protectors, 8 July 1839, Gisborne to La Trobe, 15 January 1840, and Bolden to La Trobe, 2 May 1840 in Cannon, M & Macfarlane, I (eds), Aborigines and Protectors 1838–1839, *HRV*, Foundation Series, Volume 2B, Public Record Office, Victorian Government Printing Office, Melbourne, 1983, pp. 724–726, 729–731, 732; Bassett, M, 'Gisborne, Henry Fyshe (Fysche) (1813–1841)', *ADB*.

21   Henry Bingham rather hopefully called for the squatters to have a 'more courteous line of conduct' toward Aboriginal people: Bingham to Colonial Secretary, 'Affray between Dr. Mackay's Men and Black Natives, Head Quarters, Tumut River, October 13th 1840', SRNSW, CSLR, 4/2486.1, p. 45.

22   Mackay, GE in Bride, TF, *Letters from Victorian Pioneers: Being a series of papers on the early occupation of the colony, the Aborigines, etc.*, Government Printer, Trustees of the Public Library, Melbourne, 1898, p. 211; Robinson to LaTrobe, 27 February 1841, Statement of John Scobie Anderson Mackay to Robinson, 14 Feb 1841, Robinson in Clark, vol. 2, 2000, p. 124.

23   Mackay in Bride, 1898, p. 211.

24   Megan Carter, interview, 7 October 2023.

25   Wilsone, 9 September 1839, in Serle, G, 'Manuscripts: Excerpts from the letters of Dr. David Henry Wilsone, squatter, 1839–1841', *La Trobe Library Journal*, vol. 5, no. 19, 1977, p. 57.

26   Wilsone, 18 May 1840, in Serle, 1977, p. 62.

27   William Thomas journal, 17 April 1840, quoted in Fels, MH, *'I Succeeded Once': The Aboriginal Protectorate on the Mornington Peninsula, 1839–1840*, Aboriginal History Monograph 22, ANU Press, Canberra, 2011, p. 84.

28   Gipps to Normanby, 31 August 1839, *HRA*, XX, pp. 305–306; McPherson, 2023, pp. 15–16.

29   Gipps to Russell, 3 February 1841, *HRA*, XXI, pp. 208–211.

30   Standfield, R, '"The vacillating manners and sentiments of these people": Mobility, civilisation and dispossession in the work of William Thomas with the Port Phillip Aboriginal Protectorate', *Law Text Culture*, no. 15, 2011, p. 171–172; Clark, ID & Heydon, T, *A bend in the Yarra: A history of the Merri Creek Protectorate Station and Merri Creek Aboriginal School 1841–1851*, Aboriginal Studies Press, AIATSIS, Canberra, 2004, pp. 1–2, 4, 19–22.

31   William Thomas Journal, 25 September 1840 in Fels, 2011, p. 113.

32   Presland, 2010, pp. 102–104. Fels notes that 'Winberri was a man with a "noble spirit" according to Thomas who wrote a three page description of the unusual mourning ritual for Winberri carried out morning and evening by his aged father and his only sister': Fels, 2011, p. 114.

33   'Port Phillip', *Sydney Herald*, 27 October 1840, p. 3. Some witnesses joined in the fray. John Phillips took along his new double-barrelled shotgun to assist: Phillips, J, *Reminiscences of Australian Early Life by a Pioneer*, A. P. Marsden, London, 1893 (2014), pp. 4–5. Phillips, recalling the event in 1893, suggested the 'chief', 'Gellibrand', whom he met that day, told him 'that his tribe ... intended that night to make a descent on the white fellows and tomahawk them all' but this seems unlikely.

34 Robinson, journal entry for 11 October 1840, in Clark, vol. 2, 2000, pp. 7–10 and Milliss, R, *Waterloo Creek: The Australia Day massacre of 1838, George Gipps and the British conquest of New South Wales*, McPhee Gribble, Melbourne, 1992, pp. 708–709; Standfield, 2011, pp. 179–180.

35 Gipps to Russell, 3 February 1841, *HRA*, XXI, pp. 208–211: Standfield, 2011, pp. 177–181; Thomas Papers, ML, SLNSW, uncatalogued mss, set 214 CY732; McPherson, H, '"Original Rights": Colonial invasion and Aboriginal resistance in Benalla and northern Victoria 1838–1858', Benalla Aboriginal History Group, Benalla, 2024, p. 14. Clark and Heydon's 2004 study of Merri Creek shows a more complex picture of 'native' police though places no emphasis on the Lettsom attack.

36 Parker quoted in Attwood, 2017, p. 116; Clark, 2000, p. 204.

37 Pohlman diaries quoted in Attwood, 2017, p. 51.

38 See Critchett, J, *A Distant Field of Murder: Western District Frontiers 1834–1848*, Melbourne University Press, Melbourne, 1990, esp. pp. 99–113.

39 Merrick wrote that it was 'impossible to say how many have been shot', but he was convinced 'not less than 450 have been murdered altogether'. Merrick in Stone, 2019, p. 138. Lyndall Ryan summarises McMillan's operations: 'In July 1843, following the killing of settler Donald Macalister in Gippsland, a reprisal massacre was organised by Angus McMillan, the leading settler in the region. In this case, he took the law into his own hands and covered up his action. Detailed evidence of the carnage did not emerge until many decades later when accounts were gleaned by local historians from settlers Willy Hoddinott and Charles Lucas who had grown up with two Aboriginal boys, "Bing Eye" and "Davey", who had survived the massacres. Peter Gardner has spent decades piecing together the disparate evidence to produce a compelling account of the incident. He believes that McMillan collected a party of seventeen mounted stockmen, later known as the "Highland Brigade", and after having sworn each man to secrecy, he led them on a massacre rampage. Over the next few days the party attacked at least five Aboriginal camps in the area with the aim of eradicating everyone in them ... Gardner has estimated that in this operation 170 Kurnai from an entire clan were killed': Ryan, L, 'Settler massacres on the Port Phillip Frontier, 1836–1851', *Journal of Australian Studies*, vol. 34, no. 3, 2010, p. 269; Gardner, PD, *Gippsland Massacres: The destruction of the Kurnai tribes 1800–1860*, 3rd edition, self-published, Ensay, 2001.

40 Faithfull, G, Wangaratta, 8 September, 1853, in Bride, 1898, pp. 218–222. Faithfull was certainly self-aggrandising: 'The fight I have described gave them a notion of what sort of stuff the white man was made, and my name was a terror to them ever after'. Yet to assume this is a fabrication limits the history of Aboriginal resistance. Lyndall Ryan places, I would argue, too little faith in settler descriptions of battles, preferring to assume they were generally massacres covered up: '... the evidence suggests that contemporary settler accounts of supposed "clashes" and "pitched battles" between large mobs of Aboriginal men armed with spears and small groups of colonial men on horseback armed with guns that rarely fired, had little basis in fact. Rather, the evidence suggests these accounts were often fabricated to cover up settlers' well-planned attacks on undefended Aboriginal camps at daybreak in which Aboriginal men, women and children were killed': Ryan, 2010, p. 270.

Chapter 11

1 Pratt, R and Hopkins-Wiese, J, 'The military at Moreton Bay, 1825–1842', *Queensland History Journal*, vol. 21, no. 12, 2013, p. 36; 'Moreton Bay', *Sydney Morning Herald*, 23 August 1842, p. 3.

2 'Squatting Licences – The Aborigines – Cattle Stealing', *Australasian Chronicle*, 23 August 1842, p. 2.

3   'The Blacks – Moreton Bay', *Sydney Morning Herald*, 27 September 1843, p. 4.
4   Simpson also had the escaped convicts Bracewell and Davis in his employ, with the border police as 'Interpreters and Constables', and described Bracewell as 'a very deserving man & as Interpreter extremely useful': Simpson, S, 'Quarterly Report of the Employment of each Man of the Border Police for the District of Moreton Bay from the 1st of July to the 30th of September 1843', Commissioner of Crown Lands, Reports re Border Police – Moreton Bay 1843–1846, SRNSW, CSSB, 4/7203.
5   Simpson to Colonial Secretary, 3 October 1843 in Langevad, 1979, p. 12; Simpson, 'Quarterly Report', 1 July – 30 Sept 1843, SRNSW, CSSB, 4/7203. Kerkhove and Uhr estimate the number of armed stockmen and squatters that could have been called upon as creating a total force of between ninety and 200 armed men: Kerkhove, R & Uhr, F, *The Battle of One Tree Hill: The Aboriginal resistance that stunned Queensland*, Boolarong Press, Brisbane, 2019, p. 163.
6   Simpson to Colonial Secretary, 3 October 1843 in Langevad, G, (ed.), *The Simpson Letterbook*, Cultural and Historical Records of Queensland, Number 1, 1979, Anthropology Museum, University of Queensland, Brisbane, 1979, p. 12.
7   See Marr, D, *Killing for Country: A family story*, Black Inc., Melbourne, 2023, pp. 57–65 for an overview of colonial politics and newspapers in the 1830s; 'Moreton Bay', *Maitland Mercury and Hunter River General Advertiser*, 18 November 1843, p. 2. It is unclear if the letter writer is referring to Simpson's Rosewood scrub or another sortie elsewhere and he does not include the military and other official personnel, merely 'gentlemen'.
8   Campbell, J, 'Early settlement in Queensland', *Darling Downs Gazette*, 5 November 1910, p. 6.
9   'News from the interior', *Sydney Morning Herald*, 12 October 1843, p. 3. According to Kerkhove and Uhr, Jackey Jackey survived. They suggest several 'commando groups' of squatters and stockmen with military and police attached operated in the Downs and Lockyer for two weeks between 19 and 30 September: Kerkhove & Uhr, 2019, pp. 166–169.
10 Kerkhove, R, *How They Fought: Indigenous tactics and weaponry of Australia's Frontier Wars*, Boolarong Press, Brisbane, 2023, p. 19; Roberts, T, 'Thomas John Domville Taylor (ca. 1817–1889)', Harry Gentle Resource Centre, Griffith University, 2020, <harrygentle.griffith.edu.au/life-stories/thomas-john-domville-taylor/>.
11 Simpson to Colonial Secretary, 26 October 1843 in Langevad, 1979, p. 12.
12 Campbell, J, 'Early settlement in Queensland', *Darling Downs Gazette*, 5 November 1910, p. 6.
13 'News from the interior', *Sydney Morning Herald*, 12 October 1843, p. 3. Military historians Rodd Pratt and Jeff Hopkins-Weise note that 'while no explicit record of this campaign is extant, there is strong evidence that an ongoing bush war involving soldiers and mounted settlers was waged over the next three years [and] while their primary duty was as a dray escort, there can be little doubt that during their three-year posting at Helidon this detachment was responsible for many Aboriginal deaths. Even a century after these events, human remains littered the area of Murphy's Creek and Tent Hill Creek, which local lore attributed directly to the soldiers stationed nearby. While touring through the district around 1843–44, Christopher Pemberton Hodgson [recorded encountering Aboriginal people] with fresh bayonet wounds that could only have resulted from close encounters with soldiers': Pratt and Hopkins-Weise, 'Redcoats in the 1840s Moreton Bay and New Zealand frontier wars', *Queensland Review*, vol. 26, no. 1, 2019, pp. 38–41. It should be considered, however, that bayonets were not the preserve of the military and were known to have been used elsewhere by squatters and stockworkers. The *Sydney Morning Herald*, 12 October 1843, p. 3 mentions six soldiers, and the *Sydney Chronicle*, 25 July 1846, p. 2, describes a

guard comprising a 'corporal and twelve privates'. See the *Queensland Times*, 26 October 1893, p. 5, and 28 April 1928, p. 13, and Hodgson, CP, *Reminiscences of Australia with hints on the squatters' life*, W. N. Wright, London, 1846, p. 234; Simpson to Colonial Secretary, 1 August, 31 December 1844 in Langevad, 1979, pp. 12–13.

14   While the colonial authorities turned to the military to play an active role in protecting squatters and argued that the burden should be on London's purse, in London, Colonial Secretary Lord Grey believed the colonies should take on more of their own responsibility for defence: Pratt, R, 'The Military at Moreton Bay, 1825–1842', *Queensland History Journal*, vol. 21, no. 12, 2013, pp. 824–825. See also Pratt and Hopkins-Weise, 2019, p. 40 and Kerkhove & Uhr, 2019, p. 6. The diversion of troops to New Zealand had in fact begun earlier. The fact troops were sent to Moreton Bay at all underscores the significance of the threat in the north. The pressure had been building since 1839 when the colonial office urged Governor Gipps to offer as much military support as he could to the 'New Zealand Land Company', who were planning to bring 'large Bodies of Emigrants' to New Zealand. Lord John Russell told Gipps that when 'Captain Hobson has obtained a grant or cession of territory from the New Zealand Chiefs in the Northern Island' he would then assume 'the title of Lieut. Governor of New Zealand' and should be sent one hundred troops from New South Wales: Lord John Russell to Gipps, 26 September 1839, *HRA*, XX, pp. 358–359; Russell to Gipps, 4 December 1839, *HRA*, XX, pp. 410–411. In April 1840, Gipps informed Russell he had sent a significant detachment of ninety men on the ship HMS *Buffalo* to the Bay of Islands: Gipps to Russell, 5 April 1840, *HRA*, XX, p. 592.

15   Fisher, 'From depredation to degredation: The Aboriginal experience at Moreton Bay 1842–60', in Fisher, R (ed.), *Brisbane: The Aboriginal presence 1824–1860*, Brisbane History Group Paper no. 11, 1992, p. 32; Queensland Legislative Assembly, *Native Police Force: Report from the Select committee on the Native Police Force and the Condition of the Aborigines Generally*, etc., Fairfax and Belbridge, Brisbane, 1861, pp. 6–7.

16   Bottoms, T, *Conspiracy of Silence: Queensland's frontier killing times*, Allen & Unwin, Sydney, 2013, p. 25. As Kerkhove and Uhr note, between 1842 and 1845, 'Aboriginal raids occurred all over the Darling Downs and Lockyer, temporarily evicting squatters from many runs'. So too, during 1843, 'almost all stations around Wide Bay, the Upper Brisbane and Stanley Rivers were abandoned' with 'many Wide Bay runs remaining vacant for up to four years': Kerkhove & Uhr, 2019, p. 110. In fact, there were inquiries into the deaths of what was tallied as between 1842 and 1844 in the Darling Downs and Moreton Bay districts as twenty-nine white people killed and nine wounded. The report noted that 'the charge alleged against the Govt. that no enquiry had been made is altogether without foundation': unknown, 21 December 1844, Wickham to Colonial Secretary, 19 October 1844, SRNSW, CSLR, 4/2656.2.

17   Pratt & Hopkins-Weise, 2019, p. 34.

18   Gray, WJB, 'The early days of the Big River, McIntyre and Severn', unpublished, 1902, quoted in Kerkhove & Uhr, 2019, p. 123.

19   Kerkhove, R, 'White casualties and events in the Lockyer-Downs War 1840–1850', unpublished paper, 2022, pp. 1–5; Knight, JJ, 'In the early days: The birth and growth of Brisbane', *Brisbane Courier*, 25 April 1892, p. 7. As Pratt and Hopkins-Weise note, from 1843 to 1848, the 99th and briefly the 58th regiment were mainly involved in either skirmishes with Aboriginal people, assisting parties of armed squatters in 'attacking' them, or marching to districts well after skirmishes or massacres had happened: Pratt & Hopkins-Weise, 2019, p. 37.

20   Knight, 1892, p. 7. Kerkhove has outlined the ongoing conflict after 1843 in detail. See for example his work on the Sunshine Coast-Noosa Region that covers from the early 1840s

to the 1880s in Kerkhove, R, 'Mapping frontier war on the Sunshine Coast/Noosa Region', Report for the Sunshine Coast Reconciliation Group, 2020.

21 Kerkhove and Uhr outline the conflicting and limited information about Multuggerah after One Tree Hill: 2019, pp. 204–208; 'News from the interior', *Sydney Morning Herald*, 12 October 1843, p. 3. See: French, M, *Conflict on the Condamine: Aborigines and the European invasion*: Darling Downs Institute Press, Toowoomba, 1989, pp. 102–109 for an overview of this period. Historian Rod Fisher categorised the conflict near Brisbane as essentially 'determined by the spread of pastoralism' and occurring as follows: 1842–45 from Ipswich to the Darling Downs; upper Brisbane valley 1842–46; Logan district 1844–53; Pine River 1845–58; Wide Bay-Burnett 1850–59 and Sandgate 1853–59: Fisher, 1992, p. 32. Kerkhove analysed 'Laurie's and Cilento's remarkable assertion (1959) that during the 1840s–1860s an alliance of at least a dozen Aboriginal groups openly declared war in southern Queensland and conducted a highly effective 'Black War' that temporarily impeded settlement': Kerkhove, R, 'Tribal alliances with broader agendas? Aboriginal resistance in southern Queensland's "Black War"': *Cosmopolitan Civil Societies Journal*, 2014, vol. 6, no. 3, p. 1. Ray Kerkhove estimates white casualties in what he calls the 'Lockyer-Downs War' from 1840 to 1850 (with raids into 1870s) as '84–90 casualties with 56–58 fatalities and 28–32 wounded'. He believes there were only ten to twelve Aboriginal fatalities properly recorded during this time, but the number was 'probably several hundreds': Kerkhove, 2022, pp. 1–5.

Epilogue

1 Broome, R, *Aboriginal Australians: A history since 1788*, Allen & Unwin, Sydney, 2010 (1982), p. 48. See Marr, D, *Killing for Country: A family story*, Black Inc., Melbourne, 2023, for an overview of the Native Mounted Police in Queensland, esp. pp. 250–253 for the massive and vicious response by police and settlers to the Cullin-la-ringo massacre (of whites).

2 According to Beresford, the tensions came to a head with 'with the massacre of Aboriginal people at Rufus River in August 1841', but it remains unclear whether this was in fact a battle, arguably one that turned into a massacre: Beresford, Q, *Wounded Country: The Murray-Darling Basin – A contested history*, NewSouth Publishing, Sydney, 2021, p. 86; 'The bench of magistrates and late fatal affray with the natives', *Southern Australian*, 21 September 1841, p. 3. See Foster, R, Hosking, R & Nettelbeck, A, *Fatal Collisions: The South Australian frontier and the violence of memory*, Wakefield Press, Adelaide, 2001. Richard Broome is one of few historians to have noted that often 'massacre' is not the right term for a conflict that might have begun as a stand-up battle, but then turned into a rout and then a massacre: Broome, 2005, p. 81. But the idea that a battle between warriors and Europeans with firearms is a massacre has a strong resonance in general understanding of The Australian Wars. Historian Lyndall Ryan is less concerned with whether battles end in massacres, and focuses on the motivations of reprisal, killing of livestock or 'pre-emptive strikes' that define numerous conflicts: Ryan, 'The Myall Creek Massacre: Was it typical of the time?' in Ryan, L & Lydon, J (eds), *Remembering the Myall Creek Massacre*, NewSouth Publishing, Sydney, 2018, p. 89.

3 Beresford, 2021, p. 86. In the mid-1840s, the Barkindji were, according to Bobbie Hardy, 'thoroughly roused all along the Murray'. Overlanding parties were spooked by warriors' ability to follow and watch and wait, hiding and then mounting surprise ambushes: Hardy, B, *Lament for the Barkindji: The vanished tribes of the Darling River Region*, Rigby, Adelaide, p. 51; Mitchell, TL, *Journal of an Expedition into the interior of Tropical Australia in search of a route from Sydney to the Gulf of Carpentaria*, Longman, Brown, Green and Longmans, London, 1848, pp. 16, 21, 25.

4   The report continued: 'it would appear that he was the principal in all the robberies and depredations committed by the natives, and the settlers are under great obligations to Sergeant Anderson and party, in ridding them of so formidable a person. Two others of the ringleaders, Bubbligig and Fishhook, are now in custody; great credit is due to Sergeant Anderson and his party for their praiseworthy conduct on these occasions, and I trust a lesson has been taught these benighted creatures, that they will not easily forget. Corporal Lamborn is, I understand, recovering from his wound': 'News from the interior', *Sydney Morning Herald*, 22 September 1845, p. 2.

5   The names of various groups and Nations are listed here, where they are known and used in this book. It is not exhaustive or comprehensive. Further Community consultation may reveal more. This may not be all the groups across these vast areas, and there are variations in spelling. Colonial records rarely named Aboriginal groups with their correct name, or indeed any name, using such descriptors as the 'Goulburn River Tribe' or the 'Bogan Blacks'.

6   As Kerkhove notes, resistance was not intended to be stand-up battles to kill numbers of white colonisers – it was intended to undermine the pastoral economic model, to unseat the squatters from their tenuous land occupation before they became established. Indeed, Kerkhove asks, 'was it an attempt to beat the squatters at their own game by wresting the pastoral industry out of their hands?' This strategy gave Aboriginal people the best chance in the circumstances they were facing – it was an incredibly smart, deeply thoughtful strategy based in an understanding of Country. People need land and food to survive – take this away and their guns become less meaningful. Certainly, the massive retaliations that squatters unleashed on Aboriginal people who speared or stole their cattle suggests the squatters were very much concerned about losing their economic heartblood, their largest capital investments: Kerkhove, R, 'Tribal alliances with broader agendas? Aboriginal resistance in southern Queensland's "Black War"', *Cosmopolitan Civil Societies Journal*, 2014, vol. 6, no. 3, p. 49. See also Beresford, 2021, pp. 88–89.

7   It is difficult to suggest a cost to the squatting economy in the late 1830s and early 1840s. Much evidence is anecdotal, often vague (stock could be lost then recovered) and record-keeping almost non-existent in the early periods. A detailed study of what can be discovered of sheep, cattle, crops and equipment losses would be a most valuable project.

8   Ray Kerkhove, Terry Royan, Boe Spearim and Uncle Wayne Fossey, interview, 11 June 2024, Toowoomba. As military historian Nic Grguric notes, 'Traditional Aboriginal warfare was highly localised and ritualised. Its tactics consisted of ambushes and night raids, as well as pitched battles. In Aboriginal culture, these tactics were an acceptable and traditional form of fighting. To the Europeans, however, ambushes and night raids were viewed as "treacherous" and created a sense of baffled deflation and anger at an elusive target that would not stand still for the firearm to do its work. Tactics such as these would no doubt have imposed a great psychological strain upon the minds of Europeans unaccustomed to them, especially since the brunt of frontier conflict was overwhelmingly borne by civilian settlers unused to war, rather than police or soldiers. Frustration at Aboriginal tactics led to the accumulation of a suppressed rage, stirring a desire to reassert superiority and self-respect by whatever means necessary. Settler fear was heightened in this oppressive atmosphere of distrust and misunderstanding, where one never knew when a spear might come silently flying through a window or doorway, or from the bushes': Grguric, N, 'The fortified homestead of the Australian frontier', in Clark, G & Litster, M (eds), *Archaeological Perspectives on Conflict and Warfare in Australia and the Pacific*, 2022, ANU Press, Canberra, 2022, p. 193.

9   Curr apparently berated Jack and told him if he did shoot people he would report him. Curr believed 'Jack the soldier' 'evidently thought he had a perfect right' to 'dispose of'

10   the 'lives of a few Blacks' as he chose, as long as he did not get into trouble': Curr, EM, *Recollections of squatting in Victoria, then called the Port Phillip District (1841–1851)*, George Robertson, Melbourne, 1883, p. 95.
10   Prentis, M, *A Study in Black and White: The Aborigines in Australian history*, Methuen, Sydney, 1975, p. 27. See Dennis, P, Grey, J, Morris, E & Prior, R (eds), *The Oxford Companion to Australian Military History*, Oxford University Press, Melbourne, 1995. For an overview of how historians have failed to comprehend traditional and transformed alliances in resistance warfare see: Kerkhove, 2014, p. 49.
11   *Perth Gazette and Western Australian Journal*, 16 September 1837, p. 973.
12   McCulloch, 'Gipps, Sir George (1791–1847)', *ADB*, 1966.
13   Kerkhove, R, *How They Fought: Indigenous tactics and weaponry of Australia's Frontier Wars*, Boolarong Press, Brisbane, 2023. As Ray Kerkhove notes, 'The Frontier Wars seem to have sparked major organisational changes amongst Australian First Nations including the increasing militancy of totemic cults, the forming of new and broader alliances, and the rise of more authoritarian leaders. Overall, the image is of a very dynamic and robust resistance, with many more First Nations' successes and adaptations than is currently acknowledged': Kerkhove, 2023, p. 272.
14   Wedge to Russell, 12 December 1839, Wedge to Glenelg, 22 April 1839, *HRA*, XX, pp. 447–451; Stancombe, GH, 'Wedge, John Helder (1793–1872)', *ADB*. Perhaps the greatest storyteller and land claimer in the history of Australia, William Charles Wentworth, began to write Aboriginal resistance out of his history in his 1819 *Statistical Account of the British Settlements in Australasia* and furthered it with his poem 'Australasia' in 1823. In 1840, according to Michael Persse, Wentworth and some other land speculators 'bought from seven Maori [sic] chieftains, for a song, nearly a third of New Zealand'. The claim was overturned by Governor Gipps. It would have made Wentworth the greatest landowner on earth at the time: Persse, M, 'Wentworth, William Charles (1790–1872)', *ADB*.
15   Uncle James Ingram, interview, 20 October 2023, Wagga Wagga; Uncle Bill Allen Jnr, interview, 1 December 2023 and 6 June 2024, Bathurst. Allen notes that many songlines around Bathurst run north to south following important peaks and signposts as well as riverways, but also that Windradyne travelled regularly to the coast in the 1820s.
16   As Nic Grguric notes, 'the British notion of colonial warfare at this time was one of large forces of "native" warriors who would attack en masse, generally dashing themselves against firearms. However, Australian frontier warfare involved fast-moving raids and ambushes. The tactics used by Aboriginal warriors was a cause of acute frustration to the settlers, essentially guerrilla warfare, naturally suited to the relatively small, independent tribal group': Grguric, 2022, p. 193.
17   Henderson, J, *Excursions and Adventures in New South Wales: with pictures of squatting and of life in the bush: An account of the climate, productions, and natural history of the colony, and of the manners and customs of the natives, with advice to emigrants, &c.*, W. Shoberl, London, 1851, pp. 148, 308.
18   Wedge wanted to atone for 'the Black Catalogue of crimes that have hitherto stained our career' as colonists. He suggested that colonisers be rewarded with Aboriginal land if they 'reclaimed and domesticated' Aboriginal people. Wedge thought 'reserves for townships' and supplies of 'flour, potatoes and tea and sugar as well as blankets and tomahawks' would do the trick. Tragically, a humanitarian-driven change to enforce the 'civilisation' of Aboriginal people by containment was under way: Wedge to Russell, 18 January 1840, *HRA*, XX, pp. 487–488.

19 Durrant is cautious that 'the case could be made that Aboriginal people spontaneously resisted invasion as it was happening; and that rather than it being a coordinated resistance, it was a spontaneous effort, backed by a generalised awareness that the same was happening to others much further afield': Durrant, J, pers. comm., 2 April 2024.
20 Swain, T, 'Australia', in Swain, T & Trompf, G, *The Religions of Oceania*, Routledge, London, 1995, p. 64.
21 Leichhardt, L, 1 January 1844, in Darragh, TA & Fensham, RA (eds), *The Leichhardt Diaries. Early Travels in Australia during 1842–1844*, Memoirs of the Queensland Museum, Cultural Heritage Series, Queensland Museum, Brisbane, 2013, p. 86.
22 Mitchell, 1848, pp. 17–18.
23 'Grand Corrobory', *Colonist*, 9 April 1835, p. 4.
24 *Sydney Morning Herald*, 30 June 1849, p. 4.
25 Kerkhove, 2023, p. 27. Kerkhove importantly notes that 'contemporary accounts' 'document a different narrative concerning the Frontier Wars: a narrative of Indigenous resilience and success'. He continues that: 'First Australians were not relying on inflicting massive casualties in one-off battles, but rather the "slow drip" of persistent action. In this respect, Australian resistance shared the tactics of guerrilla warfare around the globe: accumulative impact': Kerkhove, 2023, p. 27.
26 While Haydon worked to justify the historical role of police, his analysis was not unusual for the late 19th and early 20th centuries – before World War One: Haydon, AL, *The Trooper Police of Australia: A record of mounted police work in the Commonwealth from the earliest days of settlement to the present time*, A. Melrose, London, 1911, pp. 297–299; Jenks, E, *A History of the Australasian Colonies: From their foundation to the year 1911*, Cambridge University Press, Cambridge, 1912, p.16.
27 Clear, J, 'The Wiradjuri Wars: Analysing the evolution of settler colonial violence in New South Wales, 1822–1841', PhD thesis, Department of Modern History, Macquarie University, 2021, p. 271; Flanagan, R, 'The Aborigines of Australia – No. XIV: The "Rising of 1842–4"', *Empire*, 15 April 1854, p. 3.

Index

Adelaide 27, 93, 96, 160, 166, 218
Adelaide Chronicle 162
Agricultural and Horticultural Society of NSW 19
Albury, NSW 59
Allen, Uncle Bill *see* Dinawan
alliances
    between Aboriginal warriors 9, 12, 16, 64, 96, 118, 121, 176, 211, 216–17, 223, 227
    between Aboriginal warriors and bushrangers 21
    between Aboriginal warriors and convicts 24, 26–27
    between colonists 205, 226
Allman, Francis (Commissioner) 37, 149
Ambēyang Country, NSW viii, 20, 34, 43, 60, 83, 103, 117, 136, 158, 169, 188, 207, 218
Ambēyang People 34, 151–52, 154–55, 220
ambush 88, 94, 129–30
Anderson (Sergeant) 220
Anderson (station hand) 143–44
Appin Massacre 13, 86
aquaculture 84
Australasian Chronicle 206
Australian Agricultural Company 35, 141, 151
Australia Day 135
Australia Felix 2, 59
Australian, newspaper 23, 30, 37, 133, 150, 179
Australian Wars 4, 8, 16, 131, 211, 223–26, 231
Auty, Kate (historian) 5

Baaka-Darling River, NSW 26, 28, 30, 82–83, 218
Badtjala People 214
Baker (warrior) 21
Baker's Creek Massacre 35
Balfour, James 37–38
    see also Balfour and Co.
Balfour, Robert 110–11
Balfour and Co. 37

Bangerang People 176–77
Bardaji Country, NSW viii, 20, 30, 43, 60, 83, 103, 136, 158, 169, 188, 218
Barkindji Country, NSW 30, 83, 220
'Barrington River natives' people 34
    see also Birrpai
    see also Worimi
Bartley, Nehemiah 8
Bateman, William 72, 74
Bathurst Elders 233
Bathurst, NSW 22, 25–26, 28, 31, 52, 90–92, 148–49, 160, 228
Bathurst Plains, NSW 22, 84, 229
Bathurst Rebellion 25
Bathurst War 92, 229
Batman, John 40, 199
Baylie, William (Assistant Protector) 64
Bayliss, James (historian) 163–64
Bell, Marshall (Yiman man) 119
Benalla, Colony of NSW (now VIC) 1–5, 13, 59, 65–66, 70, 79, 175
Benalla History Group 232
Benalla Standard 4, 66–67
Bendigo Independent 164
Bentley, Thomas 71–73, 168
Berry Jerry run 88
Big Micky (warrior) 175
Big River, NSW 16, 32–34, 42–58, 135, 139, 142, 150, 153–54, 159, 222
    see also Gwydir River
Bigambul Country, Colony of NSW (now QLD) viii, 20, 43, 103, 117, 136, 207, 218, 220
Bigambul People 211, 220
Bila Galari River *see* Lachlan River
billabongs 65, 85, 160, 226
Bingara, NSW 32–34, 56, 141
Bingara Creek, NSW 56
Bingham, Henry (Commissioner) 46, 50, 51, 62, 63, 196, 197
Birrpai Country, NSW viii, 20, 35, 43, 60, 83, 103, 117, 136, 158, 169, 188, 207, 218
Birrpai People 35, 151, 221
Blaxland family 22

Index

Blaxland, John 181
'Blucher Tribe' People 105–06, 108
Blue Mountains, NSW 11, 84, 160, 228
'Bogan Blacks' People 38, 148, 219–20
Bogan River, NSW 16, 20, 28, 31, 53, 60, 83, 103, 117, 136, 148–50, 158, 169, 188, 207, 217–19, 222, 228
Boggabri, NSW 19, 26
Bonney, Charles 12, 59
boomerangs 46–47, 56, 98, 138, 162
Boonerong People 220
Borambil, NSW 22, 27
border police 123, 150, 153, 159–60, 163, 165, 183, 185–86, 196, 200, 208, 211, 223
Boree, NSW 28
Boru, Brian (warrior) 94–97
Bourke, John Conway (mailman) 76–78, 170–74, 176
Bourke, NSW 28, 119
Bourke, Richard (Governor) 23, 25, 38, 40–41, 86, 92
Bowman, William 37, 47, 61, 65, 69, 80, 189–91
Boyd, Benjamin 40
Bracewell (convict and interpreter) 208
Brangy (Ovens River Waywurru man) 63, 176
Brennan, Patrick 151–52
Brisbane, Colony of NSW (now QLD) 8, 13, 20, 43, 103, 107, 117, 125, 136, 206–08, 218, 220
Brisbane, Thomas (Governor) 84, 92
Brisbane Courier 215
Brisbane River, Colony of NSW (now QLD) 102, 107, 110–11, 122–23, 128, 213
British empire 19, 39, 44, 51, 102, 160, 217, 225, 232
Broken River, battle at 4–5, 80, 168, 170–71, 173, 175, 179, 186, 197, 204
Brown, George 'Black' (Sri Lankan) 104, 112–14
Brown, Jim 65, 78–79
Brown, John 65, 72, 74, 78–80
Brown, William 62
Buckinbong Station, NSW 88, 95, 97, 99, 164
Buckley, William 24
Bulgetheroon (Taungurung man) 67–69
Bundjalung Country, NSW viii, 20, 43, 103, 119, 136, 207, 218
Bundjalung People 153, 221

Bungaree (warrior) 229
Bunya Gathering 11, 13, 53, 110, 118–21, 227
Bunya Mountains, Colony of NSW (now QLD) 119–20
Bunya tree 120
Burch, Geoff (historian) 164
Burrungam People 220
bushmen 59, 84, 89, 151–52, 223, 226
bushrangers 5, 19, 21–25, 28, 32, 34, 42, 45, 46, 49, 65, 89, 147, 149–52, 222, 224, 233

campaigns
   Macquarie's 89
   Mounted Police near Moree 34
   Multuggerah's 212, 216
   Myall Creek 34
   Peninsula, Napoleonic Wars 50, 172, 182
   see also guerrilla
Campbell (squatter) 77
Campbell, Charlie 113
Campbell, James 128, 130–31, 212
Campbell, John 'Tinker' 125
Campbelltown, NSW 89
cannon 50, 56
canoe 15, 62, 66, 176
Capertee Valley, NSW 160
carbine 44, 194, 201
Carr, Aunty Wirribi Leanna 51, 233
Carroll, Uncle Robert 164, 166–67
Carter, Megan (Waywurru descendant) 63, 66, 176, 189
Casey, Thomas (stockman) 151–52
cavalry 42, 44, 50, 55, 92, 117, 137, 161, 172, 193–94
   see also Mounted Police
   see also Native Mounted Police
ceremony 10–11, 13, 120–21, 200, 227
   bora 47, 66, 119
   initiation 12, 129
   see also Bunya Gathering
Chalker, Aunty Glenda 13
Charlie (warrior) 175
Chatty (Burigaly warrior) 46
children 48, 51, 67, 109, 143–44, 151, 153, 166, 171, 194, 201–03, 205
Clarke, George 'The Barber' (escaped convict) 25–27
Clayton-Dixon, Callum (Ambēyang historian) 156

Clear, Jack (historian) 165
Cobb Station, NSW 47–48, 55–56
Cobban, George Geddes McKenzie (Lieutenant of the Mounted Police) 45–46, 55, 57, 135, 137–38
Coccombraral People 118, 221
'Cockie' (warrior) 21
Coliban River, NSW 61, 69, 187–90
Colonial Cavalry 92
Colonial Observer 124, 148–49
Colonist 228
confederacies 11, 52, 64, 121, 220
    Kulin confederacy 12
    Ngarrindjeri 11
Cooper, Aunty Cheryl 5
Coppock, John 190–92
corroboree 65, 176–77, 229
    Grand Corroboree 228
    see also ceremony
Cosby, Henry (Commissioner) 99–100, 157–59, 162–63, 165
Cosby, James (overseer) 193
Cosgrove (trooper) 193–95
counterattack 93, 118, 221
Courier-Mail 9
Coutts Crawford, James 95–96, 98
Cressbrook, Colony of NSW (now QLD) 110, 121
Croker, William Henry (Major) 23–24
Crossley, Frederick 1–2, 4
Crossley, James (overseer) 59, 61–62, 64–65, 67, 69–74, 76, 170
crow minders 107
Crown Land 40, 212
Cunningham, Alan (surveyor and botanist) 53, 102
Curr, Edward (squatter) 42, 44

'Daddy' (Wirrayaraay Elder) 144
Dallambarah People 117, 221
damper 36, 52, 67
Dangar, Henry 141–42
Darkinyung People 221
Darling, Ralph (Governor) 229
Darling Downs, Colony of NSW (now QLD) 6, 9, 15, 102, 105, 107–10, 112, 119, 123–25, 129–30, 132, 207, 210–14
Darling River *see* Baaka-Darling River
Darlington Point, NSW 85

Darug 89
Daung Wurrung People *see* Taungurung People
Davis, James 120
deserters 21, 228
Dharawal People 13, 86
Dhungala Country, Colony of NSW (now VIC) viii, 20, 43, 60, 83, 136, 158, 169, 188, 207, 218
Dhungutti, Country, NSW 12
Dinawan, Uncle Bill Allen Junior 12, 16, 224 233
disease 11, 27, 96, 109
disembowelled 189
Dixon (squatter) 77
Djadja Wurrung Country, Colony of NSW (now VIC) viii, 20, 43, 60, 64, 69, 83, 136, 158, 169, 188, 218
Djadja Wurrung People 69, 187, 189, 192–95, 220
'Doherty' (Gomeroi man) 55
Dowse, Thomas 'Tom' (journalist) 122, 126, 128, 130
Dredge, James (Assistant Protector of Aborigines) 67–68
drought 86, 96, 219, 221
Dubbo, NSW 119
Duncan, William Augustine (editor) 206–07
Dungog, NSW 35, 147
Durrant, Jacqui (historian) 69, 75, 227, 233

Ebenezer, NSW 32
Elders 13, 15, 120, 143–44, 164
emu 64, 104
Emu Plains, NSW 228
Everett brothers 152
execution 14
Executive Council 40, 50, 138, 181, 185
Eyre, Edward John 93, 166

Faithfull, George 2–3, 59, 61–63, 74, 170, 178, 187, 203–04
Faithfull, William 2–3, 59, 61–64, 72, 75–76, 78, 80, 168
Faithfull, William Senior 61
Faithfull Massacre 4–5, 65, 69, 140, 173, 175, 177
Faithfull Street 5
Faithfull Tree 3

Index

Fannan, John 73–74
Ferguson, Joseph 98, 100
financiers 15, 45, 180
fire messages 12, 53, 56, 72, 77, 82, 92, 96, 119, 144, 193
Flanagan, Roderick (historian) 6–7, 10, 14–15, 69, 138, 232
Fleming, John 34, 143–45
Flynn, Uncle Jade Yahnadarrambal 233
Fort Bourke, NSW 28–29, 219–20
Fossey, Uncle Wayne 82, 119, 221, 224
Franklin, Jane (Lady) 175, 177
Freeman's Journal 164
Frontier Wars, Australia 9, 206
fugitives 74, 79

Gabbi Gabbi People 119, 214
Gambuwal People 211
Gamilaraay *see* Gomeroi
Gamilaroi *see* Gomeroi
Gammage, Bill (historian) 85, 91, 93, 96, 165, 233
Gandangara Country, NSW 11, 60, 83, 86, 89, 158, 169, 188
gaol 22, 23, 26, 201
garrison 152, 182–83, 208, 212, 214
Geelong, Colony of NSW (now VIC) 178, 182
genocide 230
Geynyon People 220
Giabal People 102, 211
Gibson, Andrew 74, 76
Gidhabul Country, Colony of NSW (now QLD) 20, 43, 103, 105, 117, 136, 207, 218, 220
Giggabarah People 118, 221
Gilmore, Mary (Dame) 96, 164
Gipps, George (Governor) 107, 139–41, 145–46, 149–50, 159, 165, 172, 178–86, 199, 202–03, 208, 223
Gippsland, Colony of NSW (now VIC) 203
Gisborne, Colony of NSW (now VIC) 2
Gisborne, Henry Fyshe (Commissioner) 159, 196–97
Glenelg, Lord 39–40, 59, 68, 92, 140, 146, 181, 184–85, 226
Gloucester, NSW 35–36, 147
Gnarabal Country, Colony of NSW (now QLD) 105, 220

Gomeroi, Country, NSW viii, 19–20, 22, 26–27, 31, 43, 45–49, 52–53, 103, 117, 136, 207
Gomeroi People 9, 11–12, 25–27, 45–49, 52–53, 55, 57, 105, 119, 137, 139, 142, 144, 146, 154, 156, 220
'Good Morning' (Burigaly warrior) 46
Gooneburra People 108
Gorman, Owen (Lieutenant) 103–04, 107–08, 110–11, 113–15
Gormly, James (historian) 87
Goulburn, NSW 1–2, 16, 20, 43, 60–62, 64, 74–77, 81, 83, 95, 136, 157, 218
Goulburn Plains, NSW 170
Goulburn River, Colony of NSW (now VIC) 69, 74, 175, 182–83
Goulburn River Tribe 187, 197, 200–201
Government Gazette 41, 47
Grafton, NSW 153–54
Grant, Uncle Brian Mallyan 233
Grantham Station, Colony of NSW (now QLD) 112, 115, 125
Gravesend Massacre 48
Gravesend, NSW 48, 142
Greenhatch Creek, NSW 45, 54, 55
Greenhatch, Joseph 54–55
guerrilla warfare 9, 50, 56, 90, 92, 95–96, 100–101, 147, 160, 163, 165, 197, 225
Gumbaynggirr viii, 20, 43, 103, 117, 119, 136, 207, 218
Gunaikurnai People 203, 220
Gundagai, NSW 15, 85, 94, 97
Gwydir District, NSW 46, 159
Gwydir People 55
Gwydir River, NSW viii, 16, 20, 43, 50, 52, 55, 103, 117, 136, 207, 218

Hall, Ebenezer 32–34, 45
Hall, Mathew 32–34, 45
Hall, Thomas 32–34, 45
Halloran, Arthur Edward (Commissioner) 8
hanging
    after Myall Creek Massacre 14, 135, 150
    at Windmill Hill 110
Hannan, Patrick (Corporal) 57, 135, 137
Harris, Alexander 6, 7, 10, 13, 232
Hawkesbury Benevolent Society 145
Hawkesbury River, NSW 22, 32, 61, 145, 228–29

315

Hewitt, Tom (pastoralist) 154
Hobbs, Wiliam 142, 144
Hobson, Doctor 175
Hodgson, Christopher Pemberton (squatter) 107–08
Hodgson, Magistrate 113, 115
Hughes (squatter) 77
Hughy/Joey ('Bogan chief') 220
Hume, Hamilton 30, 59, 84, 181
Hume River *see* Murray River
Hunter River Gazette 155
Hunter Valley, NSW 11, 21–23, 26–27, 32, 35, 46, 50, 52–54, 139, 141, 155, 228–29
Hutton, Charles 'Captain' (squatter) 187, 189, 192–95
Hyde Park Barracks 160

infantry 42, 44, 92, 182–83, 207, 212, 225
Ingram, Ossie (Wiradyuri Elder) 164
Ingram, Uncle James (Wiradyuri) 15, 83–84, 86, 97, 224
invasion 1, 11, 227–29
Irish people 86, 187

'Jackey Jackey' (warrior) 211
'Jacky' (warrior) 54
Jaggara People 128
Jamaica 93
Jamison, Sir John 181
Jamison Station, NSW 19
Jarowair Country, Colony of NSW (now QLD) 20, 43, 102–03, 117, 136, 207, 218
Jarowair People 102, 211, 220
'Jemmy' (warrior) 21
Jibbinwy (warrior) 228
Jinaburra People 220

Kabi Kabi People 102, 109, 119, 221
Kamilaroi *see* Gomeroi
Kelly, Ned 5
Kerkhove, Ray (historian) 13, 115, 223, 231–33
K'gari-Fraser Island, Colony of NSW (now QLD) 8, 124
Kilcoy Massacre 116, 121, 227
Kilcoy Station, Colony of NSW (now QLD) 111, 116
Kilmeister 142, 144
'King Sandy' (Elder) 143

Koori grapevine 13
Kulin Confederacy 12, 176
  see also alliances
  see also confederacy

La Trobe, Charles Joseph (Lieutenant-Governor) 173, 178, 197, 200–202
Lachlan River, NSW 32, 43, 60, 83, 96, 103, 117, 136, 158, 163, 169, 188, 207, 218, 219–20
Lake Macquarie, NSW 48
Launceston Advertiser 36
Legislative Council of New South Wales 206, 230
Leslie, George (squatter) 108
Leslie, Patrick (squatter) 105–06, 108, 123
'Limestone Blacks' People 118
Limestone, Colony of NSW (now QLD) 126, 211, 213
Liverpool Plains, NSW 22, 25, 32, 35–37, 45–46, 53, 107, 154
Liverpool Plains Massacre 150
Liverpool Ranges, NSW 52
Local Aboriginal Land Council 167
Lockyer Valley, Colony of NSW (now QLD) 110–11, 125, 128, 147, 208, 212, 213, 216
Lowe, Jacob 231
Lowe, Nathaniel (Lieutenant) 23
Lynch (bushranger) 19, 21

Macdonald, George James (Commissioner) 104, 150–53, 155
Macdonald River, NSW 22, 34
Macintyre River, NSW viii, 20, 43, 103, 105–06, 117, 136, 144, 147, 154, 153, 156, 207, 213, 218, 222
Mackay, George Dr 61, 80, 177, 197–99
Mackay, William 73
Mackenzie, Colin 116
Mackenzie, Evan 21, 111, 116
Macquarie, Lachlan (Governor) 89
Macquarie River, NSW viii, 20, 31, 43, 60, 83, 103, 117, 136, 148–49, 158, 169, 188, 207, 218, 219
Maitland Mercury and Hunter River General Advertiser 209
Māori Peoples 213, 231
Marangan, Colony of NSW (now VIC) 2, 3, 65–66, 70–71, 73

Index

Maraura War 217
Marra Waree People 82
Marrambidya River *see* Murrumbidgee River
massacres
    see Appin Massacre
    see Baker's Creek Massacre
    see Faithfull Massacre
    see Gravesend Massacre
    see Kilcoy Massacre
    see Liverpool Plains Massacre
    see Myall Creek Massacre
    see Narrandera Massacre
    see Rawdon Vale Massacre
    see Waterloo Creek Massacre
McCombie, Thomas 30
McConnell, Frederic 111, 121–22, 124
McDonald (bushranger) 19, 21
McDonald, Donald Alaster (historian) 1
McDougall (squatter) 126
McIntyre River, NSW *see* Macintyre River, NSW
McLeay River, NSW 31, 152
McMillan, Angus 203
McPherson, Hamish 5, 175, 232
Meewah, Colony of NSW (now QLD) 102–15, 128–32
Melbourne Cricket Club 67, 171
Melbourne, Colony of NSW (now VIC) 4, 8, 12, 59, 64, 80, 170, 177, 180, 199–202, 220, 227
    see also Port Phillip
Merangan People 66
Merri Creek, Colony of NSW (now VIC) 200
Merriman (warrior) 175
message-sticks 13, 96, 119
Milballal (Burigaly warrior) 46
militia 36, 123, 179–81, 207, 209, 214, 223
missionaries 48, 91, 109, 116, 206
Mitchell, Thomas Livingstone (Major) 2, 26–30, 41, 47, 52–53, 57, 82–83, 131, 217, 219, 228
Monaro Plains, NSW 37
Moppy (Yaggara man) 109, 112–13
'Moppy's Tribe' 109
    see also Yaggara People
Moree, NSW 5, 33–34, 52, 57, 135
Moreton Bay, Colony of NSW (now QLD) 6–8, 102–04, 106–07, 109, 111, 115–18, 120, 122–26, 128, 130, 136, 182–83, 206–09, 211–15, 221, 232

Mornington Peninsula, Colony of NSW (now VIC) 177, 199
Morumbidgee River *see* Murrumbidgee River, NSW
Mount Alexander, Colony of NSW (now VIC) 61
Mount Brisbane, Colony of NSW (now QLD) 122
Mount Gravesend, NSW 48
Mount Harris, NSW 220
Mount Kaputar, NSW 53
Mount Macedon, Colony of NSW (now VIC) 2, 61, 187
Mount Piper, Colony of NSW (now VIC) 77
Mount Table Top *see* Meewah
Mounted Police 21–23, 26, 32, 34, 42, 44–45, 50, 59, 69, 92, 95, 123, 135, 140, 141, 145, 148, 153, 155, 157–61, 170, 177, 181–83, 189, 192–94, 199–201, 208, 210, 212, 214, 220, 222
    see also Native Mounted Police
Multuggerah (warrior) 115, 122, 125, 127–28, 130, 132, 207–09, 212, 216
Mundy, Alfred Miller (Lieutenant) 67, 170–71
Mundy, Charles Fitzroy Miller 67, 171
Mundy, Fitzherbert Miller (squatter) 67–69, 171, 187
Munro (squatter) 64, 187, 191, 196
Murrawari People 220
Murray-Darling basin 13, 15, 28, 56, 82, 103, 161, 222
    see also Baaka-Darling River, NSW
    see also Murray River
Murray, Mina 233
Murray People 195
Murray River 1, 5, 7, 12, 20, 26–27, 40, 43, 59–60, 62, 64, 77, 81–84, 86, 96, 136, 157–58, 161, 166, 169–72, 174–75, 177, 179, 182–83, 188, 218
Murrumbidgee River, NSW viii, 1, 12, 15–16, 20, 32, 43, 53, 60, 76, 82–101, 136, 157–58, 160, 162–66, 169, 171, 188, 195, 218, 222, 229
musket 14, 25, 29, 58, 62, 67–68, 71–73, 80, 87, 91, 98, 130, 132, 147, 149, 155, 191, 196–97, 201
mutilation 122, 151
Myall Creek, NSW 14, 32–34, 135, 141–42, 143, 146

Massacre 14, 114, 145, 186, 222
  trials 14, 150

Namoi River, NSW viii, 16, 19, 20, 28, 43, 45–47, 50, 52, 54, 103, 117, 136, 155, 207, 218, 222
Narawai, Colony of NSW (now QLD) 106
Narinjera People 15
Narrabri, NSW 19, 27, 45
Narrandera Massacre 164–65
Narrandera, NSW 1, 15, 83, 85, 93, 97, 163, 166–67
Narromine, NSW 220
Narrungdera Country, NSW 1, 85–86, 91, 93, 99, 101, 163
Narrungdera People 163
Native Mounted Police 123, 217, 227
  see also Mounted Police
  see also Queensland Native Mounted Police
Natty ('Namoie chief') 21
Nepean River, NSW 228, 229
New Zealand 93, 95, 213, 225, 231
Newcastle, NSW 48
Ngarigo, NSW 20, 37, 43, 60, 83, 136, 158, 169, 188, 218
Ngarrindjeri Peoples 11
  see also confederacies
Ngunawal, NSW 20, 43, 83, 136, 169, 218,
Ngurai Illum Wurrung People 64, 187, 220
Nicholson (Captain) 149
Nicholson (Doctor) 3
Ningy Ningy People 220
Nunukul People 102
Nunn, James Winnett (Major) 5, 44, 50–51, 54–57, 137, 139–40, 170, 179, 183, 186
Nyemba Country, NSW 31
Nyemba People 220
Nyirrpa Country, NSW 30, 31, 221
Nyirrpa People 220

ochre 96
O'Brien, Henry 85
O'Brien (overseer) 63
Ovens, John (Major) 84
Ovens River, Colony of NSW (now VIC) viii, 2, 16, 20, 43, 60, 62–65, 69–70, 74–78, 81, 83, 136, 158, 169–70, 172–73, 175–76, 182–83, 188, 200, 218

Palawa People 11–12
palisaded rings 129–30
Pallangan-middang People 175
pantomime 227–28
Parker, Edward Stone (Assistant Protector of Aborigines) 64, 190, 192, 202
Parris, Harry (historian) 5
Paterson, Alexander (Commissioner) 46–52
Paterson River, NSW 22
Paton, Lisa (Wiradyuri descendant) 233
Peel River, NSW 45–46, 54, 102, 144, 151–52, 154
Peels Plains, Colony of NSW (now QLD) 108
Pemulwuy (warrior) 24
Penrith, NSW 19
Phillips, John (stockworker) 161–62
Poison Waterholes Creek, NSW 157–67
poisoning 116, 118, 121, 157, 164, 166, 227
Port Macquarie 35–36, 151
Port Phillip, Colony of NSW (now Melbourne, VIC) viii, 1–2, 6–8, 14–15, 31–32, 37, 40, 59–60, 62–63, 65, 67, 69–70, 77, 80, 83–84, 93, 136, 140, 157–59, 169–71, 174, 176, 179–80, 182–89, 196–97, 200, 202, 218, 221, 224, 232
Port Phillip Patriot and Melbourne Advertiser 175
Port Phillip People 31
Port Stephens 35–36, 151
Priestly, Bill (Gomoroi man) 119

Quandamooka People 102, 221
Queen Victoria 50, 57
Queensland 6–9, 11, 13, 53, 102–03, 109, 116–17, 119, 121, 129, 131, 145, 166, 207, 211, 213–14, 216–17, 221, 227
Queensland Legislative Assembly 213
Queensland Native Mounted Police 123, 217

Rawdon Vale Massacre 35
Razorback Range, NSW 131
Richmond, NSW 37
Robertson, James (hutkeeper) 11, 122
Robinson, George Augustus (Protector of Aborigines) 64, 175, 190–91, 195–97, 201–02
Rockhampton, Colony of NSW (now QLD) 119

Index

Rogers, James 'Cocky' (station manager) 112–15
Rolleston (Assistant Commissioner) 123, 125
Rosewood Scrub, Colony of NSW (now QLD) 111, 210, 213, 216
Russell, Lord John (Secretary of State for War and the Colonies) 140–41

Scotland 116, 150, 198
'Scrammy Headed Jackey' (warrior) 21
Sievwright, Charles Wightman (Assistant Protector of Aborigines) 178
'Simon' (warrior) 62, 84
Simpson, Dr Stephen (Magistrate) 116–18, 120–26, 129–32, 208–09, 211–13
Slaughter-house Creek, NSW 142
smallpox 27–28, 109
Smith (Captain) 200
Smith, Charles (merchant) 45, 54
Smith, Joseph 74
smoke signals *see* fire messages
Smyth George Brunswick (Lieutenant) 67, 69, 170–71, 192
Snodgrass, Kenneth (Lieutenant-Colonel) 50–51, 59, 139
Snodgrass Lagoon, Colony of NSW (now QLD) 57, 135, 137
  see also Waterloo Creek
  see also Waterloo Creek Massacre
Snodgrass, Peter 77–78, 171–73, 187
Snowy Mountains, NSW 12, 84, 227
Sommerville, George 112, 115
songline 13, 119, 224
South Australia 11–12, 27, 162, 217
Spearim, Boe (Gomeroi man) 46, 119
Spearim, Uncle Paul (Gomeroi Elder) 11–12, 49, 53, 224
Stapylton, Granville (surveyor) 110
stockade 169, 179, 201–02, 212, 219, 233
  see also Fort Bourke
Sturt, Charles (Captain) 26, 29–30, 76, 83, 85, 173
Sturt, Evelyn Pitfield Shirley (Commissioner) 173
Sydney Gazette 21, 72, 74, 104, 149–50, 158, 169, 185–86
Sydney Herald 7, 22–25, 31, 36, 87, 99–100, 123, 151–52, 165, 201

Sydney Monitor 28, 31, 74, 81, 94, 154, 157, 174, 176
Sydney Morning Herald 123, 126, 155, 206–07, 210, 216
Sydney Turf Club 19
syphilis 109

'Tallboy' (Burigaly warrior) 46
Tasmania 11, 22, 56
Taungurung Country, Colony of NSW (now VIC) viii, 1, 20, 43, 59, 64–65, 67, 83, 136, 169
Taungurung People 61, 64, 67, 69, 75, 78, 175–77, 187, 192, 195–96, 202, 220
Taylor, Thomas John Domville 211
telegraph 82
Tenthill, Colony of NSW (now QLD) 125
Terribalong (warrior) 228–29
'Terrible Billy' (stockman) 34
Thatcher, Thomas 73–74, 76
Therry, Roger (Attorney General) 112–14
Thomas, William (Protector of Aborigines) 21, 64, 178, 195, 199–201
Thompson, Charles 94
Thompson, Frederick Anslow (squatter) 94–95, 97
Thomson, Charles (squatter) 87–90
Thomson, Edward Deas (Colonial Secretary) 46–47, 50, 122, 142, 179
Threlkeld, Lancelot (missionary) 48, 91–92, 139
Throsby, Charles 84
Thunderbolt's Rock, NSW 34
Thunderbolt's Way, NSW 34
tomahawks 33, 49, 124, 162, 211
Tomkinson, John (stockman) 97–98, 100
Tongerlongeter (Oyster Bay nation leader) 11
Toorbul, Colony of NSW (now QLD) 109
Toowoomba, Colony of NSW (now QLD) 102, 109, 119, 125, 128
totems 15, 84
Townshend (magistrate) 23
Turrbal People 102

Uhr, Frank (historian) 115
uniform 42, 44, 186, 211
Upotipotpon, Colony of NSW (now VIC) 79
Uralla, NSW 19, 33–34
Uren, Samuel (historian) 3, 65–66, 70, 79

Vagrancy Act 1835 24
Victoria 1–2, 5, 8, 12–13, 30, 59–60, 69, 76, 93, 169–70, 175–79, 187–88, 192, 203–04, 220, 224, 227, 232–33
Vinegar Hill, NSW 142

waddies 33, 124–25, 201, 211
Waddy, Richard (Lieutenant) 170
Wagga Wagga, NSW 83, 85, 87–88, 93, 97, 164, 167
Wailwan Country, NSW viii, 20, 43, 103, 117, 136, 207, 218
Waka Waka County viii, 20, 43, 103, 117, 119, 136, 207, 218
Walgett, NSW 19, 52
Wallamba River, NSW 35
Wangaratta, Colony of NSW (now VIC) 62–63, 73–74, 175
Wantabadgery, NSW 87
Warbreccan County, NSW 161
Warby family 86
Warby, John (Bush Constable) 89
Warby, William (squatter) 89, 90
Waterloo Creek, NSW 16, 57–58, 139–40, 179, 183, 186
Waterloo Creek Massacre 135, 138, 191, 196
Watkins, George 106
Waywurru Country, Colony of NSW (now VIC) viii, 1, 30, 43, 60, 83, 136, 158, 169, 188, 218
  see also Pallangan-middang
Waywarru People 63–64, 75, 78, 175–77, 189, 220
Wee Waa, NSW 19, 21, 45, 47
Wellington, NSW 149
Wellington (warrior) 173, 175
Wentworth, William 230
Werearai People 220
  see also Wirrayaraay
Western Wakka Wakka Peoples 102, 221
White (Colonel) 77, 80, 171, 187
Wickham, John Clements 116
Williams, Henry 93
Williams, John 97–98
Williams River, NSW 21–25, 147
Wilson, John 24
Wilsone, David Henry 13–14, 198–99
Windradyne (Wiradyuri warrior) 91–92, 229
Windsor, NSW 94

Wiradyuri Country, NSW viii, 1, 20, 22, 31, 43, 60, 83–84, 97, 136, 158, 164–65, 160, 188, 218
Wiradyuri Language 166
Wiradyuri People 12, 15, 25, 27, 32, 51–53, 75, 83, 85–86, 88, 90, 97, 99–101, 158, 160, 162–65, 220
  see also Windradyne
Wiradyuri War 91–93, 96–98, 165–66
Wirrayaraay People 141–44
  see also Myall Creek
Wirribi *see* Carr, Aunty Wirribi Leanna
Woiwurrung Country, Colony of NSW (now VIC) 177
Woiwurrung People 61, 200, 200
women
  Aboriginal 46, 62–63, 67, 71, 142, 146, 151, 176, 194, 201
  conducting ceremonies 121
  Gomeroi 48, 137
  in warfare 51, 62, 109, 138, 199, 205
  massacre of 48, 144–45, 153, 171, 203
  see also Carr, Aunty Wirribi Leanna
  see also Carter, Megan
  see also Cooper, Aunty Cheryl
  see also Chalker, Aunty Glenda
  see also Durrant, Jacqui
  see also Franklin, Jane
  see also Gilmore, Mary
Wonnarua Country, NSW 11, 20, 43, 53, 60, 83, 103, 117, 136, 158, 169, 188, 207, 218
Wonnarua People 27
Wooganbarah People 121, 221
wool 2, 39, 41, 51, 110, 128, 130, 213
woomeras 149
Wooninambi (Yaggara leader) 113, 115
Worimi People 221
Wulkidjaduwil, 'Big Micky' 175
Wurundjeri balug 200
Wurundjeri-willam 200

Yaegl People 119
Yaggara Country, Colony of NSW (now QLD) 20, 43, 103, 117, 136, 207, 218
Yaggara People 102, 104, 109–10, 112–13, 115, 121, 131, 220
Yaldwyn, William Henry 187–88, 190–91
Yass, NSW 77–78, 84–85, 93–94, 157, 160, 170, 173–74, 177, 182–83

Index

Yellamundy (Hawkesbury man) 228
Yorta Yorta Country, Colony of NSW
 (now VIC) 42, 60, 83, 135, 158, 188
Yorta Yorta People 220

Youngillums People 64
Yugambeh People 220
Yuggarapul People 102, 220

www.ingramcontent.com/pod-product-compliance
Lightning Source LLC
Chambersburg PA
CBHW030607230426
43661CB00053B/1877